WAR SCARE

WAR SCARE

Russia and America on the Nuclear Brink

PETER VINCENT PRY

PRAEGER

Westport, Connecticut
London

Library of Congress Cataloging-in-Publication Data

Pry, Peter Vincent.
War scare : Russia and America on the nuclear brink / Peter Vincent Pry.
p. cm.
Includes bibliographical references and index.
ISBN 0-275-96643-7 (alk. paper)
1. United States—Military relations—Russia (Federation)
2. Russia (Federation)—Military relations—United States.
3. United States—Foreign relations—1989- 4. Nuclear warfare—United States—History—20th century. 5. Nuclear warfare—Russia (Federation)—History—20th century. 6. Nuclear weapons—United States. 7. Nuclear weapons—Russia (Federation) I. Title.
II. Title: Russia and America on the nuclear brink.
E183.8.R9P79 1999
355'.031'0973047—dc21 98-56630

British Library Cataloguing in Publication Data is available.

Copyright © 1999 by Peter Vincent Pry

All rights reserved. No portion of this book may be reproduced, by any process or technique, without the express written consent of the publisher.

Library of Congress Catalog Card Number: 98-56630
ISBN: 0-275-96643-7

First published in 1999

Praeger Publishers, 88 Post Road West, Westport, CT 06881
An imprint of Greenwood Publishing Group, Inc.
www.praeger.com

Printed in the United States of America

The paper used in this book complies with the Permanent Paper Standard issued by the National Information Standards Organization (Z39.48-1984).

10 9 8 7 6 5 4 3 2 1

This book has been reviewed by the CIA to ensure that no classified information is divulged. The views expressed here are the author's and do not necessarily represent the views of the CIA or the Armed Services Committee.

To Frank,

my son,

in hope that he will live in a safer world,

and to the sentinels:

K. S., S. S., V. R., K. W., N. K., L. G., S. A., M. M., M.S.L., and L. O.

this book is dedicated.

Contents

Introduction ix

Part I The Missiles of November: ABLE ARCHER–83, November 2–11, 1983

1 December 12, 1979 3
2 Operation VRYAN, May 1981 9
3 The Pershing II Crisis, May 1981–November 1983 16
4 The Polish Crisis, September–December 1981 23
5 The KAL 007 Crisis, September 1983 27
6 ABLE ARCHER, November 2–11, 1983 33
7 The Death of Andropov, February 1984 45

Part II August Coup: The Fall of the Soviet Empire, August 19–21, 1991

8 Gorbachev at 20,000 Feet, August 4, 1991 53
9 Kryuchkov's Coup, August 18, 1991 57
10 The Warsaw Pact Crisis, 1989–1990 64
11 Twilight, August 18, 1991 69
12 Operation THUNDER and the Fall of the Old Guard 77
13 The Cover-Up 83

Part III The Armenian Crisis, May 1992

14 The New Russia 89
15 The U.S. Threat 99
16 The Great Debate, May 27–30, 1992 102
17 The Russo-Ukrainian Nuclear Crisis, October 1991–May 1992 109
18 War in the Caucasus: Genesis 114

Part IV The October Coup, September 21–October 4, 1993

19 Democracy of the Generals 131
20 Rutskoy 137
21 The Warning: Alexandria, Virginia, June 11, 1993 145

22 Who's Got the Button? 149
23 Ukraine and the Hot September 158
24 Live, on *Larry King* 170

Part V Northern Lights: The Norwegian Missile Crisis, January 25, 1995

25 Dangerous Men 185
26 Aurora Borealis 195
27 Dark History 203
28 Black Brant XII 214
29 Dangerous Minutes 228

Part VI The Future?

30 The West 241
31 Black Prophecies: Civilian Threat Perceptions 249
32 START: A More Dangerous Balance 255
33 Winning a Nuclear War 262
34 Flashpoints 273

Selected Sources 295
Index 323

Introduction

It will be a major political mistake of those who insist on the NATO expansion. It will definitely send the whole of Europe into the flames of war.

—President Boris Yeltsin,
September 8, 1995

The Soviet conscience, still borne by many of our citizens, leaves no room for doubt. They wonder, "who is responsible for our disintegration?" China? No. The Islamic world? No. Who then? The West.

—General Aleksandr Lebed,
March 27, 1996

The role of nuclear weapons today remains even more important than it was during the Cold War.

—Viktor Surikov,
Director, Institute of Defense Studies,
September 10, 1996

One of the reasons for Russia's increased emphasis on nuclear weapons . . . has clearly been NATO's expansion. The Cold War is over, but the threat of a new world war is only just taking on new form.

—*Novyye Izvestiya*,
January 14, 1998

NATO enlargement means the appearance of the most serious threat to our country since 1945.

—Russian Duma Resolution,
January 23, 1998

The world has never in this decade been so close as now to the brink of nuclear war.

—Former Prime Minister Viktor Chernomyrdin,
May 28, 1999

What were you doing on October, 4, 1993? I was making a desperate phone call from the headquarters of North American Air Defense and Space Command, near Colorado Springs, to my wife in Washington, D.C. I told her to take our kids out of school and head for the hills, because the Russians might launch a nuclear attack.

This was no joke. On that day, a half-dozen other intelligence and strategic warning officers from the Central Intelligence Agency, National Security Agency, and Defense Intelligence Agency made similar phone calls to their families.

I remember October 4, 1993 with the same crystalline clarity that I recall October 22, 1962. At 7:00 P.M. that Monday evening so many years ago, President Kennedy appeared on television to tell the American people that the United States and the Soviet Union were on a collision course over nuclear missiles in Cuba: "We will not prematurely, or unnecessarily, risk the costs of worldwide nuclear war in which even the fruits of victory would be ashes in our mouth—but neither shall we shrink from that risk at any time it must be faced."

I was eight years old. Fear showed in my mother's face, despite her best efforts to be brave for her children. The next day at Marcy Elementary School, my third-grade glass practiced "duck and cover" exercises, preparing for nuclear war. We formed two files in the hallway facing a wall. Girls stood on the inside file nearest the wall and boys on the outside. On the teacher's command, the girls crouched down, shut their eyes tight, and pressed their hands to their ears to protect themselves from the blinding flash and rupturing blast of a nuclear explosion. The boys leaned forward against the wall, forming an arch over the girls, to protect them from flying glass.

Just about everybody who lived through it has some recollection of the Cuban missile crisis. But do you remember August 19, 1991? May 20, 1992? October 4, 1993? Or January 25, 1995? I do, with the same sense of dread and urgency that I recall the Cuban missile crisis, and for the same reason: on these dates the world stood at the brink of nuclear apocalypse.

Yet outside of a small circle of intelligence officers, almost no one knows about these other, very recent, nuclear crises. This book is a history of our little-known brushes with nuclear war—warning that, contrary to popular opinion and the assurances of our political leaders, the possibility of a Russian nuclear attack still exists. Nuclear deterrence, the foundation of Western security for nearly fifty years, is now less stable, and much riskier, than is commonly believed. And it is growing more dangerous.

For ten years, beginning in October 1985, I served as an intelligence officer in the CIA. My principal responsibility was analyzing Soviet (and later, Russian) nuclear forces, military strategy, and operations, and the possibility of a nuclear attack. My term of service at CIA spanned from the height of Soviet power—when the possibility of communist aggression was taken seriously by most defense professionals and average citizens—through the decline and fall of the Soviet Union, to the first years of a democratic Russia. During this time I grew more and more concerned about the increasingly lax attitudes of the U.S. government toward the possibility of a Russian nuclear attack, despite the disturbing reality of a still-serious Russian nuclear threat, as described in classified National Intelligence Estimates (NIEs).

NIEs represent the collective opinion of the entire intelligence community—the Central Intelligence Agency, Defense Intelligence Agency, National Security Agency, the military services, and others—including dissenting alternative views. Up until 1995, as indicated by an unclassified study by the U.S. General Accounting Office (GAO), the highly classified NIEs portrayed a still-serious Russian nuclear threat.

However, from President Clinton to the man in the street, the overwhelming majority saw, and still see, no possibility of nuclear aggression from Russia.

My concern turned to alarm on February 28, 1996, when the U.S. intelligence community finally caved in to the politically correct view of a vanishing Russian nuclear threat. On that date Richard N. Cooper, the Clinton administration's new chairman of the National Intelligence Council, in a statement for the record to the U.S. Congress, presented the freshly declassified findings of NIE 95–19, the most recent National Intelligence Estimate. NIE 95–19, *Emerging Missile Threats to North America during the Next Fifteen Years*, published in November 1995, addressed possible proliferating missile threats to the United States, including the Russian nuclear threat. According to Cooper, NIE 95–19 concludes: "With the end of the Cold War, the United States faces a clearly diminished threat of nuclear attack by the missile forces of the former Soviet Union." Cooper added, "In our recent NIE, the Intelligence Community reaffirmed earlier assessments that the current threat to North America from unauthorized or accidental launch of Russian . . . strategic missiles remains remote, and has not changed significantly from that of the past decade."

The trouble is that many intelligence officers strongly disagree with the findings of Cooper's NIE 95–19. Dissent is especially strong among those tracking Russian strategic thinking and nuclear force modernization and operations—analysts who are closest to the problem and whose expert opinions about the Russian nuclear threat should count the most. Their more sobering views, which should have been reflected in the main findings of NIE 95–19, were ignored. The document did not allow one dissenting footnote into its easy dismissal of the Russian nuclear threat.

Many experts, including President Clinton's former CIA director, R. James Woolsey, condemned NIE 95–19. Questions were raised about whether the National Intelligence Estimate might have been biased to favor the political views of the Clinton administration. Suspicions of political bias were reinforced by the timing of NIE 95–19. Its reassuring findings about Russia and other potential missile threats were released in the middle of congressional debate over the need for defenses to protect the United States from foreign missile attack, a program strongly opposed by the Clinton administration. The rapid declassification of NIE 95–19 was unprecedented, both for its speed—declassification of an NIE normally takes at least a decade—and for the currency of the estimate. Congressional requests for declassification of earlier National Intelligence Estimates from 1993, for comparison with the 1995 NIE, were ignored, and for an obvious reason: Cooper's claim that earlier National Intelligence Estimates had said essentially the same thing as NIE 95–19 was incorrect.

A subsequent study of NIE 95–19 by the GAO found that the National Intelligence Estimate had numerous "analytical shortcomings." The unclassified GAO study, *Foreign Missile Threats: Analytical Soundness of Certain National Intelligence Estimates* (August 1996), also compared NIE 95–19 to earlier, still classified, National Intelligence Estimates from 1993. GAO concluded that the earlier NIEs presented a more sobering and worrisome analysis of the missile threat than did NIE 95–19 and were more persuasive.

It's absurd to doubt the grave nature of the Russian nuclear threat when Moscow has raised the specter of nuclear war nearly a half dozen times since 1991 and continues building nuclear blast shelters and technologically advanced strategic forces, despite a ruined economy. Even NIE 95–19 implicitly contradicted its own reassuring message about a greatly diminished Russian nuclear threat by conceding, in Richard Cooper's words, "Nevertheless, Russia continues to maintain an operational strategic nuclear force capable of delivering thousands of nuclear warheads against the United States. . . . Russia continues strategic force modernization programs, albeit within the constraints of a greatly weakened economy."

It is hard to overstate the degree of concern that's shared by some intelligence officers over the possibility of a Russian nuclear attack. Many intelligence professionals—people who serve every day on the front lines of the nuclear threat, who follow the continuing evolution of events in Russia, who monitor daily the activities of Russian strategic forces—live constantly with the reality of nuclear danger. Even as the president of the United States tells us that Russian missiles no longer target U.S. cities, and Moscow and Washington are routinely referred to as "strategic partners," many intelligence professionals and strategic-warning analysts maintain private contingency plans to evacuate their families in the event of a Russian nuclear strike. In fact, while nuclear civil defense is virtually nonexistent for the average American, some intelligence officers have recently built private nuclear fallout shelters.

If you get the feeling that there is something "wrong with this picture," then the problem is *not* with intelligence officers and strategic warning professionals. Maybe they know something that you don't. Unknown to the general public, and little known to U.S. policy makers, the world has been undergoing an extended crisis since 1980, a crisis born of the view of the Soviet—now Russian—General Staff that a nuclear world war may be imminent. A "war scare"—the mistaken belief that a U.S. nuclear surprise attack is about to occur—has gripped the General Staff, leading Moscow to ready its nuclear forces for a first strike on several occasions in the 1990s.

Oleg Gordievsky, a former high-ranking KGB officer, disclosed some of the story of the war scare and nuclear close calls during the 1980s in his book *KGB: The Inside Story of Its Foreign Operations from Lenin to Gorbachev*. However, Western academics and journalists seem not to have considered the possibility that war scare attitudes persist in the Russian General Staff. Colonel Stanislav Lunev, a more recent high-ranking defector from the GRU—the intelligence arm of the Russian General Staff—confirms in his 1998 book *Through the Eyes of the Enemy* that for the Russian military "the Cold War is not over." According to Lunev, the Russian military continues to view nuclear conflict with the United States as an imminent possibility. It continues to prepare actively for nuclear war by, among other things, plotting to assassinate U.S. political and military leaders by means of small atomic "suitcase" bombs, which can be smuggled into the United States before the initiation of a massive Russian nuclear attack.

There is a wealth of unclassified material, including Russian public statements, interviews, military writings, polls, and reports on Russian military policies and activities, that reflect the dire threat perceptions held by Russia's military leaders. They form the basis of this book. My research into these sources finds that the collapse of the Soviet Union and the internal turmoil and weakness of Russia have aggravated Russian military concerns about their vulnerability to attack and have contributed to a continuation, or heightening, of their exaggerated fears about an impending nuclear war. Such fears are dangerous to the West, because they could prompt the Russian General Staff, deliberately or through miscalculation, to launch a preemptive nuclear strike on the United States.

To most people, the notion that the nuclear threat to the United States is greater now than ever must seem fantastic. After all, in 1991 the Communist Party was replaced by Boris Yeltsin and other democratically minded political leaders friendly to the West. The General Staff and KGB, primary instruments of external threat and internal repression in the former USSR, allegedly were reformed and safely subordinated to the new Russian government. The Strategic Arms Reduction Treaties will require the United States and Russia to destroy most of their strategic nuclear weapons. Former President Bush and President Clinton have claimed that these treaties would eliminate the danger of a Russian nuclear first strike—a claim that is widely credited as true, even among treaty critics.

Yet these "facts," the basic assumptions now shaping both popular opinion and official defense and foreign policy, are at best only half true.

Although since 1991 Boris Yeltsin and some democratic reformers headed Russia, it is now clear that the democrats were never in control of Yeltsin's own government. Yeltsin's cabinet was split between reformers and reactionaries ever since the army rescued his presidency from the coup attempt of October 1993. Yeltsin's continued hold on power required concessions to the military and the forces of reaction, which includes nearly a majority of Russian voters. Reformist economic policies have been resisted—and actively sabotaged—by communist *apparatchiks*, who remain entrenched in key government posts. The democratic reformers are locked in a power struggle with the Russian Duma, which is dominated by communists and national chauvinists unsympathetic to free-market economic policies and democratic processes. These people have distinctly authoritarian preferences. In 1999, former Russian Foreign Minister Andrey Kozyrev said that the "pro-war camp" had finally triumphed over Russian democrats: "The Russian government has managed in the last 3 or 4 years to restore a Soviet-world outlook, where on the one side there is Moscow and on the other all the democratic countries. . . . Anti-NATO hysterics have been inflated in the last 3 years. Anti-Western lines of argument have increased."

Even Yeltsin's own commitment to democracy has been questionable. His support of democratic reformers coincided exclusively with his self-interest. He used the democracy movement to aggrandize political power. Yeltsin did not groom any successors, nor are there any democratic personalities with prestige and experience capable of succeeding him. Unconfirmed reports appearing in the Russian and Western press allege that even when Yeltsin was at the height of his political and physical powers, the Russian president had emotional problems and was subject to violent mood swings, fits of megalomania, and alcoholism.

Regardless of whether democrats or dictators ultimately rule in Russia, controlling the Russian government is not the same thing as controlling the country. The fall of communism broke the iron bonds that oppressed the people, but those bonds also restrained ethnic conflict and maintained the social order. Russia is now experiencing the disintegrative effects of ethnic violence and societal decay, which could lead to anarchy or to a civil war wider than the one fought in Chechnya.

Totalitarian resurgence, megalomania or madness in the chief executive, and civil war in Russia are disturbing to contemplate in a nation that still controls 30,000 nuclear weapons. Any of these factors could pose a threat to the West. A more immediate and direct threat still exists from the Russian military, especially from the Russian General Staff. Although the former Soviet General Staff and KGB have been renamed the "Russian General Staff" and "Foreign Intelligence Service" (SVR), these institutions have not been reformed in any real sense. The General Staff is manned entirely, and the SVR largely, by professionals from the old Soviet regime, former members of the communist elite, educated in Marxist-Leninist dogma, staunch upholders of the totalitarian order, and the chief warriors against the West.

To expect this militant vanguard to adopt a benign view of the West and to support the democratization of Russian society is to expect too much. Public statements and writings by members of the General Staff and the Russian military, and continued espionage activities against NATO and the United States by the Foreign Intelligence Service, indicate that they still view the West as "the enemy." Russian military writings routinely express extreme suspicion that the United States and NATO might exploit Russia's present weakness and societal turmoil. Some in the Russian military display an attitude of revanchism bordering on hysteria. Some call for the forcible restoration of the USSR and preparedness for an imminent global nuclear war.

The General Staff is probably more important to the future of U.S.-Russian relations—indeed, to the future of humankind—than are Russia's democratic reformers, because the General Staff controls Russia's vast nuclear arsenal. Much has been made in the press about the Russian president's "nuclear briefcase," which supposedly enables him to preside over Russia's strategic nuclear forces. However, the best evidence indicates that the president "controls" the nuclear arsenal only in a legal sense. Even the designer of the "briefcase" acknowledges that it is merely a communications device connecting the president to the General Staff. It is the General Staff that has the actual, technical capability to launch a nuclear strike.

Russia's president is powerless to prevent the General Staff from starting and waging a global nuclear war. Russian civilian defense experts, such as Alexei Arbatov, have warned that Russia's dangerous nuclear command and control arrangement enables the General Staff to operate autonomously, even against the wishes of civilian authority. Perhaps our proximity to disaster should be measured not by the friendly reassurances of Russian democrats but by the more malevolent attitudes displayed by the General Staff, whose finger is on the nuclear trigger.

As for the Strategic Arms Reduction Treaties (START I, II, and III), these will not eliminate or even reduce the threat of nuclear war. The unratified START ll calls for removal of over two-thirds of all deployed strategic nuclear weapons on each side by the year 2007. But even after these and deep START III reductions, Russia will still possess some 2,000 strategic weapons, more than enough to wreak global devastation.

START reductions will roll back the size of the strategic arsenals to the levels that existed in the 1960s, a period when the superpowers were so fearful of each other's nuclear strength that they embarked on the first attempt to cap the number of long-range missiles, the Strategic Arms Limitation Treaty (SALT I), concluded in 1971. The strategic forces remaining after START, on the Russian side, are likely to be more technically advanced and capable than present forces, since the START treaties do not prohibit the ambitious modernization presently being pursued by Russia.

Overshadowing all of these factors, and pointing to a still troubling Russian nuclear threat, are the recent nuclear war scares that are all presently known to no more than a few dozen people in the West. Since 1980, Soviet (and now Russian) military leaders have been so suspicious of the West and so convinced that another world war is imminent that these fears almost became self-fulfilling prophecies on several occasions in the 1980s and 1990s.

The General Staff's fearful view of recent history is all the more disturbing in that it is so sharply at variance with the Western perspective that there is no danger. There is a high risk that in the future the General Staff will again fantasize crises or imagine threats where none exist and that again the world will be brought to the brink of nuclear catastrophe. Our failure to understand the General Staff's perspective and our ignorance of the recent peril increases the possibility that the United States could, through miscalculation, unintentionally provoke a nuclear war with Russia.

The attention of the Western public has understandably been focused on the abundant good news: the reduction of nuclear weapons, the liberation of Eastern Europe, the fall of communism, the more or less peaceful disintegration of the USSR, and the budding democratization of Russia. Most are blissfully unaware of some very bad news as well, and when the ominous origins of our hopeful present are understood, it becomes clear that in the 1980s we transited the most dangerous decade of the Cold War and that in the post-Cold War era we face even more dangerous times.

This book explores recent history and current events from the perspective of the Russian General Staff. In their view, this decade and the one preceding it have constituted a protracted nuclear crisis. I'll describe several incidents from the 1980s and 1990s, at the time virtually unknown to the Western public and governments, that posed high potential risks of plunging the world into a nuclear war.

This book, in short, is about the greatest intelligence failure of the missile age, perhaps the greatest intelligence failure in modern history. Russia's prolonged nuclear war scare also raises profound questions about the stability of nuclear deterrence and about the implications of eroding deterrence stability for U.S. national security policy.

The intelligence community is not solely responsible for underestimating the Russian nuclear threat and should not be judged too harshly. Except for the notorious NIE 95–19, the intelligence community's record in other National Intelligence Estimates is better than that of most scholars. The failure to see the Soviet and Russian nuclear war scare is broadly shared by Western intellectuals and journalists, who did not recognize the abundant unclassified evidence of a crisis in Russian nuclear-threat perceptions. Besides, the intelligence community is structured to excel in analyzing narrow technical and very specific political-military issues, not large historical trends. It is in the realm of the very large—the Soviet and Russian sense of history, the future, the world, and their place in it—that the origins and existence of the still-metastasizing war scare are to be found.

Seeing the war scare requires challenging the common wisdom about Russia. Courageous individuals within and outside the intelligence community may challenge the common wisdom, but it is asking too much of any bureaucracy—and the intelligence community is a bureaucracy—to do so. Without a war scare paradigm to explain Russia's behavior, specific dangerous nuclear incidents have been rationalized as "anomalies," dangerous but temporary detours from the trend that the West prefers to see: growing East-West partnership and post–Cold War peace. I, too, would prefer this direction in U.S.-Russian relations, but the trend points elsewhere.

No classified information, sources, or methods are divulged in this book. The CIA reviewed this work to ensure that no such breaches occurred before granting me permission to publish. The review was very thorough and lasted three years. As a consumer of classified intelligence in the Armed Services Committee of the U.S. House of Representatives, I thoroughly support the principle of prepublication review to protect classified data. The fact is that unclassified and declassified sources are sufficient to tell the tale. However, the reader should know that the best evidence for the themes and events described in this book remains highly classified, locked away in the vaults of the CIA, unseen even by most of those who have national security clearances and a need to know.

I have no illusions that this book will enhance my career or increase the happiness of my family. I know that it is far more likely that "going public" will destroy me professionally. But the stakes are too high for silence. There are very few who know this story. Someone has to speak.

PART I

The Missiles of November: ABLE ARCHER–83, November 2–11, 1983

The nuclear arms race in Europe has now become the nerve center of international relations. It can become a source of a rapid and dramatic growth of a threat of new world war.

—Yuri Andropov,
General Secretary, USSR,
August 18, 1983

The threat of the outbreak of nuclear war is reaching an extremely dangerous point. . . . The task of not overlooking preparations by the adversary for launching a surprise nuclear missile attack on the U.S.S.R. . . . has acquired even greater urgency and immediacy.

—Vladimir Kryuchkov,
Director, KGB,
November 2, 1983

CHAPTER 1

December 12, 1979

On December 12, 1979, Joseph Luns, secretary general of the North Atlantic Treaty Organization, issued an official communique from NATO headquarters in Brussels that a momentous decision had been made: the United States would deploy a new class of nuclear missiles in Western Europe to answer a rapidly growing Soviet nuclear threat, one that "constituted a major and growing challenge to the security of the [NATO] alliance." The fate of NATO was at stake:

> The ministers have decided to modernize NATO's long-range-theater nuclear force by the deployment in Europe of U.S. ground-launched systems comprising 108 Pershing II launchers . . . and 464 ground-launched cruise missiles, all with single warheads.

It was the same month as the Soviet invasion of Afghanistan. One thousand miles away, across the continent and in a different world altogether, Moscow heard in Luns's words the approaching thunder of nuclear apocalypse.

Yuri Vladimirovich Andropov, chief of the Committee for State Security, known by its Russian acronym KGB (Komitet Gosudarstvennoy Bezopasnosti), was the product of a bloody history that predisposed him to see the world in apocalyptic terms. Andropov had been born into a world on the brink of war, on June 15, 1914, in Nagutskaya, northern Caucasus, where his father was a railroad worker. Andropov's infancy spanned World War I, the Bolshevik Revolution that brought the communists to power, and the counterrevolutionary campaigns of the White Terror. Five million Russians fell in these contests. At sixteen, Andropov joined the Komsomol, or the Young Communist League, while working variously as a telegraph operator, movie projectionist, and boatman on the Volga River. A brilliant labor activist and administrator, he rose rapidly through the party ranks, becoming leader of the Komsomol at Yaroslavl when he was twenty-four. Two years later, after the Soviet Union's successful but costly invasion of Finland in 1940, Andropov rose to leadership of the Komsomol in the USSR's newly conquered Karelo-Finnish Republic. By this time, at the age of twenty-six, Andropov had lived through, or witnessed, the long Red Terror of the Soviet police state, Stalin's deliberate starvation of the Ukraine, and the purge of imaginary traitors in the Red Army, estimated to have cost the lives, collectively, of twenty million.

During World War II, Andropov organized guerrilla activities in the Karelo-Finnish region and was in charge of NKVD units openly called "extermination battalions," which did guard duty and executed political prisoners. He managed slave labor and "volunteers"—forced labor by Russian women and children, many of whom perished in their effort to reach Andropov's unattainable work quotas. Andropov is suspected of assassinating a prominent comrade (Toivo Antikainen, one of the founders of the Finnish Communist Party and a guerrilla rival) who criticized Andropov's performance and tried to take his place. Twenty to thirty million Soviet soldiers and civilians died in World War II.

After the war, Andropov was sent to Moscow for special training. In 1953 he served as counselor in the Soviet embassy at Budapest, rising to become the USSR's ambassador to Hungary in 1954. Andropov's keen intellect, his mastery of the particularly difficult Hungarian language, and his understanding of Magyar culture led many Hungarians to regard him initially as an enlightened and sympathetic compatriot. Andropov bloodily dispelled these illusions by playing a leading role in crushing the Hungarian Revolution of 1956. Ambassador Andropov persuaded the Hungarian quisling, Janos Kadar, to betray the freedom fighters, led by Imre Nagy, and to open Hungary to the Red Army, which slaughtered thousands. Ambassador Andropov lured Nagy from his sanctuary in the Yugoslav embassy with promises that his personal safety would be guaranteed; he then had Nagy arrested and executed. After destroying the Hungarian revolt, Andropov, according to Hungary's former deputy foreign minister, Georg Hetai, was "the ultimate power who decided who and how many people should be executed." To this day, Andropov is known in Hungary as "The Butcher."

In 1967, Andropov assumed the director's chair of the KGB, just in time to participate in the Red Army's invasion of Czechoslovakia and the suppression of Czech efforts to reform and "humanize" communism in the failed revolution of 1968. As KGB chief Andropov contributed to, and perhaps helped mastermind, the spread of communist revolutionary movements throughout the Third World, fanning wars in Southeast Asia, the Middle East, Angola, Nicaragua, and El Salvador, and supporting pro-Soviet international terrorist movements. About three million people are estimated to have died in these adventures. Andropov ruthlessly suppressed Soviet dissidents, and he is credited with inventing the practice of confining political prisoners in mental institutions, where they could be held indefinitely and "treated" psychologically, often with drugs or surgery, for their anti-Soviet views. In 1979, Andropov was part of the "quick reaction group" that managed the invasion of Afghanistan, including the assassination of its government leaders. This developed into a war that killed another 500,000 people.

In December 1979, when NATO announced its decision to acquire Pershing II nuclear missiles, KGB chief Andropov was a lean, graying, aristocratic figure of sixty-five whose occasional wry expressions relieved an otherwise remote and sinister mien. His son, Igor, was a diplomat, and his daughter, Irina, was a journalist—professions frequently used by KGB agents as covers.

Andropov's entire life history had prepared him to expect the worst in war and in peace. KGB and Soviet military analysts told him that the Pershing II missile, once deployed to bases in West Germany, would enable the United States to deliver a decapitating nuclear strike on Moscow in six minutes. A Pershing II fired from Western Europe would not be seen by Soviet launch detection satellites, which were focused on the United States. Soviet ground-based radars would need at least a minute or two to detect and report a missile launch. This would not leave Soviet leaders with enough time to order a retaliatory nuclear strike. If Pershing II could kill Soviet leaders before they could get to their deep underground bunkers, or smash key communications nodes and thereby block or delay their launch orders, Soviet missiles and bombers would be sitting ducks. While waiting to hear from Moscow, the full weight of 10,000 U.S. strategic nuclear warheads delivered by U.S. submarines, intercontinental missiles, and bombers would vaporize the Strategic Rocket Forces, the Navy, and the Air Force. Pershing II would allow the United States to win a nuclear war—or so Andropov's people told him. KGB analysts saw Pershing II as the Cuban missile crisis in reverse.

KGB chief Andropov found the surprise-attack scenario compelling. Along with Defense Minister Dmitri Ustinov, he became a leading intellectual exponent of the theory that the United States and Soviet Union had entered a phase of supreme crisis in relations. Andropov believed that NATO's Pershing II decision had ushered in a new decade, one fraught with greater risks of a nuclear World War III. This is the message that the KGB chief carried to other Soviet leaders. Not that they needed much convincing that another world war was imminent: they all shared the same violent national history, and all had lives very much like Andropov's. An alarmist outlook seemed normal and prudent.

Leonid Brezhnev and Ustinov, the two men who mattered most in the Union of Soviet Socialist Republics, were inclined by experience to believe Andropov. Brezhnev, leader of the Soviet Union for over two decades, was born in 1906 and could remember his early life as the son of a steelworker: the purgatory of the furnaces, his father's stories of labor strikes, and the failed 1905 revolution. "All of this," Brezhnev later said, "had a decisive influence in forming my world outlook."

Like Andropov, Brezhnev grew up against the background of World War I, the Revolution, foreign intervention, and the protracted civil war between Red and White factions. He experienced the privations and the terror inherent in these catastrophes. In the revolutionary struggles, the Brezhnev family, like those of most steelworkers, sided with the Bolsheviks. Between the world wars, Brezhnev had the grim job of redistributing lands taken from peasant farmers—known as "kulaks"—millions of whom had deliberately been starved to death during the Ukrainian holocaust that Stalin called his "agricultural collectivization program." During World War II, Brezhnev saw combat in Ukraine, survived one of the Red Army's rare amphibious operations in a D-day-type landing near Novorossisk on the Black Sea, participated in the liberation of Czechoslovakia, and rose spectacularly to the rank of major general. After the war, Brezhnev climbed through the Communist Party ranks with the help of Nikita Khrushchev, whom Brezhnev and Alexei Kosygin replaced as head of the Soviet Union in the bloodless coup of October 14, 1964. Brezhnev's invasion of Czechoslovakia in 1968, which crushed Czech efforts to liberalize socialism, established the "Brezhnev Doctrine": the policy that the Soviet Union would forcibly prevent any Soviet bloc nation from abandoning communism.

The second most powerful man in the Soviet Union after Brezhnev was Dmitri Ustinov, the minister of defense. Ustinov was succinctly described by one journalist as "a stocky, sandy-haired man with gold-rimmed spectacles" who "exuded neither charm nor charisma." Nonetheless, Marshal of the Soviet Union Dmitri Fedorovich Ustinov was also a genius of logistics and industrial planning, the man who was responsible, perhaps more than any other, for the Soviet victory over the Nazis in World War II. In 1941, when the Nazi invasion had pressed the Soviet Union to the brink of collapse, Ustinov undertook the Herculean task of transplanting the USSR's imperiled war industries from western Russia to the Ural Mountains, two thousand miles away, in a matter of months. This feat was the equivalent of moving the heavy industries of the United States from the East Coast to the Rocky Mountains and restarting them at production levels to sustain a major war effort, in less than a year, all the while under enemy attack. Simultaneously, Ustinov helped organize the defense of Moscow. Within a few years the Soviet factories rescued by Ustinov far outproduced Germany in weapons and enabled the Red Army to drown the Nazis in a sea of tanks. After the war, Ustinov helped organize the Soviet space program, which launched both the first satellite and first man into orbit. Under Brezhnev, Ustinov took charge of developing the Soviet Union's strategic nuclear missile and bomber forces, in a race with the United States. He joined Andropov in proselytizing to the Politburo the gospel that Pershing II signified the coming of a nuclear world war.

Brezhnev and Ustinov, who had come of age through two world wars, had no problem believing, in the twilight of their lives, that they again faced the beast.

It was not just NATO's plans to deploy Pershing II missiles that contributed to the belief among Soviet political and military leaders that the United

States was preparing to launch a nuclear surprise attack. The modernization of U.S. strategic offensive forces, begun in the late 1970s and ongoing throughout the 1980s, had greatly increased the firepower of the U.S. nuclear arsenal. Moreover, the election of Ronald Reagan presaged in the Soviet view the empowerment of American hawks committed to a policy of aggressive confrontation with the USSR. Soviet leaders saw Reagan's "star wars" scheme—the Strategic Defense Initiative (SDI), a plan announced in 1983 to defend the United States from nuclear attack by developing space-based lasers and other new antimissile technologies—as threatening to neutralize the Soviets' own formidable nuclear arsenal, built at great sacrifice to the Soviet economy. Many on the Soviet General Staff believed that SDI was not truly a defensive program but was intended to facilitate a U.S. nuclear surprise attack by minimizing retaliatory consequences. The Soviet economy, for years on a war footing and already taxed to the limit by military spending, could not outproduce the United States in an ever-escalating arms race, especially not in the high-technology weapons deemed by the Soviets to be crucial to the future military balance.

The highest-ranking KGB officer ever to defect, Oleg Gordievsky, a former KGB colonel who fled to the West in 1985, notes that the most important factor contributing to Soviet fear of an American nuclear attack was that Soviet political and military leaders were endemically suspicious of the West to the point of paranoia. Gordievsky was the KGB's chief of station in London and was responsible for collecting intelligence against NATO. He was uniquely positioned to understand Soviet leadership views of the NATO threat. According to Gordievsky:

> In the face of Pershing, which could reach Moscow in six minutes from West German bases, and reports received from its intelligence service of an essentially new type of weapon being developed in America, which would be able to render the Soviet deterrent useless (the future Strategic Defense Initiative—Star Wars), the Kremlin panicked. Insofar as it was able to interpret them, its reactions—after the mirror-image principle—were as follows: "If we had a nuclear potential like the U.S.A. and a system which would eliminate their nuclear deterrent, would we deliver a preemptive nuclear strike against our sworn adversary? In that case, we must begin to prepare immediately for an American attack." . . . I have frequently heard people ask in recent years: "Is it possible that anyone in Moscow seriously believed that the West would commit aggression and launch a nuclear war?" The answer is, unfortunately, yes, there were such people and evidently, from 1980 to 1985, they were in the majority in the political and military leadership of the U.S.S.R.

The unbalanced Soviet view of the West is all the more apparent when one remembers that during the 1980s Soviet strategic nuclear offensive and defensive forces posed a far greater threat to the United States than U.S. forces did to the USSR. American strategic modernization was intended to head off Soviet superiority in the nuclear balance, or, in the view of some analysts, to redress a superiority already achieved by the USSR. It was not intended to impose U.S. superiority. But Soviet leaders, transferring their own aggressive designs onto American leaders, interpreted U.S. efforts to maintain parity as grasping for strategic advantage. Soviet leaders assumed that superpower relations had crossed a threshold into a permanent crisis that could last for years—much as relations between Germany and the Allies underwent a long prewar stage during the "twenty years' crisis" of 1919–1939—but that could escalate into world war at any time. Since war could come sooner or later, the prudent course was to look for it sooner.

CHAPTER 2

Operation VRYAN, May 1981

Oleg Gordievsky shuddered in the London cold as he hurried back to the Soviet embassy. Was this sudden chill due to the temperature, or because he had committed treason—*again*?

Colonel Gordievsky, who managed KGB espionage activities in Great Britain, had profound doubts about communism. His questioning had begun in 1968, after the Soviet invasion of Czechoslovakia. Gordievsky saw the rebellion as a legitimate attempt to reform and humanize socialism. Over the years, Gordievsky's doubts grew and were reinforced a hundred times over by Soviet domestic and foreign policies that struck him as either stupid or evil. Betrayal finally came in 1974, over lunch in a Copenhagen restaurant, when Gordievsky agreed to work for the British as a double agent. Remaining in the KGB while actually serving the West was an incredibly dangerous proposition, not only for Gordievsky but also for his wife, Leila, their two small daughters, Maria and Anna, and all their relations. As a KGB colonel, he knew well the fate of traitors. Another ideological traitor, Colonel Oleg Penkovsky, caught passing secrets to the West, had been skewered alive on a meat hook and then lowered into a vat of molten metal. But Gordievsky weighed the lives of millions against these risks. He had just delivered information to the British about a secret Soviet operation begun in May 1981 that put the entire world in peril.

In May 1981, Yuri Andropov listened as Leonid Brezhnev, premier of the USSR, told an audience of KGB agents and GRU military intelligence officers that the United States and the Soviet Union were on the nuclear brink. Brezhnev was preaching to the choir, and as Andropov glanced over the awestruck sea of faces, he took grim satisfaction in the fact that Brezhnev's terrifying oratory was inspired by his and the KGB's own painstaking analysis of the international situation.

Andropov rose to speak. Gordievsky would record the scene:

> The new American administration, he [Andropov] declared, was actively preparing for nuclear war. There was now the possibility of a nuclear first strike by the United States. The Politburo had accordingly decided that the overriding priority of Soviet foreign intelligence operations must henceforth be to collect military-strategic intelligence on the nuclear threat from the United States and NATO. To the astonishment of most of his audience, Andropov then announced that the KGB and GRU were for the first time to cooperate in a worldwide intelligence operation codenamed RYAN [VRYAN].

VRYAN, from the Russian acronym for "surprise nuclear missile attack" (vnezapnoye raketno-yadernoye napadenie), was also commonly known by the abbreviated acronym RYAN. It was a massive Soviet intelligence program, the largest ever mounted in peacetime, to scrutinize the United States and NATO for evidence of immediate preparations for nuclear war. The high priority of VRYAN was reflected in the imposition by Soviet leaders of unprecedented cooperation between the KGB and GRU. These rival intelligence giants were as jealous and suspicious of each other as they were of their mortal enemies in the West: the CIA and FBI, agencies they dwarfed in both manpower and resources. The KGB was the equivalent of the CIA, FBI, Secret Service, the intelligence arms of the State Department and the Department of Energy, and all federal and state police combined. The GRU is the equivalent of the combined intelligence organs of all the U.S. military services—Air Force, Navy, Army, and Marines—plus the National Security Agency. Andropov's audience seemed as astonished by the order that the KGB and GRU were to work together as by the prospect of a nuclear war.

VRYAN had priority over all other intelligence operations in both the KGB and GRU. It differed markedly from existing strategic warning programs, because it was funded and manned at a wartime level, on the assumption that nuclear war was imminent. The program monitored hundreds of indicators, some rather exotic, in order to obtain warning of an impending nuclear attack. These indicators included changes in the day-to-day posture of U.S. and NATO nuclear forces, unusual activity levels or late-night meetings at the White House, Pentagon, or other centers of allied decision making. The Soviets believed that the Western economy might betray U.S. preparations to launch a surprise nuclear attack through such indicators as increased buying of gold, which might reflect knowledge by Western elites of a coming apocalypse. Another unusual indicator viewed by the Soviets as a possible sign of impending nuclear war was a surge in efforts by hospitals to increase the blood supply. Based on close scrutiny of such Western activity, the KGB and GRU were required under VRYAN to report to Moscow every two weeks on the prospects for imminent nuclear war. The purpose of VRYAN was to supply Soviet leaders with sufficient warning of an impending U.S. nuclear attack to enable the USSR to preempt it by launching a nuclear first strike.

Striking first was always among the chief provisions of Soviet military doctrine. This is indicated by both unclassified and classified Soviet military writings, and by their strong preference for building intercontinental ballistic missiles (ICBMs) over submarine-launched ballistic missiles (SLBMs), and strategic bombers. Compared to SLBMs and bombers, ICBMs have much higher readiness and greater accuracy, making them better suited for launching a preemptive first strike. However, basing ICBMs in vulnerable, fixed silos or in garrisons makes them less survivable than SLBMs or bombers, strategic systems that are better suited for a retaliatory second strike.

Soviet *preemptive* preferences were reflected in the structure of their strategic nuclear forces, which relied on ICBMs to carry over 60 percent of Soviet nuclear warheads, while U.S. *retaliatory* preferences were reflected in a force structure that had about 80 percent of its strategic warheads on SLBMs and bombers and only about 20 percent on ICBMs. Still, the Soviets assumed the United States planned to strike first, Moscow attributing to Washington the Soviets' own strategic preferences.

ICBMs can be Launched-On-Tactical-Warning (LOTW) for a retaliatory strike: fired after incoming enemy missiles are detected but before enemy warheads arrive. LOTW depends on those critical first few minutes of (possibly ambiguous) warning, which radar or satellites would provide. This risky option would be disastrous for the Soviets, armed mostly with ICBMs, if they failed to launch their missiles in time. Preemption has its risks too, mainly of starting a war through miscalculation of the other side's intentions. However, Soviet military logic and intuition suggested that the days, hours, or minutes of strategic warning that would be needed to support a preemptive strike policy would be easier to acquire, and the warning more reliable, than the minutes of tactical warning of an incoming enemy missile that would be needed to support an LOTW policy. Preemption was also more consistent with the most important goals of Soviet military planners: to seize the initiative, carry the war to the enemy's homeland, destroy enemy forces before they could be used against the USSR, and never again be taken by surprise. They had not forgotten the lessons taught by Nazi Germany in 1941.

Soviet military textbooks written in the 1960s, 1970s, and 1980s generally endorsed the view that nuclear war could be won and that victory was likely to go to the side that struck first. For example, in *The Offensive*, a basic text used in Soviet General Staff academies, Colonel A. A. Sidorenko wrote, "Preemption in launching a nuclear strike is considered to be the decisive condition for attainment of superiority over [the enemy] and the seizure and retention of the initiative." Striking first was "decisive" in nuclear war, according to Marshal K. S. Moskalenko: "The launching of the first massed nuclear attack acquires decisive importance for achieving the objectives of war." Marshal S. S. Biryuzov advised Soviet military officers that "the first nuclear strike can immediately lead to the disorganization of the government, military control, and to the whole rear area of a country, and to stopping the systematic deployment of the armed forces and all the measures being conducted for mobilization." A few Soviet military theorists even seemed downright enthusiastic about nuclear war. Colonel B. A. Byely, in his widely read *Marxism-Leninism on War and Army*, described nuclear conflict with the West as a "sacred duty": "On the Communist side, nuclear war will be lawful and just . . . the natural right and sacred duty of progressive mankind to destroy imperialism."

Soviet plans for striking first were also explicitly spelled out in previously top secret military planning documents of the Warsaw Pact, captured by the West from East German classified repositories after German reunification. *Military Plans of the Warsaw Pact in Central Europe*, published by the German Ministry of Defense in 1992, analyzed roughly 25,000 top secret documents. Analysis showed that in exercises, typically "the WP [Warsaw Pact] took the offensive from the beginning of a military conflict with NATO." In numerous Warsaw Pact exercises, such as SOYUZ-81 and SOYUZ-83, directed by Soviet Marshal Viktor Kulikov and other senior Soviet officers, the report notes, "The use of atomic weapons was played as either a first strike or an 'answering/countering strike' [probably launch on tactical warning]." Strong preference for preemption was suggested by "the perceptions of the military leadership that employment [of nuclear weapons] should above all serve the achievement of a breakthrough of the adversary's defense." Moreover, planning documents called for Warsaw Pact "support of above all the first nuclear weapon strike." Nuclear strike plans from Warsaw Pact exercises depicted Pact first-use of nuclear weapons very early in a war. The report quotes Marshal Kulikov, commander in chief of the Warsaw Pact: "Future war will be waged without compromises until the complete destruction of the enemy. This forces the employment of the entire arsenal of means of destruction."

Moscow's ICBMs, then as now, stood ready all day, every day, to launch a nuclear first strike. Thus, VRYAN was not merely a harmless fantasy indulged by Soviet leaders but could have had fatal consequences for the world if Western intentions were misread.

VRYAN, and its danger to the West, cannot be dismissed as a concoction. Colonel Gordievsky was one of the most highly placed and most credible Soviet officials ever to defect, but one need not take Gordievsky's word. His story has been independently verified by the Russians themselves. In November 1991, after the demise of the USSR and shortly after the reorganization of the KGB into the Foreign Intelligence Service (SVR), Yevgeny Primakov, then head of SVR, acknowledged the VRYAN program but claimed it had been terminated. Another KGB defector, Yuri Shvets, who served as a spy in Washington, D.C., until the late 1980s, also acknowledged the existence of VRYAN, in a February 1993 interview, and described the same operational details as Gordievsky. "They told us that the Reagan Administration was preparing a first strike against the Soviet Union," Shvets said, "and that it was our task to ensure the survival of the motherland."

Anatoly Dobrynin, the Soviet ambassador to the United States from 1962 to 1986, acknowledged in his 1994 memoirs that Soviet leaders thought the possibility of nuclear war had sharply increased during the 1980s. He also admitted the existence of VRYAN: "While still head of the KGB, Andropov did believe that the Reagan administration was actively preparing for war and he was joined in this belief by Ustinov, the defense minister. They persuaded the Politburo to approve the largest peacetime military intelligence operation in Soviet history, known by its codename of Operation Ryon [RYAN]."

Some KGB officers working overseas, like Gordievsky and Shvets, understood the West well enough to know that the United States and NATO had no intention of launching a nuclear attack and that the VRYAN collection requirements were counterproductive. However, most KGB officers were not so enlightened. In fact, Soviet political and military leaders were convinced that the West would stop at nothing, including nuclear war, to destroy the Soviet Union.

Top secret VRYAN directives from the KGB leadership to its foreign residencies, dozens of them leaked by Gordievsky to British intelligence, make crystal clear the Soviet Union's virtual obsession during the 1980s with the immediate threat of a U.S. nuclear surprise attack. These documents are amazing, if only because they are now available to the public. Scarcely a decade ago the KGB would have killed to prevent these sensitive communications from falling into the hands of NATO.

The VRYAN directives are most remarkable for what they say about Soviet threat perceptions. For example, a top secret KGB document entitled "Chief Conclusions and Views Adopted at the Meeting of Heads of Service" bluntly expressed the view that nuclear war was imminent: "The White House is advancing in its propaganda the adventurist, and extremely dangerous, notion of 'survival' in the fire of a thermonuclear catastrophe. This is nothing else but psychological preparation of the population for nuclear war." Elsewhere, the same KGB document underscored the "growing threat of war," the "sharply increased" possibility of surprise nuclear attack, and the views that "the threat of an outbreak of nuclear war has reached dangerous proportions."

A top secret KGB directive of February 17, 1983, noted the "growing urgency" of discovering any "decision being taken to use nuclear weapons against the U.S.S.R. or immediate preparations being made for a nuclear missile attack." Another top secret KGB directive of the same date emphasized watchfulness for "surprise nuclear missile attack."

The VRYAN directives also reveal the urgency and the breadth of the KGB's search for signs of impending nuclear war. A KGB message of August 12, 1983, specified numerous activities of U.S. and NATO intelligence services that individually or severally, in combination with other activities, were considered to be indicative of preparations for a nuclear attack on the Soviet Union. The top secret *Permanent Operational Assignment to Detect Signs of NATO Preparations for a Nuclear Attack on the U.S.S.R. as Reflected in the Activity of Special Services of the [NATO] Bloc* ordered that

> The most important indications of preparation by the adversary for a nuclear attack on the U.S.S.R. which may find expression in the activity of its special services are listed below: . . . A sharp increase in the activity of all forms of intelligence . . . an increase in secret dropping of agents and operational equipment into the U.S.S.R . . . increased activity on the part of the American CIA and NSA to establish close contacts with the special services of other NATO countries . . . an increase in the number of disinformation operations against the U.S.S.R. . . . secret infiltration of sabotage teams with nuclear, bacteriological and chemical weapons into countries of the Warsaw Pact . . . reinforcement of repressive measures by the punitive authorities against progressive organizations and individuals . . . replacement of local guards by special guard detachments at particularly important state and military installations . . . restrictions on the use of telephone and telegraph network.

In this directive the KGB assumed that Western military plans were similar to Soviet war plans—mistakenly in some areas, as in preparation for bacteriological warfare. The United States had destroyed its stocks of offensive bacteriological weapons in 1972, in compliance with the Biological Weapons Convention, which banned these weapons. The Soviets had not destroyed theirs. Erroneous Soviet "mirror-imaging" is also evident in the assumption that the West would repress dissident or pacifist groups, spread disinformation, or restrict use of the public telephone system.

Some VRYAN tasking, in addition to reflecting the paranoid threat perceptions of the Soviet leaders, also displayed imperfect and even bizarre Soviet views of how Western institutions operated. One top secret KGB missive assumed that Western hospital administrators, churches, and bankers might have knowledge indicative of NATO plans to launch a nuclear first strike: "One important sign that preparations are beginning for VRYAN could be increased purchases of blood from donors . . . since the treatment of burns (the most widespread injury in a nuclear explosion) requires blood transfusions in very considerable quantity."

Over all, VRYAN tasking focused on sensible collection requirements relating to enemy war plans and the posture of his military forces. But all VRYAN tasking was extraordinarily dangerous to the West, since VRYAN falsely presumed that a NATO nuclear attack was impending. The Soviets were not troubling with VRYAN so that they could strike *second*, a goal that could be achieved without VRYAN, but *first*.

Perhaps the most disturbing aspect of VRYAN was its automated component. Intelligence collected by the KGB and GRU was fed into a battery of computers for analysis. The VRYAN computer program, designed by the KGB and Soviet military, then calculated the overall East-West balance of power—the "correlation of forces," in Soviet parlance—based on military, economic, and political strength. Factored in were numerous other variables to predict when the West would launch a surprise nuclear attack. VRYAN computations assumed that when the correlation of forces reached a certain ratio, the West would strike. The VRYAN computer program also assumed that Western preparations to launch a nuclear strike might be revealed in such obvious things as the posture of U.S. and NATO military forces, or in very subtle indicators, such as an increase of hospital blood supplies or in the price of gold. Data on thousands of such variables, some of obvious importance and others seemingly nonsensical, went into the VRYAN computers. The purpose of the VRYAN automaton was to recommend to Soviet political and military leaders when to launch a preemptive nuclear strike. VRYAN's algorithm for a nuclear first strike was the most extreme manifestation of the Soviet belief that complex political and historical phenomena could be analyzed "objectively"—that through the lens of "scientific" Marxism-Leninism, human life could be reduced to a mathematical equation.

CHAPTER 3

The Pershing II Crisis, May 1981–November 1983

More than any other single event, it was the decision by the United States and other NATO members to deploy Pershing II nuclear missiles in Western Europe that led Soviet political and military leaders to conclude that the West was preparing to launch a nuclear surprise attack. Pershing II moved the Soviets to escalate sharply their own preparations for a nuclear first-strike by instigating Operation VRYAN in May 1981. NATO had not made the decision to acquire Pershing II lightly. For two years prior to the December 1979 endorsement of Pershing II deployment, NATO member states hotly debated how to respond to the rapidly growing legion of Soviet SS-20 intermediate-range ballistic missiles (IRBMs), which were already fielded in numbers that far exceeded any reasonable Soviet defensive need. NATO Europe had no comparable missiles based on its territory with which to pose an equivalent threat to the Soviet Union or its Warsaw Pact allies. NATO members agreed among themselves on a "dual track" strategy: answer the SS-20 threat by placing U.S. intermediate-range nuclear missiles in Western Europe but propose to the Soviet Union that *both* sides ban this class of weapon altogether.

Although the decision to base Pershing IIs in Europe was made in 1979, the United States would not be prepared to deploy the missiles, which were in 1979 still under development, for several years. The first Pershing IIs were scheduled to arrive in Western Europe in November 1983. In the interim, the Soviets retained their unilateral advantage in IRBMs able to strike any target in Europe. Soviet public statements from the early 1980s are full of blunt warnings that Pershing II would increase the likelihood of nuclear war. On June 22, 1981, one month after the instigation of VRYAN, the minister of defense, Dmitri Ustinov, openly equated the Pershing II with preparations for "unleashing" World War III: "Indeed, everyone knows that the chief purpose of the scheme to deploy the new U.S. missiles in Western Europe is, by unleashing a new world war about whose preparation the Pentagon strategists are talking so cynically, to subject the FRG [Federal Republic of Germany] and other allies to a destructive retaliation strike and try to sit it out."

One month later, Defense Minister Ustinov publicly raised the specter of a U.S. nuclear first-strike: "While declaring officially that the new missiles are allegedly meant for the defense of Western European countries, Washington in actual fact is intending them for the inflicting of 'preventive' strikes on Soviet ICBMs and other vitally important installations situated inside the Western areas of the U.S.S.R." Just six months before the first Pershing IIs arrived in Western Europe, an official Soviet government statement, published in *Pravda* on May 27, 1983, warned that "deployment of these missiles would . . . sharply aggravate nuclear confrontation, and would increase the risk of the outbreak of war." Three months after this, Yuri Andropov, now general secretary of the USSR, declared, "The nuclear arms race in Europe . . . can become a source of a rapid and dramatic growth of a threat of new world war."

Soviet arms control initiatives during the early 1980s indicate that Soviet leaders were truly worried about a U.S. nuclear surprise attack. In 1981 the Soviets promoted a UN resolution making it a crime against humanity to use nuclear weapons first. In 1982 they proposed that the United States and Soviet Union pull nuclear missile submarines back from forward patrol areas. This move would reduce the possibility of initiating a short-warning nuclear attack, but more so for the Americans than for the Soviets, since the United States depends much more heavily upon submarine-launched missiles. In 1982 Premier Leonid Brezhnev pledged "no first use" of nuclear weapons and urged the United States to reciprocate. In 1983 the Soviets reversed their earlier opposition to a treaty calling for measures to avert the threat of nuclear surprise attack. This flurry of diplomatic initiatives, many involving steps for war prevention to be undertaken immediately, gives the strong impression of a Soviet foreign policy fixated on preventing, or forestalling, an imminent nuclear conflict.

At the time, Soviet war warnings and arms control initiatives were largely dismissed in the West as propaganda aimed at stopping the placement of Pershing II missiles. However, the thinking embodied in their public statements and arms control proposals squares perfectly with the mindset of Soviet leaders as described by KGB defectors and manifested in Operation VRYAN. Soviets leaders were expressing their true view that world war was imminent.

Sharply escalating social unrest and civil violence within the Soviet Union contributed significantly to Moscow's sense of crisis and of heightened vulnerability to foreign aggression. During the early 1980s, the tremendous and growing burden of the arms race overtaxed the inefficient Soviet economy. Shortages and privations of all kinds increasingly drove people to defy the Soviet police state, often at great risk; the granite facade of the "socialist worker's paradise" began to crack.

A previously top secret U.S. National Intelligence Estimate, *Dimensions of Civil Unrest in the Soviet Union*, published in April 1983, seven months before the arrival in Europe of Pershing IIs, found that "more unrest has occurred in the period 1980–82 than in any other three-year period during the 1970s." Soviet leaders were most disturbed by growing acts of civil violence:

> Violence in the Baltic states in 1978–81 reportedly included the sabotaging of a TV tower, the burning of a government furniture warehouse, and an attempt to blow up a bridge in Estonia. Six fires were set simultaneously in Latvia, including one at the Supreme Soviet building in Riga. In Lithuania, the electrical power supply to a large factory was sabotaged. In Georgia, forty-five terrorists were recently sent to prison, and four were executed, for a series of raids against the militia and military installations. . . . In Kazakhstan, in what one source described as a series of assassinations against state officials, two policemen were shot to death in their homes; for the most part, the victims have been Russians. In the Russian city of Rostov, several policemen were machine-gunned. . . . Three trains reportedly have been sabotaged in recent years. One was blown up in Chelyabinsk, RSFSR, resulting in many casualties.

The intelligence community received reports of an assassination attempt against Andropov in 1982, and the top secret NIE also reported "two apparently successful assassinations" of high-ranking Soviet officials: S. I. Ibraimov, chairman of the Kirgiz Council of Ministers in 1980, and the Azerbaijan minister of interior in 1978. The National Intelligence Estimate concluded that "Soviet elites are indeed more concerned now about the potential effects of popular discontent than they have been for the past twenty-five years." It further stated that "for the Soviets, this may be a vicious circle of greater potential significance for the 1980s than the regime has had to cope with anytime in the past three decades."

In fact, the "vicious circle" was wider, and more dangerous, than the NIE and the U.S. intelligence community acknowledged—or knew. Soviet perceptions of domestic crisis reinforced, and were reinforced by, the international crisis over Pershing II and the perceived rising threat of nuclear war. On the foreign and domestic fronts, Soviet leaders responded with desperate rhetoric and desperate measures. To the Soviet people Brezhnev and Andropov gave police terror, and to the West they gave VRYAN.

What did the United States know about Soviet perceptions that superpower relations were tottering on the nuclear brink, or of the Soviets' greater preparedness to launch a preemptive strike? Incredibly, Gordievsky's warnings to the West about the Soviet war scare and Operation VRYAN, all supported by the irrefutable testimony of top secret KGB directives from Moscow, fell on deaf ears. The U.S. intelligence community and policy makers either did not know, failed to believe, or refused to appreciate the significance of Gordievsky's revelations. Although Western leaders may have toned down some of their anti-Soviet rhetoric in response to Gordievsky's information, the aspects of U.S. defense and foreign policy that the Soviets found most provocative—Pershing II, SDI, and "rolling back" the Soviet empire—did not change at all. Indeed, the United States officially rejected Soviet war warnings over Pershing II as propaganda, in *Soviet Propaganda Campaign against NATO*, published by the U.S. Arms Control and Disarmament Agency in October 1983, one month before the first Pershing II deployments.

NIEs from the early 1980s, now declassified, are the closest thing we have to an official statement about what our government believed and did not believe about the Soviet nuclear threat. Significantly, none mention Gordievsky, VRYAN, or any of the data supplied by Gordievsky.

The National Intelligence Estimates *did* note accelerating Soviet preparations for nuclear war, an increasingly serious Soviet attitude toward prosecuting nuclear war, and other developments that should have, but somehow did not, lead the American intelligence community to conclude that the threat of nuclear war was growing.

The previously top secret NIE *Soviet Capabilities for Strategic Nuclear Conflict, 1982–92*, published in February 1983, observed that the Soviets were seeking "superior capabilities to fight and win a nuclear war with the United States" and to "assure a high probability of prevailing in a nuclear conflict." The March 1984 National Intelligence Estimate *Soviet Capabilities for Strategic Nuclear Conflict, 1983–93* made similar observations. The Soviets were pursuing "vigorous efforts to enhance their capability for strategic nuclear war" by developing "offensive and defensive weapons of virtually every type." One of the principal effects of these Soviet force enhancements was "an improved first strike capability against hardened targets." The March 1984 NIE noted that Soviet training for nuclear war had become more realistic and that the Soviets were deadly earnest about prosecuting—and prevailing in—a nuclear war. Soviet training for "global nuclear conflict" was increasingly "broad in scope" and "complex," with greater "realism"; its "increased stress placed on their personnel in combat training" was more consistent with actually preparing to fight a nuclear war that was imminent than with routine training to deter some remote and highly theoretical contingency. Yet the National Intelligence Estimates missed the implication that the Soviets saw nuclear war as a real prospect.

That Pershing II, in the Soviet view, posed an unprecedented first-strike threat and was genuinely feared was understood by the American intelligence community and reflected in the NIEs. Moreover, that preemption, striking first, was the preferred Soviet nuclear option was well understood in the National Intelligence Estimates: "Warning of a NATO nuclear strike is likely to prompt a massive Soviet preemptive strike." The NIEs hammered on the theme that in the event of war, the Soviets planned to launch a preemptive nuclear first strike. However, the NIEs also noted a crucial intelligence gap: "We are unable to judge what information would be sufficiently convincing to cause Soviet leaders to order a massive preemptive attack."

The August 1982 NIE, *The Soviet Challenge to U.S. Security Interests*, came closest to concluding correctly that U.S.-Soviet relations were becoming more dangerous:

> As the Soviet leadership moves further into a period of political succession, Soviet policies will become less predictable. The potential confluence of greater Soviet military power, increased regional instabilities, more assertive U.S. policies, and the potential for expanded U.S. military capabilities . . . could make a successor Soviet leadership increasingly willing to exploit current opportunities in what it perceives as low-cost, low-risk areas. This attitude, in turn, could increase the possibilities of miscalculation and unpremeditated U.S.-Soviet confrontations.

This warning did not go nearly far enough. The NIE implied that the spark for a future U.S.-Soviet confrontation could originate only from the Soviet side, and it saw the source of conflict as "low-cost, low-risk" issues "most likely in the Third World." In fact, Pershing II and VRYAN were high-cost, high-risk programs that placed the sides on a collision course not in the Third World but in the heart of Europe.

Despite being correct about many particulars, the National Intelligence Estimates misjudged the bottom line. As seen in the NIEs, the Soviet view of the possibility of nuclear war was no different from the Western view: remote. Moreover, the National Intelligence Estimates flatly concluded that in the unlikely event of a future nuclear war, the Soviets were not very concerned about the possibility of nuclear surprise attack. They focused overwhelmingly on a single nuclear-war scenario that pointedly excluded nuclear surprise attack: "The Soviets see little likelihood that the United States would initiate a surprise nuclear attack from a normal peacetime posture; we believe it is unlikely that the Soviets would mount such an attack themselves." The scenario advanced in the National Intelligence Estimates virtually eliminated the possibility of strategic surprise in a nuclear war, since a political crisis lasting "weeks or longer" and a phase of major conventional conflict lasting additional days or weeks would provide both sides with ample warning of impending nuclear escalation. This escalatory scenario for what was assumed to be a remote threat was the opposite of the actual Soviet scenario anticipated in VRYAN—where the expectation was that the United States was actively preparing to launch a nuclear surprise attack in peacetime, very possibly in the near future.

The intelligence community's failure to analyze correctly the important role of surprise attack in Soviet threat perceptions is all the more puzzling since some Western academics, working without benefit of classified data, were closer to the mark. For example, Mark Miller, in his *Soviet Strategic Power and Doctrine*, published in 1982, on the basis of a broad review and close analysis of unclassified Soviet writings on nuclear strategy, concluded: "It would seem perilous to ignore the implications of the long-standing doctrinal emphasis on seizing the initiative, mass, and surprise for Soviet conduct [of] war." How could the U.S. intelligence community, armed with Gordievsky's testimony and top secret KGB documents describing the Soviet fixation on nuclear surprise attack, fail to include any of this evidence in the National Intelligence Estimates? How could the NIEs draw conclusions about Soviet threat perceptions that were so wrong? It is possible that during the early 1980s the intelligence community remained ignorant of Gordievsky's message because his handlers in British intelligence did not share information with analysts in the United States. Sometimes highly placed sources with access to enemy classified data are so highly prized that their existence, and even vital information, are withheld from analysts and intelligence consumers in the military and policy communities in order to protect the source and preserve the flow of enemy secrets. For example, during World War II, data derived by cracking Germany's communications codes—data that could have aided Allied military operations and saved many lives—was often withheld from Allied military commanders. In order to avoid revealing to the Germans that their codes had been broken, and in anticipation of gaining more important data in the future, intelligence was not shared that could have mitigated the German bombing of Coventry and the Allied disaster at Anzio.

It is also possible that the intelligence community dismissed Gordievsky's testimony as part of an elaborate Soviet disinformation campaign. Moscow was, in fact, orchestrating a massive propaganda offensive against Pershing II deployment at the time. But the top secret KGB documents and VRYAN activities in Europe and North America should have proved beyond a reasonable doubt Gordievsky's veracity. Still, some intelligence officers had dwelled so long in the "wilderness of mirrors" that at least a few would have been prepared to believe that all of this had been staged.

Gordievsky's message about Soviet hypersensitivity and immediate preparations for nuclear war were certainly inconvenient for an assertive—some would says reckless—U.S. foreign and defense policy. That message also contradicted certain preconceptions about the Soviet threat that were strongly held by the U.S. intelligence and defense community—assumptions that a future world war would be unlikely to begin with a nuclear surprise attack. Indeed, American defense planners were gambling that a future war would not at first involve nuclear weapons at all. Most U.S. strategic nuclear forces were not ready for combat on a day-to-day basis but required some days of strategic warning to allow nuclear weapons to be uploaded on bombers and so additional ballistic-missile submarines (SSBNs) could put to sea. Naval, air, and ground general-purpose forces, which consumed about 80 percent of the U.S. defense budget, required some weeks or months to mobilize for a global war. A Russian nuclear surprise attack could, in the span of thirty minutes, destroy most U.S. strategic nuclear forces and virtually all general-purpose forces. The U.S. military services, and their constituent intelligence agencies, had strong institutional biases favoring a future-war scenario that would escalate to nuclear conflict gradually. The scenario advanced in the National Intelligence Estimates, wherein a nuclear war was preceded by a lengthy political crisis and protracted phase of conventional combat, provided ample time and opportunity for all U.S. services and forces to mobilize—especially the costly general-purpose forces—and to play an important role in a future war.

The failure of the intelligence community to understand Soviet threat perceptions and anticipate Operation VRYAN was extraordinarily dangerous. The Soviets may well have started thinking seriously about making a nuclear first-strike on the West the day after NATO's announced decision to acquire Pershing IIs in December 1979. Certainly, Moscow was thinking along these lines with the start of VRYAN in May 1981. Unknown to the West, VRYAN placed U.S.-Soviet relations, and Soviet strategic forces, on a hair trigger. Thereafter, Soviet interpretations of even routine U.S. and NATO activities, such as military exercises, were rendered dangerous by Soviet expectations that war was coming. As November 1983, the arrival date for U.S. Pershing IIs in Europe, drew nearer, Soviet anxieties increased, as did the potential for catastrophic nuclear miscalculation. International incidents also contributed to rising tensions in the Kremlin—in particular, the 1981 Polish crisis and the KAL 007 incident in 1983. The Soviets viewed these episodes as the possible beginnings of World War III.

CHAPTER 4

The Polish Crisis, September–December 1981

The chopper blades sliced the air like saber strokes. Bright autumn fields and forests rushed past General Jaruzelski's helicopter window. His body leaned into a sharp turn as the copter swung parallel to a highway and scudded for several minutes over roads choked with tanks and infantry fighting vehicles. Everywhere endless columns of armor, trucks, and towed artillery filled lanes, paths, and pastures with the drab greens and grays of Soviet steel.

The helicopter landed and was immediately surrounded by Soviet officers. Years later General Jaruzelski, premier of Poland, could still recall, word for word, what his host, Dmitri Ustinov, defense minister of the USSR, told him in that chopper.

General Wojiech Witold Jaruzelski was a highly improbable savior of Poland, let alone Polish democracy, but he would become, in spite of himself, both. Born in 1923 to a family of landed Polish aristocrats, staunch Catholics who hated Russians and communists with equal fervor, Jaruzelski lost everything at the age of sixteen when Germany and the USSR divided Poland in 1939. Fleeing to Lithuania, the Jaruzelskis were captured in the Soviet invasion of that country and were among the first of thousands deported from the newly captive nations to the slave labor camps in the Soviet east. Jaruzelski's mother and father died in the camps. As a teenager, Jaruzelski slaved in the coal mines of Karaganda, Central Asia, until his early convictions and loyalties had been broken. He emerged reeducated, as a "new Soviet man."

In 1943, at age twenty, Jaruzelski served alongside the Red Army in Stalin's invented "Polish Army"—little more than a pretext for Moscow to install a communist government in Poland. He saw some of the fiercest battles of World War II, in the Vistula, Oder, Elbe, and Berlin campaigns. In 1944, Jaruzelski was among those who on Stalin's orders halted offensive operations outside Warsaw, deliberately allowing Nazi SS troopers enough time to exterminate noncommunist Polish freedom fighters. The Warsaw Poles rose to support the Red Army, but their "liberators" did not advance until Stalin was sure of capturing a largely dead city. After the war, from 1945 to 1947, Jaruzelski further proved his political loyalty to Moscow by directing mop-up operations against forest bands of Polish guerrillas who refused to accept a communist Poland. He rose meteorically, and again demonstrated his reliability in 1968, when as defense minister, he authorized Poland's participation in the Soviet-led invasion of Czechoslovakia.

In February 1981 General Jaruzelski was appointed premier, the fourth new Polish leader within a year. Moscow hoped that the man in dark glasses—worn because of an abnormal sensitivity to light—would succeed where the others had failed: in squashing a menace called "Solidarity." Solidarity was a democratic labor movement dedicated to transforming Poland's political-economic system from a communist dictatorship and command economy into an elected representative form of government and a decentralized free-market economy. The movement arose in response to government corruption and severe shortages of food and consumer goods. Moscow failed to understand the popular origins of Solidarity, preferring to believe instead that the democratic movement was largely a conspiracy organized and directed by Western governments. Moscow perhaps did not realize, as the Polish government did, that popular support for Solidarity ran so deep that violence against the movement could begin a civil war. In fact, no less than the continued existence of the Warsaw Pact and the East-West balance of power was at stake. If communism fell in Poland, the future of communism throughout Eastern Europe—and eventually in the Soviet Union itself—would be threatened. In the past the Soviet Union had launched full-scale invasions of Eastern Europe—against Hungary in 1956 and Czechoslovakia in 1968—to keep communism from unraveling. These invasions had risked confrontation with the West. Numerous Soviet statements during the early 1980s condemned the West for interfering with Poland. In angry speeches before the United Nations in 1981 and 1982, Foreign Minister Andrei Gromyko charged that the United States was dominated by "military circles" who "seek domination over other countries and peoples," that the United States sought "military superiority over the Soviet Union," that the USSR was endeavoring to "ward off the threat of war," but that U.S. policy was "full steam ahead for war." Gromyko said that Western "interference" in Poland could be a proximate cause of conflict, and he warned the United States not to try to "shake loose the socialist foundations of the Polish state."

Moscow was almost as hostile toward its own ally, General Jaruzelski, warning him of dire consequences if Solidarity was not contained. In September 1981 Jaruzelski had his "chilling" helicopter meeting with Ustinov, which he would recount in a 1993 interview: "It lasted a few hours. He said the Soviet Union would no longer tolerate the situation, that it threatened the security of the whole Warsaw Pact. He took me on a whole panorama of the global threats against the Soviet Union. He mentioned Afghanistan, China. And then what really worried me was when he talked about Poland. He called us 'the third front.' In their mind, it was already a front." Later, Jaruzelski had an equally memorable meeting with the chief of the Warsaw Pact, Marshal Kulikov: "I still remember his words. I don't want to paint him as a devil—in a way I kind of liked him—but I always remember our last conversation. He told me: 'If this continues, my hand will shake.' "

According to General Viktor Dubynin, a former Soviet deputy defense minister, in December 1981 the USSR was poised to invade Poland and crush the budding Polish democratic movement. General Dubynin revealed these facts in a 1992 interview shortly before his death. He had been commander of an armored division stationed near Minsk that was part of the invasion force. He said the attack—which he helped plan—was scheduled for December 14, 1981, and targeted "an area south of Warsaw." Dubynin claimed the attack was called off only because Jaruzelski imposed martial law on Poland on December 13, the eve of the planned invasion. Ironically, the Polish premier's cruel oppression of Solidarity may well have spared the world a far graver tragedy, by canceling Soviet aggression that could easily have escalated into a confrontation with NATO.

Dubynin's admission that the Soviets nearly invaded Poland in 1981 is further confirmed by the occurrence of a major Soviet military exercise, ZAPAD-81, which commenced in September 1981. Its purpose was to conceal preparations for a war on Poland and, if necessary, a war on the West. Using the cover of a military exercise to mobilize troops for war was a long-standing Soviet practice and tenet of military doctrine. In retrospect, ZAPAD-81 certainly looked like preparation for an invasion. The exercise, one of the largest ever conducted by the USSR, featured a maneuver involving 100,000 troops. The Soviets tried to conceal the scale and nature of the exercise from NATO. According to the U.S. Arms Control and Disarmament Agency, Soviet efforts to hide ZAPAD-81 went so far as to violate the Helsinki Final Act of 1975, which required NATO and the Soviet Union to provide prior notification "of major military maneuvers exceeding a total of 25,000 troops." ZAPAD-81 intimidated the Poles into instituting martial law against the democratic Solidarity movement, which is what the Soviets wanted anyway, rendering an invasion of Poland unnecessary, as General Dubynin said.

Before Jaruzelski acted against Solidarity, invading Poland and waging a wider war if necessary was exactly what Moscow had in mind. During the months prior to the planned invasion, the Central Intelligence Agency had a highly placed source inside the Polish government monitoring the military situation in and around Poland. Colonel Ryszard Kuklinski, a Polish patriot who regarded Jaruzelski and other communists as traitors, issued his last report to the CIA in September 1981. Fifteen Soviet armored divisions, along with East German and Czech divisions, were massing along the borders. Discovered by Soviet or Polish counterintelligence, Kuklinski narrowly escaped with his life. Aided by the CIA, he fled to the United States, where he now lives under an assumed name in an undisclosed location—still targeted by the Russian intelligence services. A special National Intelligence Estimate, *Poland's Prospects over the Next 12 to 18 Months*, previously classified secret and published nine months after the USSR's near-invasion of Poland, treated the invasion as inevitable, had General Jaruzelski not imposed martial law.

The Soviets risked escalation to nuclear war by aggression against Poland in the early 1980s because of exaggerated views of a "Western threat" and because of new military and political realities that reinforced those fears. The Soviets mistakenly believed that, if the USSR invaded Poland, the United States and NATO might intervene to protect the nascent democratic movement. More than Poland was at stake. If democratic sentiment spread from Poland to other Eastern European states, it could doom the Warsaw Pact and the Soviet hold on half of Europe. In fact, the United States and NATO would not have risked war to save Poland, but in the opinion of Soviet political and military leaders, war over Poland was a real possibility.

Adding to Soviet fears that an invasion of Poland could lead to a world war was the new strength of NATO military forces in Europe. From the Soviet perspective, an invasion of Poland in 1981 would be riskier than the Soviet invasions of Hungary in 1956 and of Czechoslovakia in 1968, when NATO was much weaker. Furthermore, Poland was now more explosive than Hungary or Czechoslovakia had been, because the Polish army might fight an invasion. The Hungarian and Czech armies had not resisted. Earnest Polish resistance might ignite Western sympathy for the embattled Poles and increase the chances of intervention. The Polish army could try to *force* NATO involvement by fighting a rearguard action westward through East Germany to escape into West Germany. Many such escalatory scenarios must have plagued the Soviet General Staff as it prepared to crush democracy in Poland. No doubt, too, Soviet political and military leaders remembered well how the last world war had been sparked by an invasion of Poland. An invasion of Poland could give the United States a pretext to launch the nuclear surprise attack that the Soviets were watching for in their VRYAN project. Soviet fears of an impending Western nuclear surprise attack—and Soviet plans to foil such an attack by striking first—made the Polish situation perilous. Western troop movements, a large NATO military exercise, or even a carelessly worded diplomatic warning might have moved the USSR to act catastrophically.

CHAPTER 5

The KAL 007 Crisis, September 1983

Most passengers were probably asleep aboard Korean Air Lines flight 007 during the early morning hours of September 1, 1983, as the Boeing 747 flew the last leg of its journey from New York to Seoul, South Korea. The normal route paralleled the Siberian coast, just outside Soviet airspace. Among the passengers was Mrs. Rebecca Scruton, twenty-eight years old. A Sunday school teacher and mother of two, she had left her children with friends while taking this trip to visit her parents. Her husband had died nine months earlier of cancer. Seventy-five-year-old Jessie Slaton from Detroit was on a tour of the Far East with six other women. Edith Cruz, twenty-three, was journeying from Chattanooga, Tennessee, to the Philippines to attend her grandmother's funeral. John Oldham, twenty-seven, a Fulbright fellow and graduate of Columbia Law School, planned to spend a year in Beijing. Noelle Ann and Stacey Marie Grenfell had visited their grandmother in Rochester, New York, and were returning with their parents, Carol and Neil, to South Korea, where their father worked for the Eastman Kodak Company. Noelle Ann was aged five, Stacey Marie three.

An Su-15 interceptor from a Soviet air defense base on Sakhalin Island trailed KAL 007 through the night. The airliner, off course, had violated Soviet airspace. Radars of the PVO (air defense forces) had tracked the giant aircraft for over two hours as it lumbered over the Kamchatka Peninsula, a testing range for Soviet ICBMs, and toward Vladivostok, headquarters of the Soviet Pacific Fleet, where a third of the Navy's nuclear submarines were based. The members of the crew of KAL 007 were unaware of their navigation error. They also did not know that at least ten MiG-23 and Su-15 interceptors had scrambled to meet them.

What happened next has been reconstructed from U.S. intercepts of Soviet air defense communications. At 3:12 A.M., the Su-15 pilot reported that he had visual contact with KAL 007: "See it visually and on radar." At 3:13 A.M. he was ready to fire if so ordered: "I see it. I'm locked on target."

Air defense headquarters on Sakhalin informed Moscow of the situation and received an urgent coded message in reply. An SA-5 surface-to-air missile on the southern tip of Sakhalin Island was placed on alert, probably in case the Su-15 pilot missed. At 3:26 A.M. the Su-15 pilot fired the first of two AA-3 ANAB missiles. The first missile was a heat seeker, and it probably struck the airliner's left wing, causing an explosion. The second, radar-homing missile may have hit the passenger compartment.

The Su-15 pilot reported, "The target is destroyed."

The Soviet pilot who destroyed KAL 007, Gennadi Osipovich, recalled thirteen years later in an interview in December 1996: "I saw two rows of windows and knew that this was a Boeing. I knew this was a civilian plane. But for me this meant nothing. It is easy to turn a civilian plane into one for military use." Osipovich claims he fired warning shots but that lacking tracer bullets, they were not visible at night. "A confirmed Communist . . . Osipovich insists that the jetliner was on a spy mission. . . . He even considers himself fortunate to have received a measure of celebrity by having destroyed Flight 007," according to the *New York Times*. "One of his few complaints is that the Soviet authorities paid him a smaller bonus for shooting down the plane than he had hoped: 200 rubles minus a small fee for postage."

In a twist of fate, North Carolina senator Jesse Helms, waiting for another flight in Anchorage, Alaska, had met the Grenfell girls in the airport lounge while KAL 007 was refueling for the last leg of its doomed journey: "If I live to be one thousand, I will never forget those little girls. They played on my lap, giggling and kissing my cheeks. And when they went to get on that plane, they waved bye-bye and blew kisses at me. That's why I'll never forget those two little girls. They had a right to live."

All 269 passengers and crew aboard KAL 007 were killed. The Soviets claimed they were justified in shooting KAL 007, because although the 747 was unmistakably a civilian aircraft, it was nonetheless on a spying mission.

The KAL 007 incident illustrated the hair-trigger mindset of the Soviet military, born of its fear that World War III was imminent. Five years earlier, another Korean Air Lines 747, KAL 902, traveling from Paris to Seoul, wandered off course over the Kola Peninsula. Although fired on by Soviet interceptors, KAL 902 was not shot down but forced to land on a frozen lake south of Murmansk. The different outcomes for these similar incidents—KAL 902 was spared, while KAL 007 was destroyed—reflects the deterioration in Soviet attitudes from the détente of the 1970s to the war scare of the 1980s.

Gordievsky believes the Soviets may have shot down KAL 007 because they mistook the airliner for an RC-135, a U.S. intelligence aircraft. Their hysteria about an anticipated U.S. surprise attack led them to overreact. He disagrees with charges made at the time by President Reagan, Secretary of State George Shultz, and other administration officials that the shooting of KAL 007 was a deliberate act of cold-blooded murder. However, Gordievsky admits that one of his superior officers in the KGB confided that the Soviet military was very much aware that it was killing civilians. Soviet public justifications of the incident never admitted error or claimed mistaken identity with an RC-135. The CIA, they implied, was the real culprit:

it had used a civilian passenger aircraft for a spy mission. According to a Tass article published shortly after the shootdown, "The plan was to carry out without a hitch the . . . intelligence operation, but if it was stymied, to turn all this into a political provocation against the Soviet Union. . . . The entire responsibility for this tragedy rests wholly and fully with the leaders of the United States of America."

In 1993, an official Russian investigation of KAL 007 absolved the Soviet hierarchy of blame, arguing that the shooting was a case of mistaken identity. The Russian report claimed that a U.S. spy plane had violated Soviet airspace and that the Soviets shot down KAL 007 thinking it was the hostile intruder. However, in January 1998, General Anatoly Kornukov—newly promoted chief of the Russian air force and air defense force—who ordered the shootdown of KAL 007, said, "I will always be sure that the order was given correctly." General Kornukov is "absolutely certain" that KAL 007 was on a hostile mission.

Nine days after the KAL 007 shootdown, Marshal Nikolai Ogarkov, Chief of the General Staff, held a news conference in Moscow to justify the Soviet action: "The conclusion was made at Soviet anti-aircraft command posts: an intelligence aircraft is approaching the Soviet Union's airspace. The suggestion arises: How can this be a question of a mistake in this case? It is perfectly evident that this aircraft's flight was controlled, I would say precisely controlled. And therefore this flight was premeditated."

At the news conference Ogarkov's attitude was described as "truculent and unrepentant. . . . He declare that the dead were 'victims of the United States special services.' On being asked whether he could see a moral as well as a military aspect to the tragedy, he replied that he could not see the point of the question."

Whether the Soviets killed KAL 007 because they mistook it for an RC-135, or because they thought it was spying for the CIA, or because it was cold-blooded murder of known innocents to discourage unauthorized overflights of Soviet territory, none of these explanations justifies the act or points to any conclusion other than that the Soviets were expecting war. The United States and its NATO allies have never shot down even a Soviet or Russian intelligence aircraft, let alone a civilian airliner, in retaliation for airspace violations, because the threat posed by such intrusions does not justify so draconian a response. The Soviet destruction of KAL 007 makes sense militarily and politically only if the Soviets believed an attack on their territory was imminent.

Seymour Hersh, in *The Target Is Destroyed*, notes that, prior to the KAL 007 shootdown, in March and April 1983, "the United States Pacific Fleet was beginning its largest maneuvers since World War II in the North Pacific. During the three-week exercise, Navy warplanes from aircraft carriers *Midway* and *Enterprise* directly overflew Soviet military installations on the Kurile Islands, just North of Japan." Moreover, "three aircraft carrier battle groups, part of a forty-ship armada accompanied by Air Force B-52 bombers, specially equipped [Airborne Warning and Control System] aircraft (AWACs), and F-15 fighters, sailed . . . in the icy waters off Alaska's Aleutian Islands, 450 miles from the Soviet Union's Kamchatka Peninsula. American attack submarines and antisubmarine aircraft began operating for the first time inside the normal patrol area of the Soviet submarine fleet. In all, 23,000 American military men took part." In retrospect, knowing what we now know about Soviet threat perceptions during the period, it would not be surprising if the Soviets reacted to these exercises by gearing up, at least psychologically, their Far East air defenses for war.

A factor that increased the possibility of war, or at least ensured that incidents like KAL 007 would be interpreted by Soviet leaders as portents of war, was the death of Leonid Brezhnev in 1982 and his replacement as general secretary of the Soviet Communist Party and premier of the USSR by Yuri Andropov, high priest of VRYAN. Brezhnev was no less fearful and suspicious of the West than Andropov, but he was far less dogmatic and hostile, and less likely to act on his fears. Beefy, with thick black eyebrows his most prominent feature, Brezhnev even looked the part of "the Cautious Bully," as one Western epitaph dubbed him. Unlike many of his colleagues, he was a simple epicurean who loved to wallow in luxury, not meditate on World War III. Brezhnev used his position as premier to wangle "gifts" of automobiles from Western governments as the price of summit meetings, collecting a Rolls Royce, a Mercedes, a Cadillac, and a Lincoln "as personal fruits of détente," as one wit put it. Secretary of State Henry Kissinger would recall Brezhnev proudly showing off his hunting lodge, which included a movie theater, and asking his American guests to estimate how much it would cost in the United States. When Kissinger estimated $400,000, Brezhnev's face fell. Aide Helmut Sonnenfeldt quickly suggested two million dollars, and the premier's face beamed. A photograph of Brezhnev at a summit in San Clemente captures him appraising actress Jill St. John's derriere. He was accompanied everywhere, even to summits with the U.S. president at Camp David, by a buxom young woman, his masseuse.

KGB chief Andropov, Brezhnev's longtime neighbor and pretended friend, positioned himself to succeed Brezhnev by blackmailing the old man with threats to reveal his scandalous sex life and the alleged involvement in a jewel heist of Brezhnev's daughter, Galina. In their biography of Andropov, Vladimir Solovyov and Elena Klepikova imply he may have hastened Brezhnev's death by means of the premier's KGB bodyguards. Andropov was supported in his bid to succeed Brezhnev by like-minded colleagues Dmitri Ustinov and Andrei Gromyko, the defense and foreign ministers. General Secretary Andropov scattered Brezhnev's inner circle to the wind, posting them to positions far from Moscow, shortly after assuming leadership of the Communist Party in November 1982. There were rumors, featured prominently in the U.S. press, that the new general secretary was a closet liberal who liked American fiction and jazz, preferred cognac and scotch to vodka, and enjoyed tennis. This was KGB disinformation. Andropov added to his titles premier of the USSR in June 1983, three months before the KAL 007 shootdown. He expressed his view of the significance of the KAL 007 tragedy in a statement on September 28, about a month after the shootdown and two months before the arrival in Europe of the first Pershing IIs:

> If anyone had any illusions about an evolution for the better in the policy of the present American Administration, recent events have dispelled them once and for all. . . . During the six and one-half decades of its existence, the Soviet state has successfully endured many trials, including the crucial one [World War II]. Those who encroached on the integrity of our state, its independence and our system found themselves on the garbage heap of history. It is high time that everybody to whom this applies understand that we shall be able to ensure the security of our country, the security of our friends and allies under any circumstances. [The United States'] imperial ambitions go so far that one begins to doubt whether Washington has any brakes at all preventing it from crossing the mark before which any sober-minded person must stop.

Seymour Hersh observes that this statement "evoked the worst days of the Cold War in tone and toughness" and that "Andropov seemed to equate the crisis over Flight 007 to the life and death of the state."

President Reagan's strong public condemnations of the Soviet Union for shooting down KAL 007 and the Reagan administration's attempts to mobilize world opinion against the USSR convinced the new Soviet premier, the new KGB chief (Kryuchkov), Marshal Ogarkov, and other Soviet leaders that KAL 007 was part of an ambitious anti-Soviet conspiracy by the United States. Although Soviet leaders were aware of the mistakes made by Soviet air defenses in connection with KAL 007, Gordievsky believes that the Soviet leadership actually convinced itself that KAL 007 really was on a spy mission for the CIA, perhaps as a prelude to Western aggression against the USSR. A few days after the downing of KAL 007, on 4 September, Moscow secretly told KGB residencies overseas that KAL 007 was being exploited by the United States "to whip up worldwide anti-Soviet hysteria." Moscow directed residencies that the U.S. propaganda campaign had become "so virulent" that they should take steps "to protect Soviet nationals, buildings, ships, and aircraft" located in foreign countries from attack. Moscow further directed residencies to investigate the backgrounds of KAL 007 passengers for evidence of connections to foreign intelligence services. Moscow recalled Soviet students studying in the United States in order to protect them from violence fomented by the alleged anti-Soviet hysteria. The Soviets promoted such strong anti-Western feeling among their own people that, Gordievsky writes, returning students "were welcomed on their return home as if they were refugees from a war zone."

Soviet leaders believed that beyond anti-Soviet campaigns in Western countries, the KAL 007 crisis might provide the United States with an excuse for more ambitious acts of aggression. They feared that—like the sinking of the battleship *Maine*, which rallied Americans to make war against Spain in 1898, and the sinking of the *Lusitania*, which helped President Woodrow Wilson lead his nation into World War I—the KAL 007 shootdown could become the rallying point for a United States–led global coalition to isolate, and perhaps make war on, the USSR. Peace talks aimed at advancing NATO-Soviet cooperation on European security, which had begun in Madrid on 8 September, were terminated over the KAL 007 shooting. Soviet foreign minister Andrei Gromyko, the so-called "great survivor," who had held his post since Stalin, warned the West that "the world situation is now slipping towards a very dangerous precipice. . . . Problem number one for the world is to avoid nuclear war." Gromyko later described his meeting at Madrid with U.S. secretary of state George Shultz as highly confrontational: "It was probably the sharpest exchange I ever had with an American secretary of state, and I have had talks with fourteen of them." In response to KAL 007, Andropov placed even higher priority on VRYAN, already a top priority project. Soviet fears of a nuclear surprise attack, already near fever pitch, were escalating.

CHAPTER 6

ABLE ARCHER, November 2–11, 1983

Needle-sharp, the missile looked as if it were designed to kill by spearing its target, not by vaporizing it in a nuclear explosion. The fluttering light of the movie projector made the faces of the elite audience seem to flicker in and out of darkness as they watched a mobile missile carrier race across Yuri Andropov's wall. Dashing down a highway, then churning up dust along a country road, the ungainly vehicle charged along, its missile pointing forward, parallel to the ground—a space-age battering ram.

Vladimir Kryuchkov, the new KGB director, looked across to his boss and intoned the deadly statistics: "Missile transporter-launcher . . . a top speed of seventy-two kilometers per hour on hard-surface roads . . . missile can reach Moscow in less than ten minutes. . . ." Andropov knew it all and barely heard him now. "Delivers one nuclear warhead of fifty kilotons yield . . . ," Kryuchkov droned on.

Rolling out of a forest to the edge of a field, the machine suddenly stopped.

". . . pinpoint accuracy of fifty meters . . ."

A hydraulic arm lifted the missile upright. It vanished in an instant, becoming a blinding white star hurtling over the horizon.

Someone said, "Pershing II."

Two months after the KAL 007 tragedy, what was probably the single most dangerous incident of the early 1980s occurred during a NATO military exercise known as ABLE ARCHER–83, held on November 2–11, 1983. Gordievsky says that Soviet anxiety about a U.S. nuclear surprise attack reached its peak during this exercise which involved raising the alert level of U.S. nuclear forces based in Europe to simulate preparations for an attack. It was the first major NATO nuclear exercise to simulate Pershing II participation, and it very nearly provoked a preemptive nuclear strike in response.

In the same month as the KAL 007 shootdown, a National Intelligence Estimate was published, *Possible Soviet Responses to the U.S. Strategic Defense Initiative*. Classified secret, it included a tentative and highly qualified warning that the Soviets might respond to U.S. "actual or impending deployment" of SDI by launching a massive attack. In contrast, judging from the National Intelligence Estimates, no one in the U.S. intelligence community thought that Pershing II deployment was at all dangerous. Even the top secret NIE *Soviet Capabilities for Strategic Nuclear Conflict, 1982–*

1992, published February 15, 1983, the same year as the first Pershing II deliveries to Europe, offered no hint of awareness that "actual or impending deployment" of Pershing II could start a war. Yet two days after this estimate was published, a top secret KGB directive of February 17, 1983 warned overseas residencies that the threat of nuclear war was increasing.

Curiously, Soviet concerns that ABLE ARCHER–83 concealed an actual attack by Pershing IIs were not consistent with the missile's arrival date. The first Pershing IIs did not reach Europe until November 23, twenty-two days after the conclusion of ABLE ARCHER; Pershing II participation in ABLE ARCHER was simulated, not real. However, the Soviets almost certainly did not trust the schedule of Pershing II arrivals announced by NATO. It is possible, even likely, that they suspected the United States would clandestinely deploy a few missiles in time for ABLE ARCHER, undetected by the KGB and GRU. Even a single Pershing II armed with a "third generation" nuclear weapon—which the Soviets were correctly convinced the United States was developing or already possessed—could paralyze strategic communications in Moscow and beyond with a powerful electromagnetic pulse. One Pershing II, or a few, secretly smuggled into Western Europe for a surprise attack during ABLE ARCHER, could in the Soviet view tip the strategic balance.

Ever since the Cuban missile crisis in 1962, each side credited the other with more strategic stealth than it really possessed. For example, during the mid-1980s there was a minor flurry among Pentagon analysts over intercepted communications from communist Nicaragua or from El Salvador referring to the presence of an "SS-20 brigade." It turned out to be nothing more than the name of a new Marxist guerrilla group, seeking machismo by association with the famous Soviet nuclear missile that caused Uncle Sam so many sleepless nights. During ABLE ARCHER–83, when the KGB and GRU intercepted NATO communications with fictitious Pershing II batteries pretending to be active in West Germany, Moscow probably assumed the West had stolen a march on Pershing II deployment.

Although at the time of ABLE ARCHER–83, U.S. Pershing II missiles had not yet arrived in Europe, and many other U.S. strategic programs were still in a developmental stage, the Soviets nevertheless feared that the United States might already believe itself to be strong enough to win a nuclear war. Consider, from the perspective of a suspicious Soviet military planner, the implications of the U.S. strategic programs already completed by the time of ABLE ARCHER–83. In 1980, the United States had upgraded the Minuteman III ICBM to the Minuteman IIIA, which was several times more accurate and carried warheads having over twice the yield of those of its predecessors. It gave the United States for the first time an ICBM capable of destroying very hard Soviet missile silos. In the same year the United States also deployed the Trident C-4 submarine-launched ballistic missile (SLBM), which had warheads over twice as powerful as those of its predecessor. In 1982 the United States equipped its heavy bombers with air-launched cruise missiles (ALCMs), and in 1983 U.S. submarines were outfitted with submarine-launched cruise missiles (SLCMs). ALCMs and SLCMs could deliver a nuclear warhead with pinpoint accuracy, within yards of the target, enabling them to destroy the hardest Soviet missile silos. Cruise missiles could also fly low enough to evade detection by Soviet early warning and air defense radars; so they were perceived by the Soviets to be a new technology for accomplishing a nuclear surprise attack.

"The purpose" of these several U.S. strategic programs, according to an official Ministry of Defense publication of the period, "is to steeply increase the striking power of the strategic offensive forces, especially in preemptive surprise attacks." According to the Soviet defense ministry, the United States was seeking "attainment of military superiority over the U.S.S.R." and "the ability to win a nuclear war" so that the United States could achieve "world domination," a course that posed a "present danger" and was "pushing mankind to the brink of catastrophe." The official Soviet military press was full of warnings that the U.S. military buildup posed an increased threat of nuclear war. An example is this typical editorial, entitled "Increase Vigilance and Be Alert" published in the summer of 1983:

> The source for today's heightened nuclear danger is the most aggressive imperialist circles, which have now twice plunged mankind into the abyss of world wars but have failed to draw the necessary conclusions from the lessons of history. Impossible dreams of world domination and hatred of freedom and progress also move today's "crusaders" from across the sea. The militaristic megalomania of the present U.S. administration is pushing the Pentagon to accomplish a sharp build-up of all mass destruction weapons. Washington is inventing more and more new versions of initiation of nuclear war.

Far from being a Soviet version of yellow journalism, such missives reflected the attitudes of political and military leaders. Six months before ABLE ARCHER–83, Minister of Defense Ustinov declared that "in the U.S., nuclear war is being shifted into a possible and, under some circumstances, expedient category."

U.S. strategic programs were not, in fact, intended to make possible a surprise attack but to compensate for even more ambitious Soviet strategic programs. Significant U.S. upgrades to the offensive capabilities of its ICBMs and SLBMs were meant to compensate for the growing vulnerability of U.S. ICBMs, few of which would survive a Soviet first strike. Improving U.S. ICBMs and SLBMs was also necessary to offset the Soviet advantage in having thousands of medium-hard and deep underground shelters. The United States deployed ALCMs and SLCMs not for surprise attack but to counter Soviet air defenses that were growing so strong that

U.S. bombers would soon be unable to deliver a retaliatory blow against the Soviet Union. Soviet invulnerability to U.S. bombers could upset the balance of power and give the USSR a war-winning edge.

In the Soviet view, U.S. strategic modernization programs had significantly increased U.S. nuclear strength by 1983—perhaps sufficiently to tempt the United States into war. The Soviets may have calculated that the strategic nuclear balance would be most favorable to the United States in 1983 and not so favorable in later years, despite the expectation that it would acquire additional powerful strategic weapons in the future. The United States was scheduled to complete Pershing II deployments by 1985 and to begin deployments of the Peacekeeper ICBM in 1986, the D-5 SLBM in 1989, and perhaps begin SDI by the end of the century. However, Soviet strategic modernization programs, both ongoing and planned, might more than counterbalance these new U.S. acquisitions which were still years away. The new U.S. nuclear firepower already in place in 1983 had been acquired quickly, within the space of a few years—probably too quickly for the Soviets to deploy countervailing programs that would preserve the comfortable margins of offensive and defensive security to which they were accustomed. In reality, the Soviets had objective strategic advantages over the United States in 1983, but what mattered was their subjective perception of vulnerability.

Soviet perceptions of an imminent threat during ABLE ARCHER–83 were reinforced by events in the months preceding the NATO military exercise. In March 1983, President Reagan had announced the Strategic Defense Initiative, which, Gordievsky notes, was seen in Moscow as an act of aggression and as demonstrating "Reagan's growing belief that the U.S. could win a nuclear war." In June the Soviets saw the landslide victory in British elections of conservative Prime Minister Margaret Thatcher as reflecting the strength of the "war party" in the Western alliance. The Soviets may have believed that Western "hawks" would be most inclined to launch an attack shortly after a major electoral victory, when the "war party" would be strongest. Following Thatcher's triumph, Moscow cabled overseas KGB residencies warning that the United States "was continuing its preparations for nuclear war" and stressing again the importance of Operation VRYAN. On August 12, another cable from Moscow, this time signed personally by KGB chief Kryuchkov, again emphasized the priority of VRYAN and directed KGB agents to be watchful for evidence of a NATO nuclear surprise attack. "In this instance, as in others," Gordievsky writes of Moscow's reaction to the British elections, Soviet leaders "clearly attached a deeply sinister significance to a campaign which was in reality a normal feature of British life."

In September 1983, the KAL 007 incident boosted Soviet fears that the West might be seeking a pretext for war. The Soviets believed the United States was exploiting KAL 007 to rally world opinion against the USSR, perhaps preparing people psychologically for war. On September 28, General Secretary Andropov criticized the United States for pursuing "dangerous, inhuman policies" and a "militarist course that poses a grave threat to peace."

On September 26, shortly after midnight, the Soviet's new OKO ("Eye") launch-detection satellites reported that the United States had fired its Minuteman intercontinental missiles and that a nuclear attack was underway. Lieutenant Colonel Stainslav Petrov was the duty officer in charge of the satellites. After a few terrifying minutes, when Soviet radars failed to confirm that any U.S. missiles were on their way, Petrov figured out that the OKO satellites had malfunctioned and had given a false alarm. On his own authority, he stopped the false warning message from going farther and prevented a Soviet nuclear alert. The stress of Petrov's brief nuclear nightmare caused a nervous breakdown that ended his military career. As a reward for averting catastrophe, Petrov received, according to Russian press, "a small apartment on the outskirts of . . . Moscow . . . and a telephone without having to wait his turn." Knowing that their missile-warning satellites were defective certainly did nothing to ease Moscow's jumpiness about the impending arrival in Europe of U.S. Pershing II missiles, which would make a U.S. surprise nuclear attack harder than ever to detect. ABLE ARCHER–83 was only five weeks away.

On 26 October, one week before ABLE ARCHER, the United States launched a massive military operation that quickly liberated the small Caribbean island of Grenada from its communist regime. Grenada had been aligned with Cuba, and the USSR had been building a base to accommodate Soviet long-range military aircraft. The U.S. liberation of Grenada was the first time that the West had freed a nation from communism's grip. The Soviets probably feared that the United States might invade communist Nicaragua or Cuba next—perhaps with good reason in the case of Nicaragua, since U.S. public enthusiasm over Grenada inspired much rhetoric about liberating that nation too. It seems likely that Soviet leaders would have concluded that the invasion of Grenada might be the beginning of a Western military crusade against communism everywhere, including against the USSR itself. In *The Cold War*, Martin Walker writes that during U.S. military operations in Grenada there was "an intense burst of ciphered communications between London and Washington, as the Queen and Mrs. Thatcher protested furiously at the invasion of a Commonwealth member . . . by Britain's closest ally. That can hardly have been the interpretation put on the sudden flood of cable traffic by nervous analysts in Moscow," who suspected "ABLE ARCHER–83 . . . could be the occasion for a full-scale nuclear strike." After Grenada, Soviet vice president Valeriy Kuznetsov, renowned in diplomatic circles for his cordiality, fluent English, and long record as a troubleshooter during past East-West confrontations (including the Cuban missile crisis), accused the United States of "making delirious plans for world domination" and "pushing mankind to the brink of disaster." The Soviet press made numerous personal attacks on President Reagan, questioning his sanity and comparing him to Adolph Hitler.

All of the preceding put Soviet leaders in a frame of mind to expect the worst when, on November 2, six days after the United States crushed communism in Grenada, NATO began the ABLE ARCHER–83 military exercise. It was nothing less than a rehearsal for World War III, with U.S. nuclear forces based in Europe practicing nuclear-release procedures and going through the steps for making a nuclear strike. The Soviets were leery of NATO military exercises, because Soviet military doctrine warned that an enemy might use training to conceal preparations for an actual attack.

ABLE ARCHER was a standard, recurring NATO military exercise, based on a scenario that had been played many times in the past, but as Don Oberdofer (*The Turn*) notes, "the 1983 exercise was more extensive than ever before":

> The original plan for the 1983 exercise called for Weinberger [the U.S. secretary of defense], members of the Joint Chiefs of Staff, the supreme commander of NATO, and, in its very first discussion stages, even [President] Reagan and [Vice President George] Bush, to participate in this sophisticated test of nuclear attack procedures. According to Robert McFarlane, who had succeeded William Clark two weeks earlier as the White House national security advisor, this part of the "war game" was scaled down and most of the top-ranking civilian and military officials were taken out of the exercise because of concern about the high state of Soviet nervousness. Nevertheless, the exercise was still more realistic than in the past.

The "toning down" of ABLE ARCHER–83, by eliminating President Reagan and Vice President Bush as participants in the exercise, may have been done in deference to Gordievsky's warnings about VRYAN—but perhaps not. Proceeding with ABLE ARCHER–83 at all in the face of VRYAN was a gamble. The Joint Chiefs and the White House were behaving as if they were largely indifferent to—or ignorant of—Soviet nuclear-threat perceptions. Whether the decision to exclude the president and vice president from ABLE ARCHER–83 was informed by sensitive intelligence on VRYAN or merely based on intuition, it may have been the margin that prevented World War III.

On November 2, the first day of ABLE ARCHER–83, a nearly hysterical directive from Kryuchkov to overseas KGB agents declared, "The threat of an outbreak of nuclear war is reaching an extremely dangerous point" and that warning of "a surprise nuclear missile attack on the U.S.S.R." had "acquired even greater urgency and immediacy":

> The United States is involving its NATO allies and Japan in pursuing its aggressive designs. . . . The existing correlation of forces may be radically altered by deploy-

ment of new American medium-range missiles in Western Europe. In these circumstances, the task of not overlooking immediate preparations by the adversary for launching a surprise nuclear missile attack on the U.S.S.R. or local wars and armed conflicts threatening the security of the Soviet Union has acquired even greater urgency and immediacy.

Gordievsky reports that Soviet military leaders regarded several aspects of ABLE ARCHER–83 as highly suggestive of U.S. preparations to launch a nuclear first strike. Soviet intelligence collection of communications among U.S. nuclear forces indicated that unusual message formats and communications procedures, unlike those employed in past training practice, were used to bring NATO nuclear forces to full combat readiness. This variation from normal exercise procedures is something one would expect in a real attack, even one trying to masquerade as an exercise. A real attack would likely involve requirements different from those in exercises, requirements that would be reflected in communications. For example, an aggressor contemplating an actual attack would change communications procedures to prevent the victim from reading the aggressor's "mail" and to confuse him about the actual readiness of aggressor forces. That such a change in communications actually happened during ABLE ARCHER–83 met one of the indicators of an impending nuclear surprise attack identified in the KGB's top secret VRYAN directives.

Soviet alarm over communications anomalies in ABLE ARCHER–83 was reinforced by a too-literal interpretation of the exercise scenario, which raised the readiness of NATO nuclear forces through all alert phases to DEFCON-1, the highest readiness level. DEFCON-1 implies that the United States has placed its nuclear forces on a war footing and is ready to use them within hours or days. Nuclear release procedures, which turn off safety mechanisms designed to prevent unauthorized missile launch or accidental warhead detonation—the last steps prior to firing—normally occur at DEFCON-1. According to the previously top secret U.S. National Intelligence Estimate published in February 1983, "Soviet theater and strategic nuclear forces" would be "ready to preempt if NATO were detected beginning nuclear release procedures."

No NATO nuclear forces *actually* went to DEFCON-1 during ABLE ARCHER–83—the general alert was merely simulated, not real—but Soviet intelligence, influenced by its perception that the world political situation was rapidly deteriorating, mistook the simulated alert for the real thing.

Further contributing to Soviet misperceptions were reports from agents observing U.S. military bases in Europe that American officers were making nonroutine movements and were engaged in unusual activities. A period of radio silence observed by some U.S. military bases during the exercise also fueled Soviet anxieties. Clearing communications channels in this manner was specifically identified as a VRYAN indicator in top secret KGB directives:

> In an emergency situation and when military exercises are taking place, operation of lines of communication may be switched to the "minimize" system in which the volume of ordinary telephone calls and telegraphic messages is sharply curtailed and channels of communication cleared for transmitting urgent messages. . . . If this system is instituted in countries which have nuclear weapons, especially if it is on a global scale, this may provide a serious warning signal that the adversary is preparing for RYAN.

On November 6, while ABLE ARCHER–83 was building to a climax in Western Europe, the U.S. Navy and a Soviet nuclear submarine were playing cat and mouse in the deep Atlantic. About 470 miles off the U.S. coast, east of Charleston, South Carolina, U.S. antisubmarine surface ships and aircraft were tracking a Soviet Victor III nuclear attack submarine. This was standard procedure for training crews and for protecting U.S. vessels, and patrols by Soviet submarines in these waters were a frequent—though not everyday—occurrence.

Armed with SS-N-15 and SS-N-16 long-range nuclear torpedoes, the Victor III was designed to kill U.S. ballistic missile submarines, preferably preemptively, before they could launch their missiles. The Victor's perhaps-impossible mission was best attempted from this location, which was regularly traversed by U.S. missile-carrying submarines leaving or entering their anchorages at Charleston and Kings Bay, Georgia. In peace or war, the U.S. Navy would do what it was doing now: try to find the Victor, and in war it would destroy it. In wartime, U.S. submarines could then "flush" from Charleston and Kings Bay to hide safely in the depths, or safely launch their missiles. For these reasons, among their numerous indicators of an impending U.S. nuclear strike, the Soviets counted an attempt to destroy their attack submarines as a sure sign.

On November 6 the U.S. Navy was at peace, but its submarine hunt may have inadvertently had a wartime effect. An acoustic array being towed under water at the end of a mile-long tether snagged on something. The cable snapped. Shortly afterward the Victor III surfaced, disabled. A U.S. Navy officer on the scene later speculated the cable may have entangled the Soviet submarine's rudder. Whatever went wrong, the Victor III wallowed on the surface all the way to Cuba, buzzed continuously by U.S. reconnaissance aircraft, an object of curiosity to the U.S. Navy, of amusement to the U.S. press, and of horror to the Soviet General Staff. The presence of the Victor III off Charleston at this particular moment, in the middle of ABLE ARCHER–83, in the month the long-awaited Pershing IIs would arrive in Europe, might have been coincidence, but probably it was not.

On 6 November, halfway through ABLE ARCHER–83, and on the same day the Victor III got in trouble, KGB headquarters issued a top secret directive to agents overseas that for the first time described a time line for the expected U.S. nuclear surprise attack: "Surprise is the key element in the main adversary's plans and preparations for war in today's conditions. As a result, it can be assumed that the period of time from the moment the preliminary decision for RYAN is taken, up to the order to deliver the strike, will be very short duration, possibly 7–10 days." Moscow had apparently concluded that it was very possible, or even likely, that ABLE ARCHER–83 was ticking toward the long-anticipated U.S. nuclear offensive. Since the exercise began on November 2, given the KGB's time line of seven to ten days between a decision to strike and the actual launch of missiles, then as of November 6, a nuclear war could be only three to six days away.

"In the tense atmosphere generated by the crisis and rhetoric of the past few months," Gordievsky writes, the KGB overreacted to ABLE ARCHER–83 and mistakenly concluded that "American forces had been placed on alert—and might even have begun the countdown to nuclear war." Moscow directed overseas KGB residencies to watch particular individuals and facilities during ABLE ARCHER–83, because, as the 6 November message from Moscow observed, "preparations for the surprise attack would necessarily be reflected in the work pattern of those involved." A few days after this last message, Moscow mistakenly concluded that U.S. military bases had gone on alert, possibly in preparation for a nuclear first strike against the USSR. On November 8 or 9, Moscow sent emergency "flash" telegrams to overseas KGB and GRU elements warning them of the latest bad news and to lend even greater urgency to their request for evidence of an impending U.S. nuclear attack. Moscow made ever-louder demands of the KGB and GRU to feed Soviet political and military leaders intelligence that would reinforce their worst suspicions. Thus, Soviet perceptions of an immediate nuclear threat became self-escalating during ABLE ARCHER–83.

Probably around November 8 or 9, in response to the false alarm of a U.S. alert, and simultaneously with the KGB's flash warning telegrams, the Soviet Union alerted its own nuclear forces, posturing them for war. Oberdorfer writes that according to reliable sources in the U.S. intelligence community, "Moscow placed on higher alert status about a dozen nuclear-capable Soviet fighter aircraft stationed in forward bases in East Germany and Poland, evidently in response to what it perceived as the heightened threat arising from what it could detect of ABLE ARCHER." Martin Walker writes, "The Soviets went on to heightened alert . . . with U.S. electronics intelligence noting nuclear-capable aircraft being placed on stand-by at East German air bases."

The Soviet alert would have followed standard procedures, described in part in previously classified NIEs and Soviet top secret documents, now publicly available. At minimum, the Soviets would have moved some aircraft to their flight strips, fueled all aircraft, and checked weapons, navigation, and other electronic systems. Pilots, command staffs, and other officers and troops were recalled from leave, and everyone mustered to their combat duty posts. Base security was ratcheted to maximum, no one allowed in or out without special orders. Nuclear weapons were made ready. Command staffs removed war plans from safes and began reviewing their strike missions against NATO targets. War fever among the fanatics, fear among the normal guys, and cold sweat universally were nonstandard features of the November alert. On the Soviet side, everyone from the Chief of the General Staff down to pilots and security guards knew that this was not a drill.

On the Western side, the United States and NATO remained in the dark about the danger while ABLE ARCHER–83 was going on. It is inconceivable that the president, Joint Chiefs, and NATO allies would all have agreed to allow the war game to continue in the face of clear evidence the exercise could provoke a Soviet nuclear strike. If the United States knew about the Soviet alert when it was happening, there would have been an immediate demarche to Moscow to defuse the situation, and someone in the White House, State Department, Pentagon, intelligence community, or NATO would have leaked something about these matters to the press within days. Yet ABLE ARCHER–83 ran its course.

The previously top secret NIE *Soviet Capabilities for Strategic Nuclear Conflict, 1983–1993*, published in March 1984, four months after the Soviet nuclear alert, makes no mention of the incident. It would have been a criminal omission for a threat assessment, except that the event was not yet known to the U.S. intelligence community. National Intelligence Estimates indicate the U.S. intelligence community did not understand Soviet nuclear anxieties and did not appreciate the dangers inherent in ABLE ARCHER–83.

A previously top secret NIE, recently declassified, entitled *Implications of Recent Soviet Military-Political Activities*, indicates that by May 1984 the U.S. intelligence community was aware of the November 1983 nuclear alert: "Soviet air units in Germany and Poland [assumed] high alert status with readying of nuclear strike forces as NATO conducted ABLE ARCHER–83." The 1984 NIE also reveals other previously classified evidence of "a high level of Soviet military activity . . . large-scale military exercises, and several other noteworthy events" that were consistent with a continuing Soviet nuclear war scare after ABLE ARCHER–83 and into 1984. However, incredibly, the 1984 NIE reassured U.S. political leaders that there was nothing to worry about, that the Soviet "war scare" was mainly propaganda: "Soviet talk about the increased likelihood of nuclear war . . . has been deliberately manipulated to rationalize military efforts with domestic audiences and to influence Western political elites. Some Soviet military activities have also been designed to have an alarming or intimidating effect."

Not until seven years after ABLE ARCHER–83 did the intelligence community recant its dismissal of the Soviet war scare and admit that the increased danger of nuclear war was real during the November 1983 exercise. According to Don Oberdorfer (*The Turn*) and William Lee, a still highly classified study by the President's Foreign Intelligence Advisory Board (PFIAB) completed in 1990 overturned the complacent 1984 NIE and deemed it a major intelligence failure. Oberdorfer writes, "An extensive restudy of the evidence by the President's Foreign Intelligence Advisory Board concluded that the earlier estimates had been remiss in dismissing the possibility that the Soviet leadership actually believed the United States was planning a nuclear first strike." An unclassified 1996 study by Ben Fisher, of the CIA's Center for Historical Intelligence, repudiates the 1984 NIE: "Many Western observers dismissed the . . . war scare because they considered its worst-case scenario—surprise nuclear attack—as 'too out of touch with reality' to be credible. They based their view more on their certain conviction that there was no objective threat of a U.S. attack than on their uncertain understanding of how the Soviets saw things. Reagan wasn't Hitler, and America doesn't do Pearl Harbors. While Western observers were half right in questioning whether the Soviet war scare was 'objective' or 'rational,' they were half wrong in attributing it to scare tactics. Even fear based on a false threat can create real dangers."

The dimensions of the nuclear danger during ABLE ARCHER–83 are probably still not fully appreciated.

The nuclear alert among Soviet forces would not have been limited to a small number of aircraft in Poland and East Germany. These were the alert forces detected by the U.S. intelligence community, probably during a retrospective analysis conducted months later. Historically, when Moscow gets ready to fight, even when faced with a small conflict, it mobilizes for a big war. Everything we know about Soviet military doctrine and operational practices indicates they would not have confined their nuclear alert to a dozen aircraft capable only of a limited nuclear strike. A central tenet of Soviet military doctrine, and of General Staff military planning, was that nuclear war could not be limited but would rapidly escalate into a global conflict.

At least some Soviet intercontinental nuclear forces, most likely ICBMs, must have increased their readiness during ABLE ARCHER–83 to preempt a possible U.S. attack. ICBMs normally are at a high state of readiness, which can be increased during an alert without much visible sign detectable by an enemy. This is not true of bombers and submarines, which are "noisy" and noticeable when being manned and made ready for combat. Soviet ICBMs carried about 7,000 warheads, enough to wage a global nuclear war unaided by any other service. Since Soviet military doctrine called for attempting to neutralize an impending enemy nuclear attack by striking enemy forces before they could launch, Soviet leaders during ABLE ARCHER–83 probably came within a hair's breadth of ordering nuclear strikes against missile, bomber, and submarine bases in NATO and the United States.

The proximity of a Soviet preemptive nuclear strike may be suggested by the flash telegrams from Moscow issued on November 6 indicating that a NATO nuclear attack might occur within seven to ten days. The ABLE ARCHER–83 exercise ended on November 11, ten days after commencing, six days after the warning telegram of November 6. If ABLE ARCHER–83 had continued, perhaps even by as little as another twenty-four hours, the West might have unwittingly stumbled into a nuclear holocaust. Gordievsky believes that the world "during ABLE ARCHER–83 . . . had, without knowing it, come frighteningly close—certainly closer than at any time since the Cuban missile crisis of 1962" to nuclear war.

CHAPTER 7

The Death of Andropov, February 1984

Another dangerous event during the early 1980s was the slow death of General Secretary Yuri Andropov from kidney failure, a process that extended over many months and finally ended on February 9, 1984. Don Oberdorfer describes well Andropov's slow physical deterioration:

> After Andropov's kidneys failed in February 1983, he slowed his activities and had difficulty walking, though foreign visitors reported that his mind was sharp. . . . In July, West German Chancellor Helmut Kohl found that although Andropov was hardly permitted to walk at all, he was clear and vigorous in his arguments. Nonetheless, a West German photographer, who studied the Soviet leader through his camera's magnifying lens during a photo session with Kohl, confided that Andropov "is a man with the mark of death on his face." . . . The General Secretary's health took a sharp turn for the worse in late September or early October 1983, when he went from vacation to permanent residence in a specially prepared VIP suite in the Kremlin's Kuntsevo hospital. Sometime in the fall, one kidney is reported to have been removed. Andropov continued to try to run the country via telephone and memoranda with the help of a small group of trusted associates, including his Politburo protégé, Mikhail Gorbachev.

The KAL 007 and ABLE ARCHER–83 incidents were no doubt made more dangerous by Andropov's failing health, which increased the risk that the Soviet leader might make mistakes and act rashly. The nearness of death for Andropov might have made the prospect of nuclear war less intimidating, perhaps even tempting. Gordievsky makes the chilling observation that the leader of the Soviet Union "spent the last five months of his life . . . as a morbidly suspicious invalid brooding over the possible approach of a nuclear Armageddon."

Andropov's deathbed fixation on impending nuclear war reflected the views of the USSR's other top leaders in the aftermath of ABLE ARCHER–83. Despite its having proved a false alarm, Soviet political and military leaders remained no less convinced that a U.S. nuclear surprise attack might be imminent. In January 1984, a conference attended by high-ranking Soviet officials to judge the value of Operation VRYAN during the past two years concluded that it was indispensable and continued to deserve the highest priority. Gordievsky describes Kryuchkov's opening address at the conference, which was later circulated to KGB residencies. Kryuchkov said the threat of nuclear conflict had elevated to "dangerous proportions" and the United States was engaged in "the psychological preparation of the population for nuclear war."

After ABLE ARCHER–83, Soviet political and military leaders continued to require VRYAN reports every two weeks on any signs of an imminent nuclear attack. Further, early in 1984, Moscow levied additional VRYAN tasking on Soviet intelligence, increasing the number of indicators to be monitored as possible signs of Western preparation for launching a nuclear strike. The new indicators included: movement of GLCMs newly based in Britain, at Greenham Common; efforts by Western governments to heighten "anti-Soviet feeling" among their peoples and armed forces; and coordinated activities by slaughterhouses to increase stored foodstuffs, or by bankers to preserve economic records and the monetary system. A top secret KGB directive of January 6, 1984, entitled *Plan for Basic Measures to Step Up Still Further the Effort to Combat the Subversive Intelligence Activities of the United States Services* called for increasing the search for "signs of preparation by the ruling circles in the U.S.A. for a nuclear attack on the U.S.S.R."

It is frightening to imagine the options Andropov may have contemplated as he lay dying, convinced more than ever that the United States was plotting a nuclear surprise attack that could come at any moment. For Andropov, the most fundamental deterrent to launching a preventive nuclear war against the United States—his personal survival—was no longer a consideration. Another incident like ABLE ARCHER–83 might have been sufficient to convince the general secretary to leap into the nuclear abyss. Shortly after ABLE ARCHER–83, on November 24, Andropov announced that the USSR would implement an "analogous response" to the U.S. Pershing II deployments, by moving Soviet mobile nuclear missiles closer to Western Europe and Soviet nuclear-armed submarines closer to the United States. The object was to reduce the flight times of these Soviet missiles to pose an equivalent threat of surprise attack against the United States and NATO.

William T. Lee, a respected former senior analyst with the U.S. Defense Intelligence Agency, has suggested that the Soviet Union under Andropov was actively planning to initiate a new world war that would, once and for all, end the East-West competition in its favor. If Lee is right, the thinking of Soviet leaders may have been more dysfunctional, and the situation more perilous, than even Gordievsky supposes. It is possible that Soviet leaders deliberately exaggerated their fears of a U.S. nuclear surprise attack to subordinates in order to prepare them psychologically—as the Soviets accused the United States of doing—to launch an unprovoked nuclear first strike. The CIA's Ben Fisher also suggests that the Soviet war scare might have led to "a Soviet preemptive strike either as a result of miscalculation or by design to reverse the adverse 'correlation of forces.' "

Preempting a fictitious U.S. surprise attack would provide the excuse for premeditated mass murder, a preventive nuclear war waged because the USSR could not win its competition with the West through any means other than military aggression. Soviet leaders may have feared that their painstakingly built military machine would eventually be outclassed by U.S. strategic modernization and technological innovation. Both the Soviet economy and its society were already beginning to disintegrate, and Soviet leaders may have contemplated a preventive war while they still had a chance of winning. According to Lee, the date of this cosmic D-day was probably some time before the end of the five-year plan: 1981–85. In a retrospective interview on Hungarian television, Marshal Sergey Akhromeyev singled out 1984 as a particularly dangerous year, when he was especially concerned about a United States–USSR conflict. Perhaps 1984 was particularly significant for Akhromeyev because the United States deployed most Pershing IIs during the period 1984–85, or perhaps he knew something about Soviet war plans that he was still unwilling to admit on television.

Andropov may have died just in time. One month after his death, on March 9, 1984, the KGB residency in London sent the following flash telegram to Moscow: "In connection with our task to watch for signs of enemy preparations for a sudden nuclear missile attack against the Soviet Union, we report that on 9 March the U.S. and British armed forces conducted the first field exercise of the cruise missiles based at Greenham Common." Gordievsky writes that Moscow had as early as 1982 identified the dispersal of cruise missiles "as a signal of impending nuclear attack" and that it would "be likely to respond with a nuclear strike of its own." The new VRYAN tasking in 1984 attached special significance to activities by the GLCMs at Greenham Common as a warning of war.

The movement of GLCMs, a VRYAN indicator, took the KGB by surprise. KGB agents in Britain missed NATO preparations for the exercise and initially had no one in the London residency to tell Moscow. These circumstances panicked Guk, the London KGB chief, who reportedly exclaimed, "What's going on? The enemy are preparing for atomic war and we have no one in the residency!" Gordievsky tells us that Guk probably did not really think NATO was preparing for war in this instance. However, given Guk's extreme views, described elsewhere by Gordievsky, it is entirely possible that he meant exactly what he said. London's flash telegram to Moscow referring to "signs of enemy preparations for a sudden nuclear missile attack" was clearly a VRYAN warning. Still, what mattered was the view from Moscow, not London. Andropov's death and the resulting temporary disarray among the top Soviet leaders at the moment of the GLCM movements from Greenham Common may have spared the West from another close brush with Armageddon.

The West lost its best window into the mind of the KGB when Aldrich Ames, a senior CIA official turned KGB double agent, betrayed Gordievsky.

Recalled to Moscow in May 1985, Gordievsky was not immediately arrested, probably because the KGB hoped that if he was left free his activities would point to other traitors. Subjected to grillings and drugged with "truth serum" during an Orwellian working day, he was allowed to return home to his family in the evenings. He deliberately kept his wife Leila in the dark about his work for the West, and his ordeal, for her own protection. One evening, while grocery shopping, he kissed her a last goodbye.

British intelligence somehow spirited Gordievsky to London, leaving Leila and their daughters behind to endure six years of persecution and twenty-four-hour surveillance. She joined him in London in September 1991, bringing the children, but she could not forgive his secrecy or his abandonment of her. The marriage failed. His mother and sister never forgave him either. "The death sentence is a reward for me," a disguised Gordievsky told a reporter in 1992.

Up until 1991, Gordievsky assumed VRYAN had petered out in 1985, the year of his defection, or shortly thereafter. KGB agents working for the London residency apparently lost their enthusiasm for VRYAN. Most importantly, by 1985 the generation of Soviet leaders who had started, and believed in, VRYAN were dead. Brezhnev, Andropov, Ustinov, and Gromyko all expired within a few years of each other. In 1985 a new generation of Soviet leaders, headed by Mikhail Gorbachev, arose like a fresh breeze, blowing away old men and old ideas like so many dead, dry leaves. Yet the record of top secret KGB documents shows that Moscow remained fixated on VRYAN. On July 10, 1984, seven months after ABLE ARCHER–83 and five months after Andropov's death, KGB chief Kryuchkov personally directed overseas residencies to shorten the fuse on VRYAN, so that Moscow could react more quickly: "In order to shorten the delay in informing residencies about action to bring our Service into combat readiness, the signal 'KOSTYAR-1' has been instituted and will be transmitted when necessary to all organizations abroad. If this signal is received by a Residency [Embassy] it will mean . . . our service has been put on heightened combat alert, and the stations abroad must . . . obtain and dispatch to Center [Moscow] without delay information about specific signs of a surprise nuclear missile attack on the USSR."

VRYAN directives from February 1985, one year after Andropov's death, and the last seen by Gordievsky before his defection, warn of "the increasingly tense international situation and the American administration's persistence in striving to gain military superiority over the Soviet Union." The U.S. space shuttle was supposedly a secret weapon, a "space bomber." The KGB in Moscow sounded this familiar theme: "With the aid of this system [SDI], the Americans expect to be able to ensure that United States territory is completely invulnerable to Soviet intercontinental ballistic missiles, which would enable the United States to count on mounting a nuclear attack on the Soviet Union with impunity." In Moscow, the war scare and VRYAN marched on.

Yuri Shvets (*Washington Station*) recalls that there was less enthusiasm for VRYAN among his colleagues in the KGB residency in Washington, D.C., after Andropov's death. However, the fact is that Moscow kept pushing VRYAN tasking. In 1987, Shvet's last and most important mission in Washington involved ascertaining whether, in response to a terrorist attack in the Middle East, the United States was about to strike Libya—an act Moscow thought could blow up into a world war.

In November 1991, Russian intelligence chief Primakov publicly announced the existence of VRYAN and admitted that the program was still going strong, but he claimed he was canceling it, effective immediately. Gordievsky amended his view about how long VRYAN lasted in a 1994 interview: "The most valuable [KGB documents] were those directing secret agencies to uncover signs of Western preparation for a nuclear surprise attack on the Soviet Union. This saga had been dragging on since 1981, and, as far as I know, ended only in 1992 when instructions were suspended."

The death certificate on VRYAN is still premature.

PART II

August Coup: The Fall of the Soviet Empire, August 19–21, 1991

The Defense Ministry was a mess. . . . No one really controlled events . . . and our nuclear weapons could have been used for the devil knows what.

—General Igor Maltsev,
Chief of Staff, Air Defense Forces,
August 25, 1991

Thus, for those three days, the stability of the whole world was in the hands of people whom Gorbachev has described as adventurists, and Yeltsin—as scoundrels.

—Moscow Television Network,
August 23, 1991

CHAPTER 8

Gorbachev at 20,000 Feet, August 4, 1991

High above the Ukrainian steppes, Mikhail Gorbachev peered through the window of his presidential jet at an expansive plain stretching from horizon to horizon, broken only by rectangles of brown plowed fields and green grasslands. Below was the breadbasket of the Soviet world—and of the Slavic race since its origin. On the horizon was the mighty Caucasus, one of the world's great mountain ranges, reduced to insignificance by distance, swallowed up by the nearly incomprehensible dimensions of this land. Beyond the Caucasus lay even vaster territories: the Central Asian steppes, the forests and plains of Siberia, entire seas—the Caspian and Aral—and the homelands of a hundred ethnic groups of diverse language and heritage. The nation stretched over eleven time zones and girdled nearly half the earth. It was all led by one man.

Mikhail Sergeyevich Gorbachev was born on March 2, 1931. His parents and grandparents were communists, making Gorbachev a member of Soviet "aristocracy"—only about 10 percent of the USSR's population were allowed Party membership. In the 1950s, he attended the elite University of Moscow, where he studied law and thrived on an intellectual life dominated by Marxist-Leninist theory. All of man's existence, he learned, was a product of impersonal historical forces. Understanding these objective forces would enable one to manage global, national, and personal problems.

In all this Gorbachev was not unlike many Western university professors, political activists, and religious scholars who live the life of the mind and to whom ideas have a reality that transcends the material world. Like many Western intellectuals, Gorbachev fell in love with someone who shared his love of ideas, and, in fact, the *same* ideas: Raisa, who became his wife. She was a specialist in Marxist-Leninist economic theory and had even earned a doctoral degree in the subject.

Gorbachev was not a Stalinist fanatic advocating bloody terror and preparedness for world conquest, nor a Party hack who mouthed Marxist-Leninist pieties without grasping their meaning. He was a true believer in communism. Gorbachev's vision of communism was essentially humanitarian. He genuinely believed that it offered the fairest and most economically productive way of organizing society. He was convinced that the USSR had been thwarted in delivering prosperity and social justice by Soviet leaders and bureaucrats who, through incompetence and corruption, had mismanaged things and betrayed the true spirit of communism.

From Moscow University, Gorbachev went on to rise rapidly through various leadership positions in the Communist Party. In 1980 he became a member of the Politburo, the ruling inner circle. He was only forty-nine years old when he entered the Politburo, whereas most of his colleagues were in their sixties or seventies. He earned a reputation as an energetic problem solver of keen intellect and with experience in making the system work. After the death in March 1985 of Premier Chernenko—who had inherited leadership from the dead Andropov and the senile Brezhnev—the Politburo, weary of working with a succession of decrepit rulers, looked to the relatively youthful Gorbachev. At age sixty, Gorbachev became president of the Union of Soviet Socialist Republics—the first postwar Soviet president who was not a veteran of World War II.

As president of the USSR, Gorbachev probably did not share the alarmist views held by most other Soviet political and military leaders about an imminent threat of nuclear war from the West. The new president surrounded himself with academic reformers from such places as the Institute of the USA and Canada, many of whom had visited the United States, lived in the West, and had a better understanding of Western institutions and strategic intentions than the Soviet military did. Gorbachev certainly feared the immediacy of a nuclear war—but precisely because the Soviet General Staff seemed so anxious to launch a preemptive nuclear strike.

The war scare was in full swing among the Soviet political and military leadership when Gorbachev took the helm in 1985. Before he became president, Gorbachev probably knew about the General Staff's view that nuclear war was imminent, and perhaps he knew about the VRYAN project. Doubtless, he assumed office determined to avert a world war. The motives for his almost immediate enactment of revolutionary changes in Soviet foreign and domestic policy, surprising and mysterious to the West, become transparent if his actions are understood as reactions to the war scare. *Glasnost* and *perestroika* were aspects of a desperate emergency program to pull the world back from the brink of nuclear war.

The Intermediate-Range Nuclear Forces (INF) Treaty, the first major arms control treaty concluded under Gorbachev, removed from Europe the Pershing II missiles that the General Staff saw as so threatening. So seriously did they consider the Pershing II threat that, despite the fact that the INF Treaty heavily favored the United States, requiring the Soviets to dismantle more than two warheads for every U.S. warhead dismantled, the General Staff regarded it as advantageous.

The first Strategic Arms Reduction Treaty (START I) was intended to reduce the number of U.S. and Soviet long-range nuclear weapons and to improve relations between the sides by deescalating the arms race. While the Soviets frequently claimed that one of their major goals in START I was to avert a nuclear world war, their Western audience invariably dismissed such assertions as rhetorical excess. Through START I the Soviets also sought limits or an outright ban on "star wars," the U.S. Strategic Defense Initiative (SDI). SDI continued to be denounced vociferously as an instrument of aggression, a means by which the United States hoped to win a nuclear war. Although the Soviets failed to achieve any formal limitation on SDI, the signing of START I and the Soviet "peace offensive" that attended it undermined much of the U.S. political support for SDI.

The Conventional Forces in Europe (CFE) Treaty, like the INF Treaty, also involved lopsided Soviet concessions to the West that were apparently intended to lessen the possibility of a world war. The Soviets made major unilateral withdrawals of armor and infantry divisions from Eastern Europe even before signing the treaty. The treaty itself called for withdrawal from Eastern Europe—an obligation almost wholly met by the time of signing. Even before the CFE Treaty was signed, Soviet agreement in principle to its terms began the dissolution of the Warsaw Pact and contributed to the liberation of Eastern Europe. In effect, the CFE Treaty required the Soviets to surrender their East European empire. Gorbachev was apparently willing to do this because he understood that NATO saw Soviet forward-based conventional forces and hegemony in Eastern Europe as evidence of the nation's desire to conquer Western Europe. Withdrawal from Eastern Europe was meant to end the nose-to-nose confrontation between NATO and the Warsaw Pact, thereby eliminating a dangerous flashpoint for a new world war.

Even Gorbachev's domestic reforms furthered his foreign policy aims by assuring the West that the USSR was liberalizing and would soon cease to be an enemy. The General Staff supported many of Gorbachev's domestic reforms, because it realized that a modernized Soviet economy was needed to remain competitive with the West in the manufacture of the high-technology weapons that would dominate future warfare.

The historical record indicates that Gorbachev went to extraordinary lengths, even sacrificing the geostrategic advantages of his own country, in order to lessen the possibility of world war and to normalize relations with the West. But in striving to prevent a nuclear conflict, it is unclear who Gorbachev feared more: the United States or his own General Staff.

By 1990, Mikhail Gorbachev probably thought that he had made substantial progress toward reducing the threat of world war. His attentions now turned increasingly to a new project. It was a startling idea for a communist lawyer: justifying the existence of the Soviet Union constitutionally. When Soviet forces withdrew from Eastern Europe in 1989, Gorbachev grew alarmed as, one after another, communist regimes in East Germany, Poland, Czechoslovakia, Hungary, and other Warsaw Pact nations fell to popular revolts. The collapse of communism in Eastern Europe challenged his belief that communism, for all its imperfections, enjoyed the support of the masses. After that debacle, rumblings were heard from within the Soviet Union, from the Baltic states, from Ukraine, from the Caucasus, and from Central Asia, that the USSR was held together by force only, and that if the will of the people were obeyed, the Soviet Union would instantly dissolve into a dozen little countries.

Gorbachev, ever the intellectual, had gone to the Baltic states to prove to local leaders that it was in their best interest to remain in the Soviet Union. He even had some impromptu debates with demonstrators in the streets, and was shocked by their lack of deference to the person of the president, by their vehemence against the USSR, and by their single-minded determination to achieve Baltic independence. These experiences temporarily shattered Gorbachev's intellectual placidity and brought out the eastern despot in him—a Jekyll-and-Hyde persona that lurks beneath the surface of many men who prefer the tidiness of ideas to the complexity of real life. He secretly ordered the "Black Berets" (interior security troops) to suppress rebellion in the Baltics and ordered General Rodionov to do the same in the Caucasus. Rodionov obeyed by having his troops use picks and shovels to hack into submission student protesters seeking Georgian independence, slaughtering the unarmed teenagers gruesomely. For this act Rodionov became known as the "Butcher of Tbilisi." Gorbachev denied issuing orders inciting his generals to violence. Perhaps in secret penance for his lapse from civilized behavior, he negotiated a treaty with leaders of the Soviet republics, increasing their political and economic autonomy and easing Moscow's stranglehold on the lives of their peoples.

Now, on August 4, 1991, as Gorbachev winged his way toward his vacation palace on the shores of the Black Sea near Foros, he reflected on what he was sure would be recognized as among his greatest accomplishments. Recently he had called upon the people of the various republics of the Soviet Union to ratify the new Union Treaty, which would prove that the USSR was not a communist prison but one nation, benefiting from communism and constituted by the voluntary consent of the people. Against all evidence to the contrary, Gorbachev believed that in a fair and open debate most people living in the Baltics, Ukraine, and other republics would favor the USSR and oppose its dismemberment. His Politburo colleagues warned him that trusting the future of the Soviet Union and communism to the loyalty of the people was sure to be a disaster. But the president believed that representatives of all the peoples of the Soviet Union would sign the reformed Union Treaty, thereby transforming the USSR from an empire of conquered peoples into a legally constituted modern state. It would all happen in just two weeks, on August 20.

CHAPTER 9

Kryuchkov's Coup, August 18, 1991

Vladimir Kryuchkov was only vaguely conscious of the soft whir of the air conditioning. He was reflecting on the events he had set into motion that could, once announced to the world tomorrow, bring on a global nuclear war.

Sitting around a table in the Kremlin with Kryuchkov were his key fellow conspirators: Gennadiy Yanayev, vice president of the Soviet Union; Minister of Defense Dimitry Yazov; and General Boris Pugo. General Vladimir Aleksandrovich Kryuchkov, chairman of the KGB, was the most intelligent and knowledgeable of the group. Articulate and always armed with facts, or what he believed to be or represented as facts, Kryuchkov was a man of compelling yet subtle arguments. He never bludgeoned his intellectual prey into submission; rather he prodded, cajoled, and, most of all, insinuated. In the end, men moved in Kryuchkov's direction less because they were defeated or even persuaded than because they felt that they had independently arrived at some new insight.

Kryuchkov was not a profound theoretical thinker, but he had the enigmatic intelligence of a man accustomed to living in a world of conspiracy. He possessed the quick brilliance of a KGB salesman, whose stock in trade was persuading others to betray their countries. Although the leader of the coup against Gorbachev—no one would have been in the Kremlin bunker for that purpose were it not for Kryuchkov's salesmanship—the KGB chief was too indirect and ill at ease in broad daylight to be a natural leader. Realizing this deficiency in himself, he looked to Vice President Yanayev to serve as a civilian figurehead for the new government, and to Defense Minister Yazov to deliver the loyalty of the Army.

Yanayev and Yazov owed Gorbachev everything. Perhaps they owed him too much. Men too deeply in debt, or too extravagantly rewarded, often come to abhor their benefactor.

Gennadiy Ivanovich Yanayev, vice president of the USSR, had been rejected by the Congress of People's Deputies on the first ballot for the vice presidency. He was elected on the second vote only because President Gorbachev appealed to the Congress, insisting, "I need someone I can trust." Smooth, urbane, and personable, Yanayev was a politician who was good at making people like him. Yet he had not been particularly successful in his career, having held no posts of great importance before now. For over twenty years, from the 1960s until 1986, he worked as a propagandist in the Communist Party's international friendship societies, traveling widely in the United States, Europe, and Asia. Soviet officials who traveled abroad for "public relations" usually had ties to the KGB. In 1986, Yanayev became chairman of the Central Council of Trade Unions, where his propaganda skills largely failed to quell growing labor discontent and contributed nothing to solving a deepening economic crisis. Nonetheless, this position gained Yanayev admission to the Politburo, seat of Soviet elites, in 1990. There he attached himself to Gorbachev and became, probably because of a presumed knowledge of labor and the economy, Gorbachev's choice for vice president.

General Dimitry Timofeyevich Yazov, defense minister of the Soviet Union, was born on November 8, 1923, making him sixty-seven on August 18, 1991. He was a career officer of undistinguished record. In 1987, he was commander of all Soviet forces in the Far East Military District—where he made some effort to streamline administration and to improve the service conditions for the average soldier—when President Gorbachev suddenly promoted him to defense minister. Yazov's reputation as being among the most reform minded of the USSR's high-ranking officers apparently motivated Gorbachev to raise Yazov from a middling post to the top of the military hierarchy. Resentment blossomed among much more talented senior officers.

Despite his genuine credentials as a reformer, Yazov was much more like Kryuchkov than Gorbachev. Reflecting the still-reactionary threat perceptions of the Soviet military, the new defense minister had serious reservations about Gorbachev's agreement to the Conventional Forces in Europe Treaty. He accused the United States of exploiting the CFE Treaty to gain a dangerous advantage over the USSR, and he called for NATO to disband in response to the dissolution of the Warsaw Pact. Even though he was among the most ideologically sympathetic senior officers and owed everything to Gorbachev, Yazov betrayed his president and supported men who envied and hated Gorbachev—and him as well. In the end, General Yazov's loyalty to Gorbachev, and his own self-interest, were outweighed by his fear of the West.

General Boris Karlovich Pugo was born in Kalinin, Latvia, on February 19, 1937. He graduated from Riga Polytechnical Institute and worked briefly as an engineer, but he soon became an official in the Komsomol, the Communist Youth League. In 1976, Pugo joined the KGB, where his views on the direction of the Cold War struggle and "détente" with the United States were poisoned by Yuri Andropov's nuclear visions. Rising to the chairmanship of the Central Control Commission of the Communist Party from 1988 to 1990, Pugo investigated corruption charges against high party members, an assignment that gave him knowledge of intimate secrets, scandals, and criminal acts potentially embarrassing to the party great. In 1990 Pugo rose further, to head the Ministry of Internal Affairs

(MVD)—which controlled internal troops for maintaining public order and crushing rebellion. General Pugo was a communist "true believer" and a strict disciplinarian, who advocated the most brutal tactics against demonstrators to keep the people in line. He was fifty-four on August 18, 1991.

Other high-ranking Soviet officials in the coup leadership included Valentin Pavlov, the prime minister, and Oleg Baklanov, deputy chairman of the powerful Defense Council (the Soviet equivalent of the U.S. National Security Council) and a defense industry bureaucrat. Pavlov, Baklanov, and Yanayev were followers more than leaders, while Kryuchkov, Yazov, and Pugo were the real principals—except for Marshal Akhromeyev. He was not physically seated at Kryuchkov's table. However, unlike Kryuchkov, Akhromeyev was a profound theoretical thinker and an almost legendary military leader whose dark paradigms had helped create the intellectual climate of crisis that led—without Akhromeyev actually leading—to the perilous crossroads.

These men, on August 18, 1991, were convinced that Gorbachev's Union Treaty left them no alternative but to take desperate steps. The treaty was scheduled for ratification by republic representatives when Gorbachev returned from his Black Sea vacation on August 20. Many Soviet political and military elites believed the Union Treaty would encourage Lithuania, Latvia, Estonia, Ukraine, Georgia, and other parts of the USSR to seek independence. A weakened Soviet Union would be easier prey for Western aggression. Kryuchkov and the others had repeatedly argued with Gorbachev to abandon the treaty. It was to no avail. For months they met secretly, sometimes in a KGB safe house, to discuss the disastrous direction of Gorbachev's domestically liberal and pro-Western foreign policies. By and by, their dissent turned into conspiracy. Plans for seizing control of the government were laid and enemies lists were drawn up. Military exercises—rehearsals for overthrowing the government—were held in the Moscow area.

Outside the small inner circle of conspirators led by Kryuchkov, no one was told about the preparations for a coup. Not even the military officers conducting exercises in Moscow realized they were rehearsing to overthrow the government. Kryuchkov knew that his KGB did its job too well to risk a wide conspiracy. Informers were everywhere. Consequently, the coup against Gorbachev had an impromptu aspect, surprising even the conspirators themselves. Kryuchkov had decided—almost too late—that the Union Treaty was the last straw. He mobilized the others to act on August 18, only two days before treaty ratification and only one day before Gorbachev's return to Moscow. The generals were counting on the iron discipline of the Army and widespread hatred of Gorbachev in the military and KGB to carry off their last-minute decision to revolt.

At 4:50 P.M. on August 18, 1991, a delegation from the conspirators appeared unannounced at Gorbachev's vacation retreat at Foros, demanding to meet with the president. Gorbachev later recalled, "My first wish was to establish who had sent the people to me. I was actually working in my office at the time. Since the whole communication system was with me—the government line, the normal line, the strategic and the satellite communications—I picked up a receiver of one of the telephones. It was dead. I picked up a second receiver, then a third, a fourth and a fifth—they were all dead."

Realizing that a coup against him was unfolding, that communications with the outside world had been severed to isolate him at Foros, and that the delegation that would face him in a few minutes was his enemy, his jailer, and perhaps his executioner, Gorbachev quickly summoned his family. To Raisa, his daughter Irina, and her husband Anatoli, he said, "You must know that I will not give in to any kind of blackmail, nor to any threats or pressure and will not retreat from the positions I have taken up." They replied that they would stand by him until the end. Raisa remembered that the communists had executed the last czar and his family when he was deposed.

Gorbachev was offended that the delegation did not wait for him to complete his private moment with his family. They arrogantly barged into his office, eager for a showdown. There were General Valentin Varrenikov, commander in chief of the army; Oleg Shenin of the Politburo; Oleg Baklanov, Gorbachev's deputy on the Defense Council; Yuri Plekhanov, chairman of the Ukrainian Soviet; and Valery Boldin, chief of the president's staff. General Varrenikov was the most vociferous and rudest of the group, according to Gorbachev, and apparently did most of the talking for the delegation. Gorbachev, furious, began: "I want to ask you, who sent you?"

DELEGATION: The Committee.

GORBACHEV: What Committee?

DELEGATION: The Committee set up to deal with the emergency situation in the country.

GORBACHEV: Who set it up? I didn't create it and the Supreme Soviet didn't create it. Who created it?

DELEGATION: The situation the country is in—it is heading for catastrophe. Steps must be taken. A state of emergency is needed—other measures won't save us, we must no longer let ourselves be deluded.

The delegation demanded that Gorbachev issue a decree recognizing the State Committee for the State of Emergency as the legitimate government and recognize Vice President Yanayev as the new president. Gorbachev tried desperately to change their minds. He warned that this kind of power grab "had always led in the past to the deaths of hundreds, thousands, and millions of people." He pointed to the Union Treaty and his economic reforms as offering hope. His audience was stone faced. Finally, both sides made it clear there was no more point in talking:

GORBACHEV: Only people bent on suicide could now propose to introduce a state of emergency into the country. I will not have anything to do with it. You will kill yourselves. Go to hell! Shitheads!

VARRENIKOV: Give your resignation!

GORBACHEV: You won't get that from me. Tell that to the people who sent you here.

Armed guards took over the president's compound and converted the summer palace into a prison. For the next few days, Raisa fed her children from groceries she had purchased before the coup, fearing that food provided by their captors might be poisoned.

On August 19, from the security of their Kremlin bunker, the coup leaders would announce to the world that because of illness, President Gorbachev had been replaced by an emergency government: the State Committee for the State of Emergency. It would declare martial law, put down the rebellious republics, and reverse Gorbachev's domestic and foreign policies.

The Union Treaty was the immediate cause of the coup, but a more fundamental cause can be found in Kryuchkov's view of the threat from the West, a view representative of many, if not most, senior Soviet military and intelligence officers, and one that turned the coup into a nuclear crisis.

General Vladimir Aleksandrovich Kryuchkov had, for the past decade, believed that the United States and Soviet Union were on the verge of Armageddon, that a U.S. nuclear surprise attack could come at any time. Born in February 1924—making him sixty-seven on August 18, 1991—he began his career in the diplomatic ranks of the foreign service. In the 1950s, Kryuchkov made a career transition, leaving the Ministry of Foreign Affairs to serve as a functionary in the Communist Party apparatus. In the 1960s he moved to the KGB. A man of tremendous energy and persuasive talents, and a master bureaucrat, he rose quickly through the KGB ranks. As head of the KGB, he was widely regarded as the best-informed man in the Kremlin. Yet Marxist-Leninist ideology, the long Cold War confrontation, and perhaps even KGB disinformation warped Kryuchkov's perceptions, so that he was no longer capable of objectively assessing the Western threat. He believed ardently in the inevitability of an East-West nuclear clash. He believed that the disintegration of the Warsaw Pact and the Soviet Union's life-threatening problems with ethnic unrest and economic productivity were due, at least in part, to CIA and Western agents provocateurs.

As a protégé of KGB chief Yuri Andropov, who later became president of the USSR, Kryuchkov was cofounder, with Andropov, of the VRYAN program in the early 1980s. As chief of the KGB's Directorate of Foreign Intelligence from the early 1970s until 1988, and then as KGB chairman until 1991, he was intently focused on the U.S. nuclear threat for twenty years. Since 1980, Kryuchkov, a key player in the VRYAN program, had been the hair trigger of the Soviet nuclear strike forces.

Gorbachev and his reformist allies may have dismissed VRYAN and the war scare as fantasy, or, more likely, believed that their peace initiatives eliminated the material basis of the scare. Nonetheless, Kryuchkov, the General Staff, and "old guard" civilian leaders continued to take seriously the possibility of imminent U.S. aggression. As late as 1988, Kryuchkov, then deputy chairman of the KGB, was lecturing the Ministry of Foreign Affairs to be on the lookout for signs of a nuclear surprise attack by the United States. Kryuchkov's views of an imminent U.S. threat were widespread in the Soviet military—indeed, they were not views he originated but rather absorbed from a congenitally alarmist Soviet military culture. Military writings and official statements after Gorbachev's rapprochement with the West in 1985 continued to portray the United States as an aggressor nation bent on world conquest. Typical of this genre were General G. Konev and General V. Pokrovskiy, who in 1987, in the midst of *glasnost* and "new thinking," wrote:

> Over the period of more than forty years since the United States built the first nuclear weapon, the basic principle behind . . . American military strategies . . . has never changed: open nuclear blackmail and the threat of using nuclear weapons under any circumstances. This principle, elevated officially by Washington to the rank of a political instrument designed to achieve its aggressive hegemonistic aims, is embodied today in a doctrine of "neo-globalism," reflecting the aspirations of the most reactionary military circles to achieve world domination and relying on the use of force as the most important means of resolving foreign policy matters.

Perhaps the best evidence that, despite Gorbachev, the war scare persisted after 1985 is the continuation of the VRYAN program, which lasted at least until November 1991. Even at the time of its alleged termination, the Russian intelligence service director, Primakov, noted that the program was still consuming "huge material and human resources" and was still submitting reports on any nuclear war preparations "every two weeks." Obviously, VRYAN remained a top priority until its supposed end.

Indeed, VRYAN and the war scare probably still continue. The VRYAN obsession gripped both the KGB and the GRU. The GRU, Soviet military intelligence, is closer to the General Staff than the KGB (now the Foreign Intelligence Service, or SVR) and has not yet been penetrated by reformers. The GRU never officially renounced VRYAN. Primakov's announced termination of VRYAN applied only to his own organization, the SVR; moreover, we cannot rule out the possibility that Primakov's "abolition" of VRYAN in the SVR was an act of disinformation intended to counter Gordievskiy's revelations, published in a major book in 1990, and to reassure the West that the Cold War is really over.

The survival of VRYAN into the 1990s suggests that despite vastly improved relations between the United States and USSR under Gorbachev, the General Staff and at least some civilian elites remained convinced that world war might soon be at hand and that the nation had always to be ready to interdict a U.S. surprise attack by launching a Soviet nuclear first strike. The danger inherent in crises as well as in normalcy—even day-to-day relations between the sides involved some irritation, because of military movements and exercises—had a higher octane level than suspected by anyone in the West.

CHAPTER 10

The Warsaw Pact Crisis, 1989–1990

For Kryuchkov, Yazov, and perhaps the majority of senior Soviet military officers and bureaucrats, the collapse of the Warsaw Pact in 1989–90 was the pivot on which they turned against Mikhail Gorbachev. The General Staff's panic over the collapse of the Warsaw Pact can be best appreciated if one imagines how the U.S. Joint Chiefs of Staff would react to the collapse of the NATO alliance due to impetuous and irreversible decisions by a seemingly pro-Russian U.S. president.

When democratic revolutions overturned the communist regimes of Eastern Europe, the Western reaction was one of euphoric optimism. No one seemed to think that the situation was very dangerous. Yet Western military analysts long believed that the loss, or threatened loss, of the USSR's East European empire would be a casus belli for the Soviet Union and could lead to a third world war. This judgment was based on historical precedent and strategic logic. Historically, Russian and Soviet possessiveness toward Eastern Europe had been a contributing factor in two world wars. During the Cold War, the USSR had repeatedly demonstrated its willingness to use force to hold Eastern Europe, as evidenced in its invasions of Hungary in 1956 and Czechoslovakia in 1968. Until at least the late 1980s, the Soviet General Staff regarded Eastern Europe as indispensable to its offensive and defensive military plans. It would serve as the area in which to stage an invasion of Western Europe, and as a glacis shielding the USSR from Western invasion. But in 1989 and 1990, the assumption in Washington, London, Paris, and Bonn was that Gorbachev's benign attitude toward the democratic revolutions in Eastern Europe was universally shared by Soviet elites.

In fact, the liberation of Eastern Europe was perilous. Lothar de Maiziere, prime minister of East Germany during the democratic revolution, and Eduard Shevardnadze, Soviet minister of foreign affairs at the time, both claim that in 1989–90 the Soviet General Staff wanted to restore Soviet domination of Eastern Europe and thereby preserve the Warsaw Pact—even at the risk of world war. In a May 1991 interview, de Maiziere related that when he visited Moscow a few months after the fall of the Berlin Wall, he found "a change of atmosphere in the Politburo and the Army." He learned that "some Soviet Marshals would send tanks to the Brandenburg Gate" to stop German reunification. De Maiziere said he told West German chancellor Helmut Kohl that "we have only three or four months" to bring about reunification, because the Red Army might use the reunification issue as a pretext for reconquering Germany. Shevardnadze related much the same story, emphasizing the gravity of the threat to world peace posed by the Soviet General Staff's resentment at the loss of Eastern Europe:

> Was there any real alternative to the events of the Autumn of 1989 and the Winter of 1990? After all, these were essentially revolutions, widespread popular uprisings against the existing regimes. There was an alternative. But was it reasonable? We were urged fairly actively to apply force. . . . In other words, it was suggested that we act according to the scenarios of 1953, 1956, and 1968. . . . According to the logic of our critics, it turns out that we were obligated to act. "Even risking the policy of Perestroika?" I asked, and I heard this answer: were it not for Perestroika nothing like this would have happened in the Socialist camp. . . . What did our opponents suggest? We had to intervene in some way, to think of something. What? Place interception and covering divisions on the borders, as some said? Start the tank engines? But that is the brink of war. Yes, yes, do not be surprised—World War III. With the concentration of arms and armed forces that existed in Central Europe, any power struggle involving troops was fraught with that risk.

Consistent with de Maiziere's and Shevardnadze's stories, German chancellor Helmut Kohl revealed in 1996 that during the crisis over German reunification in November 1989, "opponents of reform in the KGB and Stasi [East German intelligence] wanted to provoke a military intervention by the Soviet troops stationed in East Germany" by feeding false reports of attacks on Soviet bases to President Gorbachev.

Shevardnadze and de Maiziere are highly credible witnesses. Both were in positions to know the thinking of Soviet elites at the time of crisis, both have proven track records for accurately reporting events, and neither has any reason to lie. The collapse of the Warsaw Pact and liberation of Eastern Europe almost sparked a major war. An attempted Soviet reconquest of Eastern Europe posed a high risk of escalating into a United States–USSR nuclear conflict, given that the Warsaw Pact crisis coincided with a still active VRYAN program and a paranoid Soviet General Staff still anticipated a nuclear surprise attack from the West. Probably the only thing that prevented catastrophe was Gorbachev's will. He would not bend to General Staff pressure to invade Eastern Europe.

After the liberation of Eastern Europe and the dissolution of the Warsaw Pact, *Sovetskaya Rossiya*, an organ of the Communist Party, bitterly criticized Gorbachev's government for losing Eastern Europe, lamenting that the loss was "tantamount to inflicting a defeat [on the USSR] in a third world war." The analogy reflected the desperate mindset of the General Staff in the aftermath of the collapse of the Warsaw Pact. The reversal in Eastern Europe and Gorbachev's role in it partially set the stage for the military coup against Gorbachev in August 1991 and for the accompanying nuclear crisis—still virtually unknown to the West—that would pose a high potential threat of world war. But first, events in the deserts of Kuwait, Saudi Arabia, and Iraq nudged Kryuchkov nearer to the edge of treason and apocalypse.

The Persian Gulf War of 1990–91 was a second major international development during Gorbachev's presidency that moved Kryuchkov and the other conspirators closer to a decision to overthrow him. In 1990, Iraq annexed oil-rich Kuwait and threatened to invade Saudi Arabia. The United States responded by leading a multinational coalition, which included some former Soviet clients like Syria, against Iraq, one of the Soviet Union's closest partners in the Middle East. Gorbachev initially objected to Western military intervention in the conflict, but he reversed himself, voicing lukewarm support for the United States–led United Nations expedition when it became clear that the United States intended to defend Saudi Arabia and liberate Kuwait with or without Moscow's blessing. Just a few years earlier, when Andropov, Chernenko, or Brezhnev ruled the USSR, a Western war against Iraq would have been unthinkable without Moscow's assent, so respected had been Soviet military power. Many Soviet military officers saw Gorbachev's abandonment of Iraq as a cowardly betrayal of an ally.

In the winter of 1991, during Operation DESERT STORM, the United States employed advanced conventional forces—precision guided munitions, stealth aircraft, and other high-tech weaponry far superior to any conventional weapons in the USSR's inventory—and smashed Iraq's military, which had been patterned after the Soviet army. The Iraqis were equipped with Soviet weapons and had been trained in Soviet tactics. For many Soviet military and civilian officials, this was further proof that Gorbachev's pro-Western and domestic reform policies had failed. Soviet power and international prestige had declined precipitously: first the collapse of the Warsaw Pact, now, one year later, humiliation in the Persian Gulf. Also, Gorbachev's vaunted domestic program had done little or nothing to make the Soviet economy competitive with the West.

Now the USSR, bereft of the Warsaw Pact, stood alone against the United States and NATO. The Persian Gulf War proved that the United States had the political wherewithal to lead a multinational coalition in a major war. The war also demonstrated that the United States possessed the high-tech conventional weapons that many Soviet military theorists believed would decide the outcome of future wars. Soviet conventional weaponry lagged far behind.

What if the United States turned its new power against the Soviet Union?

Soviet military officers warned that the United States–led war against Iraq was a move toward global domination. The chief of the General Staff Academy criticized U.S. policy in the Persian Gulf as aimed at "controlling energy sources in the region" and at establishing "a permanent military presence in the Gulf," posing a "danger" on the southern borders of the

Soviet Union that could draw the USSR into a conflict. In a May 1991 interview, General Igor Rodionov decried the shift in the balance of power DESERT STORM had brought: "The parity that we achieved with such difficulty, that unique balance of peace from which mankind could have gradually, while reducing the level of confrontation and rivalry, reached a harmonious 'post-parity' world, has been destroyed." In the same interview, four months before the coup, Vladimir Chernavin, commander in chief of the Soviet Navy, implied that the United States was contemplating a surprise attack on the USSR: "American warships armed with strike weapons have begun to appear often in the areas of Kamchatka and the Kuriles and also in the Black Sea off the coast of the Crimea. Exercises are constantly being conducted off our coasts. It has practically become impossible to differentiate the probable enemy's exercise deployments of forces from combat deployments. Deployment of the American forces for the invasion of Grenada began in the guise of an exercise."

Between the U.S. victory over Iraq in the winter of 1991 and the August 1991 coup attempt, Soviet military leaders raised the specter of a United States bent on using its military strength to impose a new world order dominated by itself. Even Gorbachev warned the United States against taking steps that could lead to a new Cold War.

In the wake of DESERT STORM and just prior to the August 1991 coup, Marshal Oleg Losik and the reformist academic Nikolai Kapranov, National Security Assistant to the USSR Academy of Sciences, urged that the Soviet military renounce its policy of "no first use" of nuclear weapons and announce a new policy *endorsing* "first use" of nuclear weapons. This was in response to numerous articles by Soviet military officers warning that the U.S. high-tech weaponry demonstrated in DESERT STORM could overwhelm Soviet conventional forces in a surprise attack. Losik and Kapranov reasoned that since Soviet conventional forces probably could not stand against a U.S. high-tech offensive in the event of war, the only recourse was to launch a nuclear first strike.

"No first use" of nuclear weapons was, in any case, merely Soviet declaratory policy. The General Staff, judging from Soviet military writings and force posture, *always* planned to strike first, regardless of the public pronouncements of Soviet political leaders. Findings released by the German government in 1991, based on examination of classified military documents found in East Germany after reunification, show that Warsaw Pact military plans called for a massive nuclear first strike, despite public disavowals of first use. But Losik and Kapranov were not advocating merely a rhetorical change in the General Staff's nuclear policy. They wanted also a substantive change that would allow a nuclear first strike earlier in a crisis or conflict, and under a much broader range of circumstances than had been planned for in the past. Whereas past General Staff planning had focused on nuclear first use to preempt an impending enemy *nuclear* attack, Marshal Losik and Nikolai Kapranov now advocated a nuclear first strike to preempt enemy *conventional* threats. Kapranov also advocated, in the event of a crisis or conflict, preemptive nuclear strikes against Third World countries that acquired weapons of mass destruction.

Of course, heavier reliance on nuclear preemption would greatly increase the chances of starting a nuclear war through miscalculation of the other side's intentions. Nevertheless, support by Marshal Losik, a hard-line military officer, and Kapranov, a liberal academic, indicates a broad constituency for a new nuclear first use policy in the spring of 1991. The new nuclear doctrine was officially adopted as Russian declaratory policy in November 1993.

The call for a change in nuclear weapons policy in 1991 speaks volumes about the General Staff's worsening threat perceptions in the aftermath of DESERT STORM. The suggestion by Losik and Kapranov that the USSR abandon the "no first use" pledge, a fiction maintained even during the worst of the war scare of the early 1980s, indicates that just prior to the August 1991 coup attempt, at least some prominent Soviets believed nuclear deterrence demanded a message of unprecedented bluntness.

CHAPTER 11

Twilight, August 18, 1991

With Gorbachev imprisoned, Kryuchkov and the other coup plotters turned their attention to a more daunting task. Kryuchkov was well aware that the overthrow of the liberal Gorbachev and a turn back toward Stalinism might provoke a civil war between constitutionalists and communists, between Russia and her imperial possessions. Then there was the question, "What would the United States do?" When revolution and civil war last broke out in Russia after the overthrow of the czar in 1917, Western expeditionary forces from the United States, Great Britain, and France invaded and tried to restore the old regime. Would the United States and NATO try to exploit the military opportunity presented by a weakened USSR? When Kryuchkov and company proclaimed a new government tomorrow, in the midst of the confusion, controversy, and possible violence that would disrupt or paralyze the government, would the United States see a golden opportunity to launch its long-anticipated surprise attack? What if the coup turned into a nuclear war? One of the Committee's first acts was to take Gorbachev's "nuclear button," the portable communications device that was kept in what appeared to be an ordinary briefcase. It enabled the possessor to order the strategic missile and bomber forces of the Soviet Union to strike.

Inherently, the coup against Gorbachev was a move toward the nuclear precipice. The men who mounted the coup, like most of the Soviet military, saw their country growing weaker and imagined the Western threat as looming larger daily. Kryuchkov, the coup's mastermind and the godfather of the still-active VRYAN program, believed that a nuclear surprise attack could come at any moment. Generals led the coup, motivated to protect the USSR from foreign aggression, while political officials and industrial apparatchiks, whose concerns were mainly domestic, followed the lead of the KGB and the army. The immediate cause of the coup may have been the Union Treaty, but more fundamental factors included Gorbachev's failure to preserve the Warsaw Pact and to maintain an army that could defeat the United States and NATO in a conventional war.

In the twilight of August 18, men had come to power in the Kremlin who were far more fearful of the West than was Gorbachev and far more likely than he to launch a preemptive nuclear strike. In the intimidating aftermath of the Persian Gulf War and DESERT STORM, the General Staff had already begun tightening the springs and gears of their military doctrine to place their nuclear first-strike policy on a hair trigger. Tomorrow the trigger would be gripped more tightly, by men with sweaty hands.

Sometime in the early morning hours of August 19, 1991, General Dimitry Yazov, defense minister of the Soviet Union, ordered the armed forces of the USSR—including the strategic nuclear forces—to prepare for war. Yazov's order was passed on to the command posts of the General Staff and the Strategic Rocket Forces. These vast complexes, accommodating thousands of personnel, were located hundreds of meters underground in nuclear blast–proof chambers hewn from solid rock. They were designed to withstand multiple direct hits from nuclear weapons. Nestled in the safety and relative comfort of these nuclear-age fortresses, the General Staff and its political leaders could launch preemptive or retaliatory nuclear strikes, survive a hammer blow from a massive enemy nuclear attack, launch follow-on nuclear strikes, and supervise military operations in a protracted nuclear war, expected to last weeks or months. In the aftermath of a holocaust, they could even direct civil defense and recovery operations to rebuild society.

Sophisticated communications systems connected the General Staff command posts to their strategic nuclear forces. A General Staff officer with Defense Minister Yazov's alert order in hand sat down at a computer terminal. He keyed the message into an encoding scrambler and pushed the "send" button. From the depths of the underground complex at Chekov, the main General Staff command post, Yazov's dark words flashed to hundreds of missile and bomber crews, armed with over 10,000 strategic nuclear warheads. Scattered over two continents and three oceans, these men and their deadly machines had waited patiently, fearfully, for years, for the command that would end their long vigil and obliterate half of mankind.

Now, Yazov's order told them: "Get ready."

Defense Minister Yazov's secret encoded order, number 8825, read in part:

> In connection with the deteriorating domestic political situation in the country, I order that:
>
> Large strategic formations, combined units, units, and establishments of all branches of the U.S.S.R. Armed Forces on Soviet territory shall move to Increased Combat Readiness.
>
> Leading personnel at Districts, Fleets, Armies, Flotillas, Corps, Squadrons . . . shall be recalled from furlough.
>
> The guard around Strategic Rocket Forces positions, arsenals, bases and dumps for nuclear and conventional munitions, armaments, and combat hardware, depots, airfields, positions, military camps, headquarters, and important military and administrative installations shall be increased.
>
> Temporary assignments, movements of motor vehicles, and flights by aircraft

> shall be restricted. Particular attention shall be paid to the observance of regulations and military discipline. . . .
>
> Leading personnel shall mount around-the-clock duty watches at headquarters of combined units and above.

Although much of Yazov's order 8825 deals with internal security matters, such as maintaining discipline and order, the phrase that leapt out at Soviet military officers was the first directive: "all branches of the U.S.S.R. Armed Forces on Soviet territory shall move to Increased Combat Readiness." Increased Combat Readiness, equivalent in U.S. military parlance to a heightened DEFCON level, placed military forces on a wartime footing in preparation for possible nuclear conflict. Secret Soviet lectures on military doctrine, acquired from the Voroshilov General Staff Academy via a defector and made available to the public in 1989 by the U.S. National Defense University, show that the term "Increased Combat Readiness" had a very specific meaning to Soviet military officers. "Constant Combat Readiness," "Increased Combat Readiness," and "Full Combat Readiness" were terms that had been drummed into their heads at the General Staff Academy. Constant Combat Readiness was the normal workaday status of the armed forces in peacetime. Increased Combat Readiness called for mobilizing the armed forces, sharply ratcheting up their preparedness for war. It implied that the possibility of war had increased significantly. Full Combat Readiness meant completing military preparations under conditions when war was considered imminent or had already erupted.

The Voroshilov General Staff Academy lectures on military doctrine state that the purpose of these preplanned military postures was to guarantee "the protection of the country from the consequences of the surprise outbreak of war initiated by the enemy." Increased Combat Readiness, in military operational terms—and in psychological terms for the troops involved—meant transitioning from a peacetime to a wartime military posture. As described in the Voroshilov General Staff Academy materials, it meant moving the armed forces to the verge of war:

> When moving the Armed Forces from a level of Constant Combat Readiness to a level of Increased Combat Readiness, normally the strength of on-call forces and means, duty units for combat, and the strength of combat patrol elements are augmented; all systems of communication and combat troop control deploy for action; the responsible duty personnel are specified in command posts; mobilization and combat employment plans for the troops are reviewed and adjusted; material reserves are prepared for transport; and other measures aimed at ensuring the rapid and concealed upgrading of the troops to the level of Full Combat Readiness, in order to facilitate the rapid accomplishment of combat missions, are taken. In this phase secret (concealed) mobilization of some units and large units, the first echelon of central rear services, and the rear services of the Ground Forces, Air Forces, and Navy is conducted; measures are taken for the technical cover of lines of commu-

> nication, and the dispersal of forces and means is effected. All of the abovementioned actions, in accordance with available time, are normally taken gradually and secretly under the guise of field exercises and other routine kinds of activities.

According to the General Staff Academy, some other steps required under Increased Combat Readiness are: "detachment of operations groups to prepared command posts; recalling troops to garrisons and bases; recalling officers absent on leave; . . . control of warning and communication system; intensification of reconnaissance activities; intensification of security at military posts, bases and objectives; taking necessary measures for protection against weapons of mass destruction; achieving a higher level of technical preparation of weapons, combat vehicles, and equipment; . . . undertaking special measures concerning rocket troops, air, and naval forces"; and "reconfirming combat alert plans." Increased Combat Readiness left only last-minute military preparations—and the political decision to attack—as the final steps on the road to war.

Orders from the coup leaders, including Yazov's order to go to Increased Combat Readiness, were generally obeyed by Soviet military forces. But they were not obeyed universally—troops in the Moscow area ultimately rejected the group's authority. However, support for the coup was generally widespread in the military. The commander of the Far East Military District, General V. I. Novozhilov, said in an interview after the coup that half of the army had supported it. Soviet press reports after the coup and testimony from senior officers indicate that Increased Combat Readiness was implemented at least in the Strategic Rocket Forces, Long-Range Aviation, the Navy, the PVO (strategic air defense forces), the KGB, and the Chemical Troops. In testimony to the Russian grand jury investigating the coup in February 1992, Minister of Defense Yevgeniy Shaposhnikov and General Konstantin Kobets related that "the majority of the orders at the time of the coup were 'sanctified' by the CPSU Central Committee, and specific commands relating to these orders were placed in the 'alert' packages of commanding officers of units and combined units. . . . On studying the documents, the commission members were haunted both by pain for the Army and by belated fear: when the troops were being made combat-ready during those August days, nuclear-powered submarines and surface ships were being equipped with nuclear warheads, nuclear charges were being slung beneath aircraft."

In the West, some have attempted to explain the move to Increased Combat Readiness during the August coup as a domestic measure intended to shore up internal security, but this explanation fails on the definition and purpose of Increased Combat Readiness: increase preparedness for war. Raising the combat readiness of offensive strategic forces (nuclear missiles and bombers) and of defensive strategic forces (reconnaissance aircraft, interceptors, and surface-to-air missiles) had nothing to do with internal security.

Nor was the move to Increased Combat Readiness merely a prudent military precaution against a remote theoretical threat from the West. Men like Kryuchkov and Yazov were true believers in the proposition that the United States posed a clear and present danger, and that the United States was actively seeking the opportunity to launch a nuclear surprise attack. General Yuri Maksimov, commander in chief of the Strategic Rocket Forces, obeyed the Increased Combat Readiness order because he too was a true believer. Less than two years before the coup, in November 1989, in a speech commemorating Missile Troops Day, he claimed that "immediately after the end of the war (in 1945) the U.S. military set about drawing up plans for a sudden nuclear attack on our country. . . . So far, there has been no change in U.S. military doctrine." In an interview after the August 1991 coup attempt, and twelve days after he placed the Strategic Rocket Forces on Increased Combat Readiness, the SRF commander's frame of mind was little changed: "The missile forces are the foundation of the strategic nuclear forces and a decisive factor in deterring and preventing war. . . . They prevent any aggressor from being tempted to wage war on our country, to blackmail it or bring strong-arm pressure to bear on it. . . . The way they [aggressors] approach a fragmented Union, deprived of its missile shield, could be different from the way they approach a unified Union. The prospect worries me."

Two senior military officers, Admiral Yuri Kaysin and General Igor Maltsev, both indicated in separate interviews after the failed coup that the reason for going to Increased Combat Readiness was the possibility of a foreign threat. After the coup, Colonel M. Ponamarev, in the official Defense Ministry publication *Krasnaya zvezda* (September 19, 1991), claimed that the United States had placed its forces on increased readiness during the coup. (The United States had done no such thing.) Ponamarev also claimed that the United States was continuing to prepare a quick-reaction force to exploit any future coup attempt.

After the coup, Yevgeniy Lisov, the Soviet deputy procurator general, headed the investigative group charged with establishing the facts of the coup. He stated in an interview that during the coup, military forces were made ready for war and that a "nuclear incident" was possible:

LISOV: The Military Districts were ready to do anything; they received all the needed instructions. All Yazov had to do was say: "Go ahead! . . . The troops—Army, KGB, and internal—had been brought to the status of "Increased Combat Readiness"—this means readiness for war.

INTERVIEWER: Was a nuclear incident possible?

LISOV: It cannot be ruled out. It could get to anything, had certain forces shown a greater interest in interfering in the situation.

The military alert was meant primarily to ready the armed forces to preempt or repel foreign aggression, including a possible nuclear attack from the United States. Defense Minister Yazov almost certainly thought that the coup would tempt the United States into considering a surprise nuclear attack. Only four months earlier, in his Victory Day speech of May 1991, when there was no obvious cause for fearing aggression by the United States and NATO, Yazov alluded to the possibility of a Western surprise attack on the USSR like the one by Nazi Germany on June 22, 1941: "We cannot fail to be perturbed by the fact that the termination of the activity by the Warsaw Pact military organization has not resulted in the creation of a bloc-free system of European security. . . . The formation of such a system in the foreseeable future becomes extremely problematical after the well-known events in the Near East [Desert Storm]. Because of this, the military-political situation is changing fundamentally, and not in our favor. Essentially the U.S.S.R. armed forces are confronted by the huge NATO military machine. . . . [The CFE Treaty] will further change the correlation of forces to the detriment of the U.S.S.R. . . . Even in the name of peace, we cannot irresponsibly disarm ourselves, lose our vigilance, and thereby create the possibility of a repetition of 22 June 1941."

Yazov so fundamentally mistrusted Gorbachev that he suspected the Soviet president might be the agent of a foreign government, or in some other dangerous way in cahoots with the West. After the coup he testified, "We talked about the situation in the country. It was unavoidable that we came to the conclusion that the President was to blame. He had distanced himself from the Party. . . . Gorbachev in recent years had been going abroad and often we had no idea in general what he was discussing there. . . . We were just not ready to become greatly dependent on the U.S.A., politically, economically, or militarily." In ordering Increased Combat Readiness, Yazov probably considered that the United States might fight to restore the deposed Gorbachev, who was an astonishingly popular figure in the West.

It is significant that Defense Minister Yazov and the Committee decided to place their nuclear forces on alert *before* announcing to the international community the overthrow of Gorbachev and the establishment of a new government. The USSR's strategic nuclear forces were ordered to an alert posture on August 19, "shortly after midnight," according to the U.S. Congressional Research Service, and no later than 4:30 A.M., according to Russian government investigators. The State Committee for the State of Emergency did not proclaim itself until 6:00 A.M., at least ninety minutes, and perhaps as much as six hours, after the alert began. Thus the first act of the new government, even before going public and officially taking power, was to have the defense minister clandestinely order a nuclear alert.

Why?

Why did the Committee not wait to mobilize strategic nuclear forces *after* the 6:00 A.M. announcement, and then do so openly, as a demonstration of the power and resolve of the new government? Why did they not wait until some *concrete evidence* of an imminent U.S. nuclear attack materialized before calling a nuclear alert? Clearly, Yazov and Kryuchkov wanted to get the jump on any enemy surprise attack. They mobilized nuclear forces before declaring a new government, because, in their view, such an announcement could start a war. They were unwilling to wait for the West to make the first move militarily. Rather than "playing it safe" by refraining from nuclear forces activities, they preferred to risk the West's discovering their secret nuclear mobilization—a considerable gamble, laden with escalatory possibilities. Of course, refraining from a nuclear alert is "playing it safe" only if one believes the risk of an enemy surprise attack is low. Rather than score *propaganda points* by publicly declaring a nuclear alert—an action that would prove the Committee was "in charge" and would rally nationalist sentiment against the presumed foreign threat—they took the nuclear threat so seriously that they preferred the *military advantages* accrued from secret preparedness for war. The timing and circumstances of the nuclear alert were consistent with a view that the coup could spark a nuclear war. The timing of the alert, ordered in advance of Western knowledge of the coup and of any possible Western military reactions, also strongly suggests that, at least to Kryuchkov and Yazov, preparedness meant being *more prepared than the other side*. Preparedness meant *being ready to strike first*.

The effect of Defense Minister Yazov's order to Increase Combat Readiness was immediate and electric. In the Strategic Rocket Forces, Long-Range Aviation, and the strategic arm of the Navy, officers and planning staffs assumed round-the-clock duty. They meticulously reviewed their parts in the preplanned strike options and their particular responsibilities under various scenarios in the nuclear war plan. At Strategic Rocket Forces and Long-Range Aviation army and division command posts, at Navy fleet and flotilla headquarters, and at scores of military commands from Murmansk, on the Arctic Ocean, to Zhangiz-Tobe, near the Chinese border, the gears of the Soviet war machine began to whir.

In Long-Range Aviation, at heavy bomber division bases in places like Irkutsk, all flights were canceled, and bombers on training missions returned to base to be made ready for war. Ground crews scrambled to fuel all aircraft, check avionics and navigation systems, and do preparatory work for uploading nuclear cruise missiles and gravity bombs.

In the icy depths of the Arctic Ocean, Soviet submarine technicians scurried between long rows of launch tubes, towers of metal several stories high, each containing a missile capable of destroying at least one city, half a world away. The sonar team scanned the vast ocean, searching for enemy hunter submarines come to destroy them. The captain ordered evasive maneuvers, just in case an enemy attack submarine lurked undetected nearby. He abandoned the peacetime patrol area and made for the wartime firing location designated by the packet in his safe marked "Increased Combat Readiness." The communications officer, a statue with headphones, listened intently. The airwaves, normally filled with the chatter of routine military communications, were now silent. He strained to hear from distant Moscow the words he most feared to hear: the launch command.

In the Strategic Rocket Forces, at the twenty intercontinental ballistic missile complexes from the Ukraine to the Siberian Far East, ICBM crews sat at their fire-control consoles, waiting for the word. The SRF's small contingent of mobile ICBMs returned to garrison, where they were surrounded by armed guards and assumed alert posture, ready to fire on a moment's notice. ICBMs were the strong right arm of the Soviet Union, carrying over 60 percent of the USSR's strategic nuclear warheads. They could be delivered at intercontinental range against targets in Europe, Asia, and North America. A single two-man missile crew for the mighty SATAN SS-18 ICBM had up to ten missiles, each carrying ten warheads—one hundred warheads altogether—at their command. Each warhead was fifty times more powerful than the Hiroshima A-bomb. Just two men had enough nuclear firepower at their fingertips to incinerate the major cities of the United States. The Strategic Rocket Forces had 308 SS-18 ICBMs, and about 1,400 ICBMs of all kinds: SS-11s, SS-13s, SS-17s, SS-18s, SS-19s, SS-24s, and SS-25s. All of this nuclear firepower was controlled by about 150 missile crews (three hundred men) plus a General Staff officer who would give them the launch codes. The General Staff preferred ICBMs over SLBMs and bombers, because ICBMs were normally kept at a very high state of readiness, prepared to launch within a few minutes, twenty-four hours a day, 365 days a year. When the SRF got Yazov's order to "Increase Combat Readiness," he was talking to a man holding a loaded pistol already aimed at another man's head. "Cock the hammer," he said.

For three days the hammer remained cocked. The nuclear forces of the Soviet Union remained on Increased Combat Readiness from August 19 through August 21, 1991. By August 22, it was over. The nuclear alert was canceled when Operation THUNDER, and the coup, failed.

CHAPTER 12

Operation THUNDER and the Fall of the Old Guard

As the coup of 1991 collapsed toward failure, its leaders became increasingly desperate, even irrational. For three days, the Soviet Union's nuclear arsenal was in the hands of men whose own world was ending. If Colonel Ponomarev's claim is true—that during the coup, the Soviet General Staff (mistakenly) believed U.S. strategic nuclear forces had gone to a heightened DEFCON level, moving to the Soviet equivalent of Increased Combat Readiness—then it seems nothing short of miraculous that a nuclear war was avoided. A top secret CIA report leaked to the press in 1996 stated that during the 1991 coup attempt in Moscow, the Russian GRU military intelligence facility in Cuba "erroneously reported that U.S. strategic forces had gone to their highest readiness levels"—grounds for a Russian preemptive strike. Perhaps the only thing that spared the world from nuclear Armageddon was the fact that the Committee was in power too briefly to act. Perhaps it was too preoccupied with trying to *stay* in power to react to the false warning that U.S. military forces were mobilizing for war. Colonel Ponomarev does not say when the General Staff concluded that the United States began Increased Combat Readiness. It might have rung the false alarm on August 21, the last day of the coup, when Committee leaders were in headlong flight or lapsed into catatonic drunkenness. Had the warning come twenty-four hours earlier, or had the Committee been more successful in maintaining control, Western civilization might not have survived the coup.

History hinged on the evening of August 20, the decisive moment for the coup. Shortly after the Kremlin announced Gorbachev's replacement by the State Committee for the State of Emergency on August 19, the only organized opposition to the coup seemed to be several hundred students and young democratic activists, led, more or less, by Boris Yeltsin. Yeltsin, a former communist aristocrat turned democratic firebrand, seized the Soviet Parliament building, which had been rechristened the "White House" by his followers, in conscious tribute to the United States and its representative form of government. Located not far from the Kremlin, the "White House" became the focus of international media attention and the rallying point for thousands. The Kremlin soon realized that it could not ignore the "White House." The Committee's authority, and its credibility as a new government, was too visibly challenged by the charismatic Yeltsin and his growing band.

Operation THUNDER was supposed to crush Yeltsin and his democrats in a lightning military raid on the "White House." Defense Minister Yazov, Marshal Akhromeyev, General Pugo, General Lebed, and some other senior military officers spent the afternoon of August 20 planning the impromptu raid, which was simple militarily but highly sensitive and unpredictable politically: it had to proceed in full view of a world media audience. Operation THUNDER called for OMON (Russian equivalent of SWAT) police troops to disperse the crowd protecting the "White House" with tear gas and water cannons. The elite Alpha Group, aided by crack airborne and KGB troops, would blast through the "White House" doors with rocket grenades and shoot their way to the fifth floor, where they would arrest or kill Yeltsin. The raid was scheduled for the late and early hours of August 20–21.

But THUNDER never materialized. Key officers on the scene refused to obey orders, and the coup plotters lost their nerve. Yevgeniy Shaposhnikov, commander in chief of the Air Force, would not send helicopters to land Alpha troops on the "White House" roof; he even threatened to bomb the Kremlin if the Committee attacked. General Pavel Grachev, a hard-bitten commander of airborne troops and a hero of the Afghanistan war, refused to let his paratroopers support the raid. The Alpha officers also refused to participate, as their commander, Viktor Karpukhin, later claimed.

These acts of disobedience were probably not motivated by a love of democracy or of Boris Yeltsin. On the contrary, as Gorbachev's aide Aleksandr Yakovlev later noted, officers like Grachev "were working both sides of the street, keeping in close contact with 'the White House' even as they were sitting in on the planning sessions of the coup. They're no democrats, but they refused to have blood on their hands for the sake of such idiots as Kryuchkov and Yazov." Moreover, civilian casualties in Operation THUNDER could have run very high. By the evening of August 20, thousands of people had rallied around the "White House." The military officers on the scene faced the distinct possibility that if Operation THUNDER went badly or killed many, or even if it was successful but highly unpopular, the Committee might deny any responsibility for what was essentially an illegal military operation—and blame the officers involved.

When Operation THUNDER failed, so did the coup. Plunged to the depths of desperation and despair, the coup leaders, who were still in control of the USSR's nuclear forces, now on alert for three days, cracked. General Shaposhnikov later expressed fear for his personal safety in his dealings with Defense Minister Yazov, a man whom he described as having gone berserk, capable of murder. A more sympathetic description of Yazov's state during the coup comes from his adjutant: "The old man suffered terribly throughout those two days, 19 and 20 August. He looked awful." In the end, the behavior of Yazov and Kryuchkov was delusional, as shown by their decision on August 21 to fly down to Foros, accompanied by industrialist-turned-conspirator Aleksandr Tizyakov, hoping to persuade Gorbachev to exculpate them. Instead, they were arrested. A witness to the arrests, Sergei Shakrai, one of Yeltsin's lawyers, said Kryuchkov "lost control of himself when he was detained. He could not control his hands or his facial expressions or recognize his own things. The man could be seen to be in a state of profound depression. . . . Yazov behaved more calmly and was in possession of himself, though he was deathly pale. The first thing he requested was help for his sick wife. . . . Tizyakov was outwardly normal, but you could sense he was bursting with spite. You got the feeling that he was ready simply to bite and tear to pieces anyone who got too close."

Kryuchkov apparently bounced back shortly afterward in prison, where he floated a masterful piece of disinformation claiming Gorbachev had been the real culprit behind the coup—a lie still believed by many, East and West. Kryuchkov's slander helped end Gorbachev's political career, giving the KGB chief a minor triumph over his hated president.

Gennadiy Yanayev, vice president of the USSR and titular head of the abortive new government, and Valentin Pavlov, another coup leader, were both drunk through most of the coup. According to Dmitri Sakharov, one of the Kremlin physicians, beginning on August 19, the first day of the nuclear alert, and thereafter, "Pavlov was drunk, but this was no simple intoxication. He was at the point of hysteria." When Yanayev was arrested in his office, the floor was strewn with empty bottles. He was so inebriated that he could no longer recognize close associates.

After the failure of the coup, Nikolai Kruchina, a high-ranking Communist Party official and supporter of the Committee, committed suicide by stepping out of his apartment window. Russian journalists claim that at least fifteen other suicides committed by coup supporters went unreported by the press.

The tough-minded General Boris Pugo, a communist true believer and disciplinarian of the masses, preferred death to democracy. In a scene reminiscent of Hitler and Eva Braun in the Führerbunker, Pugo went home to his beloved wife, Valentina, retired with her from the rest of the family to a private room, took out his pistol, shot her, then blew his brains out. Valentina had wanted death, but she was found still alive, sitting on the floor and smearing herself with blood, when the police came to arrest her husband. Valentina's grief on the death of her husband verged on madness. Pugo was both lover and hero to his wife, a giant man of destiny, now fallen. Even Pugo's bitterest enemy, the Russian prosecutor Yevgeniy Lisov, was moved in his telling of the attempted double suicide:

> We almost eyewitnessed it—he shot himself five minutes before we got there. . . . When we came in Valentina Ivanovna was practically unconscious; she was sitting

on the floor in a somnambulist state, rocking from side to side. She was wounded and was smearing blood all over her face with her hand, which is why it looked so horrible. Pugo first shot her and then himself. There were also two notes, his and hers. She writes, "Do not blame us for anything. We had to. . . ." During the last evening Pugo said at home in his son's presence—probably in order to test the reaction—that he would have to leave this life. His wife said, "Borya, if you go, I will not live without you, even a day. . . ." Pugo's father was in another room—a very old man, mentally unwell for the reason of both his age and the death of his wife. Having heard the shots, he came out, saw his son's body and the gun, picked up the gun, and put it on the shelf.

Soviet communism really fell with the suicide of its truest son, Marshal Sergey Fedorovich Akhromeyev. If the coup had succeeded, Akhromeyev might well have emerged as the de facto leader of the Soviet Union. The most senior and most respected military officer in the USSR, he was a brilliant military theoretician and strategic philosopher, one of those rare grand intellects who thought in terms of broad military, technological, geopolitical, and historical trends. Those trends, passed through the filter of Akhromeyev's personal experience as a soldier and devout Marxist-Leninist, pointed almost inevitably toward World War III. He passionately believed in the Soviet cause, that socialism was the hope of mankind for a just, egalitarian, and bountiful society, and that this bright potential was threatened by the capitalist West. Unlike most of the Soviet elite, including Gorbachev, who professed socialist brotherhood while living like millionaires, Akhromeyev was no hypocrite. Despite his high rank, making him one of the most powerful men in the Soviet Union and entitling him to luxury, he lived modestly with his wife, Tamara, in a small apartment. Admiral William J. Crowe, U.S. Navy, knew the marshal well and described him admiringly as "a warrior monk."

Sixty-eight years old at the time of the coup, Akhromeyev's formative experience had been as an officer during the World War II siege of Leningrad, where Nazi and communist fanatics had fought to exterminate each other in one of the most terrible battles of the most inhumane war in history. When Akhromeyev was carried as a hero from that killing ground, strain and starvation had reduced his frame from 170 to 90 pounds. He later rose through the ranks to become one of the Soviet Union's six field marshals, the highest military rank, signifying mastery in planning entire wars, employing combined ground, navy, air, and nuclear operations.

Despite their polar differences, Gorbachev made Akhromeyev his personal national security advisor. In that capacity, Akhromeyev visited the United States in July 1989 as the guest of Admiral Crowe, then Chairman of the U.S. Joint Chiefs of Staff. Crowe took Akhromeyev and his wife on a very human tour of the United States. Dispensing with state formalities, the tour featured rib barbecues, ordinary folks, sightseeing at the Alamo, an Indian reservation, and the spectacle of a Soviet marshal wearing a cowboy hat. Crowe and Akhromeyev genuinely liked each other, but when the tour was over, Marshal Akhromeyev looked Crowe in the eye and told him point-blank: "I still think someday you will attack us."

In the failed aftermath of Operation THUNDER, Akhromeyev stood on a chair in his Kremlin office with a noose around his neck and let himself fall into space.

He regained consciousness, surprised to find himself sprawled on the floor, still very much alive. He used the reprieve to write several letters to family, friends and colleagues—including to Gorbachev. The letters enabled prosecutor Lisov to reconstruct the scene of Akhromeyev's suicide:

> Akhromeyev was really amazing. He tried to take his life twice; in his suicide note he wrote that he would "have to make a second attempt—the first time I was not successful in committing suicide." Something did not go right. He fell down and was unconscious for about ten minutes. Then he came to, wrote five or six notes: to the cafeteria—to pay back the money he owed; to the family; to someone else; and a long note to Mikhail Sergeyevich.

In the letter to Gorbachev, the marshal apologized for breaking military regulations. To his family he wrote, "I cannot live when my Fatherland is dying and all that I have made my life's work is being destroyed. My age and all I have done give me the right to leave this life. I struggled to the end." His duties completed, Sergey F. Akhromeyev, Marshal of the Soviet Union, again stood on the chair, collared the noose—which was tied better this time—and leapt into darkness.

During the August 1991 coup, the United States was in grave danger without knowing it. A NATO or Strategic Air Command exercise, or the generation of U.S. forces to counter Moscow's escalation to Increased Combat Readiness, might have provoked the Committee to launch a preemptive nuclear strike. Any bold or unusual move by American political leaders might have had the same result. The coup leaders, moved by desperation or revenge as the coup unraveled, might have contemplated deliberately bringing on a nuclear *götterdämmerung* rather than face arrest, humiliation, and possible execution at the hands of the despised Yeltsin and his democratic masses.

Arguably, the coup attempt and nuclear alert of August 19–21, 1991 was more dangerous than the Cuban missile crisis of October 1962, and more dangerous than the Soviet reaction to the NATO theater nuclear exercise ABLE ARCHER in November 1983. Premier Khrushchev did not face imprisonment, possible execution, or feel compelled to commit suicide as a result of his failure to keep missiles in Cuba. Premier Andropov, although dying from kidney failure at the time of ABLE ARCHER–83, did not face the imminent internal collapse of the Soviet system. Unlike Khrushchev and Andropov, the coup plotters feared execution or imprisonment, and some of them preferred death to the consequences of failure. A man who is ready to kill himself, or his loved ones, is ready to destroy the world.

CHAPTER 13

The Cover-Up

In the West, Soviet military behavior during the attempted coup was reported as being restrained, responsible, and deserving of Western applause. Much was made of the recall to garrison of mobile ICBMs during the coup, a move widely misconstrued as "standing down" or somehow rendering inoperable the mobile ICBM force. But mobile ICBMs, only a tiny fraction of the Strategic Rocket Forces, can launch from garrison; their garages are equipped with sliding roofs to permit rapid launches. The coup leaders probably placed a high premium on ensuring that their orders, including launch orders, would be obeyed, and so recalled the mobile ICBMs to garrison where their crews could be directly supervised. The coup leaders may have been less concerned than normal about the vulnerability of mobile missiles in garrison, since there they are vulnerable only if attacked by surprise, and the move to Increased Combat Readiness should have minimized the chance that they could be surprised. Indeed, when missiles are at Increased Combat Readiness they are awaiting launch orders on a hair trigger. The return of mobile ICBMs to garrison was also consistent with Yazov's order calling for taking steps to enforce discipline, ensure effective control of personnel, and prevent desertions.

Disinformation from Soviet and Russian military officers has contributed to the Western misconception that Soviet military forces posed no threat in August 1991. Many officers who probably approved of, or participated in, the coup have publicly and vociferously denied complicity in order to escape prosecution. For example, General Mikhail Moiseyev, Chief of the General Staff during the coup, claimed that he had heroically assumed control of all the nuclear codes to prevent the plotters from launching nuclear weapons. But Moiseyev has since been exposed as a coup participant. Shortly after the coup, *Izvestiya* (August 28, 1991) reported that military officers all over the Union were destroying papers and evidence that would implicate them or their superiors in the coup. Boris Yeltsin's democratic Russian government also had a stake in assuring the West that there had been no danger, in order to allay fears about the consequences of instability in the former USSR and to keep Western attention, and dollars, focused on solving Russia's dire economic problems.

After the coup, Moscow's efforts to deny that there had been any danger to the West were so strenuous as to appear alarming. In an unprecedented gesture, the General Staff sent a representative to the U.S. Congress, Colonel Gennadiy Pavlov of the SRF, to describe how safeguards in command and control had precluded any danger of a nuclear attack upon the United States. Incredibly, the General Staff's generous offer to discuss their most sensitive military secret—their strategic command and control system—and to "prove" that Washington faced no nuclear danger from Moscow during the recent coup was unsolicited by the White House, unsolicited by the State Department, unsolicited by the Defense Department, and unsolicited by the Congress as a body. The General Staff offer responded to a request by Bruce Blair, then a little known U.S. academic, on behalf of a single United States senator. Oddly, after the August 1991 coup, the General Staff was suddenly eager to discuss what it previously had never been willing to discuss—the operation and recent status of its strategic nuclear forces.

Colonel Pavlov sought to disinform the U.S. Congress and the West about the danger to the United States during the August 1991 coup. If Pavlov's testimony is to be believed—that half a dozen people, each with a unique code, must all agree and all enter their codes before any missile can be launched—then the command and control system designed by the Soviets, masters of centralization, is far less centralized than ours, which requires only the president's order to launch missiles. Indeed, what Pavlov described is so cumbersome that Moscow would be incapable of launching forces rapidly in an emergency. Pavlov's claim that command and control works "by committee" contrasts unbelievably with the U.S. system, wherein contingency plans empower a number of persons individually to launch strategic forces, including individual submarine commanders. These U.S. contingency arrangements are designed to counter an enemy surprise attack or decapitation strike, to ensure the launching of strategic forces even if the top U.S. leaders are killed. In contrast, Pavlov's command and control system would be very vulnerable to surprise and decapitation—yet the Soviets always took such threats far more seriously than had the United States. Pavlov's model of how Soviet command and control works is contradicted by other Russian and former Soviet technical experts, including the chief technician who designed their system. Unfortunately, Pavlov's story was accepted at face value and widely publicized by the U.S. press and by some Western specialists who should have known better.

The coup leaders could have launched nuclear missiles and bombers at any time during the three-day nuclear alert. Except for Gorbachev, the coup leaders included all of the members of the Defense Council, which was the USSR's highest body for military decision making and almost certainly was empowered to order a nuclear strike. Since the highest-ranking military officers were among the coup conspirators, they surely knew how to control Soviet strategic forces. The coup leaders included Minister of Defense Yazov and Chief of the General Staff Moiseyev, who personally possessed two of the three "footballs," the briefcases containing special communications equipment for ordering a nuclear strike. The third "football" belonged to

Gorbachev himself, but it was taken from him when he was imprisoned at Foros. So the coup plotters had all three of the executive devices for controlling nuclear forces.

The chief designer of the Soviet "football" indicated in an interview (*Komsomolskaya pravda*, January 28, 1992) that any one of the "footballs" by itself is sufficient for ordering a nuclear strike; that there are several "footballs" for redundancy in case of decapitation; and that there are means for launching strategic forces without any "football" at all. General Geli Batenin, formerly of the General Staff and commander of an SS-18 ICBM division, acknowledged in an interview that although only the president has *legal* authority to order a nuclear strike, as a *practical* matter the Chief of the General Staff also has the authority and technical capability to launch strategic nuclear forces, as do a number of lower-ranking officers.

Would Soviet nuclear forces have launched if ordered to do so? After all, Operation THUNDER failed because officers in Moscow refused to obey Committee orders to attack the Parliament building. But Operation THUNDER was clearly illegal and immoral, even if one accepted the legitimacy of the Committee, because it entailed the use of regular troops against a "domestic enemy": Russian civilians and political figures. Calling for an attack on Russian kids in downtown Moscow was one thing; waging war against a foreign adversary—including launching nuclear strikes against the United States—was another. The Moscow garrison had been exposed more directly to the liberalizing influence of the Gorbachev regime, while nuclear troops, located in far-flung and isolated areas, were much more insulated from "new thinking" that might have led them to question authority.

At least some, and very likely all, Soviet strategic nuclear forces would have executed a launch command. Disobedience among the nuclear forces probably would have become manifest early on as refusals to go to Increased Combat Readiness, as ordered by Yazov. There is no evidence that any nuclear forces unit failed to comply with the alert command during the coup. Troops in the Strategic Rocket Forces and other nuclear services were the most elite and most rigorously trained of all Soviet soldiers. Screened psychologically and indoctrinated for robotic obedience, they operated in teams and were closely supervised to ensure compliance with orders. Their launch positions were electronically monitored to verify that commands were obeyed.

Perhaps the most compelling reason for thinking that launch orders would have been obeyed is that the overwhelming majority of SRF and other nuclear forces officers and men shared Kryuchkov and Yazov's belief that a U.S. nuclear surprise attack was a very real, if not imminent, possibility. After the coup, no one was prosecuted for obeying Yazov's order to go to Increased Combat Readiness—because the alert was universally regarded by senior military officers as a prudent precaution. Indeed, one of the few military units that disobeyed the order, the crew of a Foxtrot submarine, a nonnuclear vessel that had sailed from port and defied the Committee with offshore radio broadcasts supporting Gorbachev, *was* prosecuted for insubordination. Officers who openly sympathized with the coup but who did not actively promote it, limiting their compliance to obeying Yazov's command to assume Increased Combat Readiness, were not prosecuted, since the purpose of the alert was to protect the homeland from foreign aggression, a legitimate function of the military. Even General Shaposhnikov, who, along with General Grachev, was most responsible for defeating the coup by disobeying Committee orders, had obeyed Yazov's command. Such were the unreformed threat perceptions of the military heroes who defeated the coup.

Within one year of the coup, Pavel Grachev and Yevgeniy Shaposhnikov, respectively President Yeltsin's new minister of defense and commander in chief of strategic nuclear forces for a now democratic Russia, would be threatening the United States with World War III and placing Russian troops on alert—as if somehow possessed by Akhromeyev and Pugo.

PART III

The Armenian Crisis, May 1992

[President Bush's] order . . . caused Air Force missile and air crews at more than a dozen U.S. military bases to begin switching off nuclear-weapons related equipment that had operated continuously since the dawn of the Cold War. As a result, none of the weapons will remain ready for launch on short notice.

—*Washington Post*,
September 29, 1991

The Caucasian War did prove one thing, by the way: Local wars were going to be local nuclear wars in the 21st century.

—*Segodnya*,
January 4, 1994

CHAPTER 14

The New Russia

A few months after the failed coup attempt of August 1991, Yevgeniy Shaposhnikov peered at the wall map of his new nation in astonishment. The Soviet Union no longer existed. In its place were fifteen different countries.

Events moved so swiftly that cartographers and printing shops were unable to keep pace with the rapidly transforming face of Eurasia. Shaposhnikov's map showed the red expanse of a still-intact Soviet Union, but now covered with thick, black marker lines, drawn by hand, dividing the former USSR into the new nations. The largest of these was Russia, Shaposhnikov's new homeland. The next largest, to the west of Russia, was Ukraine, the size of France. Golden wheat fields covered this fertile land, breadbasket of Russia and outlet to Western Europe through warm-water ports on the Black Sea. Like a butcher's knife cleaving through red meat, a bold, black gash now severed Russia from Ukraine.

North of Ukraine, the knife carved out Belarus, a major industrial center, and slashed off the Baltic states: Latvia, Lithuania, and Estonia, small countries but with fine ports on the Baltic Sea. They had been Moscow's closest route to Western Europe and the world trade of London and Antwerp. Trapped between Poland, Belarus, and Lithuania was Kaliningrad, an enclave of Russian territory, now separated from the main body of Russia by over one hundred kilometers of what was now foreign frontier.

To the south, a black slash chopped off Georgia, Armenia, and Azerbaijan, with their ports on the Black and Caspian Seas. They were lands rich in fruit, milk, and especially oil. Baku, capital of Azerbaijan, was the virtual spigot of one of the largest oilfields in the world. In 1941, Adolf Hitler had invaded the Soviet Union, and lost World War II, mainly because he wanted to capture these lands, in particular the grain of Ukraine and the oil wealth of Azerbaijan. The blood of millions of Russian soldiers had consecrated these lands, and now, without a shot being fired, Ukraine, Azerbaijan, and all the rest had slipped from Moscow's grasp.

Shaposhnikov's eye traveled across the Caspian Sea, eastward. Slashing thousands of miles from south to east in a long black curve, the pen sliced open the belly of the former Soviet Union, the vast territory of Central Asia, and spilled out the new nations of Kazakhstan, Kyrgyzstan, Tajikistan, Turkmenistan, and Uzbekistan. Here was a territory the size of Western Europe, now lost to Moscow. Lost too was a vast wealth in minerals, factories, and some of the most advanced scientific and technical centers on the planet. Baikonur, to name just one of the "science cities" torn from Russian ownership, was home to the largest space launch facility on earth. Moscow's prized Baikonur Cosmodrome now belonged to the sovereign nation of Kazakhstan, a country of cattle drovers.

By the end of 1991, Russia's perimeter had been pushed back to where it had been in the seventeenth century. Gone were the territorial gains, not just those of the Soviet era, but of two hundred years of imperial Russian expansion under the czars. Gone were the gains of Peter the Great and his descendants—men who had fought for seaports, land wealth, living space, and secure frontiers enabling Russia to grow into a great modern state. Except for St. Petersburg and Siberia, most of the territorial patrimony inherited from Peter and his successors had reverted to foreign hands. It was as if the Soviet Union had entered a time machine and popped out as Russia at the end of the 1600s, hemmed into a large but in many ways economically deficient geographic space, surrounded by potential enemies, and lacking defensible borders.

This time, however, vulnerable and underdeveloped Russia was armed with nuclear weapons.

Marshal Yevgeniy Ivanovich Shaposhnikov was responsible for defending Russia. For being one of the few military officers to rally to Boris Yeltsin during the August 1991 coup, Shaposhnikov had been given the traitor Dimitry Yazov's old job: defense minister. Later, in December 1991, Yeltsin christened Shaposhnikov commander in chief of the armed forces of the Commonwealth of Independent States (CIS), thereby making him responsible for protecting not just Russia but all eleven former Soviet republics that joined the CIS as independent nations. The task seemed impossible, not least because Shaposhnikov had no troops. All of the Commonwealth states, including Russia, were busy nationalizing their armed forces. They were hypersensitive about their newly won sovereignty, symbolized by their armies, and they correctly suspected that the CIS was a device to resubordinate all military forces—and eventually the new nations themselves—to Moscow's control. The only military instruments CIS commander in chief Shaposhnikov really had were the strategic nuclear forces.

If anyone could convert the CIS from a sheaf of paper—backed by Russian nuclear weapons—into a true multinational armed alliance, it was Yevgeniy Shaposhnikov. Through diligence, intelligence, and political savvy, he had, at age forty-nine, become the youngest marshal and commander in chief of the Soviet Air Force since World War II. At age fifty he was defense minister, and then commander of the entire Commonwealth. Still he had energy enough to marry and raise three children.

He had seen the Soviet Union disintegrate with startling suddenness. The failed August coup—that failed in part because Marshal Shaposhnikov refused helicopters to the coup plotters—was quickly followed by the fall of the Communist Party, the rise of democrats led by Boris Yeltsin, and the dissolution of the USSR. Mikhail Gorbachev, restored as president, resumed his plan to convert the Soviet state into a legitimate, voluntary union. Even before its final fragmentation into a dozen states, all professing that they would build new societies based on democracy and capitalism, the imminent death of the Soviet Union was evident. Within a month after the August coup attempt, the Soviet republics were indeed acting like independent nations. Kazakhstan began talking to the U.S. State Department about jointly controlling, with Russia, the SS-18 missiles on its territory, as if Kazakhstan were already a sovereign country. Latvia, Lithuania, and Estonia entered the United Nations. Several Soviet republics restored their ancient national symbols. Tajikistan outlawed activities by the Communist Party. Boris Yeltsin, president of the Russian Republic, began boldly transferring national powers from the central Soviet government into his own hands and those of democratic reformers in the Duma, the Russian parliament. All of this happened before the end of September. Later in the fall, Gorbachev called on the Soviet republics to sign a new union treaty. The republics' leaders refused to sign, forcing Gorbachev to cancel a planned ceremony for the treaty event on November 25, 1991. On December 18, the USSR Supreme Soviet's Council of the Union drew up a draft law on the transformation of the Union into a confederation, in effect dissolving the USSR.

On Christmas Day, 1991, Mikhail Gorbachev announced on television his resignation as president of the now nonexistent Soviet Union. Also on December 25, Gorbachev handed over his "nuclear briefcase" to Russian president Yeltsin. Thus Russia replaced the vanished USSR as a nuclear superpower.

Yevgeniy Shaposhnikov looked at his map, mentally calculating the dangers that could arise in this new and unpredictable world. The subdivision of the USSR had raised a threat unprecedented in history. Tactical nuclear weapons were scattered at former Soviet Army, Navy, and Air Force bases in every one of the former Soviet republics that were now newborn nations. Strategic nuclear weapons, ICBMs, and long-range bombers were located in several of these new states. All of these new countries feared that Russia might attempt to reconquer them, and most nursed deep bitterness against Moscow for attempting to destroy their religious and ethnic identities through "Russification" and through reeducation aimed at creating a "new Soviet man." If these victim nations seized the nuclear weapons located on their territories, Russia would suddenly face a host of new nuclear threats all along its western and southern borders.

Ukraine was the most technically advanced and most independent of these troubling potential new nuclear powers, but there was a more immediate threat. Wars within and between several of the former Soviet republics had already broken out. Civil war simmered in Georgia and Tajikistan. Mujahedin "holy warriors" from Afghanistan were making cross-border raids and trying to stir up an Islamic revolution among the largely Muslim populations of the new nations of Central Asia, particularly in Tajikistan. China, Iran, and Turkey had long-unresolved territorial disputes with Russia and the former Soviet Union, and they eyed hungrily the poorly defended lands just north of their borders, lands that historically had belonged to them.

The largest and most disturbing of the conflicts erupting from the corpse of the Soviet Union was between Armenia and Azerbaijan. There, Christian Armenians and Muslim Azeris were at each other's throats in an all-out religious and territorial war. Just across the border were the Turks, hereditary enemies of the Armenians and brothers to the Turkic Muslims of Azerbaijan. Turkey's affinity for the Azeris was no doubt enhanced by the oil wealth of Baku.

Yevgeniy Shaposhnikov was well aware that the Russian Army was a hollow shell, underpaid, underfed, rusting from disrepair, a victim of economic collapse. Turkey had a modern army of 500,000 men and was a member of NATO. U.S. military forces were based on its territory. Yes, Russia had never been more vulnerable to foreign attack.

A little over one month after the coup attempt, on September 27, 1991, President George Bush made an astonishing gesture of friendship to Moscow in a televised address from the Oval Office at 8:02 P.M:

> Good evening. Tonight I'd like to speak to you about our future and the future of generations to come. The world has changed at a fantastic pace, with each day writing a fresh page of history before yesterday's ink has even dried. And most recently, we've seen the peoples of the Soviet Union turn to democracy and freedom and discard a system of government based on aggression and fear. . . . We can now take steps in response to these dramatic developments, steps that can help the Soviet peoples in their quest for peace and prosperity. More importantly, we can now take steps to make the world a less dangerous place than ever before in the nuclear age.

President Bush, inspired by the apparent victory of democracy over tyranny in the Soviet Union, and in the last year of his controversial first term with a reelection struggle impending, proclaimed what Secretary of Defense Richard Cheney accurately described as "the single biggest change in the deployment of U.S. nuclear weapons since they were first integrated into our forces in 1954." The president continued:

> After careful consultations with my senior advisors . . . I am announcing today a series of sweeping initiatives affecting every aspect of our nuclear forces on land, on ships, and on aircraft. . . . I will begin with the category in which we will make the most fundamental change in nuclear weapons in over forty years, nonstrategic or theater weapons. . . . Last year, I canceled plans to modernize our ground-launched theater nuclear weapons. . . . Last month's events not only permit but indeed demand swifter, bolder action. I am therefore directing that the United States eliminate its entire worldwide inventory of ground-launched, short-range, that is, theater nuclear weapons. We will bring home and destroy all of our nuclear artillery shells and short-range ballistic warheads . . . the United States will withdraw all tactical nuclear weapons from its surface ships and submarines. . . . I am directing that all United States strategic bombers immediately stand down from their alert posture . . . the United States will immediately stand down from alert all intercontinental ballistic missiles scheduled for deactivation under START. . . . I am terminating the development of the mobile Peacekeeper ICBMs as well as the mobile portions of the small ICBMs program. . . . I am canceling the current program to build a replacement for the nuclear short-range attack missile for our nuclear bombers. . . . I have already proposed to reduce U.S. defense spending by 25 percent.

In his address President Bush asked Soviet president Gorbachev and Russian president Yeltsin to reciprocate his historic peace offering by removing tactical nuclear weapons, standing down strategic forces, and scaling back strategic modernization. Finally, Bush kindled hope in millions that a dream almost forgotten through the long nightmare of the Cold War might at last become reality: "Now the Soviet people and their leaders can shed the heavy burden of a dangerous and costly nuclear arsenal which has threatened world peace for the past five decades. They can join us in these dramatic moves toward a new world of peace and security. . . . Now let them say that we led where destiny required us to lead, to a more peaceful, hopeful future. We cannot give a more precious gift to the children of the world. Thank you, good night, and God bless the United States of America."

On the morning after the President's speech, on Saturday, September 28, Secretary Cheney held a press conference to explain how the reductions of tactical nuclear weapons and de-alerting of U.S. bombers and half of the ICBM force—450 Minuteman II missiles—would be accomplished. Responding to a question about the vulnerability of U.S. bombers once they were taken off alert, Cheney explained that the unprecedented relaxing of the U.S. nuclear posture was premised on the assumption that a Soviet nuclear attack would be preceded by highly visible tensions and activities that would provide adequate strategic warning. Yet about a month earlier, during the August coup attempt—probably unknown to Cheney—Soviet strategic nuclear forces had nearly launched a preemptive strike that would have taken the United States completely by surprise. The "escalatory paradigm" for a nuclear war, which was predominant in the National Intelligence Estimates during the early 1980s and that had led to nearly disastrous Western carelessness during ABLE ARCHER–83, obviously still blinded U.S. perceptions in 1991.

The West's fear of possible deliberate, large-scale nuclear aggression was swept away by dramatic historical changes in the former Soviet Union. Accordingly, the United States markedly reduced the readiness of its strategic and tactical nuclear forces. It has drawn down U.S. general-purpose forces in NATO Europe, and it has made deep cuts in the defense budget, reducing the size and readiness of U.S. military forces to levels unprecedented in the post–World War II era.

World War III is no longer deemed a possibility.

Yet in the Caucasus, events were taking shape that would produce the first Russian nuclear threat against the West of the post-Soviet era. On November 9, Turkey recognized Azerbaijan's independence from the Soviet Union, raising fears in Armenia of an Azeri-Turk alliance that could upset the regional balance of power. "We must take active steps to restore the balance, otherwise a dangerous situation will develop," Levon Ter-Petrosyan, Armenia's forty-six-year-old president, told the press. Asked if Azerbaijan might become a Turkish "puppet," Ter-Petrosyan affirmed: "This is not a fear, it is a fact."

These rising tensions among minor powers, though still part of a nuclear superpower and involving a NATO ally, drew little notice in Western Europe or the United States.

President Gorbachev applauded President Bush's unilateral gesture on nuclear disarmament but said that reciprocity would require further study. Eight days later, on October 5, Gorbachev ordered the removal of all short-range nuclear weapons from ships, submarines, and naval aircraft. However, most of these tactical nuclear weapons went into storage and were not destroyed. Moreover, all Soviet ICBMs remained on alert, no changes were made in the posture of other Soviet intercontinental forces, and Soviet strategic modernization programs continued unchanged. Nor did President Yeltsin, when he inherited from Gorbachev the nation's nuclear arsenal a few months later, decrease the hair-trigger readiness of Russia's nuclear forces for war. While the United States let down its nuclear guard, Moscow continued Operation VRYAN.

VRYAN, begun in the early 1980s to provide strategic warning of an impending nuclear strike by the United States, probably continues today, even though in November 1991, as noted earlier, Yevgeniy Primakov publicly declared VRYAN terminated in the Foreign Intelligence Service (SVR), the successor organization to the KGB. Primakov's declaration was hardly to be trusted. Disinforming the West about VRYAN's continuation was certainly not beneath him; indeed, *dezinformatsiya* had been his specialty during his long KGB service, in which he posed as a foreign journalist. Primakov's alleged shutdown of VRYAN seemed timed to respond to the first public revelation of the operation's existence, by KGB defector Oleg Gordievsky in 1990. Trapped between President Yeltsin, who was seeking Western cash and admittance to the circle of democratic nations, and a still deeply suspicious Russian military, Primakov had every reason to provide false comfort to the West while actually preserving VRYAN's operation.

The GRU is stonily silent on whether it perpetuates VRYAN. The GRU never underwent even the pretense of reform and reconstruction that was pretended at the KGB and symbolized by a new name, the SVR. The GRU never even bothered to change its acronym.

When VRYAN began, the KGB and GRU both ran their own versions of the operation. Former KGB officer Gordievsky has suggested that VRYAN may have become more important in the GRU than in the KGB. Logically, strategic warning is more consistent with the mission of the GRU, which is focused on military intelligence, whereas the KGB was responsible for collecting intelligence on a broader range of issues, including economic and scientific matters. The GRU is the intelligence arm of the General Staff, and directly serves those who would share in the decision to launch a nuclear attack and who have full operational responsibility for executing the strike. For practical and operational reasons, VRYAN would be of most interest to the General Staff and GRU, which still aggressively collects intelligence on the military threat, as if the Cold War had never ended. According to French intelligence estimates, the GRU has over the last several years increased its budget and manpower and now controls about 8,000 agents overseas. French intelligence officers also believe that "the GRU's autonomy has grown considerably during Mr. Yeltsin's presidency." In a March 1996 interview, a "high-ranking GRU officer" told Russian journalist Igor Korotchenko that the armed forces of "the United States, other NATO countries, as well as Japan, China, and the states of the Near East, hold particular interest for the GRU," indicating that the United States is still regarded as a threat, along with everyone else. Two unclassified GRU reports published in November 1995 analyze the command and control of British nuclear missile submarines and of U.S. *Nimitz*-class aircraft carriers, both considered by the Russians as potential delivery platforms for a nuclear surprise attack.

A February 14, 1996, conference of the General Staff on how to predict and "resolve" military conflicts sounds suspiciously like VRYAN. The Valentine's Day conference called for "setting up a nationwide system of information gathering for the forecasting and timely localization of conflicts. . . . This would enable the country's top leadership to take the necessary decisions at early stages in the development of conflicts." General Viktor Barynkin, whose advocacy of Russian readiness to preempt a U.S. nuclear or conventional surprise attack is no secret, "stressed that it is necessary to use the full analytical potential . . . of this nerve center of the [Russian] Armed Forces . . . in the interests of preventing military conflicts or resolving them by use of military force." General Staff conferees agreed on "the pressing need for further scientific development" of means "for forecasting complex situations representing a danger to the state." Essentially, the General Staff conference was concerned with discovering "complex situations representing a danger to the state" at an early stage so that Moscow can "prevent" wars, ideally through negotiation but certainly "by use of military force." They were discussing preemption.

General V. A. Ryaboshapko minced no words about the necessity of a program like VRYAN for warning Moscow when to launch a nuclear first strike. In a summer 1996 article, published in the prestigious Defense Ministry journal *Military Thought*, General Ryaboshapko recommended that Russia prepare to "use nuclear weapons in peacetime" and that Moscow's preparations for a nuclear first strike "take a minimum of time and . . . not be discovered by technical means of reconnaissance," in order to preserve the element of surprise. According to Ryaboshapko, Russia must prepare to strike first because everyone else who has nuclear weapons is also planning to: "An analysis of conditions for the use of the nuclear potential by [other] powers indicates that their military-political leadership envisages and stipulates in advance the possibility of employing nuclear weapons in any stage of a war and even of an armed conflict [a situation short of war] should this be in the national interests."

General Ryaboshapko proposed continuing well into the next century a "supradepartmental" intelligence program for warning of enemy aggression and supporting a nuclear strike, one that should sound chillingly familiar to anyone acquainted with VRYAN:

> Considering that up to 2005 the possibility of Russia employing nuclear weapons against an aggressor . . . essentially will be the only deterring factor of a military nature, it appears advisable to create a reconnaissance-information system at a supradepartmental level based on existing components. It must provide an assessment of the threat of aggression against Russia and its allies and must determine the fact of aggression and its scale, nature and development, which will permit preparing proposals for use of tactical or strategic nuclear weapons. It is necessary to work out scientifically substantiated indicators of conditions for the transition to use of nuclear weapons.

The general's article may be taken at face value, as proposing the reinstitution of something like VRYAN, but it is more likely he was justifying the continuation of an existing VRYAN program that dangles the nuclear sword over all of our heads still.

Colonel Stanislav Lunev, the highest-ranking GRU officer ever to defect to the West, in testimony before the U.S. Congress on October 4, 1998, made it clear that the Russian military still considers nuclear war with the United States an imminent possibility: "Russian intelligence activity against this country [the United States] is much more active than it was in time of the former Soviet Union. And this activity just now is much more dangerous for this country than it was before." According to Colonel Lunev, so gravely does the Russian military regard the possibility of war with the United States that the GRU continues actively to plan to assassinate U.S. political and military leaders and to conduct nuclear sabotage with small, man-portable nuclear "suitcase" bombs smuggled into the United States. Colonel Lunev told Congress that all of this would be intended to decapitate the United States just prior to a massive Russian nuclear first strike. Lunev, wearing a black hood to conceal his identity and heavily guarded to protect him from GRU assassins, speaking in broken English, told Congress that according to Russian military plans, the GRU would preposition nuclear "suitcase" bombs in the United States prior to an all-out nuclear war: "Very well in advance, maybe few months, maybe few weeks, of course, few hours before real war would be in place against this country [the United States], Russian Special Operations Forces [Spetsnaz] need to come here and pick up [the nuclear "suitcase"] weapon system. . . . They will come here as tourists, businessmen. . . . According to their tasking, in few hours they need to physically destroy, eliminate American military chains of command, President, supreme commander-in-chef, Vice President, Speaker of the House, military commanders, especially to cut [the] head from American military chain of command. They need to destroy communications system in this country and grow panic and chaos in this country before real war would be in place. They need to destroy power stations and highly protected facilities which could not be destroyed by regular nuclear missile strike." Colonel Lunev worked as a GRU agent in the United States in the early 1990s, personally tasked with supporting Russian contingency plans to smuggle nuclear "suitcase" bombs into the U.S. He told Congress that the Russian military takes so seriously the near-term possibility of nuclear war with the United States that such bombs may already be on American soil.

Russia continues to invest heavily in technology and human resources to provide strategic warning of a possible surprise nuclear attack. Russia is upgrading its constellation of spy satellites that monitor U.S. ICBM launchers. Russia is maintaining, at great expense, its signals intelligence sites in Cuba, constantly monitoring the communications and readiness of U.S. strategic nuclear forces.

While its general-purpose forces have withered away from neglect, Russia has maintained the strategic nuclear forces at Constant Combat Readiness, ready to launch a nuclear strike on a moment's notice. This is no mean feat, and it has imposed tremendous strain on Russia's weak economy to finance, modernize, maintain, and provide spare missiles, fuel, and training to the nuclear forces. Preferential treatment is being given to the SS-25 and SS-27 ICBMs over the SLBMs and advanced cruise missiles because, as General Vladimir Belous has observed, ICBMs have the highest day-to-day readiness for striking first or responding to an enemy nuclear attack. As an added expense, Russia continues to build mobile ICBMs. Basing ICBMs on mobile launchers instead of in silos greatly increases cost but enhances survivability against a surprise attack.

Russia is investing in missile accuracy through improved guidance and the Global Navigation Satellite System (GLONASS). Accuracy buys the ability to destroy hostile missiles in their hardened silos and to smash shielded enemy command and control nodes before they can order a launch. Since November 1993 the new Russian military doctrine has explicitly allowed nuclear preemption, a point Moscow has gone to great lengths to advertise to Washington, in no small part to deter a U.S. surprise nuclear attack.

In an economy where regime stability is threatened by lack of housing for military officers and the general populace, Moscow continues to build, at tremendous expense, deep underground shelters to protect Russia's political and military leaders from a decapitating nuclear strike. One of these subterranean facilities, presently under construction at Yamantau Mountain in the Urals, is a complex of tunnels spanning an area roughly the size of Washington, D.C. The purpose of the Yamantau complex is unknown, except that it is designed to survive a nuclear war. Incidentally, in the local Bashkir language "Yamantau" means "Evil Mountain."

CHAPTER 15

The U.S. Threat

President George Bush's dramatic gesture in September 1991, retiring and standing down many U.S. nuclear weapons, failed to reassure Russian military planners. "Objective conditions," to use the Russian parlance, provided some basis for continued, or even heightened, Russian concern about the possibility of a surprise attack. Pershing II's short-warning threat against Moscow fueled the war scare during the early 1980s. The late 1980s war scare was fueled by loss of the Warsaw Pact's defensive depth and by fear of improved U.S. ICBMs, SLBMs, and the high-tech conventional weapons of DESERT STORM. The 1990s Russian war scare reacts to the same U.S. threats prevalent in the late 1980s, now grown more formidable with increased deployments and technological improvements. The 1990s war scare is also aggravated by the sharp decline of Russia's general-purpose forces, the loss of more defensive depth through the collapse of the USSR, and the disintegration of Russia's system of early warning radars, which makes a surprise attack easier than ever.

President Bush's stand-down order left the most effective U.S. nuclear forces on alert. Half the ICBM force—the more accurate and deadlier half, Minuteman III and Peacekeeper multiple-warhead missiles, carrying about 2,000 weapons—remained ready to launch on short notice. The U.S. ICBMs that were taken off alert were the older Minuteman II single-warhead missiles, collectively carrying 450 weapons. In other words, more than 80 percent of U.S. ICBM warheads remained on alert.

Bush's order did not affect U.S. ballistic missile submarines, which maintained their normal alert rates and combat patrols at sea. Until 1997 the United States was deploying increasing numbers of Trident II SLBMs. With a miss distance of merely ninety meters, they can destroy the hardest Russian ICBM silos with a single warhead. About 1,500 Trident II warheads are now operational, enough to destroy all Russian ICBM silos, submarine pens, bomber bases, and nuclear weapon storage bunkers, as well as many key command and control nodes. Launched from the Barents Sea, a Trident II would allow Moscow no more strategic warning time than that permitted by Pershing II, and it would constitute a much more effective, decapitating, threat. This partially accounts for Russia's nervousness and vocal protests against the constant presence of U.S. submarines in the Barents.

Under the Strategic Arms Reduction Treaties, the United States will retain Trident IIs, dismantling less-accurate SLBMs. U.S. missile submarines will be fewer but deadlier. In 1994, Igor Sergeyev, commander in chief of the Strategic Rocket Forces, told Ed Bradley of *60 Minutes* that the Trident is "already powerful enough to destroy almost any target in Russia" and that "the most dangerous thing about this missile may be the fear it arouses in Russia's leaders that the U.S. is seeking a nuclear advantage."

America's development of high-tech conventional weapons has continued to advance since DESERT STORM. Innovations include improved "stealth" technology, which could make cruise missiles invisible to radar. Russian military writings are full of concern that the United States could launch a surprise attack using advanced conventional weapons to destroy Russia's nuclear forces, and then blackmail Moscow into submission with the threat of nuclear annihilation. Russia's new nuclear doctrine, which threatens to preempt nuclear or *conventional* aggression, is also meant to deter this possibility.

Degradation of Russia's missile attack warning system makes Russia more vulnerable to a U.S. surprise nuclear attack. The disintegration of the USSR left many important radars, including the Large Phased-Array Radars (LPARs), outside of Russia in what are now foreign countries. Russia cannot quickly buy its way out of the radar problem by building more LPARs, which require over a decade to construct. In a July 1995 interview, Defense Minister Pavel Grachev tried to put the best face on the situation by testifying to "the reliability of the existing missile attack warning system and to the readiness of teams and crews to act in a combat situation," but he "noted the need for further technical improvement," which "would be completed by 2005, when the missile attack warning system and space monitoring system will have been completely renewed." Russian journalist Vladimir Vasilyev provides this more somber, and more realistic, assessment of the effects of the fall of the USSR on the missile attack warning system:

> A system of exceptionally great importance for all the countries that emerged from the U.S.S.R.—the missile attack warning system—was destroyed in a very brief period of time. As a result, the western, southern, eastern, and northeastern sectors are no longer covered by the radar fields of the missile attack warning system. . . . Needless to say, Russia's enemies and those who wish her ill are very happy with this outcome. But they shouldn't be, because the collapse of the missile attack warning system of the former U.S.S.R. benefits no one. The fact is that the system had the capability to effectively monitor test and combat launches of ballistic missiles in the Middle East, India, Pakistan, China, and North Korea and the seas of the Pacific Ocean. This is no longer possible.

Vasilyev's implication is clear: with gaps in its missile attack warning system, how will Russia be able to distinguish a missile strike from "the Middle East, India, Pakistan, China" or elsewhere from a U.S. nuclear attack? Russian radar blindness increases the chances for nuclear miscalculation.

Four LPARs that provided early warning of missile attacks coming out of the Norwegian Sea and Indian Ocean are not on Russian real estate. As reported by journalist Sergey Grigoryev in a January 1996 article, "Enormous breaches appeared in the ground missile attack warning system radar field inasmuch as radars at Skrunda (northwestern axis), Mukachevo (southwestern), Laki and Sary-Shagan (southern) ended up abroad. Rapid construction of new bases is very difficult under present conditions." Although Russia claims ownership of these radars, their continued operation and readiness is subject to the whims of the host governments. The Baltic states, where one Russian LPAR was located, want to join NATO, and they forced this LPAR to close—perhaps Russia's single most important early warning radar—in 1998. Nor have radars located in Russia been immune to shortages of material and trained manpower imposed by the economy. Consequently, gaps have opened in Russia's coverage of missile attack corridors, and the overall effectiveness of the early warning radar system has lowered. Lower confidence in radar warning translates into greater vulnerability to surprise attack, diminished confidence in retaliatory options like launch-on-tactical-warning, which depend critically upon radars, and increased reliance on strategic warning from the GRU and SVR to support a preemptive strike. For these agencies, war-scare attitudes are institutionally normative.

CHAPTER 16

The Great Debate, May 27–30, 1992

Nightmarish impossibilities were now the stuff of everyday life. In December 1991, while the General Staff worried about radars, border clashes between Armenians and Azeris and the fight for possession of the territory called Nagorno-Karabakh intensified. As Armenian forces pressed Azeris out of their villages in Nagorno-Karabakh, Azerbaijan imposed a blockade on the region, cutting off food, water, and electricity. An official in Yerevan, the capital of Armenia, described the situation as "a real war."

This, from a February 1992 press report: "On a snow-covered cliff, a Soviet-made field-gun points towards a mountaintop directly facing it and goes off with an ear-shattering bang. 'Damn, you missed them again,' shouts an Azerbaijani regular as he throws himself to the ground to avoid bullets. . . . This is . . . Nagorno-Karabakh." On February 19, 1992, Turkish prime minister Suleyman Demirel told his parliament that outside support of Armenia against Azerbaijan could lead to a regional war. On March 1, thousands of Muslims gathered in protest rallies in Istanbul to demand Turkish intervention against Armenia. On May 9, Armenia violated a cease-fire to seize the last Azeri stronghold in Nagorno-Karabakh.

Strategic thinking in the General Staff and Russian military continued to grow from its Soviet roots, illumined by the twilight of empire and shadowed in the darkness of growing chaos. The notion of relying more heavily on nuclear weapons and nuclear first use—first broached by Soviet officers after Operation DESERT STORM in 1991 demonstrated the technical superiority of U.S. conventional arms—continued to gain currency after the USSR and the Soviet Army both disintegrated. Officers like General Igor Rodionov, commandant of the General Staff Academy, had argued in 1991 and 1992 that the weakness of Russian general-purpose forces necessitated a compensating preparedness to strike first with nuclear weapons against the United States, NATO, or other powers that might attempt a DESERT STORM or other large-scale conventional attack against Russia.

General Rodionov and others further argued that Russia should be prepared to initiate nuclear war, even against aggressor states that possessed no nuclear weapons but he powerful conventional armies, like Turkey. In fact, as the nuclear debate proceeded in Moscow, growing Russian concerns about Turkish intentions in Armenia and Azerbaijan probably inspired this proposed change to Russia's military doctrine.

On the other side of this argument, and in a distinct minority, were officers like General Makhmut Gareyev. He agreed that Russia faced grave threats to its security, and he did not oppose a nuclear first strike against an aggressor armed only with conventional weapons, but he objected to relying *primarily* on nuclear weapons to deter or defeat an enemy. This policy, he argued, was likely to result in Armageddon. Instead, he proposed that Russia rebuild its defunct general-purpose forces, no matter what the cost, and reserve nuclear weapons for use only as a last resort.

At a crucial conference held in May 1992, General Rodionov and General Gareyev grappled with the future of Russian military doctrine, and perhaps the fate of the entire world. The nuclear debate within the Russian military came to a decision just as events built to twin crises in Ukraine and Armenia.

Perhaps as remarkable as the outcome of Russia's great nuclear debate in 1992 was the Russian military's perception that such a debate was needed. While Russia's political leaders embraced democracy and were seeking accommodation and friendship with the West, the General Staff remained essentially unreformed. Just six months after the failed August 1991 coup, Lev Ponomaryov and Victor Sheinis, members of the Russian commission investigating the coup, despaired of ever bringing all the conspirators to justice, complaining that "a number of high-ranking KGB officers who were implicated in the coup attempt still hold their jobs, and one of them, Major General Bulygin, has received a promotion and is now working in Russia's Federal Security Agency." General Konstantin Kobets, head of the coup investigative commission, publicly complained in February 1992 that at least fifty generals who supported the coup had been promoted.

President Yeltsin probably did not dismiss reactionaries en masse from the General Staff or from other government service because he was afraid of challenging their power and provoking another coup attempt. Perhaps Yeltsin also realized that changing the guard at the General Staff would be futile, since the entire generation of senior officers, schooled in Marxism-Leninism and aged in the Soviet worldview, would have more or less the same totalitarian outlook. After all, Generals Yazov and Moiseyev were hand-picked by President Gorbachev to lead the Ministry of Defense and the General Staff because they seemed more reform-minded than most senior officers; their most significant contribution to change was the failure of their attempted coup against Gorbachev.

The Russian officer corps remained essentially unreconstructed, embittered by the collapse of the USSR and defeat in the Cold War, still deeply suspicious of—and in many cases vengeful toward—the United States.

Amidst the euphoric celebration following the overthrow of Soviet tyrants in August 1991, some knowledgeable Russian officials and military reformers publicly cautioned about the General Staff's still-dangerous attitudes. Yevgeniy Velikhov, a nuclear scientist and advisor to President

Gorbachev, noted in a September 1991 interview that "the problem of the first strike continues to exist. In short: the conditions that might cause the military to make unsafe decisions continues to exist." General Yuriy Kirshin, formerly of the General Staff and subsequently director of a Russian think tank, told a Washington, D.C., audience of U.S. political scientists on September 27, 1991, that "the most important thing the United States could do to contribute to world peace" is to "convince the General Staff that the U.S. does not want to conquer the world." In the same lecture, General Kirshin said that General Viktor Lobov, then Chief of the General Staff, was "obsessed with the U.S. threat. It is all he talks about."

The year 1992 saw the first flowering of Russian democracy, Boris Yeltsin's hopeful attempts to privatize the economy and achieve a democratic social revolution, and financial aid and other assistance from the United States and Western democracies for Russia's transformation. Nonetheless, in a February 1992 interview, Admiral V. Prozorov and Captain S. Kozyrev argued that the United States and NATO continued to prepare to wage war on Russia and were getting ready to introduce a threatening military presence on the Black Sea, an act that would have constituted a casus belli a few years ago: "There is something else which alarms us. . . . Whether we like it or not, there are still two political centers in the world . . . the United States and Russia. . . . Whereas we are now obsessed with the idea of making the world homogeneous—for the sake of harmony we are sacrificing our interests regardless of the cost. . . . The question is, where are the guarantees we will avoid World War III in a new homogeneous but less stable society?"

The year 1992 also saw continued pressure for a new military doctrine that renounced Russia's "no first use" of nuclear weapons declaratory policy. On May 27–30, 1992, senior Russian military leaders and theorists held a "scientific conference" at the General Staff Academy in Moscow. The two great antagonists at the debate on military doctrine were General Rodionov and General Gareyev, a professor at the academy.

General Igor Nikolayevich Rodionov believed Russia should rely more heavily on striking first with nuclear weapons to ensure Russia's security, and that it should openly declare this Assyrian policy. One would expect such advice from "the Butcher of Tbilisi." A brilliant military theoretician, Rodionov earned the coveted gold medal upon graduating from the General Staff Academy in 1978 and, at age fifty-five, he was young to have been named commandant of the General Staff's "brain trust." Serving in Afghanistan during the mid-1980s, Rodionov was one of the few Soviet officers to achieve any significant battlefield successes. After his promotion to command of the entire Southern Military District, he in effect became Soviet military governor of the Caucasian republics of Georgia, Armenia, and Azerbaijan, just when nationalist agitation against the Soviet Union began.

In 1989, Rodionov ordered the massacre of student protesters, who were Georgian nationalists, in Tbilisi. He directed his troops to attack, swinging picks and shovels, like medieval weapons, hacking off and mangling limbs. Thus "the Butcher" earned his bloody cognomen.

That General Rodionov was not cashiered in disgrace but instead advanced to head the General Staff Academy testifies to the high value the military placed on his theoretical and battlefield capabilities. As commandant of the Academy, General Rodionov continued his outspoken warnings about the Western threat and his scathing criticisms of President Yeltsin's defense policies, once commenting that Yeltsin's death from a heart attack would be "unimportant." Despite these opinions, General Rodionov was Russia's representative in scholarly military exchanges with the National Defense University, in Washington, D.C., and with China's General Staff Academy. (Warm and personable in social settings, Rodionov is formidable in debate. He reportedly marshals facts "like highly disciplined troops on a parade ground" and argues "decisively," his intellectual victories apparently helped by an intimidating stare from eyes "like piercing blue lasers.") Eventually, in 1996, Rodionov would become Russia's defense minister.

In contrast to Rodionov, General Mahkmut Akhmetovich Gareyev believed Russia should retain its promise not to use nuclear weapons first, that it should continue secretly to plan for a nuclear first strike under extreme conditions but should not increase its reliance on nuclear weapons for fighting wars. Thinking that nuclear weapons were becoming technologically obsolete, Gareyev wanted Russia to compete with the West in developing high-tech conventional weapons, which he believed would dominate future warfare. As a professor at the General Staff Academy, Mahkmut Gareyev was officially subordinate to Igor Rodionov; however, General Gareyev had a towering professional reputation, equaled by few Russian military theorists. Serving as deputy chief of the General Staff during the mid-1980s, while Rodionov was in Afghanistan, Gareyev was one of a mere dozen senior military officers to hold such a high post. He wrote over two hundred articles and books on military and theoretical issues, and many scholars, East and West, hailed his *M. V. Frunze—Military Theorist* (1984) as the single most significant work of Soviet military theory produced in the 1980s. Born in 1923, a Tatar of Turkic ancestry, Gareyev was an energetic sixty-nine years old on the day of the great nuclear debate.

General Igor Rodionov delivered the keynote speech, entitled "Some Approaches to Developing Russia's Military Doctrine," at the May 27–30 conference. What General Rodionov said, according to one Russian witness to the conference proceedings, would not normally have been uttered, "even in a situation of strict secrecy." Mary Fitzgerald, a Western military analyst for the Hudson Institute who has an uncanny knack for obtaining Russian documents and prying into Russian military deliberations, summarizes General Rodionov's address:

According to Rodionov, the United States can reach the territory of Russia *on all sides throughout its depth* not only with nuclear weapons but also with general-

> purpose forces. Russia, on the other hand, can reach neither the United States nor many other potential opponents with general-purpose forces. . . . Therefore, Russia is left with only its strategic nuclear forces, and above all the Strategic Missile Troops (SRF). . . .
>
> In Rodionov's opinion, statements on "no first use of nuclear weapons, retaliatory strikes, and defensive nature" only repeat those past mistakes that stemmed from the "self-advertising of political leaders" and inflicted "irreparable damage" on the nation's defense. For the foreseeable future, nuclear weapons are the basic political weapon for deterring aggression and preventing war.

"It will therefore be an 'irreparable mistake,' " Rodionov charged, "if Russia does not openly declare that, in the event of aggression, it will use its entire arsenal—including nuclear weapons—to destroy the opponent and defend its interests."

The battle lines over changing Russian doctrine on nuclear first use were drawn before the conference actually convened, in weeks of long-range sparring in the military press over three key issues. The first issue was whether Russia should renounce its declaratory policy promising not to use nuclear weapons first. The "no first use" pledge had always been propaganda; the Soviets had planned to strike first against an impending U.S., NATO, or Chinese nuclear attack despite the pledge. General Rodionov and his ideological cohorts, like Colonel A. Klimenko of the General Staff, argued that Moscow should officially renounce "no first use" to bring its declaratory policy more in line with the General Staff's actual operational plans. The weakness of Russian general-purpose forces and immediate threats to Russian security necessitated strengthening nuclear deterrence by removing ambiguity about Russian plans for striking first, according to Rodionov.

Gareyev replied that publicly canceling the no-first-use pledge would be a foreign policy disaster, would provoke the United States to pursue defensive countermeasures, and could begin a new cycle in the arms race that Russia could ill afford. Gareyev also implied that renouncing "no first use," thus revealing in advance Russia's plans to strike first, would sacrifice the element of surprise in wartime.

The second issue was whether Russia should limit nuclear first use to preempting enemy nuclear attack or plan for striking first under a broader range of scenarios, including the prevention of conventional enemy aggression. DESERT STORM, General Rodionov claimed, proved that advanced conventional weapons could be used to achieve strategic missions. For example, highly accurate cruise missiles armed with nonnuclear warheads could cause damage equivalent to a nuclear war by destroying nuclear forces, nuclear power plants, chemical facilities, and other installations, inflicting grave military and environmental injury. Such weapons were instruments of mass destruction, Rodionov contended, and had erased the distinction between conventional and nuclear war.

Colonel A. Klimenko, a member of the General Staff's Center for Operational-Strategic Studies (COSS), had earlier expressed an opinion identical to General Rodionov's. Enemy attacks with advanced conventional weapons, or on strategic targets, "should be considered to be the same as if they had used weapons of mass destruction, with all the consequences that can be expected of that." As a member of the General Staff's leading think tank in reformulating military doctrine, Colonel Klimenko's view amounted to a General Staff endorsement of Rodionov's proposed new policy. That policy was summed up neatly by Colonel Klimenko: "From the onset of aggression, all limitations in the choice of forces and methods of military actions must be removed."

General Gareyev agreed that nuclear weapons could be used once an enemy began a conventional war, but he protested that *preempting* an enemy conventional attack, striking first against an enemy suspected of preparing to attack Russia with conventional forces, ran serious risks of miscalculation. Russia could start a nuclear war unnecessarily.

The third issue was whether Russia should use nuclear weapons against a nonnuclear adversary. General Rodionov spoke in the affirmative. Germany, Iran, and Turkey were nonnuclear states with strong conventional armies that the Russian Army would be hard pressed to match in its debilitated condition. Nuclear deterrence could prevent war with such states or guarantee Russian victory through application of nuclear firepower.

General Gareyev warned that such a policy could also inadvertently escalate into a global holocaust. Prudence directed that Russia rebuild its conventional forces to deter or defeat nonnuclear states, Gareyev reasoned, and that it not rely excessively on weapons of mass destruction.

A startling briefing by General Korotchenko gave the coup de grace to one side, clearing the way for the defense minister himself to declare a victor. Korotchenko gave a nuclear threat assessment that, according to a press report, "shook even scholars with the figures for our possible losses from an aggressor's first strike." The views of the military conferees supported General Korotchenko, who "was talking sense and his computations were by no means the fruit of a sick imagination but the result of profound research and a scientific assessment of the military-strategic situation which has taken shape in the world."

Defense Minister Pavel Grachev, present at the conference, applauded General Rodionov's presentation as "bold" and suggested that despite Russia's pledge not to use nuclear weapons, in the face of aggression Russia may launch a nuclear first strike.

The debate over nuclear doctrine within the military was settled decisively in General Rodionov's favor even before the May 1992 conference, which in reality was probably a pro forma exercise in crushing dissenters like General Gareyev. A draft of Russia's new military doctrine was published in the prestigious Defense Ministry journal *Military Thought* the same month that the new doctrine was supposedly being hammered out. The draft supported General Igor Rodionov's line. General Mahkmut Gareyev went into retirement shortly afterward.

CHAPTER 17

The Russo-Ukrainian Nuclear Crisis, October 1991–May 1992

The Russian nuclear debate occurred against a backdrop of unfolding crises in Ukraine and Armenia, both of which peaked while the General Staff was muscling into place its new policy that openly endorsed a nuclear first strike, even against nonnuclear states. In Ukraine, Moscow and Kiev had come nearly to blows over control of nuclear weapons located on Ukrainian territory.

Luke Sallow shook off the chill Maryland winter and dumped his Christmas mail on the kitchen table. Sorting through the greens and reds of holiday letters and postcards, he was surprised to find a plain white envelope, addressed to him in a distinctly foreign hand. It was from General Mikhail Bashkirov.

Luke had met General Bashkirov during an arms control inspection of the Russian strategic bomber base at Uzin, in Ukraine. Bashkirov was the base commander, a native Russian. Sallow's excellent command of the Russian language had pleased Bashkirov immensely, as he loved to converse in his mother tongue, not in the local Ukrainian. They became quite friendly and spent a lot of time together. But Luke also suspected that Bashkirov knew he was not just an arms control inspector but a U.S. intelligence officer—a spy. Sallow tore open General Bashkirov's note. Inside was a handwritten Christmas greeting. Funny thing, though—Bashkirov had penned it in Ukrainian.

Two months later, in February 1992, General Mikhail Bashkirov publicly renounced his allegiance to Moscow and swore allegiance to Kiev. He declared his strategic nuclear bombers to be the property of Ukraine. General Bashkirov thereby began the most perilous episode of the Russo-Ukrainian crisis.

Almost immediately following the dissolution of the USSR into a number of independent states, fears blossomed among the newly emerged nations over how to prevent a resurgent Russia from forcibly reincorporating them into a new empire. Simultaneously, Russia feared that several of its newly independent neighbors—Ukraine, Belarus, and Kazakhstan, in particular—might claim as their own the former Soviet nuclear weapons based on their territories.

Faced with the prospect of several new nuclear-weapon states on its borders, Russia began pressing Ukraine and the others to surrender all nuclear weapons to Moscow. The confrontation that unfolded over the next several years chiefly involved Ukraine, which was, after Russia, the largest and most technically competent of the newly formed nations. Kazakhstan and Belarus watched from the sidelines and probably would follow Ukraine's lead to becoming new nuclear powers if that path could be taken successfully.

Had they gained control of the nuclear weapons on their territory, Ukraine, Kazakhstan, and Belarus would have been, after the United States and Russia, the third, fourth, and fifth most heavily armed nuclear-weapon states in the world. Nothing less than the international balance of power and global stability was at stake in the dispute between Russia and Ukraine over ownership of about 1,800 strategic nuclear weapons, most of which were targeted at Western Europe and the United States.

The Russo-Ukrainian nuclear crisis flared into public view in October 1991, when the Russian and Ukrainian press alleged that an ethnic Ukrainian serving on the Russian General Staff had warned Kiev that Moscow was planning a nuclear first strike in order to prevent Ukraine from becoming a new nuclear threat to Russia. "Last week, behind the scenes in the Russian government," *Moskovskiye novosti* reported, "the question of the possibility of an exchange of nuclear strikes between independent Ukraine and the Russian Soviet Federated Socialist Republic was discussed."

Responding to these allegations, General Konstantin Kobets, military advisor to President Yeltsin, spoke in the October 18 issue of *Krasnaya zvezda*, an official Russian Defense Ministry newspaper. Dismissing the story as "nonsense that no sensible person would credit," General Kobets insisted that Russia was not planning a nuclear attack on Ukraine. Yeltsin also tried to reassure Ukrainian president Leonid Kravchuk that Russia planned no nuclear attack. Unfortunately, Yeltsin used an odd phrasing, or his words were garbled by the press in such a way that actually aggravated the situation. According to the Russian press, President Yeltsin said, "He discussed this possibility [of making a nuclear attack on Ukraine], and there were no technical possibilities for it." Ukrainian officials remained skeptical of Russian assurances and accused Yeltsin of trying to intimidate them.

In January 1992, Ukrainian People's Deputy Mykola Porovskiy, a former engineer and prominent member of the Rada, Ukraine's parliament, published an article urging that Ukraine seize control of the nuclear weapons on its territory. These weapons were still controlled by Russian military units. Porovskiy worried that if Kiev allowed Moscow to continue to control nuclear weapons based in Ukraine, his country could be drawn into a nuclear war against its will. Russia could, without consulting Kiev, launch a nuclear "preventive strike" against an unspecified third party, presumably the United States. If Moscow used Ukraine-based missiles for such a strike, nuclear retribution would fall on Ukraine's head. Porovskiy advocated that Ukraine become a nuclear power independent of Moscow.

At about the same time as Porovskiy's article, Russo-Ukrainian relations took another downward turn. In January and February 1992, Kiev and Moscow quarreled over ownership of the Black Sea Fleet and of military units based in Ukraine, amid rumors of impending war between the sides.

Close on the heels of the dispute over the Black Sea Fleet, the argument over the ownership of nuclear weapons escalated from talk to action. President Leonid Kravchuk, a silver-haired former communist ideologue who had led Ukraine to independence, ordered: "All groups of troops and forces deployed in the territory of Ukraine, except for troops which Ukraine will include in composition of strategic forces, [by] 20 January . . . must take a military oath of allegiance to Ukraine." Although President Kravchuk, known as "the crafty fox" in both Moscow and Kiev, had specifically exempted strategic forces from the oath, all troops serving on Ukrainian territory, including Russian strategic forces troops, were nonetheless pressured to switch loyalty from Russia to Ukraine.

Defiant Russian crews of six Su-24 fighter-bombers "defected" on February 13, flying from Ukraine back to Russia to keep their nuclear-capable aircraft out of Kiev's hands.

On February 17, 1992, General Mikhail Bashkirov, commander of the strategic bomber division at Uzin in Ukraine, and other senior officers pledged loyalty to Kiev and tried to force all base personnel to do likewise. Fighting broke out among troops stationed there. Based at Uzin were Bear-H intercontinental bombers equipped to carry nuclear cruise missiles, which were stored at the base. A Russian inventory of nuclear weapons, provided in compliance with the Strategic Arms Reduction Treaty, listed 168 air-launched cruise missiles (ALCMs) stored at Uzin. Russian ALCMs are highly accurate and typically carry a warhead of 250 kilotons yield, twenty times more powerful than the Hiroshima bomb.

The next day, February 18, General Igor Kalugin, commander in chief of Russian Long-Range Aviation, rushed from Moscow to the strategic bomber base at Uzin. Striding into Bashkirov's office, he fired the general on the spot. But Russia was no longer in charge. The "Crafty Fox," President Kravchuk, immediately reinstated General Bashkirov, who remained in control of the base.

Russian pilots at Uzin who were loyal to Moscow wrote a letter to Yevgeniy Shaposhnikov, commander in chief of all Commonwealth armed forces, expressing their concern over the fate of "the formidable weapons we control." The letter complained that "officers who have not taken an oath of allegiance [to Ukraine] are barred from fulfilling their duties," that discipline had eroded into violence, and that "there can be most dangerous consequences."

By February 26, cadets at the Strategic Rocket Forces Academy in Kharkov, Ukraine, had sworn loyalty to Kiev. Before this, General V. Tolubko had taken the oath. Commandant of the SRF Academy and a relation of his famous namesake, Marshal Viktor Tolubko, who had been commander in chief of the Strategic Rocket Forces, General Tolubko explained why even many Russian officers working in Ukraine might switch allegiance from Moscow to Kiev. There were reasons surprisingly mundane, unheroic, and sensible: "We have become attached to Kharkov in terms of our family roots, housing, job placement, and daily routine. Virtually no one will go anywhere else no matter how events turn out. Swearing allegiance to Ukraine guarantees us social and legal protection."

In March 1992, Ukrainian officials privately and confidentially told U.S. government officials that Kiev intended to keep the forty-six SS-24 ICBMs located on its territory. The SS-24s were train-mobile intercontinental missiles, each armed with ten warheads. Ukraine's confidence about the SS-24s was promptly leaked to the U.S. press. Three months later, in June, President Kravchuk required all officers and troops serving on Ukrainian territory—this time including personnel serving in strategic missile and bomber units—to take a loyalty oath.

Russian general Yuri Maksimov, commander in chief of the Strategic Rocket Forces, immediately protested that "these acts effectively establish dual command and dual leadership of the strategic nuclear forces" and that "if Kiev demands that missile troop officers swear an oath of allegiance to the people of Ukraine . . . this means that people on duty on the nuclear button will carry out orders not from Moscow, but from the capital of Ukraine." General Maksimov thundered, "If this process continues . . . the dispute over the division of the Black Sea Fleet, about which so much has been heard, will look like child's play compared with the struggle for possession of the strategic nuclear missiles in Ukraine."

The growing hostility between Russia and Ukraine over nuclear weapons ownership certainly alarmed Belarus and Kazakhstan, eliciting some hysterical pronouncements from the latter. Erik Asanbayev, vice president of Kazakhstan, said in an April 1992 interview that Kazakhstan intended to keep SS-18 heavy ICBMs located on its territory. Based in Kazakhstan were about 150 SS-18s, each armed with ten warheads—or some 1,500 nuclear weapons altogether. The SS-18 was the most technically sophisticated, most accurate, and most lethal missile in the entire nuclear arsenal. Kazakhstan's half of the SS-18 force—another 150 SS-18s were based in Russia—was capable of a disarming first strike against all U.S. missile silos, bomber bases, submarine pens, and command and control bunkers. It was also capable of destroying every major city in the world.

Vice President Asanbayev declared that once Kazakhstan gained possession of the SS-18s, they would be "a deterrent and guarantee of peace" at the disposal of the entire Islamic world. However, it soon became evident that Kazakhstan was probably engaging in hyperbole aimed at coercing a security commitment from the United States. In June 1992, Kazakh President Nursultan Nazarbayev asked President Bush for guarantees against a nuclear attack by Russia, China, or the United States.

Moscow was not idle as the threat of foreign takeover of Russian nuclear weapons grew more serious. According to U.S. press reports, in December 1991 "activity detected by U.S. intelligence agencies over the past several weeks indicates that . . . tactical nuclear weapons stored in the republics of Armenia, Georgia, Tadzhikistan, and Kirghizia are being moved." Three months later, on March 12, 1992, President Kravchuk ordered a halt to the removal of tactical nuclear weapons from Ukraine. Ukrainian troops controlled the railroads and manned the security perimeters outside the nuclear weapon storage depots; Russian troops manned the internal security perimeters and had physical possession of the nuclear weapons. It was a standoff. But Russia could not remove the weapons without President Kravchuk's permission.

Some Russian opinion makers began to resign themselves to the emergence of a nuclear-armed Ukraine. On March 28, a reform-minded Russian journalist, Andrey Ostalskiy, in an article entitled "Nuclear Ukraine Not End of the World," despaired:

> It looks as if the Ukrainian leaders may not be able to resist the "nuclear temptation" and . . . in a single move [join] the realm of the great nuclear powers. . . .
>
> Remember all those myths in whose grip we lived. The "nuclear free world" turned out to be one of them, a dream which did not stand up to reality.
>
> However, leaders of the U.S.S.R.—from Stalin to Chernenko—used this myth in a fairly cynical manner, as a kind of bait for foreign liberal fools. They used it and at the same time laid plans for "preemptive nuclear strikes" . . . which were devised by the General Staff. . . .
>
> With President Yeltsin in Moscow and President Kravchuk in Kiev, a full-scale Russo-Ukrainian war still seems impossible. But the political equilibrium is not permanent, and politicians are even less permanent.

Elsewhere, things went more smoothly. By May, most or all of the tactical nuclear weapons were probably out of Armenia and Azerbaijan. It was a good thing, for the dangers in Ukraine were about to be vastly overshadowed by war in the Caucasus.

CHAPTER 18

War in the Caucasus: Genesis

God had once destroyed man for his wickedness in the Great Flood. However, divine mercy spared Noah and all future life in the Ark, which, as the flood waters subsided, came to rest on dry land at Mount Ararat. Or so the Old Testament tells us. Several archeological expeditions have taken the story seriously enough to search the slopes of Ararat for remains of Noah's Ark. The mountain looms blue and mist-shrouded on the border of Armenia and Turkey, mute witness to fratricidal generations of Noah's wicked children, and an imposing reminder of the possibility of Apocalypse. Murder hears not, though God's voice is a mountain.

Russia and Turkey are hereditary enemies. In prehistory, Turkey was settled by peoples originating from the steppes of Central Asia, who retain to this day an affinity of blood, language, and religion. Russia has been an alien conqueror in lands such as Azerbaijan, Kazakhstan, and Turkmenistan, and it has labored unsuccessfully over the centuries to break the Turkic cultural tie through colonization and "russification" of native populations. Forcing Turkmen schoolchildren to learn Russian and destroying mosques did not endear Moscow to its Asian prisoners.

Satan tempted Russia and Turkey to the vanity of cosmic struggle. Orthodox Christian Russia and Islamic Turkey faced each other for half a millennium on the front lines of two great crusading religions, later supplanted by the two great "faiths" of the twentieth century, communism and capitalism. In A.D. 301 Armenia became the first nation in history to adopt Christianity as its official religion. It has been Russia's staunch ally. Up through the nineteenth century, the sides fought a dozen wars together.

The Ottoman Turks set off on a collision course with Russia in 1475, when they expanded their empire into the Crimea and the north shore of the Black Sea, taking possession of Azerbaijan and conquering Georgia by 1584. Several wars between 1676 and 1697 resulted in Russian territorial gains around the Sea of Azov. When Charles XII, Sweden's Napoleon, was defeated in his invasion of Russia by Peter the Great at Poltava in 1709, Turkey gave refuge to Charles, thereby beginning a long history of aiding Russia's great-power enemies. Russia was defeated in 1711 in the Russo-Turkish war that ensued to avenge this affront, and it was forced to raze its fortresses on the Turk frontiers. Then, in 1724, Russia seized Azerbaijan and Baku from Turkey. Wars in 1736–1739, 1770–1774, 1784, 1791, 1806–1812, 1827–1829, 1854–1855, and 1877–1878 generally favored

Russia. However, the most important of these, the Crimean War of 1854–1855, was decided in Turkey's favor by the intervention of Great Britain and France. Moscow never forgot the lesson: the Black Sea littoral, with its natural resources and strategic importance as a gateway to the Mediterranean, is a flashpoint for war with the great powers of the West.

World War I saw Turkey side with Germany, largely because Germany was the enemy of Russia. Against German advice, the Turkish commander in chief, Enver Pasha, enthralled with the romance of carving from Russia's Muslim regions a pan-Turkic empire, invaded the Caucasus. In 1915 the Turks massacred Russia's Christian allies in Armenia and forced a diaspora. The relocation policy, perhaps intentionally, turned into a holocaust, in which more than a million Armenians died.

Russia crushed Enver Pasha but was in turn crushed by Germany and by the Bolshevik Revolution. Under the 1918 Treaty of Brest-Litovsk, Turkey emerged from World War I victorious over Russia, regaining all lands lost in the Russo-Turkish wars since 1877. In 1920 Turkey again invaded Armenia. Stalin sowed the seeds of the present struggle in 1921, when he transferred Nagorno-Karabakh, even then a disputed region between Armenia and Azerbaijan, to the latter, both states being Soviet republics at the time.

Turkey remained neutral in World War II until 1945, unwilling to join the Allies since this meant siding with Moscow. When Hitler invaded Russia, Ankara signed a nonaggression pact with Berlin and carried on trade with and provided war materials to Germany. After 1945, Stalin unsuccessfully made territorial claims on Turkey.

In 1952, Turkey joined NATO, becoming with Norway one of only two NATO states sharing a common border with the Soviet Union. Ever since, the Soviets and Russians have regarded Turkey, like Germany, as the front line of the Western alliance—a potential invasion route and a possible tripwire for a nuclear conflict. During the Cold War, the USSR maintained thirty divisions, some 300,000 soldiers and 5,400 tanks, opposite Turkey. Today, now that the Soviet Army has melted away, the combined forces of Armenia and Russian troops based in Armenia amount to merely 60,000 soldiers and about two-hundred tanks. Turkey has a standing army of 500,000 men and 4,000 tanks. The NATO force in Turkey is the Sixth Allied Tactical Air Force, comprising modern jet fighters and reconnaissance aircraft of the United States, Great Britain, and France.

My wife, Ruthie, and I witnessed the birth of the Armenia-Azerbaijan War in 1988 while vacationing in what was then part of the USSR, the Soviet Socialist Republics of Armenia and Azerbaijan. Soviet president Mikhail Gorbachev's policy of *glasnost* ("openness") kindled hope among Armenians and Azeris that they would be freer to assert their national identities and act upon long-standing mutual grievances.

Our first day was spent in the Armenian capital of Yerevan. While unpacking at the undeservedly four-star Hotel Yerevan, we were amazed to see the empty boulevard outside our window suddenly fill with a sea of demonstrators waving Armenian flags and crying out against Azerbaijan. Doubly astonishing, the flags were not of Soviet Armenia but national flags of *independent* Armenia. Ruthie leaned out the second-floor window feverishly shooting photos of the scene. I hauled her back in and jerked the curtains closed, having no desire to antagonize the KGB.

On the same day, Soviet security forces, armed with light tanks and machine guns, occupied Yerevan's central square, right in front of our hotel. Ruthie, ignoring my pleas and admonitions, wandered about Yerevan, inconspicuously wearing her cowboy hat, photographing Soviet armored fighting vehicles and anything else that might even remotely be of interest to U.S. intelligence. Denouncing my cowardice, she worked her camera with a fervor and patriotic recklessness that must be unique to her profession: mortgage underwriting.

One memory in particular still gives me the shivers. Ruthie was about to photograph a heavily guarded official building but stopped when a KGB soldier waved her off. I begged her to desist, but she whirled and fired off a half dozen frames. The KGB guard ran toward us. Ruthie grabbed my hand and we disappeared, cowboy hat and all, into the milling streets of Yerevan.

Later, in response to Ruthie's queries about what was happening, our tour guide gave her an impassioned lecture about the Armenian holocaust of 1915 and Stalin's unjust annexation of Nagorno-Karabakh to Azerbaijan. The patriotic guide drew a quite accurate map of the disputed area on a napkin. She told us about Azeri pogroms against Armenians and the first killings in Nagorno-Karabakh that occurred while we were there.

The Armenia-Azerbaijan war was a grass-roots conflict. Armenian cabbies and bakers and "the man in the street" spoke of the 1915 atrocity as if it happened yesterday. They identified their own suffering as equivalent to the Jewish holocaust and were bitter that the world knew little of it. They sought redemption through military prowess, even calling Armenia the "Israel of the Caucasus." They saw Azeris as treacherous monsters.

Cabbies and bakers in Azerbaijan returned the enmity with equal ardor. When our bus arrived in Baku from Yerevan to continue our sightseeing, we were received as if from another planet. Our Azeri guide, Lali, greeted us with a loud reassurance that merely because we had toured Armenia, that did not make us Armenian or enemies of Azerbaijan. This was for the benefit of the baggage handlers and other Azeris standing around, whose eyes were knives.

Ruthie's Yerevan photos proved of great interest stateside. That we were not arrested is miraculous.

From 1988 until 1991, the Soviet Army kept a lid on Armenian-Azeri carnage, limiting the sides to pogroms, riots, and occasional shootings. The lid blew off in March 1992. In that month, soon after the fall of the Soviet Union, Moscow withdrew its last three occupying divisions from the area. Departing Russian soldiers illegally sold arms and munitions to the opposing sides, while Yerevan and Baku nationalized Soviet military bases. Now, instead of using clubs and hunting rifles, the factions had T-72 tanks, artillery, Mi-24 helicopter gunships, and some fighter aircraft. By April, an Armenian offensive had overrun most of Nagorno-Karabakh. In May, Armenia captured the whole region. Azerbaijan was clearly losing the war, and Baku appealed to Turkey.

The Ukrainian crisis and other recent events had put Moscow in a frame of mind to expect the worst as the Armenia-Azerbaijan war threatened to bring in Turkey, a NATO member. In February 1992, three months before the May crisis, a classified U.S. Defense Department study was leaked to the press, revealing that U.S. military planners were thinking about how to prosecute a war with Russia in the event that Moscow invaded the Baltic states. The Russian government and military widely condemned the U.S. research as, in the words of an *Izvestiya* article, preparing for "the start of a large-scale war against Russia by the United States and NATO."

The next month, March 1992, saw a spate of accusations by the Russian Navy that U.S. nuclear submarines were invading Russian territorial waters and had increased their activities to the point of provocation. Admiral Valeriy Aleksin suggested in a March 27 interview that the U.S. Navy was deliberately seeking confrontation: "There are people in the leadership of the armed forces of states with nuclear submarines carrying ballistic missiles and nuclear torpedoes who do not like détente." Another senior Russian Navy officer proposed to a reporter that Russia should attack the U.S. submarines: "I am 99 percent certain that it was the Americans. If this had happened ten years ago, we would have simply fired a salvo from the antisubmarine rocket-propelled depth charge launcher to a depth of thirty meters, and the submarine at a depth of sixty meters would have shot up to the surface like a cork. No one is anxious to die, and our Foreign Ministry would know exactly where to send its note."

On February 11, 1992, the U.S. nuclear attack submarine *Baton Rouge* collided with a Russian submarine in the Barents Sea near the naval base at Murmansk. Moscow exploded with denunciations from the military, claiming proof positive of the United States' immediate hostile intentions.

In the United States, on January 22, 1992, CIA director Robert M. Gates testified before the Senate Armed Services Committee that the Russian threat of conventional or nuclear attack on the United States or its allies "has all but disappeared for the foreseeable future." DIA director James Clapper agreed with Gates, saying there was "virtually no likelihood" of such an attack. However, Gates presented a darker view in remarks at the Nixon Library on March 12: "The end of the Soviet Union, the end of the thousand-year-old Russian and Soviet empire, the end of the decades-long superpower struggle and of the Cold War—these are cataclysmic events of history. And to think that they will quietly pass from the world stage without further troubling us is to be oblivious to history and naive in the extreme. The drama is not yet at an end. Forces pent up for seventy years, for seven hundred years, have been set loose, and we have yet to see, much less understand, the full consequences."

In early May 1992, with Azerbaijan losing the war with Armenia for Nargano-Karabakh, Turkey's president, Turgut Ozal, threatened to enter the conflict on the side of Azerbaijan: "Turkish troops could be moved to the Nakhichevan Autonomous Republic or Azerbaijan." This was in fact a threat to invade Armenia, since the Turkish army could not reach Azerbaijan or the Azeri enclave in Nakhichevan (cut off from Azerbaijan by a part of Armenia) without crossing Armenian territory.

President Ozal's motives for issuing a war warning to Armenia were entirely local, having to do with ethnic sympathy for Azerbaijan and alleged Armenian violations of the Turkish border. Ozal certainly had no dark design for upsetting the global balance of power or spearheading a NATO invasion of Russia. Indeed, the Turkish president's reasons for threatening to intervene in the Armenia-Azerbaijan war may have had more to do with domestic Turkish politics than foreign policy. Turgut Ozal and his attractive wife, Semra, had begun their professional lives in the 1950s as an electrician and a typist, respectively. Once married, they became an irresistible political couple, Semra working as an activist and holding important party offices in her own right. Compared by some to the Perons of Argentina, the Ozals rose to national leadership in the 1980s, prodding culturally conservative Turkey ever Westward with their progressive ideas and flamboyant style. But by 1992, Ozal's political fortunes were foundering under incessant attack from Muslim conservatives. His call to arms against Armenia on behalf of Azerbaijan—admonishing Turkey's historic enemy while offering succor to Muslim brothers—may have been a grand gesture, typical of Ozal's style, calculated to score political points with Turkish patriots and his own Muslim critics.

Turkey's foreign minister, Hekmit Cetin, repeated Ozal's threat on May 20. Russian marshal Yevgeniy Shaposhnikov, commander in chief of the nuclear forces of the Commonwealth of Independent States, warned that very day that if Turkey, a NATO member, became involved in the Armenia-Azerbaijan conflict, it would provoke World War III. Cautioning "Turkey and the United States" to abstain from the conflict, Marshal Shaposhnikov declared, "If there is military interference by another party, that will obviously place us on the verge of a Third World War." Shaposhnikov was one of the handful of men in Russia who carried a "nuclear briefcase."

Just nine months earlier, Yevgeniy Shaposhnikov's elevation to defense minister, and then to CIS commander in chief, had been hailed in the Western press as a triumph for the forces of democracy and peace. Marshal Shaposhnikov had won his democratic stars during the August 1991 coup by threatening to bomb the Kremlin if the putchists dared to storm Boris Yeltsin's barricaded "White House." As defense minister, Shaposhnikov personally participated in transferring Soviet president Mikhail Gorbachev's "nuclear briefcase" to Russian president Boris Yeltsin. The *Los Angeles Times* (December 26, 1991) put a "happy face" on the transfer and on Shaposhnikov by highlighting this exchange between the defense minister and a reporter: " 'In whose hands is the button now?' a Russian correspondent asked Shaposhnikov later Wednesday evening. 'In dependable hands,' the Marshal answered with a smile."

Shaposhnikov's unusual concern for the welfare of his men—setting an example by waiting more than a year for his own apartment, and sharing other privations endured by common soldiers—seemed further evidence of his democratic instincts and humanity. "I came from the aristocracy, His Majesty the working class," Shaposhnikov once quipped. His humor, youth, and energy were interpreted in the West as a promise of stability during a time of wrenching geopolitical change. Once asked about the national security implications of those accelerating changes, Shaposhnikov replied, "I am a fighter pilot, used to speed." Now the fighter pilot was threatening to start World War III.

Shaposhnikov's choice of words in raising his "war warning" is revealing. The United States had made no threatening moves toward Armenia and had no vital interests in the region, except the security of Turkey. Yet CIS commander Shaposhnikov assumed that because Turkey was a NATO member, and perhaps because there was a U.S. military presence in Turkey, Ankara's threats toward Armenia were originating, or at least supported by, the United States and NATO. That it was Shaposhnikov who made the initial war warning, and not Defense Minister Pavel Grachev, who had both substantial conventional forces as well as nuclear forces at his command, is also significant. As commander in chief of the CIS, Marshal Shaposhnikov had no appreciable general-purpose forces. Nuclear missiles were Shaposhnikov's only real military argument.

The day after Moscow and Ankara traded threats, events began racing out of control. On May 21, Turkish and Armenian troops exchanged gun and mortar fire over the border. Russia and Turkey immediately placed their troops near the area on alert. The Turkish Third Army and Second Air Force went on alert, probably moving to the equivalent of Increased

Combat Readiness. The Third Army comprised about 100,000 men, some one-quarter of Turkey's ground forces. The second Air Force had about two hundred jet fighters, including some seventy F-16s, half of Turkey's total air power.

Total Russian forces in the area were 5,000 soldiers and one squadron of MiG-23s, less than twenty aircraft. These were deployed on the Armenian border opposite Turkey to hold key bridges and passes against a Turkish invasion. Turkey's alert forces outnumbered the Russians by twenty to one on the ground and by ten to one in the air.

Moscow began moving two divisions down to the Caucasus to block the invasion route for a NATO thrust into Russia from the south. Armenia's poorly armed 50,000 soldiers would be little help against Turkey, and in any case they were already engaged in their war against Azerbaijan's 70,000 troops, who would support the Turks. Azerbaijan had, after all, invited Turkey in. Moscow's nerves were probably not soothed by false Turkish press reports that flights by NATO's Sixth Air Force were a "warning to the Armenians." In fact, the NATO flights were training activity, not a show of strength.

On the morning of May 21, at 8:00 A.M., Ostankino Television in Moscow broadcast, "The situation in Nagorno-Karabakh is increasing apprehensions about the involvement of new sides in the conflict, which would threaten not only the CIS but also international security. . . . The situation is also becoming exacerbated because of attacks by Armenian forces along the border with Nakhichevan."

The war was expanding to include the enclave of Nakhichevan. Armenian artillery shelled Nakhichevan for three days. According to news reports, the Azeris returned fire and counterattacked Armenian territory with "troops, tanks, and armored vehicles" but were beaten back.

Nakhichevan's health minister accused Armenian gunners of firing chemical cyanide shells—"weapons of mass destruction," by Russian definition. The veracity of Azeri claims about Armenian use of chemical weapons has never been established, and their use would constitute a disturbing escalation of the conflict. The alleged chemical attacks may have been an Azeri fabrication intended to turn international opinion against Armenia.

Gasan Gasonov, Azerbaijan's representative to the United Nations, declared that the situation was "no longer a case of a local conflict" but "a real war between two states." He called for UN observers to enter the war zone.

The Turkish parliament did not help allay Moscow's concerns that Russia and NATO were on the brink of war. Comments by numerous members of Turkey's parliament on May 21 suggested, as one Turkish newspaper headline blared, that "Majority of MPs Are for Military Solution." Safa Giray, Turkey's former minister of defense, a senior member of parliament, and leader of one of the main political parties, actually called for NATO intervention, "as was the case in Iraq," alluding to Operation DESERT STORM, Moscow's nightmare. Giray said that Armenian intransigence would provide a good test for the reliability of NATO and the United Nations, because "no matter what these organizations say, Armenia ignores their calls and continues its own way."

Abdullatif Sener, another senior Turkish MP and political leader, said that Turkey was obligated by treaty to intervene against Armenia: "The Kars and Moscow Treaties make Turkey a guarantor state. Turkey should fulfill the requirements mentioned in those treaties. Volunteers who want to go there [to Azerbaijan] should be granted permission. Nakhichevan should be supplied arms for defending itself." Opposition party members criticized the Turkish government for not moving aggressively enough against Armenia.

Geydar Aliyev, chairman of Nakhichevan, condemned CIS commander Shaposhnikov's threat. But at a May 21 press conference, Aliyev agreed that the situation could lead to a world war: "Marshal Shaposhnikov follows the old pattern of thinking, intimidating everybody with a Third World War, to which, admittedly, the aggravation of the situation on the Nakhichevan-Armenian border can lead." He implied correctly that Russia was in league with Armenia. "Russian military formations," Aliyev complained, "refuse to help the Azerbaijan people to repulse the Armenian aggression against part of sovereign Azerbaijan." Issuing a threat of his own, Geydar Aliyev pointed out that Turkey had the legal right to intervene on the side of Azerbaijan under the Kars Treaty of 1921.

On the evening of May 21, Ankara television reported that General Dogan Gures, chief of the Turkish General Staff, had abruptly concluded an official visit to Egypt and rushed back to Turkey. Deplaning at Ankara's Esenboga Airport, General Gures declared, "The Turkish Armed Forces are ready to fulfill any duty assigned by the political authority." Russian defense minister Grachev and Gennadiy Burbulis, President Yeltsin's security advisor, flew down to Yerevan to hold secret discussions with Armenian president Levon Ter-Petrosyan on the growing crisis.

On the following day, May 22, in Portugal, Andrey Kozyrev, Russia's forty-year-old foreign minister, was at the Lisbon Conference to seek financial aid from and normalized relations with the United States and other Western countries attending the forum. Obviously because of last-minute orders, the pro-Western and normally soft-spoken Kozyrev had the unpleasant task of repeating Marshal Shaposhnikov's war warning to Turkey and the United States. At a hastily convened press conference, Kozyrev announced to his Western colleagues and benefactors, to whom he had just expressed "profound gratitude" for their financial support, the bad news: "Russia has warned Turkey that, in the event of an attack by the Turkish Armed Forces against Armenia, Russia will come to the latter's rescue." The diplomatic Kozyrev did not specifically warn the United States, but there was no need, as the purpose of making such a declaration before the assembled representatives of NATO and the United States was clear. A shaken Kozyrev later tried to reassure the West, and perhaps himself, by noting informally as an aside that he "does not believe that there may be a Turkish armed intervention. Even so, the warning has been made."

On the same day, Armenian forces continued to pound Sadarak, in Nakhichevan. The entire population, 14,000 people, was evacuated, and Azeri forces trickled into the besieged town.

At the Azerbaijan mission in Moscow, the deputy speaker of the Azeri parliament, Tamerlane Garayev, aimed a press conference at the Kremlin as Sadarak burned. He condemned CIS commander Shaposhnikov's warning against Turkish intervention as deliberately encouraging Armenian aggression: "These statements further encourage the aggressor occupying Azerbaijan territory and provide carte blanche for further unpunished actions." One journalist directed what was probably a planted question to Garayev, asking "whether Russian special services are involved in Armenian troops' capture of Shusha." Garayev assumed a posture of objectivity: "That can only be proved following the investigation, which is not yet complete." Then he again threw Azerbaijan's gauntlet in Moscow's face: "If events in the region continue to develop in this way, the Azerbaijan leadership will ask Turkey to immediately engage in military intervention to repulse the Armenian aggression."

On May 23, the morning edition of *Izvestiya*, a Russian newspaper that often served as a government mouthpiece, replied to Tamerlane Garayev and the Azeri Mission by reiterating CIS commander Shaposhnikov's and foreign minister Kozyrev's warnings: "An invasion by NATO member Turkey could be seen from the legal standpoint as an invasion of the CIS by NATO, which would run the risk of a clash with one of the parties to the treaty of collective security recently signed in Tashkent." The Tashkent treaty committed Russia to use nuclear weapons in defense of Commonwealth members, including Armenia. "Moreover, before 'crossing the Rubicon,' " *Izvestiya* cautioned, "the Turkish Army would first have to deal with the Commonwealth Armed Forces guarding the border—with all the consequences this would entail, and most probably not just for the Caucasus."

On June 1, Russian defense minister Grachev declared that "Russia will regard the dispatch of foreign troops to neighboring states and the buildup of troops and naval forces at its borders as a direct military threat to the [Russian] Republic." In a warning obviously aimed at the United States, Grachev also noted that "factors of military threat also include the existence of powerful armed forces in some states, mobilization possibilities and a system of their deployment close to Russian borders, as well as attempts at using political and economic pressure and military blackmail against Russia."

Andrey Kozyrev's prediction at Lisbon was right. Turkey blinked. After about a week, both sides relaxed their military posture. No Turkish invasion of Armenia occurred. Not even Turkish volunteers or military supplies went to Nakhichevan or Azerbaijan. It was not Russia's 5,000 troops and fewer than twenty aircraft in Armenia, overwhelmingly outnumbered by Turkey's Third Army and Second Air Force, that deterred Ankara; Turkey could easily have swept these Russian forces aside. The deterrence was CIS commander Yevgeniy Shaposhnikov and his nuclear saber.

Shaposhnikov's was an unnecessarily dangerous diplomacy that sought to deter a nonexistent threat. Turkey's invasion of Armenia would not have been the beginning of general NATO aggression against Russia. Indeed, despite the rhetoric of its parliament, Ankara may have had no intention of invading Armenia. Turkey's alert of its military forces may have been defensive, in reaction to alleged Armenian attacks on Turkish territory. But if Russian words are taken at face value, Moscow was prepared to wage a world war against the United States based on wholly independent actions by Turkey in Armenia-Azerbaijan, a region in which the United States had no ambitions and only the most tangential of interests.

Russian concerns about the vulnerability of their southern flank, and about a possible wider war resulting from outside intervention in the still tense Armenia-Azerbaijan standoff, have not cooled. In 1993, during a meeting with Turkish officials in Ankara, Russian defense minister Pavel Grachev reportedly warned Turkey to stay out of "our" Azerbaijan, slamming his fist on the table to emphasize his point.

Up until 1994, Armenia and Azerbaijan continued to wage a fierce seesaw war for possession of Nagorno-Karabakh, the territory changing hands three times. In May 1993, a Russian-backed coup in Azerbaijan replaced President Abulfez Elchibey, an Azeri patriot and the most ardent proponent of collaboration with Turkey in Central Asia, with Geydar Aliyev. Moscow may have assumed that Aliyev, a former KGB official, would be more accommodating to Russian interests in Azerbaijan. President Aliyev resisted Moscow's pressure to allow the basing of Russian troops in his country, but he did agree to a cease-fire and peace negotiations with Armenia in May 1994.

The peace talks have gone nowhere. Armenia remains in possession of 20 percent of Azerbaijan's territory, including Nagorno-Karabakh. Sporadic violence continues in the disputed areas. War could erupt again at any time.

Moscow's suspicions of Turkish-NATO designs on the oil wealth of Azerbaijan, and of NATO penetrating the Caucasus as a means of threatening Russia, still smolder. The glowing embers of Moscow's fears are sometimes fanned by the Turks and by NATO regional exercises. In 1993, Turkish analysts argued for forging an alliance with Ukraine, which seemed on the verge of acquiring nuclear weapons, in order effectively to press Turkey's interests in Azerbaijan against Russia.

In a November 1995 article, Russian Navy Captain V. Simonenko suggested that NATO exercises indicated preparations for aggression in the region:

> Year in and year out the growing aggressiveness of the NATO Unified Command Authorities in Southeastern Europe and in the Mediterranean basin has become firmly extended to the Black Sea region where peacekeeping exercises like "Cooperative Partner" . . . are being conducted regularly. . . . What are the actual intentions of the NATO command authorities and the Turkish government, specifically, for the further "mastery" of the Black Sea and its coast? Fro chwhere do they see the potential threat of the outbreak of a military conflict or something similar here, for what reason and at whose initiative?

A panicky article subtitled "Turkish Military Presence in Georgia Possible in Near Future," published in December 1995, claimed that Turkey was about to occupy Azerbaijan and Georgia on the pretext of their candidacy for membership in NATO's Partnership for Peace: "A future Turkish military presence in the Transcaucasus cannot be ruled out, since both Georgia and Azerbaijan have signed the NATO Partnership for Peace Program. (Turkey is a member of the NATO bloc.)" In 1997, Russia and Armenia signed a military alliance amid Azerbaijani claims that Armenia is seeking nuclear weapons and President Yeltsin's warning that "already the United States is declaring [the Caucasus] is in their zone of interest. . . . The Americans . . . are beginning to penetrate this zone." In April 1998, the Russian press noted nervously the visit to Azerbaijan of Turkey's top military commander, who publicly backed Azerbaijan's claim to disputed Nagorno-Karabakh, saying the Armenian occupation threatened Turkey. In February 1999, Azerbaijan rejected membership in Russia's Commonwealth of Independent States, explaining that "Azerbaijan cannot participate in a 'security system' in which one country (Russia) provides military support to another (Armenia) at war with a third (Azerbaijan) within the same system." Also in 1999, Azerbaijan expressed interest in joining NATO and invited the United States to establish a military base on its territory. In April 1999, Armenia joined Russia's air defense system and Moscow began beefing up its military presence by basing more MiG-29s and advanced S-300 SAMs in Armenia. In March 1999, Russian MiGs violated Azeri air space.

Nothing has really changed since May 1992. All of the elements remain present for another close call in the Caucasus. In 1994, some surprisingly specific information surfaced on the nature of the nuclear threat in May 1992.

In a 1994 article by Russian journalist Pavel Felgengauer, published shortly after interviewing his friend General Staff chief Mikhail Kolesnikov, who warned of Turkey's "ambitions" in Southern Europe, Felgengauer described a hypothetical future war between Russia and Turkey. Russia wins the theoretical conflict by making a nuclear strike on Turkey, against a military base belonging to the United States.

Pavel Felgengauer is known to be well connected to the Defense Ministry and the General Staff, organizations that frequently use his articles to speak unofficially. Western analysts have found Felgengauer's writings a reliable guide to Russian military thinking. His writings have often predicted developments or represented points of view that later have been officially acknowledged.

Felgengauer's article, "Caucasian War at Center of World Policy in the Year 2000" (subtitled "Nightmare"), appears to describe nothing less than an actual nuclear strike plan considered by the Russian General Staff against Turkey and the United States during the Armenian crisis of May 1992. Published in *Segodnya* in January 1994, less than two years after the events of May 1992, the article pretends to be a fictional account of future possible events. But there are a striking number of parallels between Felgengauer's scenario and what actually happened in May 1992, too many to be dismissed as mere coincidence.

Felgengauer's scenario has Turkey invading Armenia in May 1995—the same threat the Russian military thought it had faced in 1992, and during the same month, May. In the supposedly fictional scenario, the proximate cause of Turkey's intervention is Armenian attacks in Nagorno-Karabakh and on Nakhichevan—the proximate cause of the May 1992 crisis. In Felgengauer's scenario, the attacking Turkish forces are Turkey's "Third Field Army . . . with the support of combat aviation"—the Turkish Third Army and Second Tactical Air Force were the units alerted in May 1992. In Felgengauer's scenario, "Russian motorized rifle and armored forces" were "located at the Turkish-Armenian border," just as in May 1992. In the "fictional" scenario, Russian forces in Armenia "had almost no air cover. . . . Turkish aviation dominated the battlefield." In May 1992, Russia's air power based in Armenia, fewer than twenty MiG-23s, was outnumbered ten to one by Turkey's Second Tactical Air Force.

In Felgengauer's scenario, Russia warns Turkey, "Russia would use all means at its disposal to stop the aggression," a nuclear threat also implicit in Shaposhinkov's specter of a new world war in May 1992. However, in Felgengauer's story, "Turkey said it would not yield to nuclear blackmail, obviously figuring that Russia would never opt for nuclear weapons against a non-nuclear power that was also a member of NATO." As we have seen, one of the provisions of Russia's new military doctrine debated in May 1992, and officially declared in November 1993, just two months before Felgengauer published his article, was to allow Russian nuclear first use against nonnuclear states aligned with nuclear states through an alliance, like NATO.

In Felgengauer's fictional scenario, Russia makes a preemptive nuclear strike on a U.S. radar station in Turkey, near Kars: "The Russian Supreme

Military Council decided to make a preemptory strike on Turkey. A radar station in the vicinity of Kars was targeted. The 100-kiloton air burst, after which there was no noticeable radioactive fallout, destroyed the station. The civilian population practically didn't suffer."

There is in fact a U.S. radar base near Kars. The Russian nuclear-weapons inventory for bombers does in fact include a weapon having an estimated yield of a hundred kilotons. A nuclear weapon can, in fact, be burst at a certain height for optimum destructive effectiveness, producing little or no fallout. Standard targeting procedures for limiting collateral damage call for such air bursts, to minimize radioactive contamination of the civilian population. Such targeting procedures would very likely be employed during a limited nuclear strike, especially one for demonstrative purposes. This esoteric aspect of nuclear strike operations is common knowledge among nuclear targeteers, but it is not otherwise widely known, even among civilian nuclear strategists.

In Felgengauer's scenario, Russia wins its nuclear war against Turkey and the United States:

> Washington's reaction [to the destruction of the U.S. radar] was sluggish. No one wanted to begin a world nuclear war because of some half-destroyed villages in the Caucasus Mountains. And especially the weak and unpopular Clinton Administration. . . . The Russian president general announced that another, more powerful nuclear strike would be made on Turkey in 24 hours. But as a result of many hours of negotiations via the "hot line," a joint Russian-American settlement was developed that Turkey would have to accept.

The Russian military probably believed that its nuclear diplomacy in May 1992 had thwarted Turkish aggression and settled the immediate crisis in Russia's favor. This was achieved, of course, without the actual necessity of nuclear war.

Russian journalists, unlike their Western counterparts, do not typically have access to detailed information on the numbers and locations of Russian and foreign military forces. Yet Felgengauer gets these details right. This, and his accurate description of a little-known technique on nuclear strike operations, indicates that one or more of Felgengauer's numerous contacts on the Russian General Staff or in the defense ministry gave him inside information.

Someone on the Russian General Staff or in the defense ministry talked to Pavel Felgengauer about the events of May 1992 while they were still fresh, because they wanted to send the West a message. The message was twofold, an account of what had recently happened during the Armenian crisis, and a warning for the future. In May 1992, Yevgeniy Shaposhnikov was not bluffing. As a contingency against a Turkey-NATO invasion of Armenia, Russian military planners were prepared to make a demonstration strike on the U.S. radar base near Kars with a hundred kiloton nuclear weapon and to make additional nuclear strikes if necessary. The warning for the future is Felgengauer's last sentence: "The Caucasian War did prove one thing, by the way: Local wars were going to be local nuclear wars more often in the twenty-first century."

PART IV

The October Coup, September 21–October 4, 1993

What's wrong with a military dictator?

—General Aleksandr Lebed,
September 8, 1994

There is no real civilian control over the military today. . . . There is still no real government in Russia: bureaucrats do what they like, without fear. In the military itself, you have a democracy of the generals.

—Sergey Rogov,
November 28, 1993

In the future, Russia will frankly acknowledge its nuclear first strike policy. . . . Russia may acknowledge the possible preemptive use of nuclear weapons at an early stage of conventional war.

—Alexei Arbatov,
General Vladimir Dworkin,
June 11, 1993

CHAPTER 19

Democracy of the Generals

Gravestones stood around them like soldiers; gray granite sentinels, hard and cold, in parade formation, row upon row, forever at attention. Within this honor guard of stone, hundreds of Russian military officers, brightly festooned with ribbons, stood at attention around a single grave. Carved upon the stone was a name—Akhromeyev.

Marshal Sergey Fedorovich Akhromeyev: master strategist, coup plotter, and suicide. Days after hanging himself to atone for the failure of the August 1991 coup, "pro-democracy" vandals exhumed Akhromeyev's grave, stripped off his marshal's uniform, and left his desecrated corpse lying naked in the dirt.

Now, one year later, the marshal was again a hero.

Time had transformed Akhromeyev into a farsighted prophet and martyr. Akhromeyev's reputation, large in life, loomed even larger in death. The disintegration of the Soviet Union, the agonized withering of the Russian Army, and the unfulfilled promises of Boris Yeltsin's new Russia had drawn a cadre of military officers and others to Akhromeyev's resting place. They came on August 19, 1992, the anniversary of the failed coup.

"Some regard this as a day of victory," muttered Colonel Stanislav Terekhov, leader of the militant Officer's Union, "but we see it as a day of mourning in a degraded country."

Red flags lowered over Akhromeyev's grave in an overgrown cemetery, near the ruins of a church. Pink roses brightened a grim portrait of the marshal, dressed in full uniform, his chest heavy with his country's highest honors.

A black leather trenchcoat stepped forward: Colonel Viktor Alksnis, the "Black Colonel," so dubbed by Russian democrats for his fierce, authoritarian attitude. "I stand before you a reactionary, a hawk, a bastard," he had once defiantly told the Russian parliament. Now he called upon the silent mourners to swear an oath upon the grave of the fallen Akhromeyev, an oath that they would one day restore the Union of Soviet Socialist Republics. As if from one voice, the chanting of hundreds boomed into a sky dark with clouds: "I vow, I vow!" The officers punched the air with their fists: "I vow, I vow!"

Defense Minister Pavel Grachev stared hard at the page. Anarchy, civil war, and world war stared back at him. In March 1993, Grachev sat in the comfortable confines of his Defense Ministry office, reading a most uncomfortable poll, recently published by General Vladimir Dudnik, one of the few high-ranking officers who supported democratic reform and the Yeltsin government. Dudnik's poll bluntly warned that the Russian Army's "right-communist orientation" posed a threat to democratic rule:

> Only 19 percent of the military servicemen supported the government, while 56 percent were opposed to it. . . . The President's popularity in army circles is relatively low. He is supported completely by 30 percent, 10 percent are categorically opposed to him, and 60 percent did not define their position. No less than one-third of the officer's corps speaks out for the re-creation of the U.S.S.R. . . . Two-thirds favor the introduction of a regime with a firm hand (but not the hand of Yeltsin) and a state sector in the economy.

Grachev dropped the page, watching it swing wildly left and then right on its way to the floor. In his bones he could feel disaster coming. There was no longer any question about *whether* it would come, only when and how big.

Pavel Sergeyevich Grachev was ill-prepared to serve as defense minister. Born in the village of Rva, just south of Moscow, on January 1, 1948, he was young to hold Russia's highest military post. Of undistinguished background—his father was a metal worker and his mother a milkmaid—he had no highly placed relatives to help him master the Russian military bureaucracy. But he had a friend: Boris Yeltsin.

General Grachev spent virtually his entire military career, twenty years, in the airborne infantry, serving seven years of combat duty in Afghanistan, where he rose to command a division. In August 1991, as a recent graduate of the General Staff Academy and commander of all airborne infantry, he sided with Boris Yeltsin against the coup plotters. As a reward, President Yeltsin made Grachev, now a confidante and drinking partner, minister of defense in 1992. But Grachev's narrow background, limited combined-arms training, promotion over numerous more senior and better-qualified officers, and close association with the despised Yeltsin made him an unpopular leader among Russian military officers.

There was worse. President Yeltsin reportedly caught Grachev funneling stolen defense ministry funds into a secret German bank account—but forgave him the "indiscretion." Rumored to be the godfather of organized crime in a Russian military festering with corruption, the defense minister was also accused of assassinating a journalist—GRU-style, with an exploding briefcase—who was investigating military criminality. Yet President Yeltsin stood by his defense minister, preferring a friend and political dependent as his military chief, over who knew what enemy. October 1993 would put that friendship to the test.

Evidence of mutiny in the Russian Army crossed Grachev's desk nearly every day since the last coup attempt. Not even elite military units armed with nuclear weapons were immune. According to rumors circulated in the Russian press, in December 1991, an admiral of the Baltic Fleet threatened a nuclear strike against St. Petersburg unless his men were paid. The story was probably apocryphal, but the point is that the situation in Russia had deteriorated so far that such nightmares were plausible enough to make the papers.

Most of the nightmares were indisputably real, however. Sailors really had starved to death in the Pacific Fleet. Riots and full-scale mutinies really had broken out in many military commands. In January 1992, the commander of a mobile missile unit, blocked at Panemune by Lithuanian border guards from returning to Russia, threatened to "wipe Panemune off the surface of the earth" with a missile attack. The unit ended up shooting its way across the border.

In 1993, troops at the Baikonur Cosmodrome, Russia's largest military space center, mutinied. Inspectors from the Russian defense ministry found a battery of SS-25 mobile intercontinental nuclear missiles out in the open, completely deserted. All the operators and guards had abandoned their posts to forage for food.

In March 1994, at a mobile ICBM unit near Barnaul, a Russian soldier armed with a submachine gun killed his commanding officer and several others. According to Russian press accounts, "the guards on duty did not retaliate, fearing that bullets might hit fuel tanks of nuclear missiles deployed at the site. In that case, a catastrophe would have been inevitable."

In September 1994, according to Russian officials and press reports, "the Moscow region electricity authority cut off power to the strategic nuclear arsenal, which has enough firepower to wipe out human life on the planet, because of unpaid bills." The combat readiness of Russia's strategic nuclear forces, which have independent auxiliary electric power supplies, had reportedly been unaffected by the power cut. Nonetheless, as the Russian military newspaper *Krasnaya zvezda* put it, "if the independent electric supply had not cut in, it could have resulted in loss of command and control over Russia's nuclear missiles." Civil-power authorities later admitted error and claimed not to have known that the customer they were punishing was the Strategic Missile Forces Command Center.

Russian central control is one of the main means of preventing an unauthorized missile launch. Blunders involving Russia's strategic nuclear forces evidence a profound failure of governmental order and also sheer incompetence, both of which could pose a global danger. Another example of Russian governmental failure occurred in 1993, involving General Aleksandr Lebed. As the controversial commander of Russia's Fourteenth Army, based in Moldova, Lebed appeared determined to remain in permanent occupation of that independent nation—in open defiance of Moscow. He successfully resisted efforts by both President Yeltsin and Defense Minister

Grachev to remove him from command, finally resigning voluntarily in 1995 in order to run against Boris Yeltsin in the 1996 presidential election. Infamous for inflammatory public remarks, Lebed seemed to calculate his rhetoric to encourage military revolt. "Can you imagine the situation of the soldier who comes home today to Tula or Ryazan and old women spit in his face?" Lebed asked the press in 1993. "It all happened before, in 1917, when the nation split into White and Red. History teaches us nothing." Polls showed that Aleksandr Lebed was one of the most respected and popular military officers in Russia. In a September 1994 interview, he spoke contemptuously of President Yeltsin, declared democracy an impossibility for Russia, and asked rhetorically, "What's wrong with a military dictator?"

Defense Minister Grachev was neither an economist nor a political scientist, but he could see that President Yeltsin's domestic program was failing. During 1991, 1992, and 1993, Yeltsin and reform-minded elites had tried to transform Russia into a capitalist democracy by privatizing state industries and holding honest elections. The radical free-market surgery only seemed to add joblessness to the normal scarcities of the moribund Russian economy. Capitalism was alien to Russian managers and workers. The czars had tolerated a small entrepreneurial class, but this had been exterminated by the commissars. Russia passed from feudalism to socialism—both paternalistic, communal systems—without ever experiencing the competitive, highly individualistic free market that had been the norm in the West since the industrial revolution.

In January 1993, the huge Russian textile factory at Ivanovo, which produced one-quarter of all fabrics in the former Soviet Union, halved production and laid off thousands of workers. Warehouses stood empty. Cotton and other raw materials were unavailable for future production. Other basic industries followed the same pattern of rapid decline. Hyperinflation made the ruble worthless. Once officially valued as roughly equivalent to the dollar, the ruble plunged to an exchange rate of five hundred rubles against one dollar. Millions of Russians saw their savings evaporate under "capitalism."

By 1993, Boris Yeltsin's bold attempt to turn Russia toward democracy and free markets had been shipwrecked on the shoals of a hostile Supreme Soviet, the Russian parliament, dominated by reactionaries, communists, and ultranationalists. Communist apparatchiks embedded in the state and industrial bureaucracies were resisting and sabotaging Yeltsin's moves toward economic privatization. Voracious crime and corruption ate Russia's newborn entrepreneurs alive.

Food and housing shortages, widespread unemployment, and an explosion in crime convinced many Russians that their political and economic institutions had failed utterly and that Russian society was sliding toward anarchy. Rampant street crime, which victimizes Russian citizens every day, and organized crime, which offers uranium and advanced military hardware for sale on the international black market, were virtually nonexistent under the former Soviet police state.

Homelessness among about 180,000 Russian military officers had driven many to desperate measures to care for their families, including selling weapons and illegally serving as mercenaries in local border conflicts. The deterioration of their quality of life had many Russian military officers pining for the "good old days" of empire, and soured many on the Yeltsin government: "You can forgive Yeltsin our pauper's pay, the destroyed health of our wives and children, our eviction from warm houses virtually into open fields," cried one officer in 1993. "But we cannot forgive that lands conquered by our fathers and grandfathers, and our people living on them, have been given away for less than a pinch of tobacco." Such was the voice of a man ready for revolution.

Russia's burgeoning internal crisis could threaten the West directly if it led to irresponsible or criminal behavior among soldiers entrusted with weapons of mass destruction. Among Russia's military officers, the country's deepening internal problems and growing disrespect for political authority contributed to an increased sense of vulnerability to external threats, and to greater willingness to act against those threats independently. Deputy Defense Minister Andrey Kokoshin, in a July 1994 interview, admitted that "a real threat arose somewhere at the beginning of 1992 of losing controllability of the Armed Forces. . . . Both Grachev and I understood that urgent decisions were needed with respect to ensuring controllability of the Armed Forces." Kokoshin acknowledged that internal problems with the Russian armed forces threatened global security: "It was clear to us what enormous might there was in the hands of our Army, and it could become extremely destructive not only for our country, but also for the entire international community." He also said that Russia, and perhaps the world, was running out of time: "History has set aside for us a certain time for reform, but we do not think it is endless."

Sergey Rogov, a prominent civilian defense expert and deputy director of the Institute of the U.S.A. and Canada, made Andrey Kokoshin seem like an optimist. In Rogov's view, given in a November 1993 interview, the Russian military was already out of control: "There is no civilian control over the military today. The end of 1991 saw the collapse and withering away of the Soviet state, and there is still no real government in Russia: bureaucrats do what they like, without fear. In the military itself, you have a democracy of the generals."

In 1993 the Russian military appeared—and it still does today—to be pursuing a number of military programs autonomously, without the knowledge or approval of Russia's president or other civilian leaders. For example, in both 1993 and 1994 Russian defectors Val Mirzayanov and Vladimir Pasechnik told the U.S. intelligence community that Moscow was secretly developing chemical and biological superweapons in direct violation of arms control treaties. Mirzayanov and Pasechnik were scientists who had recently worked on the programs. Former CIA director Robert Gates testified before Congress in 1993 that the agency believed the Russian military was working illegally on biological weapons, without the knowledge of Russia's civilian government.

An uncontrolled Russian military could disobey its political masters and destroy the West. Ever since the collapse of the USSR, Russia's political leaders and General Staff spokesmen have repeatedly told Western audiences that a war between former Soviet states, or a civil war within Russia, would somehow likely mushroom into a world nuclear holocaust. Presumably, escalation would occur because the Russian military would get out of control. It is not clear whether this was a scare tactic to solicit help from the West, a friendly warning—or a threat.

Certainly, some Russian military officers did not mean such remarks as a friendly warning. If nuclear war offers no prospect of victory, revenge should not be underestimated as a motive for toppling the pillars of civilization. Consider the views of the "Black Colonel," Viktor Alksnis, expressed in December 1991, after the disintegration of the USSR:

> It is impossible to predict the future of our nuclear weapons today. I talked to a commander of a submarine equipped with nuclear arms. He told me that he would immediately carry out the maximum strike possible if anyone should try to put our nuclear weapons under international control. He will not wait for an order from Moscow, he said. The current [situation] constitutes a greater danger for the West than before. I do not rule out that from a peaceful period we could move toward a period of war. A civil war in the [former] U.S.S.R. would lead to a Third World War.

"I am sorry for those people in the West who are now applauding the decline of the last empire," Colonel Alksnis threatened. "If our state truly collapses, it will take the whole world with it into the grave."

CHAPTER 20

Rutskoy

General Aleksandr Vladimirovich Rutskoy, vice president of Russia, heard in the words of the "Black Colonel" the voice of reason. Rutskoy, like the communists and ultranationalists, saw the CIA behind Russia's decline, and as a clear and present danger to Russia's survival. Although the central pillar of President Boris Yeltsin's foreign policy was to build a strategic partnership with the United States, his own vice president did not hesitate to demonize the United States, sharing his CIA conspiracy theory with *Pravda* correspondent Boris Slavin on May 18, 1993:

SLAVIN: Might some people have an interest in the collapse of both the [Soviet] Union and the Russian economy?

VICE PRESIDENT RUTSKOY: There is nothing accidental in this world. In 1991 CIA Director Gates wrote that the breaking away of the republics from Russia would only be the start of the process. Subsequently the Army would have to be dismantled and work done to ensure that the population became impoverished.

In Aleksandr Rutskoy's view, the United States was well on its way to delivering the final blow to Russia: "We are incapable of ensuring the country's defense; the Army has collapsed completely."

A youthful and energetic forty-seven in 1993, Vice President Rutskoy was a dynamo who worked eighteen-hour days and, during his leisure hours, played tennis and lifted weights. Rutskoy was a popular figure in his own right, a war hero born in Russia's heartland city of Kursk to a family with a military tradition. Upon graduating from the Gagarin Air Force Academy in 1980, Rutskoy became the third generation of his house to join the officer corps. In Afghanistan, he flew over four hundred ground-attack missions between 1985 and 1988, missions that had been made extremely hazardous by Stinger missiles supplied to the Afghan rebels by the United States. Shot down twice, Rutskoy survived to tell the tale.

The second time down, he was taken prisoner by Mujahedin warriors and held for several months. Although slowly starving at the hands of his brutal captors, he still refused Western offers to defect and emigrate to Canada. Ultimately exchanged in return for a captured Pakistani spy, Rutskoy had withered from his normal weight of 220 pounds to a mere 110. Proclaimed a Hero of the Soviet Union, the highest Soviet military honor, Aleksandr Rutskoy became a nationally respected figure overnight. His courageous war record earned him the vice presidency in June 1991, when Russia was still a republic of the USSR. In August 1991, Rutskoy helped organize the defense of Yeltsin's besieged "White House"; correspondent Vasily lzgarshev credits him as being one of the three military officers chiefly responsible for Yeltsin's victory over the communists.

However, by 1993 Vice President Aleksandr Rutskoy was convinced that Boris Yeltsin was leading Russia down the wrong path. He openly blamed Russia's deteriorating condition on President Yeltsin and his reformist policies. "Yeltsin's administration is criminal and should be tried in court for its economic reforms," Rutskoy told British television in February 1992. "I want only one thing: to stop this corrupt and criminal chaos which is called reforms," he said in April 1993. Shortly before the October 1993 coup attempt, Rutskoy aimed this barb at Yeltsin through the Russian press: "What can I tell those who ruin Russia by remaining in an endless state of drunkenness and booziness?" In public remarks, the vice president often suggested that Yeltsin and his democratic reformers had deliberately conspired to destroy the Soviet Union and weaken Russia's defenses.

Zbigniew Brzezinski, former U.S. national security advisor to President Jimmy Carter, predicted in March 1993 that if Vice President Rutskoy ever assumed the mantle of the presidency, "we would probably see a much more demagogic nationalistic and somewhat imperialistic foreign policy. . . . Demagogic in the sense that he's awfully good at manipulating slogans and symbols. . . . Nationalistic in terms of emotional appeals to the deeply embedded national instincts of the Russians. And imperialistic in the sense of a determination to recreate some larger entity reminiscent of the former Soviet Union."

Rutskoy could be dangerously impulsive. In July 1993, he unapologetically admitted that he had once telephoned the president of Georgia, Eduard Shevardnadze, while President Yeltsin was traveling abroad and threatened that "if Georgia did not immediately change its policy in South Ossetia," he would "command an air squadron to bomb Tbilisi [Georgia's capital] at once." Rutskoy also acknowledged that many of his aides and associates were former KGB officials, whom he valued "because they were good experts in various fields."

In Aleksandr Rutskoy's view, Boris Yeltsin had sacrificed Russia's empire and military strength for no appreciable domestic advantage, and at great risk to national security. Like his nemesis of August 1991, Vice President Rutskoy convinced himself it was his duty to save Russia. "If God permits us to live another five years," he told a journalist working for Ostankino Television in July 1993, "you will see what assessment will be given of those who have destroyed the Soviet Union, which was respected by the whole world and which ensured a balance of power and stability in the world."

Defense Minister Pavel Grachev heard the words of the "Black Colonel" and Vice President Rutskoy. He saw the growing chaos in Russia infecting the military, and he worried. He worried that men like Alksnis and Rutskoy might take matters into their own hands and act against Moscow—or against Washington. Despite the mounting seriousness of internal threats to Russia, Grachev was more concerned about foreign threats to Russian security. In this, he was very much like Rutskoy. He worried that the United States, or some combination of foreign powers, would be tempted, tempted by Russian weakness, tempted to eliminate forever the possibility of a resurgent Russian challenge to Western dominance, tempted to deliver a nuclear or conventional coup de grace.

"We must be realists; things are no longer the same. The nature of a future war, if it breaks out, will be radically different. Even if only conventional high-precision weapons are used, it will immediately turn into a nuclear-chemical war," Defense Minister Grachev told the press in a February 1993 interview, justifying the need to maintain Russia's nuclear preparedness. General G. Ivanov, Grachev's director for military organizational development in the defense ministry, explained in a March 1993 press interview "the need to 'detect' promptly, in conjunction with the Foreign Intelligence Service and the Internal Affairs, and Security Ministries, an armed attack which is being prepared against the Russian Federation. . . . We do not intend to be the first to start a nuclear war. But the level of the Russian Federation's strategic nuclear forces must be a guarantee of stability and the prevention of a large-scale conventional or nuclear war." General Ivanov did not explain what role the new military doctrine envisioned for the interior ministry and security ministry in warning of a nuclear war, since these ministries were responsible for police activities, riot control, and maintaining domestic order. Did the new doctrine regard Russian internal crises as an increasingly plausible cause for a nuclear war?

Worsening social and economic problems and sharpening internal military divisions aggravated war scare attitudes in the Russian military in the months leading up to the October 1993 coup attempt. A particularly authoritative example of Russian fixation on world war is a June 1993 article written by no less a person than the Russian minister of defense, General Pavel Grachev. The rare appearance of an article by the defense minister in the official government publication *Military Thought*, Russia's most prestigious journal of strategic studies, gives the article the weight of official doctrine rather than mere personal opinion. Claiming also to speak for President Yeltsin, Grachev asserted that Russia's highest military priority was "deterrence of any aggressor from unleashing a world nuclear or conventional war." Grachev wrote that deterrence of nuclear or large-scale conventional conflict is to be accomplished "by maintaining the strategic nuclear forces in a state that ensures the conduct of retaliatory operations with the required effectiveness under any conditions." Later in the article, Grachev defined "retaliation" to mean, or include, Russian use of nuclear weapons in a *preemptive or preventive first strike*.

In his description of Russian military doctrine, Grachev paid lip service to "the end of the Cold War" and "a reduction in the probability of large-scale wars in the near future," but most of his remarks belied these reassurances and made clear that World War III remained the focus of Russian military thinking. In a thinly veiled reference to the United States and NATO, he emphasized that "we have observed the aspirations of certain states (coalitions) for supremacy in individual regions and in the world as a whole"; that "there are 530 divisions, 42,000 tanks, and 12,000 combat aircraft [of potentially hostile nations] concentrated near Russia's borders . . . an impressive instrument of war"; and that "military force remains one of the main instruments of policy of a whole series of countries." Grachev stressed that preparedness for nuclear war remained Russia's top priority. "It is obvious that at the present time and in the foreseeable future, nuclear weapons will remain the defining element of European and global stability. Therefore, we regard the strategic nuclear forces to be the most important guarantee of ensuring the military security of Russian and its allies." As if to make certain that no one missed his last point. Defense Minister Grachev's article was followed by another, by Russia's top nuclear officer. The commander in chief of the Strategic Rocket Forces, General Igor Sergeyev, writing in the same issue of *Military Thought*, offered another rare article—it is not usual to see articles by the defense minister and SRF chief—reiterating most of Grachev's themes.

War scare attitudes were not confined to the elite of the Russian defense ministry and General Staff. Russian navy captain and former missile submarine commander Anatoliy Gorbachev spoke plainly in an article published in March 1993, titled: "From the Nuclear Abyss to Catastrophe for Russia—That Is Where the START II Treaty Is Leading." Captain Gorbachev excoriated the Strategic Arms Reduction Treaty as weakening Russian nuclear forces, in his view the only restraint preventing the United States from starting World War III:

> Only a gullible person could hope that with [the START II Treaty] the world will become a safer place than it used to be. Let us be totally honest: it was the U.S.S.R. which restrained the United States from geopolitical aggression, and it was never the military monster or the empire of evil that the now triumphant U.S. imperialism actually was and still is. . . . In a word, the future world bandit is getting stronger in every respect, knocking Russia off its feet and treading it as yet invisibly into the dirt. But what will things be like then, when a real monster will acquire the full freedom to punish the whole world?

The article indirectly condemned President Yeltsin, who had publicly embraced START II, as ignorant of Russia's security needs and careless of national pride.

A March 1993 lecture by Colonel Yevgeniy Morosov claimed that the United States and NATO might invade Russia in the near future. "NATO is directing its forces of the so-called central European military area against the Moscow region, forces which, under normal conditions—the term 'peaceful conditions' refuses to pass my lips—consists of up to thirty-six divisions and thirty-five brigades and regiments." Colonel Morosov warned, "In the event of a decision to attack, these units could be extended to ninety divisions, including 4,000 fighter aircraft, within one month." Morosov argued that in the face of such a threat, Russia was "unprotected and defenseless." In language reminiscent of *Mein Kampf*, he lamented, "This is how low our proud country, our great Army, have sunk. We have not been defeated on the battlefield, but we were stabbed from behind with a poisoned dagger." According to Colonel Morosov, the withdrawal of Russian forces from Germany may have started the clock ticking toward World War III: "Yet, to prevent disturbing NATO's military planning, the withdrawal times have been revised, that is to say shortened. Once this year is over, we are absolutely at the mercy of NATO, or rather of the United States."

In a June 1993 speech titled "The Third World War Is under Way," Colonel Stanislav Terekhov alleged to other Russian military officers that the United States was *already* waging a war of subversion and sabotage against Russia, preparatory to military conquest. Terekhov would join the coup in October 1993. Suspicion of the United States ran so deep among many Russian military officers that even U.S. gestures of good faith were interpreted as parts of a sinister design. For example, in July 1993, Secretary of Defense Les Aspin announced the cancellation of Strategic Defense Initiative ("Star Wars") research on high-tech defenses against nuclear weapons, a program much feared by the Russian General Staff. Some Russian military analysts accused Aspin of deception, claiming that the United States continued to work on SDI under another name.

In a February 1993 interview titled "I Put My Trust in Facts," General Vladimir Achalov, one of Russia's most senior military officers, left the unmistakable impression that the United States posed an immediate military threat to Russia: "Of course, if U.S. politicians' peace-loving words and assurances are to be believed, armed forces can be eliminated altogether. But I prefer to put more trust in facts and I cannot turn a blind eye to the way in which the United States is behaving in relation to Iraq and Yugoslavia, with the provocative effrontery of a world policeman. . . . I might be accused of inflaming passions. But, as far as I know, nobody has denied the reports about NATO strategists' elaboration of operations plans for its peacekeeping forces on the former Union's territory."

Seven months after this interview, General Achalov would become one of the leaders of the new coup against President Boris Yeltsin.

Hostile attitudes toward the West were not limited to the Russian military but were also expressed by many Russian civilian leaders, including some prominent in the Yeltsin government. In January 1993, Andrei Chernenko, a high-ranking official in the security ministry, accused foreign spies of meddling in Moscow's affairs, of fueling separatism and civil violence in parts of the country, and spreading disinformation and slander about Russia abroad. In February 1993, after interviewing members of the Russian parliament, journalist Sergey Shevykin concluded, "The antipathy that the parliamentary majority harbors for U.S. imperialists knows no bounds."

In a February 1993 interview, the mysterious Vladimir Zhirinovsky, a member of the Russian parliament and notorious leader of the proto-fascist Liberal Democratic Party of Russia, expressed the view that "the United States is an empire of evil, the nucleus of hell, which is behind the beginning of every war. . . . [The United States is] aspiring to rule the whole world." Zhirinovsky was no kinder to President Yeltsin's government, which he claimed was in collusion with the United States to destroy Russia:

> I spit on the Russian Ministry of Foreign Affairs. They are criminals, CIA agents, a nest of Americans! That scoundrel [Foreign Minister] Kozyrev will not die a natural death. How can you pursue that kind of foreign policy! How can you betray such a great country! Or take that Shevardnadze! A scoundrel, a CIA agent too, it is his fault that we had all of Eastern Europe demolished, he has undermined Russia's authority in the world.

Zhirinovsky announced in the interview—entitled "Saddam, We're Proud of You!"—that in defiance of Moscow, his followers were illegally going to Iraq to help Saddam Hussein fight the United States. A number of armed Russian ultranationalists did, in fact, appear in Baghdad when the United States was launching air strikes to enforce UN sanctions against Iraq.

Vladimir Volfovitch Zhirinovsky's diatribes are extreme, even by the rhetorical standards of communist propagandists during the height of the Cold War. Nonetheless, judging from Zhirinovsky's popularity, his inflammatory talk against the West resonates with many ordinary Russians. How did Zhirinovsky, a product of Russian democracy—he was unknown during the Soviet period—come to hate the West and Russian reformers so?

Surprisingly little is independently verifiable about Zhirinovsky's background—highly unusual for such a prominent political figure, even in Russia—and rumors abound. Allegedly, the virulently anti-Semitic Zhirinovsky is himself a Jew. Another story claims he is secretly on Boris Yeltsin's payroll and deliberately spews wild rhetoric to scare voters away from the nationalists and communists. If that is true, Yeltsin's "Zhirinovsky stratagem" has backfired badly. Still another account claims Zhirinovsky is a KGB agent. It is a plausible hypothesis given his training in several foreign languages: English, German, French, and Turkish; moreover, Zhirinovsky served on the Soviet Peace Committee, a KGB front organization. Less plausibly, some allege that Zhirinovsky still works for Russia's intelligence services and is their candidate for president.

Zhirinovsky certainly talks like a KGB fanatic. He has pledged that if he ever becomes president of Russia, he will blackmail the United States by threatening to launch SS-18 ICBMs at U.S. cities unless the West pays Russia tribute. If the United States refuses, Zhirinovsky promises to engage the U.S. in nuclear Russian roulette, trading city for city, vaporizing one metropolis at a time as he repeats his demands. Many such psychotic ideas are proposed in Zhirinovsky's latest book, *I Spit on the West*. Despite these views, or perhaps because of them, Vladimir Zhirinovsky remained one of the most popular and influential politicians in Russia.

The views of a Zhirinovsky, of General Achalov, or, for that matter, the more balanced but still profoundly suspicious views of a Defense Minister Grachev or General Ivanov, were ripe for nuclear miscalculation, especially when mixed with an international or domestic crisis.

While Grachev was publishing his landmark June 1993 article on the still-serious danger posed by the United States and the increased importance of nuclear vigilance, a U.S. professor at Stanford University, Scott Sagan, published *The Limits of Safety*. Sagan's book recounted "numerous instances of safety violations, unanticipated operational problems, bizarre and dangerous interactions, and unordered risk-taking" in the management of the U.S. nuclear arsenal during the Cuban missile crisis and into the 1970s.

For example, despite President Kennedy's order that U.S. forces refrain from any actions that might be interpreted in Moscow as signs of an imminent nuclear attack, the U.S. Air Force flight-tested an ICBM at the height of the crisis, on October 26, firing the missile from Vandenberg Air Force Base in California to a point in the Pacific Ocean. The Air Force then proceeded to upload nuclear weapons on other missiles at Vandenberg. "No one in Washington apparently imagined the possibility that Soviet intelligence might learn of the launch just as it was taking place, and interpret it as part of an actual attack," Sagan wrote.

On the same day, another U.S. intercontinental ballistic missile was flight-tested from Florida, passing over Cuba en route to the South Atlantic, alarming U.S. Strategic Air Command headquarters in Omaha. SAC officers, who had not been notified of the missile test, were informed by a radar site at Moorestown, New Jersey, that an ICBM had been detected, Sagan recounts, and apparently they briefly mistook it for a Soviet missile flying toward, instead of away from, Florida.

After midnight on October 25, 1962, during the Cuban missile crisis, a security guard at a military base in Duluth, Minnesota, saw an intruder climbing the security fence. Fearing an attack by Soviet terrorists, he sounded the base alarms, which accidentally tripped air-raid klaxons at nearby Volk Air Field, causing nuclear-armed F-106A fighters to scramble for takeoff before being recalled. The Soviet "terrorist" turned out to be a bear. Sagan uses the incident to illustrate the danger of what he terms "cascading accidents" involving nuclear weapons. It could happen again, and at any time.

CHAPTER 21

The Warning: Alexandria, Virginia, June 11, 1993

Cars whipped past my open window, their bright colors receding in my rearview mirror like shrinking balloons of blue, red, white, and glittering chrome. As usual, I was late. Weaving in and out of the noonday traffic on 395 South, just a few miles outside Washington, I nearly missed the King Street exit, and felt the "Gs" of force press me against the driver's-side door as I careened my Dodge Colt into Alexandria. The Center for Naval Analyses (CNA), a quasi-private institution with government connections, like the RAND Corporation, was just a mile down King Street, right next door to Copeland's, my favorite restaurant. Several of us planned to skip the Center's usually uninspired catered lunch and dine on the fine Cajun cuisine at Copeland's—after the Russians had briefed us.

Inside the usually somber Center for Naval Analyses, the atmosphere was almost festive. Many assumed that the presentation we were about to receive would be another nail in the coffin of the Cold War. General Vladimir Dworkin of the Strategic Rocket Forces and Alexei Arbatov, a well-known Russian civilian defense intellectual, would be speaking on "Emerging Russian Nuclear Strategy and Doctrine."

Just a few years ago, of course, it would have been unthinkable for a Russian general to come to Washington to explain the General Staff's nuclear strategy to an audience of U.S. military analysts. Most of us had spent entire careers trying to divine Russia's nuclear strategy from obscure scraps of data. Now, no less a figure than the director of the Main Research Institute of the Strategic Rocket Forces, the single most important military think tank in Russia, proposed to lecture us. Adding to the thrill was that Arbatov, perhaps Russia's foremost academic nuclear strategist, was also going to speak. Arbatov was a member of the Russian parliament's Committee for Defense, the equivalent of the U.S. House Armed Services Committee, and director of the Center for Geopolitical and Military Forecasts, a Russian academic think tank. His reputation as a pro-Western reformer and critic of the Russian military whetted not a few people's expectations of glad tidings from the former USSR.

Dworkin and Arbatov stood at the podium together and bluntly declared to the smiling faces gathered before them that Russia had adopted a nuclear first-strike policy and could launch a preemptive strike early in any future confrontation.

Arbatov spoke, reluctantly and even painfully, as General Dworkin glowered at us: "In the future, Russia will frankly acknowledge its nuclear first-strike policy. It is obvious that, for the new military doctrine to call for nuclear deterrence of conventional war, implies abandoning the 'no first use' pledge, since logically this requires readiness to use nuclear weapons first. . . . Russia may acknowledge the possible preemptive use of nuclear weapons at an early stage of conventional war."

Stunned silence.

A woman from the U.S. Air Force tried to put the best face on this nuclear bombshell with a question crafted to steer the threat away from the United States: "Does the shift away from 'no first use' imply the 'Americanization' of Russian military policy; that is, the use of nuclear deterrence to deal with overwhelming Chinese forces?"

Arbatov, eager to please, offered, "The 'first use' option is not directed at all against the West or the U.S., but rather obviously against China. But should NATO extend itself eastward and move directly up to Russia's border, then Russia would feel threatened, and the 'first use' option would apply against NATO as well."

Relief started creeping back into the audience. Then General Dworkin, speaking through a translator, sternly corrected his subordinate, saying that Russia's nuclear strategy did not make "any conscious effort to imitate the U.S." and that Russian nuclear plans for striking first "made no distinctions between nations." A chastened Arbatov chimed in: " 'Americanization' is not an appropriate description of Russian policy."

The USAF woman tried again to lead the Russians to "politically correct" ground, asking plaintively, "Does readiness to use tactical nuclear weapons first to deter conventional war also apply to *strategic* nuclear weapons?"

Her question invited Arbatov to deny a first-strike role for those weapons—strategic nuclear weapons—that could reach the United States, and Arbatov again tried to come to the rescue.

"First use of nuclear weapons really applies only to tactical nuclear weapons, not strategic ones," he answered in rapid English, with a furtive glance toward Dworkin's translator.

But General Dworkin obviously knew what Arbatov was up to—and obviously understood English as well. The General answered before his translator could finish rendering Arbatov's reply into Russian. Visibly annoyed, Dworkin shot Arbatov down.

"The military doctrine does not distinguish between tactical and strategic nuclear weapons."

I put a question to General Dworkin: "Going back ten years ago, to 1983, when Soviet leaders said that nuclear war was imminent and that the U.S. might attack, did they really believe it? And who was in control of the nuclear weapons when President Andropov and, later, President Chernenko, were so sick?"

General Dworkin ignored my question about the war scare, replying only, "I didn't know who was in control of the nuclear weapons then, but I can say they were under control."

Alexei Arbatov, looking steadily at General Dworkin, stated firmly, "Real control over nuclear weapons has never been in the hands of the political leadership. It has always been under the control of the defense minister and the General Staff." Relaxing, he turned to me and replied, "As to whether the leadership really believed nuclear war was imminent or that the U.S. was about to attack, I never worried about that. I was never afraid of a surprise attack. But what I *was* worried about was that each side might, through fear and misunderstanding, make mistakes, and escalation could occur. A minor incident might happen and it might escalate because each side feared the other and misunderstood the other. So that was enough to worry about. But those days are over."

Alexei Arbatov smiled nervously.

We exited the Center for Naval Analyses like moles pushing up through earth, blinking into the blazing glare of Virginia's summer sun. No one felt like eating at Copeland's.

Waiting in our office mailboxes was another bitter pill. Moscow had made available an English translation of Defense Minister Grachev's article on the new military doctrine, appearing in the June 1993 *Military Thought*. He suggested that Russia might launch a nuclear first strike, not only in response to an enemy conventional attack in progress but also against "an aggressor who is preparing to attack." Thus, just four months before the October 1993 coup attempt, the General Staff tried to make sure the United States understood Russia's more aggressive policy allowing a nuclear first strike. The Russian military clearly considered the communication of this new policy a matter of urgency, since it was still in draft form and had not been officially published. Nor had it received the formal approval of President Yeltsin.

One month later, in July, Russia conducted an unusual and alarmingly realistic strategic-forces exercise that culminated in a simulated nuclear attack on the United States. As reported in the press, "The nuclear exercise, detected by U.S. intelligence sensors . . . involved all the strategic forces of the former Soviet Union—silo-based and mobile missiles, strategic bombers and nuclear submarines, according to officials familiar with intelligence about the exercises which lasted several days, and caused alarm in some parts of the Pentagon among officials who thought such activities had ended along with the Cold War."

Within weeks, Grachev would face another coup attempt. Like Defense

Minister Yazov and KGB chief Kryuchkov before him, Pavel Grachev and the General Staff would see the coup as creating an opportunity for a U.S. surprise nuclear attack. Defense Minister Grachev, perhaps even more so than his predecessors, was thoroughly committed to striking first.

CHAPTER 22

Who's Got the Button?

"This is an enormous threat, given the volatilities and civil wars in the former Soviet Union, which may well place [nuclear] weapons into aggressive or erratic hands almost overnight," Sven Kraemer, a former senior member of the U.S. National Security Council remarked a few weeks before the October 1993 coup attempt. Kraemer reminded the press that Russia retains a "superpower arsenal capable of destroying the United States in a matter of minutes."

Yet there seemed little consciousness in the Clinton administration or elsewhere of the immediacy of the nuclear threat. Secretary of State Warren Christopher, speaking at the University of Minnesota, reassured American students at the Hubert H. Humphrey Institute of Public Affairs that the threat of nuclear war had been reduced. However, Christopher implied, the threat "could return" if Boris Yeltsin's drive toward democracy were derailed by Russian reactionaries.

In fact, what Christopher called the "shadow of nuclear confrontation" had never gone away. It had materialized as recently as August 1991 and May 1992. Within five months of Christopher's speech, it would do so again.

During the October 1993 coup—as today—Western complacency was—and is—based on the assumption that Russian civilian leaders who embrace democracy and are friendly to the West are the people that matter most in Russia. This is a grave miscalculation. The General Staff, still a bastion of paranoia and totalitarianism, matters *more* than Russia's president and civilian leaders, because it controls the former USSR's nuclear arsenal. As noted earlier, although only the president of Russia has the legal authority to order a nuclear strike, the General Staff has the *technical capability* to launch a nuclear attack on its own, even against the president's wishes.

General Geliy Batenin, formerly of the General Staff and Strategic Rocket Forces, warned the West in an October 1991 interview that actual technical control of strategic forces does not reside with the Russian president but with the military:

INTERVIEWER: So let me recapitulate then. As I understand it, launch orders can be sent automatically, even without the participation of the president, in an emergency situation.

GENERAL BATENIN: Military personnel can, technically, launch missiles from their facilities. Technically. But not legally.

INTERVIEWER: How far down the chain of command can you go and still have someone capable of launching a weapon?

GENERAL BATENIN: I would say down to the level of the General Officer on Duty in charge of the Central Command Post of the Armed Forces. [Russian military writings indicate that the "General Officer on Duty" can be of lower rank, sometimes a colonel.] In principle, he has in his hands the technical means to implement strategic decisions.

INTERVIEWER: Can he initiate?

GENERAL BATENIN: Using his authority, he can issue orders to unlock nuclear weapons in two areas: to unlock the PALs [permissive action links] on the delivery systems, and, most important, unlock the nuclear weapons themselves. To do this it would be necessary to activate one of the operational plans, by which all operations, both human and machine, would proceed according to a set schedule. The operational plan is put into operation: and that's it. Everything would proceed automatically.

General Geliy Viktorovich Batenin, former commander of an SS-18 ICBM division, was, at the time of his disclosures about Russia's "nuclear button," a senior military advisor to both the defense ministry and foreign ministry on nuclear forces and arms control. He is the highest-ranking and most authoritative Russian to have publicly described in detail how Russia's strategic command and control system works. His warnings about the dangers inherent in Russia's command and control system are highly credible, because of his background and proven record of honesty and friendship toward the West. He is one of the few senior Russian military officers who genuinely supports reforming Russian politics, the economy, and military along democratic, Western lines. He has frequently risked his career by publicly opposing General Staff policies, taking positions intended to end East-West confrontation and build a cooperative partnership between the United States and Russia. In telling a Western reporter how Russian nuclear forces are controlled, Geliy Batenin probably risked his life.

Unfortunately, few Western specialists are even aware of the interview with General Batenin. Instead, they rely on the General Staff's reassuring, but misleading, version of Russian command and control, which was related to Congress by Colonel Gennadiy Pavlov on September 24, 1991. General Batenin, speaking to the U.S. press shortly afterward, was trying to provide an antidote to Pavlov's disinformation.

In fact, no one in the West knows for sure how Russia's command and control system for strategic nuclear forces works. The most visible and best-understood parts of the system, though not the most important, are the "nuclear briefcases," attaché cases containing communications equipment that allow top Russian leaders to talk with each other and with the General

Staff. Three men in Russia carry "nuclear briefcases": the president, the defense minister, and the Chief of the General Staff.

Contrary to the view popularized by Soviet disinformant Colonel Pavlov, "votes" from two or more "nuclear briefcase" holders are *not* required to order a launch of the nuclear forces. Nor is Pavlov's story credible that military service chiefs would get to vote or veto a nuclear-launch decision. Contrary to Colonel Pavlov, Russia's nuclear command and control system does not, in all likelihood, require any consensus among the defense minister, the General Staff, and service commanders. Such a cumbersome system would consume precious time during an emergency and almost guarantee that the enemy would land the first blow. Moreover, such a system violates the basic military principle of unity of command, which places a single person in charge. It makes no sense that service commanders would be able to veto a launch decision by their better-informed superiors in the General Staff. Pavlov's nuclear command and control "democracy" makes no sense, given that the General Staff's main concern was with an enemy nuclear surprise attack that could kill the top echelon of political and military leaders and decapitate the nuclear forces.

Most Russian sources, and the most authoritative sources, imply or state explicitly that any individual holding a "nuclear briefcase" can order a nuclear strike. General Batenin, General Dworkin, General Boldyrev, Alexei Arbatov—as well as the "nuclear briefcase" designer—all indicate that Soviet and Russian strategic command and control was designed mainly to *guarantee* nuclear strike execution, not inhibit it. This is consistent with the purpose of the "nuclear briefcases," first introduced during the early 1980s as an insurance policy against a U.S. surprise nuclear attack aimed at the top political and military leaders. Giving "nuclear briefcases" to the president, defense minister, and Chief of the General Staff increased the odds that *one* of these men would survive an enemy attack and authorize the launch of Russia's nuclear forces. If only one briefcase holder survives, a nuclear strike can still be authorized. Requiring the survival of two or more briefcase holders in order to authorize a strike would defeat the purpose of the system: to provide redundance, an insurance policy against leadership decapitation.

But then, the "nuclear briefcases" are not even technically necessary to launch a nuclear strike. They are merely portable communications devices: a telephone to the General Staff in the event a surprise nuclear attack comes when the president, defense minister, and General Staff chief are all traveling, at a restaurant, or otherwise unavailable by secure communications. But any of these men could authorize a nuclear strike from a pay phone if that happened to be more convenient than the "nuclear briefcase."

Nor do the "nuclear briefcases" have launch codes necessary to unlock missile and warhead safety mechanisms prior to firing. The word of the president, defense minister, or Chief of the General Staff authorizes a nuclear strike—makes it legal—but is not technically required to launch the forces. It is probably not even legally required, in the event that these men are killed or disconnected from the General Staff. As top civilian defense expert Alexei Arbatov, with the concurrence of SRF General Vladimir Dworkin, told a U.S. audience on June 11, 1993: "The so-called football [nuclear briefcase] means nothing. It is only a communications device, a phone so the President can call up the SRF command post. But it is purely administrative and for political show. It has nothing to do with operational control of the weapons. The military had effective control [ten years ago] and they still have it now."

The General Staff controls all of the electronic, mechanical, and operational means for waging nuclear war. Giving the General Staff the ability to launch missiles on its own was in Russian eyes not a stupid and dangerous oversight but a prudent insurance policy against a nuclear attack that killed all the "nuclear briefcase" holders before they could authorize a strike. In Russia's nuclear command and control system, redundancy is designed to guarantee that a strike will be executed—even in the teeth of a highly effective surprise attack.

Located at the deep underground command post at Chekov, the General Staff owns all the codes and communications systems technically necessary for executing a nuclear strike. It is the *real* apex of Russia's nuclear command and control system. General Staff duty officers at Chekov who manage Russia's nuclear forces day to day, could launch a strike on their own, independently or even against the will of President Yeltsin and senior officers not present at Chekov. On this virtually all Western analysts agree.

More controversial is whether launch codes exist at operational levels *below* the General Staff, as an insurance policy against a surprise attack that destroys Chekov or disrupts communications between the General Staff and its strategic forces. Theoretically, launch codes providing an independent capability to execute a nuclear attack under some contingencies may reside with commanders in chief of the nuclear services; commanders and staffs of ICBM and bomber armies and submarine fleets; commanders and staffs of ICBM and bomber divisions and submarine flotillas; and individual ICBM launch crews and submarine commanders. Under this system, an unauthorized launch by lower levels would be prohibited by iron discipline, by the vigilance of higher operational levels and by local launch codes never being used for training, but being stored securely for use only as a last resort.

Some credible Russian military officers, with firsthand knowledge of Russia's strategic command and control system, have stated or implied that launch codes do exist at lower operational levels—with individual ICBM launch crews and aboard submarines. General Batenin insists that crews of SS-25 mobile ICBMs can independently launch their missiles. Navy captain Viktor Ryzhkov told an interviewer that launching SLBMs legally "requires a governmental order from the political leadership" but that, as a practical matter, "the missiles can be launched at any time." The commander of a Typhoon missile submarine claimed during an interview that his most important job was to prevent an unauthorized launch of nuclear missiles. This suggests the existence of firing codes aboard individual Russian submarines. A classified CIA study obtained by the *Washington Times* in October 1996 concludes that units below the level of the General Staff, including Strategic Rocket Forces command posts and individual submarine commanders, "have the technical ability to launch without authorization of political leaders or the General Staff." The CIA report also warns of "conspiracies within nuclear armed units" to commit nuclear blackmail.

General Korobushin and some other Russian military officers have told U.S. command and control specialist Bruce Blair that in the event a nuclear surprise attack kills all or most commanders able to launch Russia's missiles, Russian strategic nuclear forces will launch on their own, through an automated system known as DEAD HAND. This is supposedly a computer linked to the strategic forces and to sensors scattered around Russia. The sensors are designed to detect nuclear blast and radiation effects. If, in the absence of orders from its human superiors, DEAD HAND decides that Russia is under nuclear attack, the computer will assume those superiors are dead and launch doomsday. How or whether DEAD HAND can distinguish between a U.S., Chinese, British, French, Israeli, Indian, Pakistani, or North Korean nuclear attack is unclear. Perhaps distinguishing between aggressors and neutrals is irrelevant to Moscow, once Russia's elite are corpses. Or, DEAD HAND may be disinformation. Russian military officers may have concocted it to dissuade the United States from attempting a nuclear surprise attack. A February 1999 Russian article on command and control acknowledges, "Reports have appeared repeatedly . . . about the so-called dead hand, the system of automated sanctioning of the use of nuclear weapons. To this day there is no unequivocal answer to the question of whether or not in fact it exists."

In January 1993, a Russian Army major was discovered hiding in a government building near the Kremlin and was arrested. He confessed that he was lying in wait to assassinate President Boris Yeltsin. In March, the Russian parliament escalated its long feud with Yeltsin by attempting to curb his presidential powers. Yeltsin counterattacked, claiming sweeping emergency authority, which parliament challenged by threatening impeachment and a trial of the president in Constitutional Court. Crowds of pro- and anti-Yeltsin demonstrators formed outside the parliament building. On March 3, according to Russian and Western press reports, "Top generals demanded . . . that President Boris Yeltsin resolve the nation's worsening political crisis. . . . Leaders of the Defense Ministry and the military's General Staff told Mr. Yeltsin during a Kremlin meeting to take firmer steps to end his power struggle with parliament." The same day, a conciliatory Yeltsin told the parliament, "If we don't agree, Russia will be torn into fifty or sixty feudal states. It will mean a thousand-year war."

The struggle between president and parliament went on. President Yeltsin tried drafting a new Russian constitution that would curtail parliament's power. On May 15, parliament speaker Ruslan Khasbulatov warned that Russia's internal political struggle could end in nuclear catastrophe: "Alongside the general weakening of our very statehood—and we are a state with nuclear missiles—such actions by people in power as the adoption of the constitution may lead to the final collapse of the Russian Federation and loss of control. And that means that those nuclear, biological, chemical, and other types of weapons that are very dangerous to the environment and to other states may end up out of control."

The Yeltsin government may have attempted unsuccessfully late in 1991 to eliminate the threat to its sovereignty, and the nuclear threat to the world, by wresting operational control of Russia's nuclear arsenal from the grip of the General Staff. In December, General Vladimir Lobov, who replaced General Mikhail Moiseyev as chief of the General Staff after the failed August 1991 coup, was suddenly forced to resign amid unconfirmed reports that he was plotting a new coup against Yeltsin. General Viktor Samsonov, Lobov's successor as General Staff chief, apparently did not inherit Lobov's "nuclear briefcase," perhaps indicating President Yeltsin's mistrust of the loyalty and judgment of the General Staff.

Alexei Arbatov indicated in a Moscow television interview on November 29, 1991, just prior to General Lobov's dismissal, that the president, the minister of defense, and the General Staff chief all had "nuclear briefcases." The head designer of the "nuclear briefcase," whose identity was concealed by the Russian government, noted in an anonymous interview on January 28, 1992, that "until quite recently" the chief of the General Staff had a "nuclear briefcase" but that Defense Minister Yevgeniy Shaposhnikov had now "made it quite clear" that only he and President Boris Yeltsin had them. On March 20, 1992, in a roundtable discussion in which I participated, Leon Gouré, a respected U.S. scholar of Soviet and Russian military strategy, corroborated Shaposhnikov's claim. He related that during a conference he attended in Moscow in February 1992, General Igor Kalugin, commander in chief of Long-Range Aviation, Russia's strategic bomber force, mentioned that both President Yeltsin and Defense Minister Shaposhnikov had "nuclear briefcases" but that General Samsonov, the new chief of the General Staff, did not.

If Yeltsin attempted to deprive the military of day-to-day control of Russia's nuclear arsenal, he did not succeed. The "nuclear briefcases" designer and General Geliy Batenin both indicated in their interviews that the "nuclear briefcases" were only one of several means, and not even the most important means, of launching the nuclear forces. As the new Chief of the

General Staff, Samsonov retained access to, and authority over, the command posts and chain of command that can independently unlock nuclear warheads and launch Russian missiles and bombers. In any case, the Russian minister of defense, always a senior military officer loyal to the General Staff, retained his "nuclear briefcase." Later, press reports and authoritative Russian and Western sources confirmed that General Mikhail Kolesnikov, Samsonov's replacement as Chief of the General Staff, had a "nuclear briefcase." General Viktor Boldyrev, chief of Russia's nuclear command and control "briefcase" program until his retirement in 1993, affirmed in a June 1994 interview that the Chief of the General Staff, along with the president and defense minister, all continued to have "nuclear briefcases." Indeed, Boldyrev stated that not only does the Chief of the General Staff have a "nuclear briefcase" but that he, General Boldyrev, worked for the Main Directorate of the General Staff. So the General Staff has overall operational control of the "briefcase" program.

General Boldyrev further noted that the "nuclear briefcases" were not the only means for launching the strategic forces. He said this could be accomplished by other means, including a home telephone: "Whoever has communications—be it the command and control of strategic forces or a home telephone—that is who rules the dance." General Boldyrev specifically noted that the General Staff had not designed Russia's strategic command and control system to be "a system for the president that is closed and not under the control of anyone else."

Alexei Arbatov has minced no words in pointing out that the Russian military alone retains operational control over the strategic nuclear forces. In a 1992 *New Times* article, he warned that the Russian military, not Russia's political leaders, control the strategic nuclear forces and that Russia's political leaders would be powerless to stop the military from launching a nuclear attack. Arbatov compared President Boris Yeltsin's role in Russia's nuclear decision-making process "to that of a chimpanzee used for testing: he will just have to push a button when a lamp comes on." Arbatov emphasized that the Russian approach to command and control of nuclear weapons "amounts to depriving the political leadership of the right to make a decision to use nuclear weapons." He explained that "at the top level of government, positive control has always taken precedence over negative control. The monopoly of the military in working out the control system and operation plan . . . has materialized in a concept which guards not against an accidental strike due to a mistake, a nervous breakdown, or a technical problem, but against failure to respond to an attack promptly and on a massive scale. . . . This is a reflection of a typically militaristic mentality—the main goal is to crush the enemy; deterrence is just a sideline."

Ironically, after the failed coup of August 1991, military reactionaries attempted to strengthen their control over nuclear weapons by the formation, with President Yeltsin's probably unwitting assent, of the new Strategic Deterrence Forces. For the first time, all the long-range nuclear services—the Strategic Rocket Forces, strategic missile submarines of the Navy, and bombers of Long-Range Aviation—were to be placed under a single commander in chief, General Yuri Maksimov, nemesis of the West. Maksimov was an "old thinker," who cooperated with the coup plotters in August 1991. He was instrumental in placing the Strategic Rocket Forces on alert during the coup, and in the immediate aftermath of the coup, issued jeremiads about the Western threat. Yet, somehow, Maksimov managed to convince the Russian democrats that he was, in reality, a military reformer. Fortunately, Russia's economic crisis—and perhaps opposition by the General Staff, jealous of its dominant role at the apex of Russia's command and control pyramid—prevented the Strategic Deterrence Forces from becoming more than a name. This may change soon.

After General Maksimov's retirement, he was succeeded by General Igor Sergeyev as commander in chief of the Strategic Rocket Forces. Sergeyev is another hard-liner who spent his entire career in the SRF training for nuclear conflict. In 1999, "missile man" Sergeyev is minister of defense and his brother-in-law, General Vladimir Yakovlev, is chief of the Strategic Rocket Forces. Together, they are advocating a reorganization of Russian command and control that would make the Strategic Deterrence Forces an operational reality, combining the several nuclear services into one, and putting the top "missile man"— Yakovlev—in charge of "the button." So the "nuclear shooters" themselves would be in control.

It is not clear if the proposed reorganization would transfer the technical capability to launch a nuclear strike away from the General Staff and to the Joint Supreme Command of Strategic Deterrence Forces (OGK SSS, Obeydinennoe Glavnokomandovanie Strategicheskikh Sil Sderzhiivaniya), the name of the proposed new command for managing nuclear operations. The proposed reorganization may give an additional operational level, the OGK SSS, along with the General Staff, the independent technical capability to launch all nuclear forces. Sergeyev, in his public remarks, and Maksimov, in a February 1999 article advocating the reorganization, emphasize that OGK SSS will be subordinate to the General Staff. The General Staff reportedly opposes the reorganization.

The OGK SSS is bad news. With the consolidation of the several nuclear services into a single unified force, the ability to launch *all* nuclear forces will be extended to yet another, and lower, command echelon, the commander in chief of the SSS (Strategic Deterrence Forces). If Sergeyev and Yakovlev succeed, they will make more dangerous an already too dangerous situation. Will nuclear "missile men" themselves be more inclined to push the button than the General Staff? Probably. The General Staff at least has a great many officers from the conventional forces, who are less inclined than strategic forces officers to see nuclear weapons as a "silver bullet."

Regardless of the outcome of the latest struggle over control of Russia's nuclear forces, this fundamental perilous reality will remain unchanged: those military officers who are most fearful of the "U.S. threat" will continue to be in a position to act on their fears, independently of Russian political leaders, if need be.

In October 1993, Defense Minister Pavel Grachev and General Mikhail P. Kolesnikov, Chief of the General Staff, were two of the three men in Russia who carried a "nuclear briefcase." As such, either of these men could order a nuclear strike from a sidewalk cafe, if they so desired.

Russia's nuclear command and control system, which emphasizes guaranteeing launch execution over prohibition of an unauthorized launch, is consistent with the priorities of the General Staff during the Soviet period. In the halcyon days of Soviet military power and discipline, when the present command and control system was designed, a coup, civil war, or mutiny that could defeat the system was inconceivable.

CHAPTER 23

Ukraine and the Hot September

Ukraine continued to stir the simmering cauldron of Russian fear. Just as Boris Yeltsin and Viktor Rutskoy were about to come to blows over who would lead Russia—a confrontation that the General Staff believed might tempt the United States to strike—Ukraine grasped for nuclear weapons.

"Moscow-Kiev Clash. This Seems to Be Washington's Persistently Pursued Aim," proclaimed the title of an article by Russian journalist Manki Ponomarev in the official Defense Ministry newspaper, *Krasnaya zvezda*, on August 20, 1993. "Certain forces in the United States would not be averse to aggravating the problem [of a nuclear-armed Ukraine] instead of settling it, so that, by exacerbating it, they could fragment the independent states that have emerged from the ruins of the U.S.S.R., drive a wedge between them, and pit them against each other. This would apply primarily to the most powerful and important among them—Russia and Ukraine."

The goal of the United States, according to Ponomarev, was to provoke a Russian-Ukrainian nuclear war by encouraging Ukrainian nuclearization with one voice while saying to Moscow with another, in Ponomarev's ventriloquism of Washington: "Look, perfidious Kiev does not want to part with its nuclear arms. It has an ulterior motive. Is it not time to switch from warning statements to preventive actions using force directly?"

It did not occur to Manki Ponomarev that Russian words and deeds, and not least Moscow's political instability, gave Ukraine ample cause to go nuclear. Ukraine certainly noticed public drafts of Russia's new military doctrine that offered a pretext for reoccupying Ukraine and other former Soviet republics and that emphasized the importance of a nuclear first strike. Russia's message was not lost even on the Estonian parliament, which was prompted to hold one of its sessions in a nuclear bomb shelter. Estonian prime minister Mart Larr said that he "would not take refuge in such shelters in the event of a bombing raid, since they were constructed during the years of Soviet power, and Russia knows both their location and the communications system." An Estonian press report carried the headline "Every Estonian Must Know Where [the] Missile Will Come From." The reference was to Russia.

Ukrainian aspirations to become a nuclear-weapons state aggravated the multiplying anxieties of the Russian General Staff, which was already in a panic that military weakness and internal instability might invite foreign aggression. Most Russian military officers agreed with Colonel Viktor Alksnis, an extremist on most issues, that Ukraine's self-interest in preserving its national sovereignty made Kiev's gambit to keep the nuclear missiles on its territory inevitable: "The fate of Ukrainian sovereignty depends upon its access to the nuclear button. If the Ukraine has this access, the West will have to recognize the Ukraine."

In the summer of 1993, as President Yeltsin and Vice President Rutskoy separately toured various military commands, soliciting support from the generals for their coming showdown with each other, Ukraine made its move. On July 2, 1993, the Ukrainian parliament declared all nuclear weapons on its territory to be the property of the Ukrainian government. At the same time, the Ukrainian Ministry of Defense, in violation of agreements with Russia and the United States, took possession of nuclear-weapon storage sites on its territory and subordinated the sites and the units guarding these sites to the Ukrainian 43rd Army.

On August 4, the Russian Ministry of Foreign Affairs responded with an official statement in bellicose language that, by the standards of normal diplomatic discourse, amounted to a warning of war: "This policy by Kiev is causing concern in the world and is leading to very serious consequences for international stability and security, and the whole system of international relations. In declaring herself in possession of nuclear arms, Ukraine is moving toward breaching the international obligations which she had accepted regarding her non-nuclear status, at the same time throwing down a challenge to international law and order, and sowing nihilism in international relations."

In an August 6, 1993, article, Pavel Felgengauer, a Russian journalist well connected to the General Staff, wrote that according to Russian missile experts, the ICBMs based in Ukraine could be retargeted to strike Russia. One of these ICBMs, the SS-24, numbered "46 total" based in Ukraine, "each having up to 10 warheads with a capacity of up to 550 kilotons." The SS-24s alone carried 240 warheads, enough to destroy every major city in Russia. "If necessary," Felgengauer's Russian military sources told him, the ICBMs in Ukraine could "quite accurately hit Paris, London, Hamburg, or Copenhagen, and, after possible retargeting, would be able to hit Moscow or St. Petersburg."

A combination of pressure and incentives from Russia and the United States persuaded Ukrainian president Leonid Kravchuk to reverse his course away from nuclear weapons. Russian imposition of a natural gas embargo, which crippled the Ukrainian economy, combined with U.S. offers of generous financial aid and security guarantees to Ukraine, induced President Kravchuk on September 3, 1993, to agree in principle to return all nuclear weapons, and the Black Sea Fleet, to Russia. Ukraine would keep the missiles, bombers, and fuel for these systems located on its territory, but surrender all nuclear warheads to Russia. One month later, the October coup attempt in Moscow shook the agreement to pieces.

October 1993 saw Russians slaughtering each other in the streets of Moscow on behalf of Rutskoy and Yeltsin. Fear of Russia and an outcry from the Ukrainian parliament that giving up nuclear weapons betrayed Ukraine's interests, moved "the Crafty Fox," as President Kravchuk was known in both capitals, to reverse himself again. He indicated that Ukraine would retain the most modern and destructive nuclear weapons on its territory, the SS-24s.

His slamming on the brakes to stop nuclear disarmament was motivated in part by the new Russian military doctrine, published in draft form in May 1992 and discussed in the international press. One provision of the doctrine asserted a right to launch a nuclear first strike against any nation that did not sign the nuclear Non-Proliferation Treaty and give up nuclear weapons—a barely disguised threat against Ukraine. Other provisions legitimated a Russian initiation of offensive military operations and asserted Russia's right to defend from oppression ethnic Russians living abroad. This last proviso was widely interpreted as a flimsy pretext for future Russian invasion of its neighbors and reestablishment of the Soviet empire.

When the new Russian military doctrine was made official in November 1993, with the offending provisions intact, President Kravchuk spoke against it: "There has never been a precedent set in the world whereby a state would defend people of any nationality if they are citizens of another state. . . . Ukraine will defend Russians living in Ukraine."

Kazakh president Nursultan Nazarbayev saw shades of Nazi Germany's rationale for invading Czechoslovakia in the new Russian military doctrine: "When they talk about protecting people who are not citizens of Russia but of Kazakhstan, I recall the times of Hitler, who started with 'protecting' the Sudeten Germans."

Russian foreign minister Andrey Kozyrev seemed to verify the worst fears of Ukraine and Russia's other neighbors when, in the same month that Russia's new military doctrine was published, he announced that the former Soviet republics were a "zone of interest and special responsibility" for Russia. Foreign Minister Kozyrev came close to declaring Ukraine to be Russian property when he remarked, "We would not like NATO to protect Ukraine from Russia. We ourselves can defend Ukraine from anyone."

President Bill Clinton's assessment of the Russian-Ukrainian situation and of the nuclear threat to the United States was upbeat, giving the impression that these problems were vanishing fast or were already gone. Following the Vancouver summit with President Yeltsin in April 1993, President Clinton announced "a new security partnership with Russia and the other states" that would "accelerate the deactivation of nuclear weapon systems." In later remarks, President Clinton continued the theme that the United States and Russia had forged a "partnership in working to reduce the threat of nuclear weapons."

If popular opinion is any guide to reality, Russian and Ukrainian views about the status of the nuclear threat were ominous, and they contrasted sharply with Western euphoria. In response to a poll question—"Has the collapse of the Soviet Union increased the probability of an accidental or deliberate nuclear strike?"—38 percent of those questioned in Russia and 24 percent in Ukraine thought the risk of a nuclear strike had increased; only 4 percent of Russian and 5 percent of Ukrainian respondents thought the nuclear threat had decreased; 24 percent of Russian and Ukrainian respondents thought the threat remained unchanged; the rest were undecided. A false air raid warning that panicked the people of Kiev in late October underscored Ukrainian jumpiness over their long argument with Russia.

Events in Moscow in September and October 1993 gave Ukraine—and the rest of the world—good reason to be nervous. In those months, Russian hard-liners, led by General Aleksandr Rutskoy, Yeltsin's vice president, attempted to overthrow the president.

Rutskoy had been elected vice president on Yeltsin's politically progressive platform. But the general and his reactionary allies in the Russian parliament had their own agenda: termination of Boris Yeltsin's pro-Western policies, and restoration of the USSR.

Yeltsin recognized the threat to Russian democracy posed by the Supreme Soviet and Congress of People's Deputies, Russia's parliamentary bodies, early on. On December 9, 1992, the parliament rejected Yeltsin's choice for prime minister, Yegor Gaidar. Gaidar was Yeltsin's chief engineer for transforming Russia's socialist economy into a capitalist free market, and had served as acting Prime Minister until parliament refused to confirm him. He was accurately "condemned" by his communist enemies as a "neoclassical liberal." Gaidar's defeat figuratively severed Yeltsin's right arm, provoking him to denounce the parliament as a "serious danger," whose goal was to "make short work of the government, the president, the reforms, and democracy" and to restore "the totalitarian Soviet Communist system, cursed by our own people and rejected by the whole world." The parliament "blushed" from "vulgar abuse [and] the dirt the congress is filled with, due to the sick ambitions of failed politicians," rare color even for the earthy President Yeltsin. Over the next two days, December 10 and 11, 1992, pro-Yeltsin and pro-Soviet demonstrators clashed in the streets.

In the months leading up to the October 1993 coup attempt, Vice President Rutskoy broke with Yeltsin and played the "white knight" to a discontented Russian public. The people suffered grievously under the still unreformed economy, and they were frightened and wounded by the sudden collapse of the USSR. Communists and nationalists in the Russian parliament succeeded in blocking President Yeltsin's legislative efforts to liberate Russia's economy and society from socialist calcification. The long political stalemate in parliament threatened to derail the reform movement, topple Yeltsin's government, and kill any hope of building a free society in Russia.

During the summer, in anticipation of a confrontation with the parliament, President Yeltsin alluded several times to a coming showdown, predicting a "hot September."

Aware that Russia's deep political divisions could soon produce a civil war, the General Staff moved to protect its control over vital military installations in the Moscow area, beginning in December 1992. On December 14, according to the Russian press, "more than 100 generals gathered in the Strategic Missile Forces Staff, a highly classified facility of the Russian Ministry of Defense," to review "the hasty formation of *Spetsnaz* [special-purpose] subunits around Moscow." Spetsnaz were GRU commandos, trained, in the words of the press report, "to carry out raids, terrorist acts, operational reconnaissance, and other actions in an enemy's rear area. The units are characterized by a high level of fighting spirit, with proficiency and discipline exemplary." In 1979, during the Afghan war, Spetsnaz had conducted a lightning raid against the capital in Kabul, toppling the Afghan government and contributing significantly to the initial success of the Soviet invasion. In the event the NATO-Soviet confrontation turned hot during the Cold War, Spetsnaz units would, according to a U.S. Defense Department study, "conduct reconnaissance and sabotage on a wide assortment of military and political targets," including "ship and submarine bases, airfields, command and intelligence centers, communications facilities, ports, harbors, radar sites, and—of prime importance—nuclear weapon facilities."

Spetsnaz were hastily assigned a new mission in the winter of 1992. Instead of conducting deep penetrating offensive operations against foreign enemies, the elite units were assigned guard duty on key Moscow military facilities. The mission was not to thwart a coup but to protect the General Staff's capability—no matter what political upheaval might happen in Moscow—to prosecute a nuclear war. The ranking officer at the December 14, 1992, meeting assigning Spetsnaz to Moscow was General Igor Sergeyev, commander in chief of the Strategic Rocket Forces. Spetsnaz units were allocated to strategic facilities that would detect and respond to a nuclear surprise attack.

According to one Russian correspondent, "sources close to the General Staff" told him that Spetsnaz units were needed "on an urgent basis" to protect "Moscow area military installations. These installations as a rule belong to subunits of the Strategic Missile Forces, Antiballistic Missile Defense, and Missile Attack Early Warning System and are especially well protected." The organs of the civilian government, Boris Yeltsin's Kremlin, the parliament building, the mayor's building, and civilian television stations were not accorded Spetsnaz protection.

Under an operation called HARD SIGN, Spetsnaz moved into Moscow clandestinely. Up to two Spetsnaz divisions may have discreetly relocated to the Moscow area by the time of the October 1993 coup. "The personnel are currently undergoing a course in survival under extraordinary conditions, intensive instruction in hand-to-hand combat, and . . . patriotic indoctrination," according to the December 1992 press leak. "It is assumed that the training will be completed by summer."

In September 1993, President Boris Yeltsin was still locked in a losing struggle with the hard-line parliament and with Vice President Rutskoy to advance free market reforms. Yeltsin took desperate, and probably illegal, steps to break their stranglehold. On September 1, 1993, he dismissed General Rutskoy from the vice presidency. Rutskoy and First Deputy Prime Minister Vladimir Shumeiko, a crooked Yeltsin loyalist who was also dismissed to make Rutskoy's firing look nonpolitical, were charged with corruption—Rutskoy allegedly had an illegal Swiss bank account, and Shumeiko was accused of misappropriating government funds for baby food. "For simple hygiene reasons, I should not be bracketed together with Shumeiko in a single decree," Rutskoy said scathingly.

President Yeltsin stripped Rutskoy of his security guards and official posts but could not force the general to step down. Legally, General Rutskoy remained Yeltsin's successor in the event of presidential impeachment—which the parliament had already proposed—or in the event of Yeltsin's death, which was always a possibility.

On September 17, Yeltsin announced he was bringing back Yegor Gaidar, the free-market economist who had been forced out as Yeltsin's prime minister by the parliament the previous December. Then, four days later, on September 21, Yeltsin announced on national television that he was dismissing parliament because it no longer represented the will of the Russian people. Defiant, the Supreme Soviet immediately voted to impeach Yeltsin. Led by Ruslan Khasbulatov, Supreme Soviet chairman, the parliament decreed that General Aleksandr Rutskoy was Russia's new president.

Rutskoy mobilized several hundred fanatical followers to fortify the parliament building against attack and called on the Russian people and the armed forces to overthrow President Yeltsin for violating the constitution. He named General Vladislav Achalov the new minister of defense, "firing" Pavel Grachev. Yeltsin appointees were replaced with General Rutskoy's own men in the other "power ministries." Viktor Barranikov was named by parliament as security minister, and Andrey Dunaev, interior minister.

Unlike the U.S. secretary of the interior, who manages national parks and the like, Russia's ministers of security and interior command 180,000 soldiers equipped with armored vehicles and helicopters—an army known as the MVD. The MVD troops' purpose was not to combat foreign enemies but to crush internal dangers to the Russian state arising from riots, labor unrest, or popular revolution. Whoever controlled the MVD troops would in effect control the national police force.

Ruslan Khasbulatov, the Supreme Soviet chairman, called for nationwide strikes to force President Yeltsin to step down. A mob of nationalist and communist hard-liners swarmed to the Supreme Soviet building, still known as the "White House," where Boris Yeltsin had made his stand for Russian democracy in August 1991. They began building barricades.

The September 1993 confrontation was becoming an eerie mirror image of August 1991. On September 21, 1993, President Boris Yeltsin sat in the Kremlin, where the forces of totalitarianism in August 1991 had plotted the abortion of Russian democracy. Now those forces occupied Yeltsin's "White House" and were throwing up barricades around the birthplace of Russian democracy, as if by mimicking Yeltsin's moves they could reverse the verdict of August 1991 and bring back Soviet Russia.

In fact, the old Russia still lived in the "power ministries." At first, Defense Minister Pavel Grachev and his colleague, Viktor Yerin, interior minister, asserted that they would remain neutral in the contest. In effect, they refused to defend President Yeltsin's government, a stance they deemed virtuously apolitical. "Neutrality" of the army and of the internal security troops of the MVD would go far toward ensuring victory for Yeltsin's enemies.

Amid all this, on September 21, the same day President Yeltsin and the Supreme Soviet tried to abolish each other, the Russian Navy accused U.S. submarines of violating territorial waters and of engaging in suspiciously aggressive levels of activity around Russia.

General Rutskoy's firing of Yeltsin's ministers, Grachev and Yerin, rapidly persuaded them that neutrality was not in the "national interest." On September 22, Defense Minister Grachev and Interior Minister Yerin publicly sided with President Yeltsin, spurning the authority of the Supreme Soviet.

Affirming his support for President Yeltsin, Pavel Grachev said that the military leadership "has unanimously declared its obedience to the minister of defense and Boris Yeltsin, the country's president." Denouncing the Supreme Soviet's appointment of a new defense minister as "illegal," Grachev nonetheless continued to imply that the military would not actively oppose the coup, as its real business was guarding against foreign threats. Grachev and Yerin's new loyalty to President Yeltsin was no doubt strengthened by a parliamentary resolution passed on September 22: obstruction of parliament by President Yeltsin and his followers was decreed a crime, punishable by death. Defense Minister Grachev and Interior Minister Yerin had already been "fired" for disobeying the Supreme Soviet. If President Yeltsin lost his struggle, they faced execution.

Looming civil war and the prospect of parliament-approved assassination would have been enough to occupy any Western political or military leaders. However, another threat, this one imaginary, loomed more ominously than the real ones. On September 22, scarcely twenty-four hours after the beginning of the crisis, and on the same day they were marked for death,

President Boris Yeltsin and Defense Minister Pavel Grachev declared to the world press through the defense ministry that "the nuclear chain of command remains as it was before yesterday's events. The nuclear button is in the hands of the president and the defense minister. There is only one president and one defense minister and they are Yeltsin and Grachev."

Why such a proclamation? To reassure the West that hard-line zealots had not captured Russia's nuclear arsenal? To reassure the Russian public that the Yeltsin government was still "in charge"—by brandishing nuclear weapons, the ultimate symbol of power? These motives probably contributed to the nuclear declaration and the strategic-forces activities that followed, but they are not a sufficient explanation. Over the next eleven days of crisis, Defense Minister Grachev and the Russian military spent most of their time and energy preparing for a nuclear war.

Two weeks before the struggle between President Yeltsin and General Rutskoy turned into a full-blown crisis, it was becoming obvious that Russia would face another coup attempt and possible civil war, and the General Staff began looking for signs of a U.S. nuclear surprise attack. Beginning on September 7, the Russian military undertook the highly unusual precaution of launching, in rapid succession, several spy satellites designed to monitor enemy communications and strategic missile, bomber, and naval forces. There was nothing routine about these satellite launches, which would have been an extraordinary feat when the USSR was still intact and the Baikonur Cosmodrome maintained in perfect condition. In September 1993, the Baikonur space center was in the middle of a foreign country, Kazakhstan, which begrudgingly tolerated Russia's continued use of the facility. Baikonur existed in a state of semi-siege due to its odd political status, which aggravated the ravages of economic scarcity. According to Russian press accounts, living conditions had so deteriorated that a recent mutiny at the Cosmodrome had burned down "three barracks, three staff buildings, a club, a hospital, and a library." Twenty-one thousand people fled Leninsk, the town supporting the launch site. The facility was short of trained manpower, requiring an additional 2,500 military officers. Defensive perimeters were drawn to protect the launch pads and key facilities, and the new spacecraft blasted off from pads surrounded by a "Wellington's square" of armed guards.

The surge of spy satellite launchings was a clear sign that the General Staff feared that the West might move militarily to exploit Russia's internal crisis. Previously top secret U.S. National Intelligence Estimates from the early 1980s, now declassified, regarded the rapid launch of reconnaissance satellites as an indicator of preparation for a possible nuclear conflict. However, some in the West now suggested that the satellites were intended to help the Russian military monitor events inside Russia and inside Russia's own navy, presumably for signs of mutiny, during the coup attempt.

Shortly after the satellite launchings, a highly respected U.S. aerospace journal, *Aviation Week & Space Technology*, pronounced that the Russian spy satellites were intended to "improve the military's ability to eavesdrop on communications in Russia and the Commonwealth of Independent States, photograph intelligence targets, and monitor naval operations [by the Russian Navy] around Russia's borders." The *Aviation Week* article did cite the opinion of Geoffrey Perry of the Kettering space observer group, who noted the Russian satellite launches "were surprising given the tight Russian budgets and lack of Russian Navy assets at sea. The launch of a new ocean surveillance satellite . . . is even more unexpected for similar reasons."

The article did not attempt to explain why Russia would want to take high-resolution satellite photographs of its own territory when it had enough ground-based means and manpower in the military and intelligence services to observe events everywhere in Russia. The Russian security services routinely monitor Russian civil and military communications. The additional satellites were superfluous for domestic purposes in September 1993.

The satellites launched during the attempted coup added little or nothing to the military's ability to monitor internal events, but they did significantly increase the ability to observe potential foreign military threats, as the satellites were expressly designed to do.

On September 7, 1993, six days after President Yeltsin sacked Vice President Rutskoy and started the leadership crisis, Baikonur Cosmodrome launched KOSMOS-2262. According to *Aviation Week & Space Technology*, KOSMOS-2262 was the military's "most advanced high-resolution imaging spacecraft." KOSMOS-2262 was designed to observe the readiness of foreign nuclear and military forces by photographing missile silos and command posts, bomber bases for signs of aircraft on strip alert or being uploaded with cruise missiles, and submarine ports to see if additional missile boats had put to sea. KOSMOS-2263, Russia's most advanced satellite for eavesdropping on radio transmissions, and used for spying on foreign military communications, followed on September 16. One day later, September 17, Russia lofted KOSMOS-2264, its most advanced ocean surveillance satellite, normally used for following the activities of foreign navies and submarines. Such satellites try to ascertain the locations and alert status of U.S. aircraft carriers and ballistic missile submarines; they also listen for U.S. "emergency action messages" ordering alerts or actual aircraft and missile strikes.

A fourth satellite was scheduled for launch on September 23, two days after the Supreme Soviet declared General Rutskoy president and one day after the defense ministry reminded everybody that President Yeltsin and Defense Minister Grachev still commanded Russia's nuclear arsenal. Owing to technical problems, the satellite was rescheduled for launch in early October. This last, according to Russian press reports, was probably a military communications spacecraft intended to enhance the responsiveness and readiness of Russian military forces, including strategic nuclear forces.

The unusual rapidity of the satellite launches and their missions—to provide detailed photography of foreign military bases and forces, collect foreign military signals intelligence, monitor foreign naval operations, and enhance Russian military communications—speaks volumes about General Staff threat perceptions during the 1993 coup attempt.

TSENTER, meaning "center," also spoke louder than words, proclaiming the Russian military's concern that the leadership crisis might invite an enemy surprise attack. On the second day of the coup attempt, September 22, the same day the Supreme Soviet threatened him with the death penalty, Defense Minister Pavel Grachev told journalists that a military exercise of the strategic nuclear forces, code-named TSENTER, had commenced. This was odd news. The Russian military should have had better things to do during a coup attempt, and potential civil war, than play nuclear war games—if TSENTER *was* a game. Odd, too, was the announcement of TSENTER, broadcast worldwide by Moscow Radio—in English. Ordinarily, the Russian military does not advertise major exercises or other training events. It tries to keep them secret.

The TSENTER-93 exercise, according to the Russian defense ministry, practiced "control of strategic nuclear forces" and "repulsion of an enemy aerospace attack." In other words, the supposed theme of TSENTER-93 was practicing intercontinental and submarine missile launches to defeat enemy missile, cruise missile, and aviation strikes. "Aerospace attack" in Russian military doctrine refers to strikes by nuclear or high-tech conventional forces, or a combination of both. "Repulsion" of, or "repelling," such an attack, in Russian military doctrine, is accomplished by both offensive and defensive means. It is, therefore, a common euphemism for a Russian preemptive strike.

TSENTER-93 almost certainly provided clandestine cover for raising the combat readiness of Russia's strategic forces, so as not to alarm or provoke the West while preparing secretly to preempt or retaliate against a possible Western attack. Using an exercise to hide real mobilization and preparation for military operations is commonplace in Russian and Soviet military writings.

Another suspicious event suggestive of a wartime mindset among Russia's military leaders during the 1993 coup attempt was Grachev's announcement, on September 22, that extraordinary measures would be taken to "step up the protection of all facilities, above all arms and ammunition depots; and . . . pay special attention to guarding nuclear weapons sites." Grachev told the press, "Special attention was being paid to guarding and transporting nuclear weapons." This implied disturbing possibilities, even if it was aimed only at a domestic threat. However, such precautions were also standard operating procedure under Increased Combat Readiness, when raising the alert status of forces in preparation for war. "Intensification of security at military posts, bases, and objectives" is listed by the General Staff's Voroshilov textbook as among "the principal measures for raising the status of troops to the level of Increased Combat Readiness." Other principal aspects of Increased Combat Readiness included "intensification of reconnaissance activities," "taking necessary measures for protection against weapons of mass destruction," "achieving a higher level of technical preparation of weapons," "undertaking special measures concerning rocket troops," and "reconfirming combat alert plans."

Grachev's ordering of heightened security at nuclear depots could be explained as a prudent precaution to prevent General Rutskoy's followers from seizing nuclear weapons, but Rutskoy's forces, barricaded in the "White House" and surrounded by the MVD troops, were nowhere near any nuclear-weapon storage casernes. Still, if the Army were to split between General Rutskoy and President Yeltsin, Rutskoy's forces would suddenly be everywhere.

Were Defense Minister Grachev's military precautions intended primarily to support President Yeltsin, or to guard against a U.S. nuclear surprise attack? The "support Yeltsin" hypothesis is contradicted by Grachev's orders on September 22 to the Russian armed forces: "Double-check all instructions with regard to the chain of command and only obey instructions issued by himself [Grachev] or by the Chief of the General Staff." The order excludes by omission any requirement to obey orders from President Yeltsin, the commander in chief, a stunning "mistake" at a time when the president's authority over the military had been directly challenged just the previous day.

Defense Minister Grachev's order did not neglect to remind troops to obey the Chief of the General Staff, General Mikhail Kolesnikov, a hardline hawk and personal enemy of Grachev. What Grachev and Kolesnikov had in common was that they were both military officers and both held "nuclear briefcases." Grachev, while supporting President Yeltsin politically against the reactionary Rutskoy, may have had less confidence in Yeltsin's military instincts if faced with an impending or incoming U.S. nuclear strike. Kolesnikov, on the other hand, could be counted on "to do the right thing."

The alert of General Lebed's 14th Army is hard to explain in any other way except as a preparation for possible foreign attack. According to a September 23 press report, "General Aleksandr Lebed, the commander of the 14th CIS Army, has ordered the start of Operation Morning Dew, which consists of placing on alert the troops stationed in the Dneister region."

The 14th Army, stationed in Moldova, is far from Moscow—hundreds of kilometers distant—and geographically separate from Russia, trapped between Romania and Ukraine. Lebed's army was a heavily armed enclave of Russian troops, a bristling shell left behind in Eastern Europe by the receding tide of the Russian Army. Lebed's forces could offer neither help or hindrance in a power struggle or civil war within Russia; however, the 14th Army was, along with Kaliningrad, Russia's westernmost outpost in Eastern Europe, and would be part of Russia's first line of defense against NATO.

On September 28, the Russian press reported that nuclear submarines and ships of the Pacific Fleet based on the Kamchatka Peninsula had gone on alert, probably to Increased Combat Readiness. The alert was ascribed to "a planned training action, since flotilla commanders can raise their alert status without orders from Moscow." However, training merely simulates the heightened combat readiness of a real alert. It does not in fact raise the alert status, as had been reported of Kamchatka, unless the "training" is merely a guise to conceal a real nuclear alert. Nor is it likely that local commanders on Kamchatka would independently conduct training or "raise their alert status without orders from Moscow" while TSENTER was still tasking forces nationwide. Some activity was happening in the fleet sufficiently disturbing to provoke top regional political authorities to tell the Russian press, "the oblast's inner Soviet denies any part in it."

Most likely, the two flotillas on Kamchatka had gone on alert, probably moving to Increased Combat Readiness, along with Russian strategic forces nationwide, under the pretext of Defense Minister Grachev's phony exercise, TSENTER.

The alert condition described at Kamchatka would have entailed getting Russian submarines in port ready to fire their nuclear missiles from pierside. Special communications are available at Russian submarine docks connecting them directly to the General Staff, so that vulnerable submarine missiles in port can be launched from Moscow on short notice, a unique capability not shared by missile submarines of the United States, Britain, France, or China. Russian sub-launched ballistic missiles are designed with sufficient range to strike the United States while anchored at Russian docks, while U.S. submarines cannot perform a pierside launch because they lack the necessary dockside communications, and because their missiles do not have sufficient range to reach Russia from U.S. ports.

Moscow went to great trouble and expense to give its submarines a pierside launch capability, for one reason: to defeat an enemy "bolt from the blue" surprise attack. "Defeating" such an attack entails launching the missiles before the boats are struck, either while enemy missiles are en route—or preemptively.

CHAPTER 24

Live, on *Larry King*

While Russia was frantically launching advanced reconnaissance satellites, reminding the world that only Yeltsin and Grachev possessed the "nuclear button," and alerting the 14th Army and strategic nuclear forces in the midst of a coup—in Washington there was no fear. The only concern in Washington was that Moscow might lose control of its nuclear weapons to General Rutskoy or his mutinous followers.

On *Larry King Live*, Foreign Minister Andrey Kozyrev reassured Americans that they had nothing to fear, because Moscow remained in control of its nuclear missiles:

KING: . . . Since your country has nuclear weaponry and it is in a position now of some instability, what would you say to the people of the United States? Should they be very worried?

KOZYREV: Well, I think the nuclear weapons are under some control, and this is another argument in my mind, at least, for Yeltsin to stay. . . . So if and when the presidential election takes place, there is no possibility of shaking military command, because he is commander-in-chief in the so-called vatem or whatever. The control of nuclear weapons is in his hands.

Foreign Minister Kozyrev's remarks betrayed ignorance of his own nation's nuclear command and control system. There is no institution or device called the "vatem." Kozyrev confused Yeltsin's legal role as commander in chief with actual operational control of the nuclear forces, which Yeltsin did not possess. The latter error may have been deliberate, of course. Kozyrev knew that Americans liked President Yeltsin and would find it comforting to think he controlled Russia's hundreds of missiles and thousands of warheads.

At his confirmation hearing on September 22 to become President Clinton's new chairman of the Joint Chiefs of Staff, General John Shalikashvili told the Senate Armed Services Committee that there was no nuclear danger as long as Russia's nuclear weapons remained "under solid central control": "I believe they [the nuclear weapons] are under control. . . . In the past we have been gratified to find out that those weapons had remained under solid central control, and I have no indication that is not the case at this moment." Shalikashvili may have been unaware that the Russian version of "central control" gave charge of the nuclear arsenal to the General Staff, the alma mater of dangerous reactionaries like Rutskoy and Achalov.

General Shalikashvili went on to testify that grave nuclear risk would arise if central control were lost: "I cannot think of a greater nightmare scenario than if there were some breakdown of law and order and control of those weapons in a country like Russia. . . . The danger really is if lower level commanders, subordinate commanders, were to choose sides. That probably would be the sort of unraveling effect that ought to give us all great concern."

Apparently, the future Joint Chiefs chairman could not imagine a still greater nightmare. What if the Russian General Staff, deeply suspicious of the United States and with a long record of overreacting during crisis situations, miscalculated again and used its central control to launch a massive, coordinated preemptive nuclear strike against the United States?

Even as General Shalikashvili testified before Congress, Defense Minister Grachev announced the commencement of TSENTER, and Russia's strategic nuclear forces, under the "solid control" of the General Staff, quietly prepared for global nuclear war.

Back in the Russian "White House," General Rutskoy and his parliamentary rebels were laboring—without benefit of electricity or water—to take over the country.

Fortunately for President Yeltsin, the coup plotters had not plotted well. Rutskoy was naively counting on parliament's defiant refusal to adjourn, and its entrenchment at the "White House," to ignite a spontaneous military and popular revolt against Yeltsin. During the first few days, General Vladislav Achalov, Rutskoy's rabidly reactionary "defense minister," feverishly tried to contact various military commands and cohorts and order them to mutiny against the Yeltsin government.

Defense Minister Grachev knew Achalov, his colleague-turned-adversary, and guessed his dangerous game plan. "The extremist-minded Vladislav Achalov, appointed as minister of defense by the dissolved parliament," Grachev said on September 22, "will take up arms without a second thought, something he has demonstrated on several occasions during the events in the Baltic states, Georgia, and in August 1991 where, with his help, blood was spilled. . . . This would not be a series of local conflicts," Defense Minister Grachev warned, "but the start of a real civil war."

General Achalov did not have any significant success in inciting an armed military rebellion. Although there was little fondness for Boris Yeltsin in the Russian armed forces, few military officers were willing to risk life and limb for the parliament's "new government," which controlled nothing outside the narrow confines of its barricades. Besides, General Achalov's ability to communicate with the military was severely limited by the primitive phone system at the "White House." Its telephones were tied into Russia's underdeveloped civilian network, and they were still based on switchboards; they were not part of the military's regular high-tech communications. In desperation, telegrams were sent to all military district and fleet commands, urging them to rescue Rutskoy's government. When the police turned off the power and the water, General Achalov couldn't even take a shower, let alone order Russia's legions to rise.

On September 26, cut off from the outside world, Rutskoy promised his small army now manning the barricades that if Yeltsin's troops tried storming the "White House," he would "fight to the death."

President Yeltsin was also getting desperate. For about two weeks, the future of Russia hung precariously in the balance while the military and interior ministry did little or nothing to crush the coup. The longer the crisis lasted, the greater the chance that the General Staff or subordinate military commands might actively support Rutskoy.

Although Generals Rutskoy and Achalov apparently did not know about it, because of their poor communications, General Vladimir Dudnik, one of the few senior officers who ardently supported Yeltsin, later "intimated there was some substance to the rumors that the staffs of several military districts [the Leningrad, Volga, Ural, and Siberian districts], as well as the Pacific Fleet, supported the parliamentary forces." Pacific Fleet commander Admiral Georgiy Gurinov was a blatant Rutskoy loyalist. During the summer, when Yeltsin and Rutskoy were openly heading for a showdown, just weeks prior to the coup, Admiral Gurinov invited the rebellious vice president to visit his command, where together they toured military units in the Far East.

Support of the "White House" during the coup by the Pacific Fleet and military districts must have been passive or political, but not military—otherwise, from Leningrad to the Far East, Russia would have exploded into civil war.

Members of the General Staff, including the chief of the General Staff, Mikhail Kolesnikov, and the commander in chief of the Air Force, Petr Deneiken, found ways to communicate secretly with the besieged "White House" behind President Yeltsin's back. General Dudnik maintains that, as in August 1991, the General Staff and defense ministry played both sides of the street, participating in planning sessions to support Yeltsin while informing and advising General Rutskoy.

For the first week of the crisis, "White House" occupants probably outnumbered the police that were intended to contain them. Not until September 28, eight days into the coup attempt, did MVD troops from the Ministry of Interior surround the "White House" with armored vehicles and barbed wire, demanding that the occupants surrender their arms within twenty-four hours. This tardy show of force undermined its own support of Yeltsin. Parliament was asked to give up its guns not because of rebellion against the legitimate government, but because the armed Rutskoyites posed a threat to the neighborhood.

The next day, September 29, when the deadline passed and the "White House" still refused to disarm, the MVD pushed its deadline for surrender forward to October 4. Siberian political leaders on September 29 threatened to secede from Russia if President Yeltsin did not rescind his decree dissolving parliament. The military's reluctance to act decisively on behalf of President Yeltsin underscored the weakness of his hold on power.

On September 30, more MVD armored vehicles arrived at the "White House," and General Rutskoy knew he was running out of time. Spontaneous combustion began on Saturday, October 2, as anti-Yeltsin demonstrators blocked traffic around Moscow in an attempt to disrupt the normal life of the city. Rutskoy demanded access to television as a condition of negotiations, but he was prudently refused.

The general decided to strike. He needed communications to reach the people, to reach the military, to fan the rising flames of rebellion. He called on his supporters outside the "White House" barricades to take up arms against Yeltsin.

As in any "banana republic" coup, one of General Rutskoy's main objectives was to seize the television station. Dominating Moscow's airwaves by taking the Ostankino television facility would convey the illusion that a new government had been installed and was in control, a fiction that would become fact if the masses, or the military, could be rallied behind Rutskoy. The military mattered more. Other facilities targeted for takeover included key military headquarters in downtown Moscow. As in ancient Rome, all roads led to Moscow, except that in the twentieth century, the "roads" were electronic communications on civilian and military frequencies. Seizures of military command and control nodes in Moscow would give General Rutskoy access to the official communications used to direct the Russian armed forces, including the strategic nuclear forces. The military equivalent of Ostankino television station was in a bunker under the defense ministry.

On Sunday, October 3, at 2:00 P.M., thousands of General Aleksandr Rutskoy's loyalists, many of them well-armed veteran soldiers, gathered at October Square under the giant statue of Lenin. Riot police attempted to disperse the growing mob, but they were routed, savagely beaten, and pursued through the streets, pelted with bottles and bricks.

Fifteen thousand Rutskoy loyalists—an army of veterans, communists, neo-Nazis, and thugs, waving red banners and armed with assault rifles, grenade launchers, crowbars, and bare fists—surged toward the "White House." At 2:20 P.M. they rolled over another police line trying to block their drive. At 3:00 P.M. they punched through police trying to hold Krimsky Bridge, the last defensive line protecting the MVD cordon around the

"White House." Between 3:30 and 4:00 P.M., through volleys of gunfire, the mob stormed the last police barricade. Smashing water-cannon trucks and overturning riot-control vehicles, they threw themselves across the barbed wire and overwhelmed the MVD troops.

General Rutskoy appeared before his conquering horde and gave it marching orders to seize key communications and government centers. "Driven by what appeared to be an equal mix of spontaneous hooliganism and planned military action," as analyst Stephen Foye later put, it, "the anti-Yeltsin forces burst forth from the parliamentary center to do Rutskoy's bidding."

Led by General Albert Makashov, former commander of the Volga-Ural Military District and a fierce nationalist, the rioting legion seized the mayor's building from police in less than five minutes. General Makashov appeared on the mayor's balcony above the crowd and directed it to form for an assault on the heavily guarded Ostankino television station, some distance away. Thousands of Rutskoyists had gathered outside the Ostankino facility by 6:00 P.M. At 6:30 P.M. President Yeltsin reluctantly declared the obvious, that a state of emergency existed in the city—a further admission of his helplessness.

General Makashov and General Viktor Barranikov led the assault on the Ostankino television station, beginning about 7:30 P.M. Around 8:00 P.M., the Rutskoyists rammed a truck through the building's barricaded doors and blasted clear the lobby with grenades. It was a fierce battle, which left over sixty dead and four hundred wounded.

"This is the free territory of the U.S.S.R.!" bellowed a triumphant General Makashov above the din of gunfire and explosions.

The assault on Ostankino knocked Moscow's three television stations off the air, but before the Rutskoyists could complete their conquest of the building and begin broadcasting rebellion, the MVD troops counterattacked with twelve armored personnel carriers.

Just when television broadcasts from Ostankino flickered out at 8:00 P.M., the deputy minister of defense—and Yeltsin loyalist—General Konstantin Kobets formed an emergency operational staff for putting down General Rutskoy's revolution. General Kobets had organized the defense of the "White House" for Yeltsin during the August 1991 coup, two years earlier. The General Staff remained uncommitted about ordering the Army to rescue the Yeltsin government until 10:00 P.M., when the battle for the streets was swinging back in Yeltsin's favor. Most published accounts claim that the MVD recaptured the Ostankino television before 11:00 P.M.; however, some Russian journalists on the scene reported that General Rutskoy's forces were still very much in control until much later.

Sometime past midnight, on the disputed streets of Moscow, Russian journalist Irina Savvateyeva found absurd the endless radio reports that "the situation is being controlled . . . [that] troops loyal to the president are entering the city." Savvateyeva could see for herself that "in actual fact, there are neither troops . . . nor practically any militia on the streets of Moscow":

Outside the government building on Staraya Ploschad there are precisely three militiamen and not a single militia military vehicle. (How can one fail to recall here Yazov, who in the past was in a matter of hours able to surround the entire Kremlin . . . with armored personnel carriers?) The taking of the Winter Palace comes involuntarily to mind. This is evidently how things were then too—they calmly marched past and calmly took it by storm. . . . If anyone was "controlling" the situation anywhere, they certainly were not forces loyal to the President.

Hearing that the ITAR-Tass news building had supposedly been liberated "from the putchists," Savvateyeva found instead "a Rutskoyite in a dappled uniform, rigged out from head to foot (only his eyes shine through the slit of a mask), [raising] his assault rifle at an approaching vehicle. He commandingly waves his free hand: 'Faster, faster!' "

Izvestiya reporter Vasiliy Kononenko found that "the Kremlin is in a state of siege. . . . All gates are blocked by trucks. They have been placed under guard by presidential regiment platoons in full combat gear, and firefighting subunits are prepared to go into action at any moment. God forbid!" President Yeltsin was prepared to make a quick getaway; Kononenko saw that "there are two presidential helicopters on Ivanovskaya Ploschad."

Reports vary on the danger posed to the defense ministry and other buildings housing strategic communications. During the fighting on October 3, according to one Western account, "in the Defense Ministry, desperate commanders were reduced to guarding their own building and its nuclear weapons codes: each entrance was secured by a deputy minister and a three-star general."

However, General Staff chief Mikhail Kolesnikov told journalist Pavel Felgengauer after the coup attempt that the defense ministry building, also known as the General Staff building, was not even attacked by what he describes as well organized "squads" of singing Rutskoyites:

FELENGAUER: Following the events of 3–4 October, General Grachev acknowledged that the nuclear command and control center was located in the General Staff building. How serious was the threat of the seizure of the General Staff building in the evening of 3 October? How reliable generally is the system of control of the nuclear forces?

GENERAL KOLESNIKOV: A very dependable system of control of the use of our entire nuclear triad has been created, exists, and is functioning successfully in the Armed Forces of the Russian Federation and the highest command and control bodies in the General Staff. . . .

> The provocation in the evening of 3 October, when militarized squads of supporters of the Supreme Soviet appeared in the area of the General Staff in Arbat Square, was, of course, extremely unpleasant. Officers coming on duty, who work on a Sunday also, were not allowed into the building, and there were threats of physical reprisals. . . .
>
> In response, we implemented measures to reinforce the security of the buildings of the central staff of the Ministry of Defense, including the administrative building, which everyone calls the General Staff building. We were prepared to act, had the armed formations engaged in any provocative actions.
>
> Fortunately, this did not happen. About 2200 [10 P.M.] these squads formed up in organized fashion and moved off in columns, singing, in the direction of the "White House."

General Kolesnikov understates the danger to the defense ministry building on the night of October 3. In fact, it was attacked. Perhaps the general was offering false reassurance to the West, as was done in the aftermath of the August 1991 coup, when the General Staff actively sought to reassure Washington that Russia's nuclear command and control system was immune to the effects of political instability. Perhaps, too, General Kolesnikov may have wanted to minimize political and legal damage to General Rutskoy's followers, who an apparently admiring Kolesnikov portrayed as far more disciplined and self-restrained than they deserved.

General Rutskoy's rampaging horde was unable to capture the defense ministry or any other military communications facility. His forces did break the siege of the "White House" and temporarily seized the Ostankino television center, but their assaults were repulsed from the CIS Joint Armed Forces Headquarters, the Ministry of Communications, and the defense ministry building.

Spetsnaz, the special forces deployed months earlier to key nuclear command and control nodes, inadvertently saved the Yeltsin regime. Months earlier, as noted, the General Staff and General Igor Sergeyev, commander in chief of the Strategic Rocket Forces, had secretly moved Spetsnaz units into the Moscow area to defend key communications nodes against seizure during a coup. The idea was to ensure that, even in the middle of a civil war, Russia would still be able to wage a global nuclear war. The military girded for a possible U.S. nuclear surprise attack during the long anticipated showdown between Yeltsin and Rutskoy. What the General Staff got, instead, was a second chance for Russian democracy.

On the night of October 3, President Yeltsin finally had enough of his defense minister's procrastination. He telephoned Pavel Grachev and ordered him to send in the army: "I am sending you the appropriate edict. I will take full responsibility."

Grachev replied simply, "Understood."

Russian press headlines later pointed an accusing finger at Grachev for his long delay, asking, "Where Was the Army? It Was Ascertaining Who the People Were Behind." The press accurately concluded that Grachev "did everything possible to prevent the Army being drawn into bloodshed" and "held the troops back to the last, as far as this was possible." Yet the same newspapers, while accusing Grachev of complicity with the coup plotters, also shared his ambivalence about intervening with the Army: "A split in the Army means civil war. . . . A peaceful outcome is needed! Do not allow bloodshed! Do not let things slide into the abyss of civil war!"

On the morning of October 4, a Monday, Grachev finally broke the stalemate. In his words: "Some thirteen hundred troops were brought into Moscow on 4 October to collaborate with MVD and internal troop subunits. These troops being subunits of the Taman and Kantemir Divisions, a separate motorized rifle regiment, and a paratroop regiment from Naro-Fominsk . . . subunits from the Tule and Ryazan Paratroop Regiments were also brought into Moscow." The defense minister admitted two days later, during a press interview on October 6, that during the Moscow action some of his troops, chosen for loyalty, had switched to General Rutskoy's side. Fortune's balance was precarious, and it might have tipped in Rutskoy's favor, had he succeeded in capturing the defense ministry or other buildings having military communications. General Grachev's armor settled matters.

At 7:30 A.M., Grachev's tanks, modern T-72s and T-80s, rumbled onto the Kalinin Bridge and began lobbing shells into the "White House." Thousands of onlookers watched history being made from across the river. Konstantin Zlobin, Ruslan Khasbulatov's press secretary, who was holed up with his boss on the sixth floor of the "White House," described the scene:

> They fired very accurately. Bullets and shells kept pounding straight at the windows, shattering glass and piercing the walls and furniture, as if our attackers were working from a detailed layout of the building and were methodically wiping out one floor after another. The fire spread down our corridor; people were running to and fro in a panic. Suddenly, a powerful blast shook the adjoining wing of the building. The screams grew more shrill.

General Rutskoy had a well-deserved reputation for courage over the deadly skies of Afghanistan, but he lost his nerve under the hammering of Grachev's artillery. According to Zlobin, he hid behind a desk and screamed into a telephone at Valeri Zorkin, his ally on the Constitutional Court: "Valeri, they will kill us all! Go ahead, call the foreign embassies. . . . Valeri, I implore you, Valeri—you're a believer, damn your mother! You will have this sin on your soul. They are murderers; do you understand that or don't you?"

It is well that the Rutskoyites had not captured the nuclear button.

General Rutskoy's troops fought their uneven battle, men against tanks, with the courage and fanaticism of Stalingrad. They answered Grachev's artillery with the cry, "We're dying for Soviet power, but we will not surrender!" A chorus of women's voices from an upper floor of the "White House" could be heard through lulls in the battle singing an old Russian ballad that begins, "Shine, my star, shine. . . ."

At noon, after five hours of artillery fire, Grachev's elite Alpha Group penetrated the "White House" and began room-to-room fighting. At 6:00 P.M. the rebel leaders and most of their followers gave up. Russian television, back on the air, showed "President Rutskoy," Ruslan Khasbulatov, and Generals Achalov and Barranikov being paraded out of the shell-torn "White House," surrendering with hands over their heads in military fashion. Buses took them straight from the "White House," and their bid for national leadership, to Lefortovo Prison. About three hundred diehards in the basement and on the blazing upper floor of the "White House" fought on into the evening.

Some two hundred people were killed, and five hundred were wounded in the two days of violence. These losses were trivial compared to what might have been.

Nothing less than planetary survival was at stake during the failed coup of September–October 1993. As during the coup of August 1991, the Russian General Staff again feared that the West might see the disruption among Russia's armed forces and populace as an opportunity for launching a surprise attack. As noted earlier, Russian preparations for war were manifold. Reconnaissance satellites were surge-launched on an emergency basis to provide warning of an attack. The 14th Army, part of Russia's first line of defense against NATO, went on alert, and TSENTER, Defense Minister Grachev's strategic forces "exercise," beginning "coincidentally" at the same time as the coup attempt, provided cover for readying Russian nuclear missiles to perform a retaliatory or preemptive strike.

Russia's war preparations were scarcely noticed in the Western press and, when noted, were misconstrued as being focused inwardly against the coup, not against the United States. Public commentary by Western political and military leaders, like General Shalikashvili, expressed concern that General Rutskoy or his followers might seize control of nuclear weapons. This was a legitimate fear. But no alarm was raised over the more immediate threat posed by TSENTER and other strategic activities initiated by Grachev and the General Staff, who were portrayed in the Western press as pro-Yeltsin "good guys."

A few in the West were not so naive. At least some U.S. intelligence and defense professionals were deeply disturbed by TSENTER and by the possibility that what they were witnessing was not an exercise but the real thing. However, almost no one had the courage to challenge the "politically correct" interpretation that TSENTER was harmless training.

On October 3–4, during the most violent phase of the coup attempt, the General Staff suddenly "flushed" more than a dozen airborne command posts, aircraft equivalent to the U.S. LOOKING GLASS, and designed to manage nuclear operations in the event that Russian underground command posts are destroyed or disabled by enemy nuclear strikes. A major training event might include flying a few airborne command posts, but never as many as went aloft on October 3–4. On the other hand, flushing the airborne command posts is a textbook Russian move in preparation for an enemy surprise attack, which the General Staff probably regarded as most likely during the height of the coup attempt.

On the other side of the world, news about the scrambling of Russia's airborne command posts temporarily disrupted a major analytical conference being held on October 3–4 at North American Air Defense–Space Command (NORAD-SPACECOM) Headquarters in Colorado Springs, Colorado. Were the Russians merely training for nuclear conflict, or actually mobilizing for the real thing?

No one called the president, but several of us phoned our families in Washington, D.C., and told them to evacuate to places we knew would be safe in the event of a nuclear war.

Was TSENTER training, or the real thing? About two weeks after the coup attempt, Yevgeniy Makoklyuyev answered the question. During the leadership crisis, the Russian General Staff placed the strategic defense forces on alert, a sure sign that it feared the possibility of a surprise nuclear attack. In an October 20, 1993, interview, General Makoklyuyev, First Deputy Chief of the Air Defense Forces, spoke frankly and acknowledged that during the September–October struggle, Russian Air Defense Forces had undertaken a forcewide alert:

IVANOV: I was interested to know whether the air and space situation had changed at all when Russia was on the brink of civil war?

GENERAL MAKOKLYUYEV: There were no violations of the state border during this period. Although, since foreign aircraft including military aircraft, were flying very close to our territory, during that week fourteen surface-to-air missile divisions were put on alert status one, eighty-five additional radar stations were brought on line, and the number of fighters on duty in the air increased fourfold.

General Makoklyuyev described a major, virtually unprecedented, mobilization of most of Russia's strategic defenses to readiness for war. Such mobilization is normally matched by corresponding increased strike readiness in the strategic offensive forces, especially among ICBMs and combat-ready nuclear missile submarines. TSENTER was not an exercise. The

Russian General Staff was not "war gaming" a nuclear alert—the alert was real, and extraordinarily dangerous. The West watched with cool detachment the Yeltsin-Rutskoy struggle unfold in distant Moscow; there was no real sense of immediate or personal danger in Washington or among American citizens. The Russian General Staff, in contrast, watched the United States and U.S. strategic forces for one false move; it watched with the same intense animosity and suspicion that attended ABLE ARCHER–83, the 1991 August coup, and the May 1992 Armenian crisis. As in those crises, the desperate and confused circumstances surrounding the October 1993 coup attempt greatly increased the possibility of nuclear miscalculation. An ill-timed U.S. or NATO military exercise, or some other seemingly inconsequential Western act, perhaps as trivial as a national blood drive or a jump in the price of gold, might have been misconstrued by the GRU and General Staff as having apocalyptic significance.

TSENTER lasted twenty-four days, from September 22 to October 15, beginning with the coup attempt and continuing for eleven days after the coup failure—just long enough to guard against foreign aggression while the Yeltsin government reasserted its hold on power. TSENTER's length was unprecedented for a training event. Normally, major military exercises last just a few days, not weeks.

On October 8, one week before TSENTER terminated, the *New York Times* broke a story alleging the existence of a Russian doomsday machine called "DEAD HAND." Based largely on information from General Korobushin, a senior Russian military officer and former member of the General Staff, the *Times* story claimed any attempt to launch a decapitating strike on Russia's nuclear command and control system would fail, because the DEAD HAND computer system would automatically launch Russia's nuclear forces. According to General Korobushin, a U.S. nuclear surprise attack on Russia would be futile.

Political instability in Russian domestic politics could cause a global nuclear war. The events of August 1991 and September–October 1993 will probably be replayed in the future, perhaps a number of times. In 1994, shortly after the October 1993 coup attempt, Russian military cadets—the next generation of General Staff officers—were already grumbling publicly against Yeltsin. Opinion polls showed that the Russian cadets would make the rebellious General Aleksandr Lebed, who was in 1994 an overt enemy of President Yeltsin and the West, the new minister of defense. Defense Minister Pavel Grachev was said to be "near despair" over cuts in the defense budget, and he became openly critical of what he regarded as a betrayal of promises made to the military by President Yeltsin. Rumors began circulating that General Kolesnikov, Chief of the General Staff, was plotting another coup against the government. Defense Minister Grachev was fired for allegedly plotting a coup against President Yeltsin during the

Russian Presidential election of 16 June 1996. Ironically, Grachev was replaced by General Lebed, a harsh Yeltsin critic and presidential rival who joined Yeltsin's government only when it became obvious Lebed would lose the election. In the fall of 1996, Lebed fell victim to allegations that he was on the verge of springing a coup. A 1997 study by the U.S. Congressional Research Service, *Russian Conventional Armed Forces: On the Verge of Collapse?*, concludes that the very weakness and deteriorating condition of Russia's nonnuclear forces threatens regime stability and Western interests: "Present trends are literally unsustainable and, if allowed to continue for another year or two, raise the prospect of some military calamity such as implosion, mutiny, or coup." Political violence against prominent Russian reformers, such as the assassination in December 1998 of Galina Starovoitova—the most pro-Western member of the Duma, who was shot three times in the head—does not bode well for the future of Russian democracy. In 1999, appointments by then Prime Minister Primakov, himself a former KGB spymaster, of veteran KGB espionage agents to head Russia's major television, radio, and news organizations are also worrisome. In May 1999, Primakov joined the army of prime ministers fired by President Yeltsin, and was replaced by General Sergei Stepashin, another former KGB official, who is also an MVD officer and architect of the Chechnya war. Coup rumors persist because the basic conditions that led to previous coup attempts continue to exist.

However, in October 1993, in the bright aftermath of General Rutskoy's defeat, statements and headlines from the capitals and newspapers of the West amounted to a collective sigh of relief. President Boris Yeltsin, champion of Russian democracy, had again prevailed. Yet fifteen months later, Yeltsin would come closer than any previous leader to pushing "the button" during the most dangerous twelve minutes of the nuclear-missile age.

PART V

Northern Lights: The Norwegian Missile Crisis, January 25, 1995

I have indeed used yesterday for the first time my "little black case" with a button, that is always carried with me.

—President Boris Yeltsin,
January 26, 1995

For the first time . . . the "footballs" of the president, the defense minister, and the Chief of the General Staff . . . were switched into an alert mode, which gave the president the technical possibility . . . by merely pressing the button, to authorize the Armed Forces to use Russian nuclear weapons. For the first time!

—Nikolay Devyanin,
"Nuclear briefcase" designer,
February 5, 1995

For a while the world was on the brink of nuclear war.

—Sergey Yushenkov,
Duma committee chairman,
January 27, 1995

CHAPTER 25

Dangerous Men

The military aide stood, ashen-faced, before General Mikhail Kolesnikov. Gripped tightly in both his hands was a briefcase— a crushing, agonizing, weight that he wished the general would take.

It was an ordinary-looking briefcase, indistinguishable from any you might see on the street—save for the small light near its handle. The light was glowing. General Kolesnikov knew that the light *never* came on—except during drills of the strategic forces, who practiced launching missiles during hypothetical nuclear surprise attacks. But there were no drills involving the "nuclear briefcase" scheduled for today.

In a single fluid motion, the aide popped the latches, and the briefcase opened. The pedestrian exterior of the case, of inexpensive simulated leather, seemed to proclaim the simple domestic comforts of the average bureaucrat or businessman: a newspaper, a coffee thermos. The high-tech mechanism within shattered this image. The aide laid the bizarre contraption before General Kolesnikov. It looked like something from Mars.

Inside the briefcase was a view screen flashing data and messages against an electronic map of Russia. The information originated from Russia's vast array of early warning radars, satellites, and aerospace command posts—the largest and most sophisticated data collection and processing complex on the planet, all spilling into General Kolesnikov's little briefcase.

As soon as the "nuclear briefcase" was opened and its screen came into view, General Kolesnikov noticed the light in the north: a glowing dot in the vicinity of the Norwegian Sea signified a missile launch. Fired just a few minutes earlier, the missile was rapidly rising from an area known to be regularly patrolled by U.S. submarines and suspected to be a preferred missile launch site for a U.S. surprise attack. If it was a sub-launched missile, it could reach Moscow in less than ten minutes.

General Kolesnikov glanced over the row of buttons immediately below the screen in his "nuclear briefcase." Depressing these in a particular sequence would launch Russia's strategic missiles and bombers. Was this the end of the world? The date on the screen was January 25, 1995, 0627 A.M. Zulu (Greenwich mean time).

If the most important goal for the United States, and mankind, is to avoid a nuclear war, then the most important men in Russia are those who are empowered, either through political authority or technical capability, to launch nuclear weapons. By this standard, the Chief of the General Staff is the most important—and the most dangerous—man in Russia. He is the only figure known to have both political authority and direct control of the technical means for executing a nuclear attack. As a "nuclear briefcase" holder, General Kolesnikov had the political authority to order a nuclear strike, and as chief of the General Staff, he controlled the codes for unlocking and launching Russia's nuclear forces.

I met General Kolesnikov in the autumn of 1992 at a Washington, D.C., conference intended to bury the Cold War. A Russian version of General George Patton in his bluntness and barely concealed ire, he openly mocked the proceedings, saying that the General Staff still based its planning on the presumption that the United States is "the enemy." He was visibly agitated at being expected to extend an olive branch. On the second day of the conference, when all other Russian military officers donned civilian clothes at the urging of their foreign ministry colleagues, General Kolesnikov proudly remained in uniform.

Kolesnikov despised Defense Minister Pavel Grachev, a man he considered an incompetent weakling and a tool of addlebrained civilian reformers. On the topic of reforming the Russian armed forces, General Kolesnikov was decidedly reactionary: "I am by no means sure that the new army must differ fundamentally from the former one. . . . When creating the Russian Army, we must in no way forget the traditions of either the old Russian Army, or of the Soviet armed forces." The general openly referred to Grachev, theoretically his superior, as a "prostitute." Kolesnikov spoke with the bluntness of a man who has no master. Indeed, when it comes to control of Russia's armed forces, no one *is* superior to the Chief of the General Staff.

Mikhail Kolesnikov's views were basically unreconstructed from the war scare attitudes of the early 1980s. He freely shared his opinion of the Western threat with the press and of the possibility of a nuclear confrontation "in the very near future":

> Russia's military-political situation could not be worse. The U.S.S.R.'s collapse destabilized the situation in Eurasia. There is a real danger that the process of sovereignization will follow the Yugoslav precedent. The intensification of armed conflicts between former Soviet republics could lead to direct intervention by the West (NATO forces), including intervention on the pretext of ensuring international control over the nuclear potential.

According to General Kolesnikov, "The emergence in the place of the U.S.S.R. of a new center of strength, of Russia first and foremost as a potential rival to these powers, does not accord with the long-term interests of the United States, the NATO bloc as a whole, or Japan." Therefore: "A situation could emerge in the very near future whereby precisely the nuclear-missile potential constitutes a real factor deterring Russia's breakup and loss of national sovereignty."

In the May–June 1995 issue of *Military Thought*, General Kolesnikov saw "an explosion-like growth in world and regional military-political crises, local wars, and armed conflicts." He linked the frequency of such phenomena to the occurrence of global conflicts, writing of current crises and small wars: "Their total number is more than seven times that [of those which occurred] between the last two world wars."

Mikhail Pavel Kolesnikov, in January 1995, was the man closest to Russia's "nuclear button." Though little known in the West, he was the single individual in all mankind whose judgment was most crucial to the question of whether or not our futures would be consumed in a nuclear holocaust. Kolesnikov believed another world war was imminent.

Other Russian "dangerous men" who, on January 25, 1995, had the authority to order, or the technical capability to execute independently, a nuclear strike were: President Boris Yeltsin; Defense Minister Pavel Grachev; General Viktor Barynkin; the half dozen commanders in chief of the nuclear services; and the duty officers in the General Staff Command Post. If you would know the kind of characters in Russia who have power in their hands to murder your children, know these men.

President Boris Yeltsin and Defense Minister Pavel Grachev were the other two "nuclear briefcase" holders. Yeltsin has been a conflicted, enigmatic figure, seemingly torn between Russia's czarist and communist traditions of aggressive dictatorship, and the promise of "a new Russia" rebuilt on foundations of international peace and democracy. As a product of the *nomenklatura*, the Soviet Union's bureaucratic elite, Yeltsin broke with communism when his career suffered seemingly irreversible setbacks at the hand of President Mikhail Gorbachev. Was Yeltsin's conversion to democracy genuine, or the result of wounded pride and opportunistic grasping for an alternative way to power?

The West knows Boris Yeltsin as the champion of democracy who defied communism from atop a Soviet tank in August 1991, leading the Russian people to victory and a new society. Less well known is the Yeltsin who rigged elections, winked at human rights abuses by the secret police, and tolerated international treaty violations by the military. The contradiction between the democratic Boris Yeltsin of the popular imagination and the genocidal horrors of the war in Chechnya is so great that the West often acts as if the Chechen conflict was somehow an act of nature, a product of reflexive Russian aggression, of a faceless imperialism—anything except Boris Yeltsin's war.

On the other hand, Yeltsin was riding a tiger. The General Staff is only nominally controlled by the president. Yeltsin owed his survival to the intervention of the military against the coup forces in October 1993, and he was still paying off his praetorian guard. In part because Yeltsin had no *real* power base, he stayed on top by playing factions against one another. This explains why the Kremlin has democratic reformers and authoritarian militarists in the same cabinet. Byzantine power struggles and contradictory policies result. It is a dangerous game, but, arguably, it was the only game Yeltsin could play.

Yeltsin raised the specter of World War III over NATO expansion. He also had a problem with alcohol, and questions arose periodically about his psychological stability. Intimates of the president claim that a drunken Yeltsin boasted that his "nuclear briefcase" was proof of omnipotence.

Despite his occasional rhetorical convergence with communists and ultranationalists, Boris Yeltsin was the most pro-Western leader in Russia's nuclear chain of command. A reformer, whatever his motives, Yeltsin did more than anyone else to promote Russian democracy and improve relations with the West. He also came closer than any national leader, East or West, to pushing the nuclear button, during the missile incident in January 1995.

Pavel Grachev was a hard-liner in all but his friendship with President Yeltsin, who promoted him to defense minister. Far less qualified than other military officers to serve in that post, Grachev was promoted by Yeltsin, over the heads of better men because Grachev was one of the few senior officers Yeltsin could trust, or so Yeltsin thought. For all his affable, smiling ways, Pavel Grachev was deeply corrupt, even by the low standards of a Russian military rotten with corruption. He embezzled a fortune from the defense ministry, and there is reason to believe he was chieftain of an organized crime ring within the military. Yet, despite Grachev's crooked ways, Yeltsin preferred his dishonest friend as defense minister to an honest political enemy.

Grachev was an outspoken proponent of Russia's new military doctrine, endorsing heavier reliance on nuclear weapons—and striking first with them. Grachev warned that NATO expansion eastward "lays the foundation for future dangerous crises" and may lead Russia to "put the strategic nuclear forces on a different status." The defense minister's vision of future war was derivative of the war scare, with its emphasis on the sudden use of weapons of mass destruction right from the start: "If a war begins it will be an air-space offensive operation by both sides. . . . Even if we do not use nuclear weapons, a nuclear-chemical war will still begin, because there will be zones of flooding and zones of radiation and chemical contamination."

This thug and nuclear hawk held one of Russia's three "briefcases" in January 1995. Pavel Grachev's extraordinary ideas on the necessity of preparing to launch a nuclear first strike and on the dangers of NATO expansion elicited little interest from the Western press. Imagine the press reaction if the U.S. secretary of defense held such hawkish views, and was a crime lord to boot. However, unlike Russia's defense minister, the U.S. secretary of defense lacks the political and technical wherewithal to launch nuclear weapons independently.

General Viktor Barynkin, chief of the General Staff's Main Operations Directorate, managed the day-to-day operations of all Russian military and nuclear forces. Barynkin certainly had the launch codes, and he may also have had the political authority to order a nuclear strike, which may not be limited to "nuclear briefcase" holders, who probably are merely the most visible persons legally entrusted with this responsibility.

Viktor Barynkin's frequent contributions to military journals hammered endlessly on the U.S. and NATO military threat to Russia, particularly the immediate threat of a U.S. nuclear or strategic-conventional surprise attack. In an article entitled "Is Russia at Risk of War?" General Barynkin answered in the affirmative, noting U.S. plans to expand NATO into Eastern Europe: "What is advancing rapidly eastward [NATO], toward Russia's borders, is not a network of joint enterprises producing consumer goods, but a mighty structure designed to use force to establish its own order of things. . . . And why are [NATO's] peaceful intentions always accompanied by large numbers of civilian deaths? As has happened, for instance in Yugoslavia."

Barynkin's answer to the various threats he saw was that Russia must "ensure the maintenance of a high level of combat readiness of the strategic nuclear forces." General Barynkin also wrote, "Reliance on military force is sometimes the most persuasive argument."

In a November 1995 article, Barynkin suggested that judging from history, Russia's present military weakness meant that the nation would soon be attacked: "Russia was not ready for the 1612 war, it was not ready for the 1812 war, it was not ready for the Crimean War, it was not ready for the 1914 world war, and it was not ready for 1941 either. . . . History itself provides us with an object lesson that, in the overwhelming majority of cases, military aggression against Russia has been carried out when the country has been experiencing hard times."

Some of Viktor Barynkin's views were extreme, even by General Staff standards. For example, he was convinced that during the Falklands War, Britain was prepared to launch a nuclear strike on Argentina. On the other hand, his article suggested that this view derives from the General Staff's intelligence arm, the GRU, which would make the bizarre idea of Britain getting ready to vaporize Buenos Aires a mainstream General Staff opinion. Such thinking is significant. It implies that at least General Barynkin believed the West could launch a nuclear first strike on the flimsiest of pretexts, during a remote and minor conflict where Western victory is virtually guaranteed, for goals as trivial as the Falkland Islands.

These men, and the dozen or so duty officers managing the General Staff command post, were legally or technically capable of launching all the strategic nuclear forces of Russia. Any one of these men could send the thousands of warheads on Russia's ICBMs, SLBMs, and bombers flying toward our shores.

Others could probably do so, also.

The commanders in chief of the several nuclear services are probably technically capable of independently executing that portion of Russia's nuclear arsenal under their direct control. General Igor Segeyev, commander in chief of the Strategic Rocket Forces, controlled Russia's intercontinental missile forces, armed with nearly 5,000 warheads, each capable of leveling a city. Because of the dominant role played by the Strategic Rocket Forces in Russian military planning and in the command and control system, the SRF chief may be a fifth member of Russia's nuclear elite—along with the president, General Staff chief, defense minister, and General Staff chief of operations—all capable of executing all Russian strategic forces. Admiral Felix Gromov, commander in chief of the Navy, controlled Russia's submarine missile fleet and its 1,500 warheads. General Igor Kalugin, commander in chief of Long-Range Aviation, controlled the strategic bomber force, with nearly 1,500 nuclear weapons. As commander in chief of the Ground Forces, General Vladimir Semenov had 20–30,000 tactical nuclear weapons at his disposal.

As commander in chief of the Air Defense Forces, Viktor Alekseyevich Prudnikov controlled Russia's 10,000 surface-to-air missiles, most of them having nuclear capability, and the hundred antiballistic missiles protecting Moscow, all of which are nuclear armed. An argument could be made that the Air Defense Forces chief was no less important than the Chief of the General Staff in avoiding, or in starting, a nuclear war. The ADF was responsible for operating and interpreting data from the radars and satellites that would provide early warning of a nuclear strike.

The Air Defense Forces under General Prudnikov continued to display the same hair-trigger mentality that during the Soviet period resulted in several attacks on foreign civilian airliners in the mistaken belief that they were on spy missions or part of a surprise attack. On September 12, 1995, the Air Defense Forces killed two Americans by shooting down their sport balloon, which had strayed near a Russian ICBM base in Belarus. Despite the uneven contest between a balloon and helicopter and jet interceptors, no efforts to signal or fire warning shots were made by the ADF pilots. They deliberately machine-gunned both balloon and gondola, slaughtering the presumed "spies."

In a 1995 article, Viktor Prudnikov expressed the view that the world was on the brink of crisis and that world leaders were trying "to minimize the likelihood of a general nuclear and conventional war breaking out, but the actual processes are distinguished by extreme complexity and contradictoriness. Centers of tension are rising in some areas, especially on the southern and western strategic axes, with the danger of armed conflicts escalating." Prudnikov's writings emphasized the importance of continued readiness to respond to a surprise strike by nuclear or advanced conventional forces, even in peacetime: "In peacetime, aerospace defense troops and forces must continuously reconnoiter the air and space enemy, discover the beginning of a nuclear missile and aerospace attack on a timely basis, and notify the Supreme High Command." In January 1995, it was Prudnikov's Air Defense Forces that triggered a nuclear alert over what they thought might be a U.S. nuclear surprise attack.

This cast of characters controlled Russia's nuclear arsenal during the missile crisis of January 25, 1995.

The roster of Russia's nuclear commanders has some new names today, but the new members share the reactionary views of their predecessors. Grachev and Barynkin were removed in June 1996, arrested by General Aleksandr Lebed for allegedly plotting (in a men's room) a coup against President Yeltsin. Yeltsin had fired the unpopular Grachev—his erstwhile friend—cutting a political deal with the popular Lebed, a potential Napoleon and Yeltsin's personal devil, in order to win reelection. For General Barynkin, who had participated in the unsuccessful attempts to overthrow President Gorbachev in August 1991 and President Yeltsin in October 1993, it was his third try at a coup.

President Yeltsin tried to keep his hardline military off balance, and so prevent a challenge to his government, by periodically firing his top military leaders, resulting in a kaliedoscopic succession of nuclear commanders marching through the Kremlin. So far, the hawks have left the Kremlin peacefully, only to be replaced from the General Staff's endless supply of new hawks. One day the generals may decide not to go peacefully. The Kremlin is playing Russian roulette with its own General Staff, men who control Russia's nuclear arsenal.

The winners over Grachev's dismissal, at least momentarily, were General Mikhail Kolesnikov and General Igor Rodionov. Kolesnikov temporarily replaced Grachev as defense minister, while retaining his own post as Chief of the General Staff. Mikhail Kolesnikov became the only man in history to hold simultaneously both of Russia's most powerful military offices—defense minister and Chief of the General Staff—giving him two of Russia's three "nuclear briefcases." Plus, Kolesnikov controlled the General Staff's missile launch codes.

However, in the fall of 1996 Kolesnikov was outmaneuvered by Rodionov and replaced by General Viktor Samsonov, another hard-liner, who had run the General Staff during the Soviet era.

Rodionov, the "Butcher of Tbilisi," considered by many to be guilty of crimes against humanity in Georgia, held the defense minister's "nuclear briefcase" until May 1997. In December 1996, Rodionov, the chief architect of Russia's new military doctrine that endorses a nuclear first strike, warned of a possible nuclear war over NATO enlargement.

Rodionov and Samsonov were fired by President Yeltsin in May 1997, officially because they had failed to reform the military. Unofficially, the two "nuclear briefcase" holders were fired because at a stormy meeting of the Russian Defense Council, they insulted President Yeltsin and were openly defiant.

Today, Russia's top nuclear commanders are General Igor Sergeyev, the new defense minister, and General Anatoly Kvashnin, the new Chief of the General Staff.

Igor Sergeyev's entire professional life has been spent in the Strategic Rocket Forces, preparing for nuclear war. His elevation to defense minister reflects, in the view of most Western analysts, the expanded role and importance in Russian strategy of nuclear weapons. Defense Minister Sergeyev is more diplomatic than his predecessor, better at following the foreign ministry's lead in pretending to show a friendly face to the West. But this is the same Sergeyev who in 1993 wrote that preparedness for nuclear war should be Russia's top military priority and in 1994 reacted to NATO's plans for enlargement by rattling the nuclear sabre. Christmas Day, 1997, Sergeyev spent celebrating deployment of Russia's first SS-27 intercontinental missile, that the one-time launch control officer, now defense minister, boasts is the most advanced ICBM in the world. In January 1998, Defense Minister Sergeyev again raised the spectre of war over NATO expansion.

Sergeyev as defense minister may prove to be the most aggressive nuclear hawk ever. In January 1999, several senior officers of Russia's Missile Attack Warning System—themselves nuclear hard-liners—resigned in protest over Sergeyev's plan to merge their service with the strategic missile troops, in effect subordinating the warning function to the "shooters" in the strategic offensive forces. According to some critics, Sergeyev's reorganization might make Russia more inclined to "shoot first and ask questions later."

As discussed earlier, Sergeyev is also attempting to establish a new command and control echelon for the Strategic Deterrence Forces that would give the top "missile men" the technical capability to launch all nuclear forces. The Joint Supreme Command of Strategic Deterrence Forces (OGK SSS) is intended to increase combat efficiency. It will also give the capability to launch forces to those Russian officers who are the strongest advocates of the new nuclear warfighting doctrine. Nikolai Sokov of the Monterey Institute observes in a February 1999 article that Sergeyev's OGK SSS manifests that, "Nuclear weapons are acquiring a special role in Russia's defense policy . . . including a prominent role in possible local and regional conflicts . . . these weapons might need tighter coordination and control to become usable in possible future conflicts."

The new Chief of the General Staff, Anatoly Kvashnin, is so fundamentally hostile to the West that he cannot even bring himself to behave diplomatically. In September 1997, Kvashnin accused an official U.S. delegation of trying to encircle Russia with NATO, implied the Cold War was still on, and claimed that NATO peacekeeping exercises threatened Russia. In August 1997, General Kvashnin declared that the Russian military needs "large strategic formations," which must be "ready for immediate action." As Chief of the General Staff, Kvashnin holds a "nuclear briefcase," giving him political authority to order a nuclear strike at any time, and he has direct control of the codes and technical apparatus needed to launch nuclear missiles.

As of February 1998, General Anatoly Kornukov is the new commander in chief of Russia's recently combined Air Force and Air Defense Forces. The Air Defense Forces warn of incoming attacks and provide leaders with critical information for making a decision on launching Russia nuclear missiles and bombers. General Kornukov is the commander who in September 1983 ordered the shootdown of civilian airliner KAL 007, thinking it was on a hostile mission. Questioned about this decision fifteen years later, on January 22, 1998, General Kornukov still believes that KAL 007 was part of a mysterious U.S. threat. He has no regrets that he ordered the airliner destroyed, a decision that killed 269 tourists. In January 1999, during a television interview, General Kornukov said that, in response to U.S. air strikes on Iraq during operation DESERT FOX, Russian nuclear forces went on alert "just in case."

The new commander in chief of the Strategic Rocket Forces, since July 1997, is General Vladimir Nikolayevich Yakovlev. According to a 1997 article by General Yakovlev, the United States has been planning for nuclear aggression and seeking strategic superiority over the USSR, and now Russia, since 1946. Yakovlev's take on the 1962 Cuban missile crisis is that surreptitious Soviet placement of nuclear missiles in Cuba was a good thing—a "complex and responsible mission to prevent an American invasion of Cuba"—and achieved a peaceful victory for Moscow: "The real threat to the territory of the United States that emanated from this missile formation largely facilitated a peaceful resolution of the Caribbean crisis. This was the first victory that was attained by peaceful means." The youthful, forty-three-year-old General Yakovlev applauds the primacy of the

Strategic Rocket Forces in Moscow's defense plans, because "the SRF's missile systems have the highest combat readiness" and the highest "stealthiness of preparation for their combat employment." The SRF, in other words, is best suited for launching at any moment a nuclear surprise attack.

CHAPTER 26

Aurora Borealis

Stars bit through the Norwegian night. The watchers scanned the northern skies, straining to catch the first glimpse of the phenomenon.

Then it appeared.

A few waves of color flashed beneath the stars, tentatively at first; then came the silent explosion of natural fireworks shimmering on high, rubies and amethysts thrown against black silk. Ghostly blues and purples danced eerily, a huge windblown curtain suspended in the darkness.

Aurora borealis: named for the Roman goddess of dawn, the northern lights have awed Norse and Inuit peoples for millennia. As recently as 1862, Confederate soldiers witnessing the extraordinarily rare appearance of the aurora borealis in Virginia, over their victorious battlefield at Fredericksburg, interpreted the phosphorescent streamers in the sky as a sign that the cause of Southern independence was blessed by the Almighty.

Meteorologists and geophysicists remain scarcely less fascinated by the northern lights. According to *Webster's*, the aurora borealis is an electromagnetic storm "caused by the emission of light from atoms excited by electrons accelerated along the planet's magnetic field lines." Despite the authoritative ring of this definition, there is still much not understood about the physics of the northern lights. Scientists Jan Holtet, of the University of Oslo, and Craig Pollack, of the U.S. National Aeronautics and Space Administration (NASA), conceived the idea of lofting a physics package, a miniature automated laboratory, above the atmosphere into the ionosphere in order to advance human understanding of the aurora borealis and of the geomagnetic sphere that surrounds our planet. The package would have to be carried above the vicinity of the magnetic North Pole. Norway, close to the pole, was the logical launch site. The package had to be delivered to an altitude above one thousand kilometers. Balloons and low-altitude rockets, the usual tools of meteorologists, could not reach such heights, so something more powerful was needed. The experiment required a missile.

Science moves more slowly than politics. When missile exploration of the aurora borealis was first proposed in the late 1980s, Western Sovietologists and military analysts did not even consider, or dismissed as impossible, the notion that the Soviet military might disobey their political masters in Moscow and launch an unauthorized nuclear strike on their own. The "impossibility" of an unauthorized nuclear attack crumbled with the Soviet Union. Undisturbed by changes in the political world, however, U.S. and Norwegian scientists marched toward their missile rendezvous with the Northern Lights, scheduled for January 1995. By 1995 Sovietology had become an antiquarian pursuit, and an unauthorized launch of missiles was regarded by many in the West as the only conceivable way that Russia might start a nuclear war.

Russia's president has no technical means to prevent the General Staff from launching nuclear missiles on its own. Military control over Russia's nuclear forces, without any technical veto power by Russia's political leaders, is especially disturbing, not only because of the questionable loyalty of Russian military leaders, but also because of the often byzantine power struggles among the military elite. Even a high-ranking Russian military officer, if fired or demoted, faces for himself and his family poverty and homelessness in an increasingly anarchic Russian society that offers few private-sector employment opportunities and few social protections against the ravages of a primitive market economy.

It is frightening to contemplate that men whose personal fortunes are so precarious hold the fate of the world in their hands. We in the West live our everyday lives unaware of, or indifferent to, desperate contests within the Russian military for control of the nuclear arsenal. Sometimes these subterranean struggles break into the light of day.

For example, on July 25, 1993, Pavel Grachev abruptly took possession of the "nuclear briefcase" belonging to Marshal Yevgeniy Shaposhnikov. As commander in chief of the nuclear forces of the Commonwealth of Independent States, Shaposhnikov supposedly represented the nuclear interests of Ukraine and other CIS nations as well as Russia. Grachev's seizure of Shaposhnikov's "nuclear briefcase" was done unexpectedly, without conferring with the leaders of Ukraine or other non-Russian CIS member states.

Grachev probably wanted to symbolize dramatically Russia's claim that all former Soviet nuclear forces—including those located outside Russia in the now independent nations of Ukraine, Belarus, and Kazakhstan—belonged to Russia. He probably also wanted publicly to humiliate Shaposhnikov, who was a potential rival for Grachev's job as defense minister. After the incident, a wounded Shaposhnikov bitterly remarked that "the Russian military agency could not wait to deprive me of control over the nuclear forces."

On November 5, 1995, the Russian and Western press reported that when President Yeltsin was temporarily incapacitated by a heart attack, his "nuclear briefcase" was illegally taken by General Aleksandr Korzhakov. This chief of presidential security was a Rasputin-like character who supposedly had some mysterious hold on Boris Yeltsin. Korzhakov believed in spiritualism and psychic phenomena, was notorious for using wiretaps and police surveillance against personal political rivals in the Kremlin, had his own private army, and was generally regarded as a candidate to lead a future coup.

Russian journalist Maksim Chikin, in an article entitled "Whose Hand Is Reaching for the Nuclear Button?", and the *London Sunday Times* reported that after President Yeltsin's stroke,

> [Defense Minister] Grachev was out of the country, his first deputy Andrey Kokoshin was in a bad way after celebrating his birthday, and it [the "nuclear briefcase"] was left to General Aleksandr Korzhakov . . . who said: "Whoever has the button has the power." [Prime Minister] Chernomyrdin sat silently, unwilling to precipitate a crisis of greater dimension.
>
> The next day Sergey Medvedev, Yeltsin's press secretary, solemnly announced that the black box—which contains the hotline telephone for ordering nuclear strikes—was at the president's side. But it is unclear who will be advising the stricken president on when to lift the receiver. The only person allowed into his room has been his wife Naina.

Under the terms of Russia's 1993 constitution, the prime minister, Viktor Chernomyrdin, should have received Yeltsin's "nuclear briefcase." Chikin and the *Sunday Times* were alarmed by General Korzhakov's playing with nuclear fire. His actions also boded ill for the peaceful transfer of power in Russia: "It is uncertain whether such transfer of power can be effected in Russia. If Korzhakov and his Kremlin cronies were to try to hang onto power over Yeltsin's body, the worst-case scenario, say defense analysts, would be a coup by the disgruntled army and fighting in Moscow's streets of the kind witnessed two years ago." Some analysts can imagine even worse scenarios, since Korzhakov's control of nuclear weapons during a coup or civil war would be similar to the events of August 1991 and October 1993. Korzhakov, the master schemer, fell victim to Kremlin intrigue and lost his position in the June 1996 elections.

Political gamesmanship and career predation exacerbate an already high-stress environment of conflict and overdeveloped threat sensitivity, which could easily breed psychological instability among Russia's top nuclear guardians. Scarcely a year after the October 1993 coup, on January 25, 1995, Russia's nuclear commanders would see a mysterious missile coming out of the north. The unexpected blip on their radar screens—signifying a rocket hurtling skyward—appeared at a time and from a place that fit the General Staff's textbook scenario for a nuclear surprise attack. Another text, published in November 1993, told them what to do about it.

"For the first time since the dawn of the nuclear age, there are no Russian missiles pointed at America's children," President William Jefferson Clinton declared in his January 23, 1996, State of the Union address. It is a claim he has made many times since he and Russian president Boris Yeltsin signed the so-called "detargeting agreement" in Moscow on January 14, 1994. Under the agreement, officially called the Moscow Declaration, according to a White House statement "by May 30, 1994 no country will be targeted by the strategic forces of either side. For the first time since the earliest days of the nuclear age, the two countries will no longer operate nuclear forces, day-to-day, in a manner that presumes they are enemies."

The Clinton administration has said in effect that the Moscow Declaration eliminates the Russian nuclear threat. Yet both Russian and U.S. experts overwhelmingly hold that the detargeting provisions of the Moscow Declaration are nonbinding, unverifiable, and militarily inconsequential. For example, Russian general Viktor Yesin, chief of the Strategic Missile Forces Main Staff, noted in an April 1995 interview that "the missiles' target coordinates can be unloaded and reloaded. Missile specialists believe that the SMF's actual combat readiness following Boris Yeltsin's generous gesture of friendship to the Americans has not diminished." Anton Surikov, a senior advisor to the Russian Ministry of Defense, acknowledged in a March 1995 interview, "When it was decided to detarget missiles, the decision was mostly of a political, propaganda character," because "technically it is not difficult to retarget a missile very quickly." Less than one month after detargeting was supposed to take effect, during a major Russian strategic forces exercise held on June 22, 1994, Russian missile launches simulated strikes on the United States.

Despite clear proof that the Moscow Declaration is worthless propaganda, the Clinton administration continues to tell the American people that the detargeting agreement has substantially reduced the nuclear threat to their children. Never mentioned by the administration are Moscow's official statements of Russia's new military doctrine and nuclear strategy, which are even more aggressive than Soviet-era policy in that they endorse a nuclear first strike.

The real winner of the failed October 1993 coup attempt was not President Yeltsin but the General Staff. Ever since the military doctrine conference of May 1992, in which General Igor Rodionov trounced General Mahkmut Gareyev in arguing for the repudiation of Russia's pledge never to use nuclear weapons first, the defense ministry and General Staff had agitated for President Yeltsin to abandon officially Russia's "no first use" declaration. Foreign Minister Andrei Kozyrev and President Yeltsin had strenuously resisted this proposed reversal of openly stated policy, which amounted to a "first strike" declaration. They feared strong Western disapproval and a possible return of the Cold War. But the October 1993 coup made military demands for reversal of the "no first use" policy irresistible. Rescued by the Army, President Yeltsin realized that his future power and the preservation of Russian democracy depended on the continued willingness of the military to resist or refrain from the violent overthrow of the government. One month after saving the Yeltsin presidency, the General Staff got its new military doctrine.

Russia officially repudiated its "no first use" promise in November 1993, with the publication of a document, made available to foreign readers, entitled *Basic Provisions of the Military Doctrine of the Russian Federation*. The official purpose of *Basic Provisions* was to describe and reconcile—in diplomatic language crafted to be inoffensive to a Western audience—the fundamental, and often conflicting, assumptions of Russia's political-military leaders about the new international environment, possible threats to Russia, and principles guiding defense policy. The immediate, and probably most important, purpose of the document was to warn the West not to try to exploit Russian weakness. The warning was backed by the withdrawal of the "no first use" pledge.

General Vladimir Dworkin of the Strategic Rocket Forces and Defense Minister Pavel Grachev had earlier proposed heavier reliance on nuclear first strikes to preempt a U.S. conventional attack. Despite its "peace loving" tenor, *Basic Provisions* goes even further than Dworkin or Grachev in expanding the conditions under which Russia might launch a nuclear first strike. The language of Armageddon is convoluted and overlaid with diplomacy, but the meaning is clear enough:

> The aim of the Russian Federation's policy in the sphere of nuclear weapons is to eliminate the danger of nuclear war by deterring the launching of aggression against the Russian Federation and its allies.
>
> The Russian Federation: will not employ its nuclear weapons against any state party to the Treaty on the Non-Proliferation of Nuclear Weapons, dated 1 July 1968, which does not possess nuclear weapons except in the cases of: (a) an armed attack against the Russian Federation, its territory, Armed Forces, other troops, or its allies by any state which is connected by an alliance agreement with a state that does possess nuclear weapons; (b) joint actions by such a state with a state possessing nuclear weapons in the carrying out or in support of any invasion or armed attack upon the Russian Federation, its territory, Armed Forces, other troops, or its allies.

In the first paragraph, Moscow is still trying to "eliminate the danger of nuclear war" by using nuclear weapons to deter not just nuclear aggression but "the launching of aggression" generically—and not just against Russia, but against Russia's allies, notwithstanding the fact that the Cold War was supposed to be over. In the second paragraph, Moscow promises not to use nuclear weapons against signatories to the 1968 nuclear Non-Proliferation Treaty who do "not possess nuclear weapons"—which makes the United States and other nuclear powers fair game. But the paragraph goes on to list the exceptions that allow Russia to attack virtually any state. Few nations lack an "alliance agreement" of some kind with one of the nuclear powers. Few are without bases, communications facilities, or trade connections that could be construed as lending "support" to one of the nuclear-armed powers. For example, under the new Russian military doctrine, if Turkish border guards fired on Armenians, Russia could respond to Turkish "aggression" with nuclear missiles, because Turkey is allied to a nuclear-armed state through NATO. As was demonstrated by the May 1992 Armenian crisis, this example is not far-fetched.

In addition to broadening Russian nuclear options to allow Russian nuclear strikes against nonnuclear states, *Basic Provisions* also lengthens the list of provocations that Russia would consider sufficiently grave to justify a nuclear strike. The revised list includes a broad range of conventional military threats: "Deliberate actions by the aggressor which aim to destroy or disrupt the operation of the strategic nuclear forces, the early warning system, nuclear power and atomic and chemical industry installations, may be factors which increase the danger of a war using conventional weapons systems escalating into a nuclear war." In other words, if you drop a conventional bomb on a Russian radar or oil refinery—a "chemical industry installation"—Russia reserves the right to launch a nuclear strike. This is just a diplomatic way of saying that in a war, almost any war, even if the other side refrains from using nuclear weapons or has no nuclear weapons, Russia plans to launch a nuclear strike. Nearly any conventional conflict between Russia and a foreign power would place at risk the "nuclear tripwire" installations listed in *Basic Provisions*.

In contrast to the *Basic Provisions*, Soviet military plans for nuclear preemption allowed a first strike to preempt an impending *nuclear* attack by the United States, NATO, or China. The Soviets did not consider other nations plausible nuclear adversaries. Under old-style Soviet doctrine, *conventional* attacks—even from the United States—were to be defeated by general-purpose (conventional) forces.

Today's post–Cold War Russian military doctrine is more destabilizing—and more dangerous—than Soviet Cold War military doctrine.

And it only gets worse.

Russia's new military doctrine not only may *allow* the *option* of launching a nuclear first strike, it appears to *require* a nuclear first strike, if this is deemed the most effective course of military action to defeat the enemy: "The forms, methods, and means of conducting combat operations which best accord with the prevailing situation and ensure that the initiative is seized and the aggressor defeated *must* be chosen" (emphasis added).

Two prominent Russian defense intellectuals who normally reflect very different perspectives on the same issues have independently arrived at the same conclusions about Russia's new military doctrine. Sergey Rogov is a doveish, pro-Western academic and deputy director of the Institute of the USA and Canada. General Makhmut Gareyev is a hawk who remains suspicious of the West, and, until his retirement, was one of the Russian military's most prominent doctrinal experts. In fact, Gareyev participated in the internal debate over Russia's new military doctrine and unsuccessfully argued against the provisions broadening Russia's nuclear first-use policy, a defeat that coincided with his retirement from the military. But Gareyev had been in a position in the military hierarchy to know the intent and operational implications of the new doctrine.

In separate articles and commentary published in May and June 1994, Sergey Rogov and General Gareyev concurred that because the new doctrine allows Russian nuclear first use, it contradicted claims that Russian doctrine is essentially defensive. They agreed that the new doctrine promoted operational practices that would be destabilizing in a future conflict or crisis. In Sergey Rogov's words, the doctrine demonstrated "a readiness to lower the nuclear threshold to the maximum extent" by allowing nuclear first use against conventional aggression "at an early stage of armed confrontation," and it could even involve "an immediate escalation of a nuclear conflict" by Russian "massive [first] use" of nuclear weapons. As Rogov puts it, "If Russia can use nuclear weapons first, then the conclusion about their 'massive use' can be interpreted as a hint that we may undertake an immediate escalation of a nuclear conflict."

General Gareyev, who was privy to the General Staff's thinking when the new doctrine on nuclear first use was being drafted, wrote that the policy "is undoubtedly geared toward being the first to launch military operations." Gareyev warned that Russia might launch a nuclear first strike, not only in response to an enemy conventional attack already under way, but to preempt enemy preparations for such an attack. According to General Gareyev, Russia might start a nuclear war based on vague strategic warning or "totally unproved aggressive intentions" attributed by Russia to another state:

> As the international situation becomes more complex, the actual desire not to delay and be the first to successfully use nuclear weapons would prompt a dangerous rivalry—who would use them earlier, thus whipping up an already exacerbated situation and encouraging the delivery of a preemptive strike. In such conditions it would be difficult to determine why nuclear weapons were used and who was the first to use them. This will create a breeding ground for sundry speculations and concealment of aggression. Preemptive actions could be taken and nuclear weapons could be used in "response to totally unproved aggressive intentions" by one state or another.

Gareyev is no pacifist, nor is he a fan of the West. He is not even averse to striking first with nuclear weapons during a conventional war that is already under way—"The first use of nuclear weapons in the course of a war that has already been launched is another matter"—but the new doctrine allowing Russian initiation of a nuclear war, based on the mere suspicion of hostile intentions, chilled even General Gareyev's hawkish blood.

Gareyev and Rogov also agreed that the new doctrine implies, or was influenced by Russian military officers who believe, that it is possible to *win* a nuclear war. Moscow's new military doctrine, relying more heavily on nuclear weapons and striking first, may seem to many in the West like madness. Judged by Western values and historical experience, Moscow's military policy appears not merely irrational but malevolent. Yet it is hardly fair to judge Russia by Western standards, since that nation has long existed in brutality that is alien to the West. The past will continue to shape Russian consciousness and decisions. Even if it survives as a democracy, Russia cannot escape its dark history.

CHAPTER 27

Dark History

Armored corpses lay in heaps—some with arrows protruding from open mouths, blood matting their beards—as smoke rose into the cold air from the ruins of ancient Muscovy. Thousands of Mongol ponies had carefully picked their way along the frozen Oka River, which that winter had been transformed into a highway into Russia. Year after year, the Khan's warriors had traveled farther westward in this way. For centuries, ice, snow, and frigid air had made the winter season a time of safety for the people of Rus. The elements immobilized local enemies, and no European army could march very far through waist-deep snow and still have energy to swing sword and axe in pitched battle.

In the thirteenth century, mounted armies suddenly burst out of Asia to follow the frozen rivers into the heart of what is now Russia. Powerful compound bows allowed the Mongols to shoot Rus foot soldiers from horseback at a distance. Rus battle tactics, massing in a densely packed formation of heavily armed foot soldiers, made them easy targets, and the Mongols enslaved the Rus for two centuries.

The Mongol horse and bow and their trick of traveling in winter gave them advantages over the Rus that were no less decisive than the machine gun and tank would prove to be in later wars. The greatest Mongol advantage was that their weapons and tactics were entirely unfamiliar to the Rus, giving the Khan's warriors the element of surprise.

Half a millennium later, at the Battle of Austerlitz in 1805, Napoleon surprised the Russian army through an elaborate series of deceptions that misled it into believing that the French were weak and demoralized. This misconception lured the Russians to attack, and soon they found themselves incapable of resisting Napoleon's innovative use of artillery. Bonaparte had introduced the tactic of massing cannon against a portion of the enemy's line in order to blow a hole through his ranks; through it, the French would charge to victory.

At the climax of their losing battle, the tattered Russians found themselves crossing a frozen lake. Bonaparte administered another shock, by cracking the ice beneath their feet with cannon balls. Whole regiments spilled to a frigid death. The Satschwan waters, gaudy with gold braid and beribboned uniforms, looked like the scene of a drowned opera company.

A famous painting by Jacques Louis David depicts Russia's surrender in the aftermath of Austerlitz. A triumphantly mounted Napoleon soars over the crouched figure of a muscular Slavic officer, who tenderly kisses the toe of Bonaparte's boot. Few artistic works so well capture abject humiliation or represent that unforgettable moment in the Russian historical memory.

In 1914, surprise came in the form of the machine gun and Germany's use of railroads to outmaneuver and outsupply the Russians. At Tannenberg, the Russian army suffered nearly 200,000 casualties and prisoners, their corpses thickly carpeting the cratered mud on the battlefield that was East Prussia.

In 1941, surprise came from the blitzkrieg of German massed armor and air assault, which killed or captured over two million Soviet soldiers in five months of Operation Barbarossa. Reversing this colossal defeat, and eventually achieving victory, required the sacrifice of thirty million Russian lives.

These are the images of war engraved in the historical imagination of Russian soldiers and military scholars. From this perspective, warfare is the story of a series of technological and tactical innovations unleashed with decisive effect against a victim nation—often Russia—in a surprise attack. General P. A. Zhilin's *The History of Military Art* begins the cycle of innovation and surprise with the charioteers of ancient Egypt. Zhilin sees this recurring pattern in every historical period, up to our own "revolution in military affairs": the nuclear missile age. Zhilin's Soviet-era text is still required reading in the Russian General Staff Academy, and it is representative of most Soviet and Russian military historical thought.

The average Russian citizen is significantly more concerned about the possibility of surprise attack and the consequences of military unpreparedness than the average American, who has only Pearl Harbor as a reference point. Imagine how differently Americans would think if the United States had suffered a dozen Pearl Harbors—on its mainland and in its heartland—and you begin to appreciate Russia's concern about surprise attack. Reminders of the 1941 blitzkrieg are everywhere in Russia, and not just in monuments. Bullet-pocked churches, mass graves, and the remains of trenches and antitank ditches, softened by erosion and a carpet of green grass, are in almost every village in European Russia. When Americans want to see a battlefield, they travel to Gettysburg. Russians have only to walk to the local park, or look in their own backyards.

During the fifteen months between the October 1993 coup attempt and the missile crisis of January 1995, events conspired to feed the Russian military's naturally suspicious nature and keep the General Staff on edge, convinced it was sitting on an international powder keg. Moscow sometimes lashed out. In June 1993, whether as a pretext or out of real concern about alleged abuses against ethnic Russians living in Estonia, President Yeltsin made a thinly veiled military threat, supposedly against his Baltic neighbor but broadcast in English to a world audience: "[The] Estonian leadership has misinterpreted Russia's good will and has 'forgotten' some geopolitical and demographic realities. The Russian side can recall them." In July Foreign Minister Andrei Kozyrev warned the United States not to "interfere" in Estonia. In January 1994, in response to the detention of two Russian generals in Latvia, Defense Minister Grachev placed an airborne division on alert.

In 1994, civil war broke out in Russia, as Moscow invaded Chechnya to prevent that breakaway republic from asserting its national independence. Russian troops were waging "peacekeeping operations" in the now independent nations of Armenia, Azerbaijan, Georgia, and Tajikistan to suppress local wars and insurgencies, and to deepen the dependence of these governments on Moscow.

A sense that Russia had weak leadership and was rudderless reinforced among senior Russian military officers feelings of vulnerability and a continued preference for dictatorship. In 1994 a German research institute conducted a poll of Russian military officers and concluded that most senior Russian military officers were "a group of men deeply disenchanted with Russia's place in the world and their place in Russia—as well as fearful of the future and resentful of the past." The poll, based on a sample of 615 senior officers, including sixty generals and admirals, found that officers ranking major and above believed that "without authoritarian rule [Russia] cannot overcome chaos," that "Western types of democracy are not suitable to Russia," and that the "main foreign policy task must be to reestablish Russia as a great power respected throughout the world." The poll results revealed that senior Russian military officers "are overwhelmingly in favor of a strong hand to guide the state and evidently feel that such a hand is presently lacking."

The Russian military's capacity for bizarre conspiracy theories that see the black hand of the West behind almost any outrage remained undiminished. In 1994, the GRU, accused of murdering a Russian journalist investigating military corruption whose briefcase mysteriously exploded, claimed that the CIA had committed the deed in order to undermine GRU efforts to save Russia from the West:

> When the Soviet Union broke up, the foreign press and also, sometimes, our own, wrote that a colossus with feet of clay had collapsed and that its successor, Russia, would become a raw materials appendage of developed Western countries. Informed Western special services made a different assessment of Russia's role. They declared: "Yes, we have won the Cold War, but we are not yet the victors." They warned: "Do not be in a hurry to bury Russia, for it is very strong. Some serious work still has to be done to turn our wishes into reality."

This paranoid accusation against the West verges on self-caricature, but it is not so amusing when one remembers that the GRU is the intelligence arm of the General Staff, responsible for providing strategic warning of a nuclear attack.

In view of Russia's increased vulnerability, General Lev Volkov, in a June 1994 article, warned that "the United States and NATO have the possibility of inflicting a 'non-nuclear' strike against the Russian strategic nuclear force." Not satisfied that Russia's new doctrine allowing nuclear first use went far enough, General Volkov called upon Moscow to put the United States and NATO on notice by officially declaring that "a premeditated attack with the use of conventional weapons on the strategic nuclear force means the guaranteed start of a nuclear war."

And then there was Bosnia.

At the same time that Sergey Rogov and General Makhmut Gareyev tried to warn the world about Russia's dangerous new nuclear doctrine—even as General Volkov called for a still bolder doctrine—Moscow raised a nuclear specter over the Balkans.

Bosnia, 1994: Serbs and Muslims struggled for control of the country in a civil war that recognized no noncombatants and no neutrals, not even among children. It was not merely a civil war but a war of genocide. Bosnian Serbs deliberately targeted civilians—including children—with sniper and mortar fire. They raped Muslim women, warring against their bloodline. Atrocities straight out of the Dark Ages were committed on both sides by medieval minds armed with modern weapons.

The American people saw the victimized children of Bosnia on television, crying, bleeding, horribly injured. They didn't like it.

High above Sarajevo, the F-15 pilot could see the blue Adriatic. A U.S. aircraft carrier task force, with enough air firepower to flatten every military target in Bosnia, hung back over the horizon. U.S. satellites and reconnaissance aircraft had pinpointed the locations of Serb artillery and mortars on the hills surrounding Sarajevo. The guns were pounding the ancient city—one of Europe's cultural treasures—into dust. These were people who fired at anything that moved: men, women, or children.

The F-15 descended on the Serb gunners, delivering bombs with surgical precision, sending the medieval mortarmen to their fiery reward. The Kremlin didn't like it.

Numerous articles by Russian military officers published recently and over the past few years warn that local conflicts currently under way, in states on the periphery of Russia, could escalate into a global nuclear war. This view is also reflected in the new Russian military doctrine published in November 1993. The mechanism, as implied in Russian writings, that escalates a local conflict into a nuclear war appears to be intervention of the United States or its allies into conflicts on Russia's periphery. From such a vantage point, the West could then invade, surround, or encourage the breakup of Russia. Because of the superiority of Western conventional forces and resources, Russian military efforts to prevent these developments would mean recourse to nuclear weapons.

Russian military scientists also note that protracted local conflicts, if they escalate into large-scale war, are likely to do so unexpectedly. Colonel V. Cheban, a widely published and highly respected Russian military theorist, warned in a 1994 article that prolonged small-scale conflicts can conceal from view the emergence of a major war. "Any conflict is genetically predisposed to transformation into major wars."

General Viktor Barynkin of the General Staff, who was responsible for the daily management of Russia's general-purpose and nuclear forces, agreed with Colonel Cheban. In a June 1994 article appearing in the prestigious Defense Ministry journal *Military Thought*, Barynkin concluded that small, currently ongoing conflicts may contain the seeds of world war: "Analysis of the tendencies in the development of the military-political situation in the world shows that it is unstable to the point of crisis. Therefore . . . any armed conflict may deteriorate into a local war which . . . may grow into a large-scale war." This thinking colored Russia's foreign policy toward the ethnic conflict between Muslims and Serbs in Bosnia. Ever since the disintegration of Yugoslavia into warring factions in 1991, Russia had objected to unilateral Western military involvement to quell the dispute, while tolerating ineffectual United Nations peacekeeping efforts, over which Russia, as a UN Security Council member, had veto power.

The conventional wisdom holds that Russia resisted decisive Western military action to end the conflict because the West sympathized with the Muslim underdogs while Russia favored the Serbs, who are Slavic, have historical ties to Russia, and were winning the war. But Russian words and deeds indicate that Russia sees much higher stakes in the Balkans than the fate of a minor ally. More likely, Russia fears that Western "peacekeeping" in former Yugoslavia would provide an excuse for permanently introducing a large Western military presence that could use the region as a staging base to threaten Russia. The fear of a more assertive U.S. and NATO military policy in the Bosnian war climaxed in 1994 in a display of Russian nuclear saber rattling.

"You can freeze-frame every moment of the final destruction of the Stari Most bridge. On the videotape timer, the moment is exactly 3:32 P.M. on 9 November 1993. In its last milliseconds of existence, tank shells smash into the west side of the parapet in a cloud of brown dust. Then the entire sixteenth-century bridge—'a rainbow rising up the milky way,' as a traveler to Mostar described it 400 years ago—falls in a slow, lazy way into the waters of the Neretva, to be met by a majesty of spray. The tape ends. Press the rewind button and you can rebuild the bridge, the spray falling back into the gorge, the old Turkish stones rising mystically upwards to recompose themselves in their magical span." So journalist Robert Fisk described one destructive act of the war in former Yugoslavia.

The roots of the conflict there twine back to A.D. 395, when the Romans divided their empire into east and west halves, along a line that split the Balkans between Latin Rome and Greek Constantinople. The division later became cultural, religious, and ethnic, separating Roman Catholic Serb from Eastern Orthodox Croat. Ottoman Turks introduced Muslims to the Balkans and dominated the Serbs for five hundred years, finally losing control of the region by 1878 to the Austro-Hungarian Empire. In 1914, the heir to the Austro-Hungarian throne and his wife fell victim to Serb assassination on the streets of Sarajevo, thereby setting off World War I. During World War II, Germany exploited Yugoslavia's ethnic fractures, recruiting Croats to serve the Nazi cause, murdering some 350,000 Serbs, Jews, and Gypsies in a local holocaust. After the war, Field Marshal Josep Broz Tito's communist government squeezed Yugoslavia together again with an iron fist. Tito's death in 1980 and the general collapse of communism in Eastern Europe in 1991 unleashed Yugoslavia's long pent-up rivalries, which exploded into a war among Croats, Serbs, and Muslims.

The United States might have stayed out of it were it not for General Ratko Mladič and the emotive power of modern journalism. In April 1994, the Serbian general upset peace negotiations and humiliated United Nations forces by overrunning the Muslim enclave at Goradze. Mladič's troops rounded up Muslim men for imprisonment, while women and children were ejected from their homes. The bodies of hundreds of Muslims were later found in mass graves, executed by a bullet to the head. Just one month earlier, Ratko Mladič's daughter had committed suicide because, according to some Western diplomats, she was appalled at her father's butchery.

"Terror was their weapon—the Yugoslav Army's artillery bombardments, Chetnik mass murders, concentration camps like Trnopolje for men of military age, where barbaric things were done, systematized rape of women—so that whole populations would flee, compelled at gunpoint to leave everything behind," William Tribe wrote in February 1994, relating Ed Vulliamy's eyewitness account of Serb brutality. "Cattle trucks, stuffed with suffocating women and children, carried some away; others walked. Vulliamy accompanied one procession from Sanski Most to Travnik, running a gauntlet of Serbian fighters shouting 'Butcher them!' and 'Go to Allah!' They encountered the remains of some who had gone before them and indeed been butchered—Vulliamy trod on a severed hand in the dark."

Early in 1994, in response to a series of highly publicized Serbian atrocities against Muslim noncombatants, the United States and other NATO countries warned the Serbs that further atrocities might provoke NATO air strikes and other military steps in retaliation.

In an article issued to the Western press in March 1994, Russian foreign minister Andrei Kozyrev vehemently condemned the United States and

NATO for their warning, claiming it evidenced "a chauvinistic wind blowing in Washington" and proved the United States had "an almost manic desire for a world with just one great power: the United States." Kozyrev reminded his Western audience that "Russia remains a superpower . . . because of its arsenal of nuclear weapons and missiles . . . also because of its natural resources, technological skills, and strategic location." Foreign Minister Kozyrev countered the U.S. ultimatum to the Serbs with an ultimatum of his own: "The NATO ultimatum on Sarajevo was made while Russia was not involved in any way. It is unacceptable to exclude Russia from attempts to solve the situation in Bosnia, where Russia has present and future interests." This was strong stuff from Kozyrev, the most pro-Western minister in the Russian hierarchy. The following month, Russian defense minister Pavel Grachev railed against NATO air strikes on the Serbs, claiming they could "make the whole conflict explode beyond control."

Victims of the war in Bosnia walked across the newspapers and televisions of the West in a seemingly endless line. On June 9, 1994, in response to continued Serb predations against Muslims in Bosnia, the U.S. Congress voted to exempt Bosnia from a UN-imposed arms embargo on former Yugoslavia, allowing the United States and NATO to arm Bosnian Muslims against the Serbs. On June 14, Foreign Minister Kozyrev voiced Russia's opposition to ending the arms embargo on Bosnia and raised the specter of a return to the Cold War: "If one great power or both start supporting their clients, it would bring the world back to the worst years of the Cold War." Kozyrev went further, warning Congress that its vote could bring on World War III: "If American legislators try such steps in favor of the [Bosnian Muslims] it would create a new political situation. . . . It is definitely a way to a new world war."

One week after Foreign Minister Kozyrev's warning about "a new world war" over Bosnia, the Russian General Staff conducted an unusually large and realistic exercise of all strategic nuclear forces, simulating the waging of a nuclear conflict. This highly publicized training event was probably intended to reinforce Kozyrev's threat. A number of features gave the strategic forces exercise of June 22, 1994, the unmistakable flavor of nuclear diplomacy.

The publicity surrounding the exercise, including television coverage of the actual launching of an SS-25 ICBM, was unprecedented. Strategic forces exercises are almost always conducted in secret.

President Boris Yeltsin took part in the exercise from the General Staff Headquarters at Arbatskaya Square, and he personally ordered the ICBM's launch. Film footage showed an animated Yeltsin sitting at a table surrounded by military officers, a sea of green in their perfectly tailored uniforms, bright with ribbons and the red trouser stripes of the General Staff. It could have been a scene from the eighteenth century of the czar and his attendants. Or were they his captors? No civilians were present to advise the president during the nuclear exercise.

Participation by a head of state in a strategic forces exercise is unprecedented in the history of the Soviet Union or Russia—or in the history of the United States, for that matter—a point deliberately made to the press by Chief of the General Staff Mikhail Kolesnikov. Defense Minister Pavel Grachev and Kolesnikov also played in the exercise and advertised their participation to the press, even having themselves televised entering the underground nuclear command post at Chekov. Their small figures disappeared into the maw of a bombproof elevator shaft, a hulking ziggurat of gray concrete, to be swallowed down through a mile of solid rock to the cavernous nuclear fortress below.

The announced official purpose of the exercise was to demonstrate "the combat vigil arrangements and the procedure for the control of the country's nuclear forces in realization of the agreement between Russia, the U.S., and Britain" on detargeting. The "detargeting agreement" of January 1994 was supposed to decrease the combat readiness of the sides and thus the threat of surprise nuclear attack or of war through miscalculation. Shifting missile aimpoints to uninhabited areas, or canceling existing missile aimpoints, was supposed to require time-consuming retargeting of missiles before they could be used against another country. However, live Russian television coverage of an ICBM launch from the far northern military base at Plesetsk during the exercise showed in living color that the detargeting agreement was a meaningless scrap of paper. A Russian TV commentator witnessing the launch said in effect, perhaps unwittingly, that the accord on detargeting was hollow: "The speed with which officers at the Plesetsk test range executed the relatively sudden launch order provides sufficient grounds for confirming Russia's status as a nuclear power, ready to defend itself within a matter of minutes."

The rapid missile launch was also impressive for its warlike realism. Unlike U.S. strategic missile tests, usually conducted by scientists using a pristine ICBM under ideal conditions, Russian soldiers fired a workaday rocket as if in combat. Lieutenant Colonel Sergey Sergeyev's missile was from one of several missile divisions on forest maneuvers. He had bounced his mobile SS-25 ICBMs through the woods, pushing through branches and brush along narrow wilderness trails and fording unbridged streams to his launch site. Sergeyev's rocket was eleven years old, not fresh from the factory. In the words of the Russian press, "The division fired from a regular launcher a missile that had been placed on alert duty in 1984."

Russian television showed a missile transporter, an immense green flatbed truck, with its launch tube fully elevated, pointed straight up at the sky: a six-story cannon. White smoke erupted from the mouth of the canister. Suddenly, a long dark shape nosed through steaming vapor. Forty-five tons of missile seemed to hang suspended in midair for an instant, then a burst of light obscured all but the missile, which shot up out of sight at incomprehensible speed. An SS-25 ICBM had never before been fired in public.

These images of the men and missiles of the Strategic Rocket Forces—rough and ready like Sergey Sergeyev, able to blast away an intercontinental missile on a few minutes notice—loudly proclaimed the insignificance of the detargeting agreement.

The exercise also featured a promptly executed SLBM launch and an ALCM launch from a Blackjack, Russia's most advanced strategic bomber. Half a continent away from Plesetsk, in the icy depths of the Arctic Ocean, a Russian submariner bathed in the fluorescent glow of nuclear-generated light transcribed a code-word message from the General Staff. "A Northern Fleet . . . missile-armed submarine commanded by Captain 1st Rank Aleksandr Zheltyakov, on alert duty in an area of the Barents Sea," *Izvestiya* reported, "launched a ballistic missile in the direction of the test range on order from Moscow."

Bomber crews got the launch message high above Zheltyakov, above the vast whiteness of the arctic ice. Not by Boris Yeltsin's order but "on a command from the Air Force central command and the General Staff central command," according to purportedly "confidential" information passed on to the Russian press, "the crew headed by Lieutenant Colonel Sergey Danilchenko launched a long-range cruise missile." Danilchenko briefly glimpsed his flying robot, like a gray crucifix, hurtling toward the curved horizon.

Both the ICBM and SLBM launches were aimed at the same place, the Kamchatka Peninsula, and were sequenced to strike "within a short time of each other." The launches went perfectly. Over Kamchatka, twin white contrails from two missile warheads streaked across the heavens, almost converging in a giant V. It was a formidable display of technical competence and military prowess.

The date of the exercise, June 22, coincided with the anniversary of Germany's invasion of the Soviet Union in World War II. Russian officers told the press that "the choice of the launch date—22 June—was not accidental." This comes close to an admission that Russia was using the nuclear exercise to warn someone not to contemplate attacking Russia, now or in the future.

One day after President Boris Yeltsin's participation in the nuclear exercise, he flew to Corfu to sign a trade agreement with the European Union, a consortium of most of the nations of Western Europe. The connection between Russia's strategic nuclear forces exercise and the Corfu summit of European leaders was not lost on the Russian press. *Izvestiya* reported that timing the nuclear exercise to occur just before the Corfu meeting was deliberate, intended to impress upon the world that Russia was still a superpower. At Corfu, Yeltsin made it clear that he sought more than merely respect for Russia—he also sought to avoid a crisis that threatened European stability. On June 24, during the televised ceremony of the European Union trade agreement, attended by numerous state leaders, President Yeltsin told his slightly bewildered Western audience that the "consequences of the Cold War continued to poison the international atmosphere," that in some respects there remained "a growing threat of confrontation," that European stability must be maintained, no attempt made to isolate Russia, and a solution found to the Yugoslavian crisis.

Russian deputy foreign minister Vitaliy Churkin, who accompanied Yeltsin to Corfu, used the occasion to tell the world press that there was an imminent danger of a "big war" breaking out in Yugoslavia, that the "war could start as soon as the summer ends," and that if Russian peace proposals were "not accepted during July, the great calamity will result." This, combined with the recent television spectacle of the Russian president launching an ICBM, and the recent talk about a new world war arising from the Bosnian crisis, constituted, by the normal standards of diplomacy, a war warning.

President Yeltsin and Foreign Minister Kozyrev, both democrats and pro-Westerners, probably did not see any threat to Russia from U.S. and NATO policy in former Yugoslavia, although their words and deeds said the opposite. Indeed, their behavior contradicted the whole thrust of their policy of rapprochement with the West. Very likely, Russia's nuclear saber rattling over Bosnia was part of the price Yeltsin had to pay to reward the military for defeating the 1993 coup attempt against his government. Unable to buy off the military with budgetary concessions—the deteriorating Russian economy simply cannot sustain the defense budget wanted by the General Staff, except for some of the highest-priority programs—President Yeltsin was compelled to appease the General Staff with concessions on military and foreign policy. This would explain, for example, why Yeltsin would agree to the internationally embarrassing new Russian military doctrine of November 1993 endorsing Russian nuclear first use.

The General Staff, which has always had operational control of Russia's strategic nuclear forces, appeared now to be the "power behind the throne" on both Russian military and foreign policy, leaving Yeltsin in charge only of domestic policy. Yeltsin and Kozyrev spoke not for themselves but for the General Staff, which somehow saw in the Bosnian crisis of June 1994 a possible NATO threat that needed nuclear discouragement. Once again we may have been close to the nuclear brink. How close, only the General Staff knows.

However, four months after the Bosnian crisis, the Russian Defense Ministry went directly to Washington to make absolutely sure the United States understood Moscow's new nuclear doctrine. The defense ministry and General Staff were especially anxious that Washington understand the circumstances under which Moscow would launch a first strike.

As if to be certain that the United States got the message on Russia's new strategy, a document entitled *Russia's Nuclear Doctrine* was given to U.S. assistant secretary of defense Ash Carter by the Russian defense ministry in October 1994. It was an unprecedented act. Never before had any nuclear-armed state spelled out so frankly, for the benefit of a potential adversary, preemptive aspects of its nuclear strategy. Simultaneously, General G. D. Ivanov, Assistant Minister of Defense for Military Policy, briefed Carter and an audience of senior U.S. military officers and analysts.

His briefing and the accompanying document provided a more in-depth and explicit explanation of Russia's commitment to nuclear first use than had the 1993 doctrine *Basic Provisions. Russia's Nuclear Doctrine* pointedly states that Russia might launch a nuclear first strike in most conflict situations. Russia could use nuclear weapons first in three of four scenarios against adversaries that correspond to the United States or other nuclear powers; allies of the United States or other nuclear powers "acting together with or being supported by a nuclear state"—that is, practically any nation in the world; and nonnuclear states acting alone but "bound by an alliance agreement with a nuclear state"—again, practically any nation. The one scenario in which Russia did *not* use nuclear weapons was against a nonnuclear signatory to the Non-Proliferation Treaty, acting alone and with no support from or alliance with a nuclear state. To make sure there could be no misunderstanding on the U.S. side about Russia's first strike policy, *Russia's Nuclear Doctrine* includes an illustration depicting Russia launching a nuclear first strike in three of four scenarios.

Russia's Nuclear Doctrine describes itself as advancing an "expanded understanding of deterrence," wherein "lies the possibility of employing nuclear weapons first against a non-nuclear state." It admits, "Russia's new military doctrine includes a harsher, stricter component in its nuclear policy with respect to surrounding countries. Objectively, the multifaceted nature of new threats to peace justifies this component." The Russian military may already have translated its new doctrinal concepts on nuclear first use into actual operational plans. In a 1993 article, General Andrey Nikolayev noted that "the draft fundamentals of military doctrine and the concept of the military-technical policy *have been prepared*" (emphasis added), including first and foremost "new views and approaches to the use of strategic nuclear forces." When General Ivanov was briefing the U.S. Department of Defense on Russia's new nuclear doctrine in October 1994, the U.S. National Aeronautics and Space Administration (NASA) and Norway were making preparations to launch their new missile. Blast off was now only three months away. No one in the West made the connection between Russia's deeper commitment to a nuclear first-strike strategy and a possible need for greater caution in Western behavior. For the West, the central assumption was that the Cold War was over—for everyone.

CHAPTER 28

Black Brant XII

By the autumn of 1994, the missile had made the journey from mind to metal. Prototypes had been successfully flight tested by NASA off the coast of Virginia. The rocket, designed for weather and earth-science research, was ready for its Norwegian launch.

It was an ambitious project, by far the largest space vehicle ever to be flown from Norway. Known as the "Black Brant XII," the rocket was about the size of a Pershing II, the U.S. nuclear missile that during the early 1980s had started Moscow's long fixation on nuclear surprise attack.

While Black Brant was nearing its launch date in January 1995, Moscow increasingly felt itself set upon by a hostile world. Concerns over NATO expansion, and the war in Chechnya in particular, flared in December and January. Many Russian elites blamed the United States for tensions with the Baltics and other former Soviet republics, believing that the United States was actively stirring up antagonisms to keep the former Soviet Union divided and to perpetuate Russia's internal troubles and military and economic weakness. In September 1994, according to the *Washington Post*, Yevgeniy Primakov, director of the Foreign Intelligence Service (SVR), the successor to the KGB, warned the West not to "stand in the way of economic and political reintegration among former republics of the Soviet Union." Primakov's remarks were echoed in an official Foreign Intelligence Service report titled *Russia-CIS: Does the Western Position Need Correction?* In an unprecedented gesture, Primakov made the report available to the public. He wrote that Western critics were showing "unwillingness to see Russia strengthen as a great state" and that because the West was modernizing its offensive arms, the Russians must "preserve and strengthen their own strategic offensive forces."

The universe of Russian opinion—pro-Western reformers and anti-Western militarists alike—regarded U.S. plans to allow Poland and other Eastern European states to join the NATO alliance as a betrayal and as dangerous to Russia. Russia's threats in response to NATO expansion moved Polish president Lech Walesa to tell President Clinton, during Clinton's July 1994 visit to Warsaw, that he feared a war with Russia might be impending. A keen observer of his Russian neighbor, Walesa set the likelihood at "only 40 percent optimistic Moscow will not order troops into Poland" and "60 percent apprehensive" about a possible Russian invasion.

In December 1994, President Yeltsin warned the United States against NATO plans to expand eastward, briefly awakening the international media with his remark that "Europe is in danger of plunging into a *cold peace*," an obvious allusion to revival of the Cold War. At about the same time, Russia vetoed a United States–sponsored proposal in the UN Security Council intended to cut off supplies supporting Serbian aggression in Bosnia. This was Moscow's first Security Council veto on a major issue since February 1984, a decade earlier.

In addition to Russia's rising tensions with the United States over (imagined) U.S. interference in the former Soviet republics and over the very real issue of impending NATO expansion, there was Russia's war in Chechnya. In December 1994, one month before Norway's missile launch, the Russian Army invaded the breakaway Chechen republic to reassert Moscow's control and to deter secessionist tendencies among other republics, which, if unchecked, could end in fracturing an already debilitated Russia.

The invasion was badly bungled, resulting in many Russian casualties and bogging down into a protracted war. Some generals mutinied, refusing to obey orders. In January 1995, Russian troops were mauled in a battle for the Chechen capital, Grozny. It was a battle that proved to the world that the Russian Army had deteriorated into a hollow shell. On the eve of Norway's missile experiment, the Chechen conflict provoked a crisis in Moscow over Boris Yeltsin's competence to lead. Reformers and hard-liners alike questioned the matter. Another coup was in the air.

Yegor Gaidar, a progressive pro-Westerner and Yeltsin's former prime minister, said that the Chechen war proved President Yeltsin had either been converted to hard-line policies or had become a powerless figurehead ruled by Russia's generals. The Russian press shared Gaidar's opinion. In a 1995 article titled "Boris Yeltsin Joins the Party of Force," journalist Valery Vyzhotovich wrote, "It looks as if the president does not notice he has become the captive of 'power' ministries and his own secret service. Under the pseudonym of 'Yeltsin,' the Russian policy makers are Lobov [chief of the Russian Security Council], [defense minister] Grachev, Yerin [Russian Security Council], Stepashin, [General] Korzhakov, [General] Barsukov. . . . It seems to the president that Korzhakov, Barsukov, and others who stand behind him and are armed make up the guard. But they are the wardens."

The Chechen disaster heightened Moscow's sense of vulnerability and its dependence on nuclear arms. In a January 1995 hearing before the Senate Armed Services Committee, General James Clapper, director of the Defense Intelligence Agency, said that the shortcomings of Russia's general-purpose forces displayed during the invasion of Chechnya would make Moscow more reliant on its nuclear arsenal in order to support "their continued claim to major power status, as their conventional forces have obviously declined." As if to verify General Clapper's testimony, a Russian article featuring an interview with General Igor Sergeyev, commander in chief of Russia's Strategic Rocket Forces, aimed a nuclear threat at the United States for promoting NATO expansion: "Russia is the only country in the world capable of destroying the United States in half an hour—just as the United States can destroy Russia, incidentally—but the Washington of today, for some reason, considers such nuclear missile discussion 'an irrational manifestation of Cold War thinking.' The Clinton Administration has decided to effect NATO expansion, disregarding protests from Moscow. But our Strategic Missile Troops continue to maintain their round-the-clock combat alert status all the same."

Tensions between Russia and Norway over NATO expansion and other issues were particularly acute during the period leading up to the launch from Norway of Black Brant XII on January 25, 1995. After the collapse of the USSR in 1991, Oslo had resurrected a border dispute with Moscow, laying claim to half of Russia's polar possessions—over 150,000 square miles of territorial waters and islands rich in oil and fisheries. These territorial claims were constant sources of irritation, and they remain today a sore point between Moscow and Oslo. As NATO expansion moved from the realm of speculation to an explicit NATO goal in December 1994, just weeks before the launch, Moscow looked nervously at its northern neighbor.

The General Staff was especially fearful of a greater NATO presence in Norway, which was the only NATO state that shared a common border with Russia, and which was located uncomfortably close to some of Russia's most important strategic facilities. NATO missiles and aircraft forward-deployed in Norway would be a scant two hundred kilometers from Murmansk, home of Russia's Northern Fleet and its largest nuclear submarine base. From Norway, NATO would be positioned to launch short-warning attacks against Russian strategic warning radars, and even against Moscow itself. Just weeks before Norway's missile launch, the Russian military press complained of more numerous and aggressive joint military exercises between NATO and Norway.

On December 11, the Russian defense ministry added another nuclear threat, specifically against Norway, to General Igor Sergeyev's December 1994 nuclear threat against the United States and an expanded NATO. Delivered through Alexander Zhilin, a Russian military journalist, it read:

> According to a source at the Defense Ministry in Moscow, the military think that any future NATO maneuvers close to the Russian nuclear defense network based on the peninsula give NATO a chance to test the "Norwegian Springboard" scenario for rapid deployment of Western forces in the Russian north in case of conflict.

Thus the changes in Norwegian policy make Russian nuclear bases near Murmansk susceptible to attack and call for countermeasures against the new national security threat, the source says.

"Since the lack of funds and low military preparedness of Russian ground forces precludes any physical redeployment up north, the 'countermeasures' are likely to mean corrections in the operational plans of Russian strategic nuclear forces," indicating a retargeting of strategic weapons against the Norwegians. "I don't think that will increase Norway's security," Zhilin commented sarcastically.

NATO formally proposed to expand the alliance to include Eastern European states at an international summit of the Conference on Security and Cooperation in Europe held in Budapest during December 1994. General Igor Sergeyev, chief of the Strategic Rocket Forces, leveled his nuclear threat at the United States shortly thereafter. All through December and into January, Moscow's disastrous invasion of Chechnya unfolded. It was a major humiliation, as Russian tanks and troops were slaughtered by Muslim rebels on the streets of Grozny.

On January 25, just one month after NATO affirmed its plans to move east, and merely days after the worst of Chechnya and General Clapper's prescient congressional testimony, Norwegian and NASA scientists launched their meteorological rocket into what they thought were clear skies.

Norway's missile launch would have gone more smoothly had someone bothered to forewarn the Russian military about it. Scientific-sounding rockets were no strangers to the skies of Norway. Over the past three decades, since 1962, Oslo had fired 607 missiles for scientific research, always being careful to inform Moscow of the event in advance. The launch of January 25 was no exception.

Oslo could not specify the exact day and time of its missile launches, because this depended on the weather. Such imprecision about missile firings was "part of the procedure because the weather decides when a launch can be made," Ingvard Havnen, of Norway's Foreign Ministry, later explained. "This is the procedure we have followed for thirty-two years." On December 21 and again on January 16, the Norwegian government informed the Russian embassy in Oslo that a scientific missile launch was impending. "We told them what type of rocket was going to be fired, where it was going to land, and we indicated a time period from January 15 to February 5 with a daily window from 5 A.M. to 12 A.M.," according to Norwegian rocketry director Kolbjoern Adolfsen.

Someone on the Russian side, probably an inexperienced, minor functionary either at the foreign ministry or the defense ministry, failed to pass this information on to the General Staff. The military operators of the Air Defense Forces, the Strategic Rocket Forces, and the other nuclear services remained in the dark that a peaceful Norwegian missile launch was impending.

Mikhail Demurin of the Russian foreign ministry later said that Norway's launch notice "clearly stated the timing and the areas of water which ships should stay away from in order to avoid the remains of a spacecraft accidentally falling on deck." An anonymous Russian general, who sounds very like Anatoliy Sokolov, commander of Russia's northern early-warning radars, later told the press that the wording of Norway's missile launch message to "notify the upcoming launch of a meteorological rocket to seafarers" was taken too literally by Russian bureaucrats. "Foreign Ministry officials took a literal attitude toward that request: sailors knew of the event. Not the military."

Nikolay Devyanin, chief designer of the Russian president's "nuclear briefcase," later blamed the Norwegians for being vague in their missile launch notification about the precise launch time, seeing in this "an arrogant attitude toward a nuclear power." However, Devyanin also conceded the possibility that "the note and coded cable by the Norwegian side got into the Defense Ministry and ended up in its offices, thus failing to reach duty-shift personnel of the Missile Attack Warning System (MAWS)." General Anatoliy Sokolov, in charge of the MAWS radars facing Norway, put the blame elsewhere: "The information that this was a geodesic missile got bogged down somewhere at the Foreign Ministry level."

However it happened, this clerical error nearly caused a global nuclear catastrophe.

In the early morning light of January 25, 1995, Kolbjoern Adolfsen gazed admiringly at the needlelike missile gleaming on its launch pad. The Black Brant XII was Norway's largest rocket ever. "This was the first time we fired a four-stage rocket," Adolfsen later told the press. "It was twice as big as any rocket we have ever fired in the past."

NASA had provided the funds and technical expertise to help develop the missile, and discarded U.S. military boosters were used in Black Brant's construction. Engines that formerly might have lobbed a nuclear weapon would now carry aloft a scientific package to study the spectral northern lights.

Unlike previous, and substantially smaller, Norwegian rockets, which merely popped straight up a few hundred kilometers before falling back to earth, Black Brant XII was designed to travel higher and farther, following an arcing ballistic trajectory for some 1,500 kilometers. Earlier Norwegian rockets were toys by comparison. Tall but thin, like some impossibly large pencil, Black Brant towered sixty feet into the air—the height of a six-story building—roughly comparable in length to the U.S. Pershing II or the U.S. Trident II submarine–launched ballistic missile.

As the countdown started toward launch, the brightening gloom of Norway's polar dawn illumined the bleakness of the Andoya Island rocket range, a rock washed by the arctic waters of the Norwegian Sea. Gulls wheeled over the ocean, brilliant white, looking for fish. *Steel* fish also lurked in these seas, U.S. submarines carrying on their endless nuclear vigil.

On endless vigil, too, were the officers and men of Russia's Missile Attack Warning System (MAWS). Every hour of every day, Russia's northern "HEN HOUSE" and Large Phased-Array Radars looked out over the Norwegian Sea and beyond, watching for the radar signature of a missile launch from a U.S. submarine, or of an incoming intercontinental ballistic missile.

The northern radars at Murmansk, Skrunda, Baranovichi, and Pechora and the anti-ballistic missile radar outside Moscow watched the most likely corridor for a U.S. nuclear attack. The northern radars monitored especially closely the launch areas for U.S. submarine missiles fired from the Barents or Norwegian seas. These could reach Moscow in the shortest possible time, allowing the least warning of an incoming missile attack. U.S. intercontinental ballistic missiles fired from North America at Moscow would also pass through the field of view of the northern radars.

Radar and satellite early warning work is tough, fatiguing duty, involving long hours in unpleasant places. Russian journalist Oleg Falichev found that at one MAWS facility, a single officer, "Colonel Sergey Lobov . . . is personally . . . responsible for the . . . United States; that is, for monitoring the territory of America. So you can imagine the workload that falls on such people as him, and the iron nerves that they must possess." Falichev describes well the overworked exhaustion of Russia's "iron men" of the Missile Attack Warning System:

> At times, the officers who perform alert duty are so exhausted at the end of a shift that they don't feel either their hands or their feet. Honor and praise to them. . . . One day that time may come when the professionalism of the military personnel will . . . not come to their rescue. When all of the sores and plagues will very urgently appear all at once. . . . What then?

This grueling duty was usually conducted in barren, arctic places like Murmansk and Pechora, or in politically hostile surroundings like the Baltic states, where the newly foreign local population hated Russian officers and any reminders of the former Soviet empire. Under such pressures, even iron men can make mistakes.

The elite officers of the Missile Attack Warning System performed their duty with the seriousness of men who could not afford error. Ever since Matthias Rust, Germany's boy aviator, embarrassed the radar men by flying a tiny Piper Cub–sized aircraft through Russia's dense air defenses in May 1987—then compounding Moscow's humiliation by landing in Red

Square—the Air Defense Forces had seemed more determined than ever to "shoot first and ask questions later." General Viktor Prudnikov, commander in chief of the Air Defense Forces, which included MAWS, did not forget that his predecessor had been fired over the Rust affair. He urged his troops to ever-greater vigilance. Their hair-trigger readiness, still too sharply honed today, accounted for the killing of the two U.S. sports balloonists who drifted near a Russian ICBM base in 1995.

Norway's missile would be launched into airspace watched most carefully by the Air Defense Forces and MAWS for signs of a nuclear surprise attack, monitored by overworked radar crews, who thought that if World War III ever came, it would most likely come at them first, and come with the swiftness of a missile launched almost in their faces.

If a nuclear surprise attack occurred, the General Staff and the radar duty crews expected to see missiles launched from U.S. submarines first. These could be fired close to Russian territory and arrive in ten minutes or less, leaving little time for Moscow to order a retaliatory strike. Intercontinental ballistic missiles fired from North America would arrive in half an hour, appearing on Russian radar screens perhaps ten minutes after the first submarine missiles were detected—in some cases, after U.S. SLBMs had already struck. U.S. bombers carrying cruise missiles would arrive hours later, long after the main strike had been delivered by U.S. strategic missiles. Intermediate-range ballistic missiles, which had posed a short-warning threat from bases in Europe, had been dismantled in the 1980s under the terms of the Intermediate-range Nuclear Forces Treaty. Therefore submarine ballistic missiles, particularly those launched close in from the Barents or Norwegian seas, were the key to detecting a surprise attack in the 1990s.

In the months preceding Norway's launch of its science missile, the Russian Navy repeatedly complained about allegedly increased U.S. submarine patrols in the Norwegian and Barents seas, even penetrating Russian territorial waters. In the view of the Russian General Staff, the leading edge of a massive U.S. nuclear surprise attack would probably be from submarines launching missiles in this forward area. A particularly worrisome scenario for the General Staff, much discussed in their theoretical military literature of the 1990s, was the possibility of an electromagnetic-pulse (EMP) attack. A nuclear weapon detonated above the atmosphere would generate a powerful electromagnetic wave, much like a supercharged radio signal that, while not directly injurious to people, would overload and burn out electronic systems over a broad area of the earth's surface. The United States unexpectedly discovered the EMP effect in 1962, during a nuclear test called FISHBOWL. Conducted in outer space above Johnston Island in the Pacific Ocean, FISHBOWL knocked out rows of street lamps in the Hawaiian Islands, thousands of kilometers away. The Soviets probably knew about the EMP phenomenon earlier, from high-altitude nuclear tests conducted above the Arctic, which would have affected Archangel, Murmansk, and other northern Russian cities.

In a 1991 issue of *Military Thought*, General V. Belous, a prominent Russian military scientist, wrote that "EMP . . . is capable of disabling electronic gear, communications and power transmission lines, radios, and radars at great distances." He noted that a single nuclear warhead detonated at an altitude of three to four hundred kilometers over North America would generate a powerful electromagnetic pulse covering the entire continental United States. Such an attack would, according to General Belous, "disrupt operation of electronic equipment on virtually the country's entire territory for the time necessary to disrupt retaliatory operations." EMP's potential to disrupt command and control, paralyzing retaliatory systems long enough for an enemy to land his nuclear knockout punch, was termed by some U.S. analysts "the chaos factor."

In the 1990s, the General Staff was aware of U.S. research into super-EMP nuclear weapons, which would generate a particularly powerful electromagnetic pulse capable of destroying even protected electronic systems. "From the early 1980s, U.S. military scientists . . . aimed at creating . . . a super-EMP [weapon] with intensified electromagnetic radiation output," General Belous accurately observed. "They figure to use it to increase the intensity of the field at the Earth's surface to several hundred kilovolts per meter." A super-EMP weapon would deliver a shock to electronic systems more powerful than a bolt of lightning, and against which circuit breakers and other EMP protection devices would be useless. In 1991 General Igor Rodionov, chief of the General Staff Academy and future defense minister, predicted the possible "appearance of third generation nuclear weapons," such as a super-EMP warhead, "in the next few years."

A super-EMP warhead could be designed small enough for delivery by a submarine-launched missile.

One of the General Staff's blackest nuclear nightmares was a scenario in which a U.S. submarine launched an EMP attack on Russia. A solitary EMP warhead could disable radars and other early warning systems, isolate the leadership in Moscow by destroying strategic communications and military computers, and even paralyze missiles in silos or in flight. The precursor EMP strike would be followed by a massive U.S. nuclear attack, involving hundreds of ICBMs and SLBMs, that would complete the destruction of Russian strategic forces.

The virtue of an EMP precursor attack by a single missile is that it could be disguised as a training test, an accidental launch, or scientific experiment, denying Russia precious minutes of strategic warning until delivery of the paralyzing electromagnetic pulse. Ideally, in a surprise EMP attack that allowed Russia the shortest warning and least reaction time, an SLBM would be fired from a forward location having the shortest flight time to targets in Russia. The best locations for such an attack are off the coasts of Russia and Norway, in the Barents or Norwegian seas.

On January 25, 1995, at 0624 A.M. Zulu, Black Brant XII blasted off from the Andoya Island rocket range on the edge of the Norwegian Sea. The long steel finger, trailing flame, accelerated rapidly as it climbed toward its target altitude for geomagnetic experimentation, about 1,500 kilometers. Seconds later, Russian radars of the Missile Attack Warning System, including the Pushkino anti-ballistic missile radar just north of Moscow, detected the high-velocity rocket. It was accelerating rapidly to an altitude that could carry it on a ballistic trajectory toward Russia. Now the effects of the bungled handling of Norway's missile launch notification, the failure to warn military operators about the impending launch, started to assume dangerous dimensions.

"The launch was detected by several Russian MAWS radars," according to "nuclear briefcase" designer Nikolay Devyanin, one of the foremost experts on Russia's command and control and early warning systems. "Automatic processing of initial flight parameters showed radar-duty shift personnel that they were not expecting such a missile."

Radars are unable to geolocate the launch origin of a missile with a precision better than several tens of kilometers, especially during their boost phase. To Russian missile attack warning radars, the Black Brant XII racing skyward had a launch origin not precisely at Andoya Island but in a vast region extending dozens of kilometers into the Norwegian Sea. The unexpected missile could be an SLBM launched from a forward-deployed U.S. submarine.

Frantic queries to the military high command proved futile. No one, including the General Staff, "had any advance information on the Norwegian missile," MAWS General Anatoliy Sokolov later said. According to General Sokolov, commander of the northern early warning radars, "the launch of a civilian missile and a missile carrying a warhead—particularly early on in their trajectory—are virtually identical. And we were simply obliged to treat it very seriously."

The last thing General Sokolov and the officers of the Missile Attack Warning System suspected was that they were making a mistake in regarding the unidentified missile as a threat. Even in the aftermath of the Norway missile fiasco, General Sokolov argued that Russia's Missile Attack Warning System does not make mistakes:

> The early warning system was . . . developed to detect a missile attack on the country and to provide the military-political leadership with the information necessary to adopt the final decision regarding the use of our own nuclear forces within as short a time as possible. At the same time the reliability of the information is ensured at several levels. At the first echelon, by the space-based ballistic missile launch detection system. At the second echelon, by the over-the-horizon detection

> systems stationed around the perimeter of the former Union in Pechora, Murmansk, Skrunda (Latvia), Mukachevo and Sevastopol (Ukraine), Mingechaur (Azerbaijan), Balkhash (Kazakhstan), and Irkutsk. We realize that even if we tell a lie only once we suffer a loss of confidence in us. . . . Only educated officers who have undergone special training are allowed on combat alert duty.

"The system carries a tremendous safety margin and has several levels of defense," General Sokolov told the press after the Norwegian missile incident, "which preclude false information being given to the military-political leadership."

As Black Brant XII raced toward its apogee, Russian radar officers could see its stages fall away on their cathode ray screens, ghostly dots breaking off a streaking comet—an ominous sign.

Previous Norwegian missiles had only a single stage; after a brief powered flight to a low altitude, the entire rocket would fall straight back to earth. Black Brant, however, resembled a U.S. submarine-launched, multiple-stage, ballistic missile.

The automated radar system, which would compare incoming data on the missile, its stages, and engine blast to those on Western missiles stored in a computer inventory, may have even recognized one of the U.S. military boosters used in the stages of Black Brant. This would trigger an automated threat message to the radar operators. Moreover, the unidentified missile's velocity, altitude, and trajectory resembled that of an SLBM.

"Judge for yourself," General Sokolov later challenged the press. "At 0923 [Moscow time], the operational duty officer reported the detection of a ballistic missile. . . . What kind of missile was it? What was it carrying? We had no notification of upcoming work. The missile . . . had it been launched on the optimum trajectory, the range would have [been] 3,500 kilometers. And that is the distance to Moscow."

"Approach time to Moscow is five to six minutes, but it is just within arm's reach to the Kola Peninsula [where the bulk of Russia's Navy, the Northern Fleet, is based]. What is to be done?" Nikolay Devyanin asked. He later described the ambivalent mood of the Russian radar officers, who were on the verge of panic, torn between a paralyzing terror and a mechanical dedication to duty:

> There was no time to ask their superiors for advice, but they did not want to become scapegoats for another [Matthias] Rust [the German youth who flew through Russian air defenses to land in Red Square]. In this situation the duty officers made the sole possible decision: to work according to plan, as prescribed by instructions, and as has been practiced dozens of times in drill sessions.

Officers of the Missile Attack Warning System decided that the unidentified rocket on their screens was a threat. They alerted higher command echelons that a possible nuclear attack was in progress. This they did by activating "KROKUS," a system that flashed a missile threat warning to the "big board," a global situation screen covering an entire wall in the General Staff Command Post, located south of Moscow, hundreds of meters underground. In turn, the officers on duty in the General Staff Command Post decided that the threat was serious enough to activate "KAZBEK," placing the "nuclear briefcases" and the strategic forces on alert.

Nikolay Devyanin describes the alert process—and the pressures of decision making—during the missile incident:

> Combat information about the missile launch went through MAWS channels to corresponding command points, including the Russian Armed Forces top command points, which are incorporated in the KAZBEK system and are linked with the "footballs" [nuclear briefcases] 24 hours a day. Here, all information about a flying ballistic missile, with indications of the time and place of launch, immediately popped up on MAWS terminals: the KROKUS panel. For the general on duty to make a decision to put the KAZBEK system on alert mode and pass the report about the launch of an enemy missile to the "footballs" [nuclear briefcases] was both easier (a combat alert report was already glowing on his display) and more difficult (a dressing down from the top level for the bother and panic could follow immediately). Even so, he had no one to consult either, except the "football" [nuclear briefcase] users: his minister and the Chief of the General Staff. Be that as it may, it appeared that the best option was to follow the instructions.

General Sokolov, commander of the Missile Attack Warning System radars that notified upper echelons of the missile threat, admitted that on receiving the bad news, the Russian military high command "were all stressed, as were the Air Defense Main Command and the Defense Ministry." General Sokolov later unapologetically affirmed that he reacted to the missile threat "just as I should in the worst-case scenario." He also affirmed that Boris Yeltsin was alerted to the missile threat "within a matter of minutes after its launch." Nikolay Devyanin detailed how this was done, by activating the "nuclear briefcases" for President Yeltsin, Defense Minister Pavel Grachev, and Chief of the General Staff Mikhail Kolesnikov. There is no better guide to the Russian nuclear alert process than Devyanin, who designed the "nuclear briefcases"—which in his account he calls "footballs," using the American slang term for these doomsday devices:

> A few seconds to unblock the duty officer's work place, to enter a formal report, and press the "transfer" button, and alarm signals flashed virtually at once on all "footballs." The KAZBEK system went into alert mode. A few seconds later the duty officer's display began to read: his report had reached the "footballs" and had been received by the users. At the same time, a telephone conference call was ar-

ranged between the president, the defense minister, and the chief of the General Staff.

"Next stage actors are 'football' operating officers," Devyanin continued. "Their task—in the event the system is put into alert mode—is to seize it and go (run) to report it, without thinking. Which they did."

The military officer in charge of President Boris Yeltsin's "nuclear briefcase," always close at hand to the president, saw a light flash on his device, signifying a nuclear alert in progress. He immediately interrupted President Yeltsin and opened the device. He quickly briefed the president on the situation displayed on the computer screen inside the case. He probably also refreshed the president's memory on how to operate the device. The electronic display depicted the same missile threat information displayed on the "big board" in the General Staff Command Post. A possible U.S. or NATO nuclear missile launched from Norway or the Norwegian Sea was rapidly ascending, but the target azimuth was still unknown. Would it fly toward Russia?

A row of buttons in the briefcase allowed a choice of nuclear strike options, probably ranging from limited strikes against selected targets in individual nations to a massive strike against all strategic targets everywhere. This latter option would obliterate military, economic, and administrative targets in the United States, Western Europe, Japan, China, and all the nations tied to those by alliances or military cooperative relationships—essentially the entire world.

As the warning message from MAWS activated President Yeltsin's briefcase, the same message raced through the ether to Russia's strategic nuclear forces.

Captain Sergei Ivanko looked around his brightly lit bunker, a launch control capsule for a regiment of SS-18 ICBMs, Russia's most powerful nuclear missile, called the SATAN.

Serving in the capsule—Ivanko's home away from home during interminable shifts that sometimes dragged on for weeks—was like living in a transistor chip. Electronic arrays, panels of lights, switches, and cables covered the walls. Beneath his feet he could see through little holes in the metal floor to the level below, also packed with electronics and machinery.

Judged by a tape measure, the place was actually roomy, offering more space than his entire family had when he was growing up. Seven people—his two parents, grandmother, sister, his two brothers, and himself—had lived together in a tiny apartment in Nizhny-Novgorod. The launch control capsule was larger by far and had to be shared with only one other person, his partner, Lieutenant Viktor Yashin. Moreover, the capsule was air conditioned, and the heating system worked well. Outside, the howling blizzards of January went completely unnoticed by Ivanko and Yashin, toasty in their underground bunker. This pleased Ivanko.

Still, the crowded family quarters in Nizhny-Novgorod *seemed* somehow roomier. Perhaps knowing the launch control capsule was dozens of meters underground created a sense of claustrophobia. Or maybe it was the occupation. Ivanko would sometimes lie in his bunk and imagine what it would be like to be trapped down here in a war. He could visualize the enemy missile launch, the rocket exploding out of its silo like an angry god, its warhead flashing over the North Pole, plummeting like lightning through the atmosphere, striking somewhere overhead, probably not more than one hundred meters away, the shock wave collapsing the massive concrete walls of the bunker, like closing a book on an insect.

Captain Ivanko hoped that would never happen. But if it did, he wanted to be sure of retribution. Once they received launch codes from the General Staff, he and Yashin would insert their launch keys, turn them simultaneously, and fire the ten SS-18s of their regiment. Two men would deliver a hundred nuclear warheads against the United States—enough to devastate every major city in America. Scores of other launch crews in other launch-control capsules would hurl thousands of additional warheads at America.

Maybe it was mere vengeance, but when Ivanko thought about what an enemy nuclear attack would do to Russia, to his family—the leveled cities, children dying from burns and radiation sickness, his dear wife vaporized in a flash of unbearable light—it felt like justice.

Captain Ivanko knew that when the moment came, if it ever came, he and Yashin would have to act swiftly. There would be no vengeance or justice if the enemy missile reached them before they could turn the keys.

Then, like a waking nightmare, it happened.

The red light on the launch control console flashed on. An electronic klaxon sounded in shrill urgency. An emergency message clattered over the teletype, a noise like chattering teeth. *Nuclear alert. Not a drill.*

Ivanko and Yashin plugged in their headphones, straining to hear further orders from Moscow. They pulled their seatbelts tight, sinking slightly into the padded chairs designed to hold them fast and protect them from bouncing off the walls, should their bunker survive a nuclear shock wave. They inserted their launch keys. They waited. The time was 0628 A.M. Zulu on January 25, 1995.

As President Yeltsin stared at his "nuclear briefcase," contemplating his choices, the alerted missile crews of the Strategic Rocket Forces and the strategic naval forces stood by. When the missile attack warning message was disseminated on KROKUS and KAZBEK, all of the command posts and individual crews at ICBM launchers, aboard missile submarines, and for strategic bombers were simultaneously alerted.

Every hour of every day, Russia maintains the Strategic Rocket Forces and some missile submarines on Constant Combat Readiness, always prepared within a few minutes to launch thousands of nuclear warheads against strategic targets worldwide. Hundreds of additional warheads would become available as Russia's nonalerted submarines and bombers received the alert message and sprang into action. But mobilization takes time. Bomber and submarine crews must scramble to their duty posts, aircraft must be fueled, and bombs and cruise missiles removed from storage bunkers and uploaded.

Constant Combat Readiness is Russia's insurance policy against a nuclear surprise attack. Moscow is always prepared, at any moment, to execute fully any nuclear strike option against any nation or combination of nations. Russia is always ready to wage any of a dozen possible nuclear wars. At 0628 A.M. Zulu on January 25, President Boris Yeltsin had 4,700 strategic warheads at his disposal, ready to launch at the push of a button.

CHAPTER 29

Dangerous Minutes

A hotline connected President Yeltsin to General Mikhail Kolesnikov, Chief of the General Staff, who was studying the missile threat on his own "nuclear briefcase." General Kolesnikov controlled the nuclear codes. He had the technical capability to execute a nuclear strike, with or without President Yeltsin's assent. Legally, however, the decision to go to war is the president's. Quickly obtaining Yeltsin's permission to launch a nuclear attack was the entire purpose of the briefcase, and the purpose of the hotline to the General Staff.

As President Yeltsin and General Kolesnikov conferred, only about four minutes had passed since the launch of Norway's Black Brant. The "nuclear briefcases" indicated it was a possible U.S. or NATO nuclear missile launched from the vicinity of the Norwegian Sea, still rapidly ascending. Black Brant was rocketing toward its apogee, hurtling nearly straight up, so its target azimuth, its intended impact area, was still unknown.

Although a nuclear alert had been initiated, General Sokolov later indicated to the press that there was still doubt about the missile's identity. This must have been the case. Doubt about whether a U.S. nuclear attack was in fact in progress must have been communicated to President Yeltsin and Kolesnikov via their briefcases; otherwise, a preemptive nuclear strike surely would have been launched.

As they watched the progress of the mysterious missile on their briefcase screens the pressure and burden of responsibility on Boris Yeltsin and Mikhail Kolesnikov was crushing. If the missile was an EMP precursor attack, its detonation would be followed by the massed launch of U.S. intercontinental and submarine missiles. *Now* was the time for a Russian preemptive strike, before the electromagnetic pulse paralyzed the strategic forces, and while U.S. ICBMs and bombers were still sitting at their bases, vulnerable. Russian launch detection satellites would have confirmed that U.S. ICBMs had not yet fired, meaning that the opportunity for a Russian first strike had not yet passed—or meaning that whatever was happening, it was not a U.S. nuclear attack.

General Kolesnikov suspected a nuclear surprise attack was under way, and he almost certainly contemplated a preemptive strike. The next day, after the Norwegian embassy had explained to Moscow the Black Brant missile program and its peaceful, scientific mission, the Chief of the General Staff continued to believe that it had been, in reality, a new NATO military missile. "The rocket launched Wednesday from Norway can be ranked as a new operational-tactical missile," Kolesnikov told the press the day after the missile crisis. He admitted his grave concerns of the previous day: "A rocket launched from a certain area is always a serious event."

Reflecting General Kolesnikov's doubts about Norway's claims that Black Brant was peaceful, an anonymous general, probably Anatoliy Sokolov, commander of the northern MAWS radars, asked the press after the crisis, "What kind of meteorological rocket is that which is multistage and flies farther than 1,000 kilometers along a ballistic (parabolic) trajectory, rather than 300 to 500 kilometers straight up?"

A spokesman for A. Chernikov, director of Russia's Central Aerological Observatory, told the press the Black Brant was not a science rocket but a military missile of intermediate range:

> To judge from its long flight range and height of climb, the Norwegian rocket does not belong to the class of meteorological rockets. The latter are launched vertically, and then the equipment descends by parachute not far from the launch site. The height of climb of meteorological rockets is usually approximately 100 kilometers, with a maximum of 500 kilometers. The Norwegian one climbed to a height of over 1,400 kilometers and flew along a ballistic trajectory. Rockets of this kind are classed as intermediate-range combat "surface-to-surface" missiles.

The Pershing II had been an intermediate-range missile.

Despite Norway's best efforts to prove otherwise after the crisis, Russian expert opinion remained convinced that Black Brant was a military missile. When the missile was still flying, Russian missile experts had doubts about the threat, but not enough to refrain from calling a nuclear alert, not even enough to change their minds afterward about the military nature of the missile. During the missile crisis on January 25, President Yeltsin and General Kolesnikov must have been advised—and probably thought for at least several minutes—that their "briefcases" were showing an incoming U.S. nuclear attack.

Watching the unidentified missile, Yeltsin clearly thought that there was a real possibility of nuclear war. The next day he unexpectedly told an audience, who had assembled to hear about economic issues, that he had, for the first and only time in his presidency, seen his "nuclear briefcase" and its doomsday button in an active mode, with Russia's military high command at his elbow: "I have indeed used yesterday for the first time my 'little black case' with a button that is always with me. . . . I immediately contacted the Defense Ministry and all the military commanders that I require and we were following the path of this missile from beginning to end." President Yeltsin said that he had considered shooting down the missile with an antimissile, a contingency that became unnecessary as the missile's trajectory headed away from Moscow: "We had calculated that it would fall far from our shores. We therefore did not shoot it down."

The nuclear close call of January 25 apparently put tremendous psychological strain on Yeltsin. Nikolay Devyanin, who disapproved of his president's "spilling the beans" about the nuclear crisis, chalked up Yeltsin's confession to nerves: "Had Yeltsin himself not told about the incident the following day, the story would have hardly received such a resonance. The president's reaction is probably natural for a man who had been in a stress situation."

President Yeltsin and General Kolesnikov tracked the flight of Black Brant on their briefcases for between three and seven minutes before it became clear the rocket was not headed toward Russia. It reached its apogee about twelve minutes after launch, at which point it had flown half its trajectory on a northeasterly course, a fact that should have been plain by then to Russian radars. The anonymous Russian general who spoke afterward claimed that by this point the crisis was over: "After the rocket emerged onto a ballistic curve, the direction of its flight became clear, and we could see that it would in no way touch on Russian territory, but land in the Spitsbergen region—we calmed down and took no serious measures, although we tracked it to the very last second of its flight." Contrary to the anonymous general, Moscow may have worried about a possible threat from Black Brant even after it became clear the rocket was flying away from Russia. In an EMP attack, the threatening dimension is altitude, not direction. An EMP warhead detonated at Black Brant XII's apogee of some 1,400 kilometers could have covered all of European Russia with an electromagnetic field. Moreover, an electromagnetic pulse is most powerful when the warhead is detonated nearer the magnetic North Pole. Maximum EMP effects at the earth's surface would be, depending on missile trajectory and other factors, hundreds of kilometers *downrange* of the detonation point. Thus, under some circumstances, the most effective trajectory for an EMP attack on Russia would be toward the magnetic pole, even if this meant flying a course *away* from Russia.

Perhaps for this reason, and not mere idle curiosity, the Missile Attack Warning System, President Yeltsin, and Chief of the General Staff Kolesnikov stayed glued to their screens after apogee, watching Black Brant complete its flight. At 0648 A.M. Zulu (0948 A.M. Moscow time), the missile impacted near the ice-covered Spitsbergen archipelago. Black Brant had traveled a rainbow trajectory, peaking at an altitude of 1,453 kilometers and terminating at a distance of 1,564 kilometers uprange of Andoya Island. The flight lasted twenty-four minutes. The latest war scare was over.

The next morning, on January 26, President Boris Yeltsin returned to his normal schedule and flew to Lipetsk. It was a routine political "parish call" on Russia's version of a rust-belt manufacturing town, one that had fallen on harder-than-usual times. The theme of Yeltsin's visit was supposed to be the economy. "The president and journalists were shown the high quality refrigerators, audio and video equipment, and other quality output at the Novolipetsk Metallurgical Combine and the 'Lipetsk-Kompleks' Agrarian Joint Stock Exchange," journalist Vasiliy Kononenko wrote. "Workers at Lipetsk's enterprises gave the president a quiet welcome, without any hysterical placards making political demands. And it seemed as though the president had forgotten big-time politics for a while."

Then President Yeltsin shocked his audience by departing from his speech on the economy to describe, almost as an afterthought, his glimpse into the nuclear abyss a few hours earlier:

> Yesterday I used my "attaché case" for the first time. . . . I called the defense minister and the relevant services and asked them what kind of missile it was and where it had come from. Within a minute I had the information—the entire flight of the missile had been monitored from start to finish. . . . They [those who launched the missile] clearly did not expect us to detect the missile on our radar. Maybe someone had decided to test us out? In short, we had cause to thank our military. The army has shown that it is not weak, as the mass media are claiming.

General Mikhail Kolesnikov, Chief of the General Staff, made a similar comment later that same day. General Kolesnikov insisted that Norway's science rocket was actually a new military missile. He acknowledged that Norway had warned Russia of a missile experiment two weeks in advance, but had neglected to provide a precise launch time. Kolesnikov offered this version of events following the missile blastoff:

> Our early warning stations' equipment automatically began tracking the rocket. The rocket launch was detected straight away by three stations in European Russia. The equipment is quite indifferent as to what kind of rocket it is—whether it be military or civil—but a rocket launch from a certain area is always a serious event. The hardware was supposed to respond to a rocket, and so it did. It was a small rocket, incidentally, and we Russian military feel particularly satisfied that our systems got a fix on the "baby." [The] subsequent train of events is easy to picture: the rocket launch was shown on a panel, and this made us conduct a kind of unplanned drill, precisely tracking its launching and landing positions. From the very start of the rocket's flight a direct special communications line between the president, the defense minister, and the chief of the General Staff was activated.

President Yeltsin and General Staff chief Kolesnikov may have been trying to put a "happy face" on another Russian military disaster, close on the heels of Chechnya, this one involving nuclear weapons. Instead of admitting that Russia had dangerously overreacted to Norway's missile launch, Yeltsin and Kolesnikov tried to focus attention on the proficiency and high combat readiness of the strategic forces. However, both men continued to imply that there *was* in fact, some sort of Western threat on January 25, even if it was only NATO probing Russia's defenses or the launch of a new military missile that warranted Moscow's nuclear alert. If President Yeltsin and General Kolesnikov knew by January 26 that Norway's missile was no threat and the nuclear alert was an error—and if their propaganda goal was to underscore Russia's military proficiency—then continuing to misrepresent Norway's science missile as a military threat and the alert as justified would be self-defeating. Such a course would only draw attention to the error and raise further doubts about Russian military competence. Yet this is precisely what Yeltsin and Kolesnikov did. Neither man ever admitted Russia's nuclear alert was a mistake.

It is at least plausible that on January 26, President Yeltsin and General Kolesnikov meant what they said. Perhaps they still believed the Black Brant was a military missile designed to probe Russian radar defenses and test their vigilance. Perhaps, even after the immediate missile crisis, they still feared Western aggression might be imminent. "Exposing" the Western missile ploy and praising Russian military readiness might help deter an impending U.S. nuclear surprise attack.

The world press tended to dismiss Russia's nuclear alert as propaganda. Unfortunately, an initial report by Russia's Interfax news service claimed that Moscow's antimissile systems had intercepted Norway's rocket. The report was false. It was quickly disproved, and it encouraged the Western press to focus on the wrong issue. Most Western press coverage amounted to a sigh of relief that Russia had not shot down Norway's rocket experiment. This journalistic slant ignored the fact that Russia's nuclear alert was far more dangerous than the downing of a mere meteorological rocket. In fact, Moscow had contemplated shooting down Black Brant, which was tracked by ABM radars. These could coordinate interception by an antimissile. Boris Yeltsin admitted at Lipetsk that shooting down the missile had been initially considered, but eventually deemed unnecessary. Apparently a leak to Interfax from a senior Russian military officer was misconstrued, making the contemplated interception of Norway's missile a missile actually intercepted.

On January 26, the day after the nuclear alert, the page-one story in the *Los Angeles Times* was headlined " 'Missile Attack' on Russia Was Just a Science Probe; Defense News Agency Is Falsely Informed That a Weapon Was Shot Down." The *Los Angeles Times* thought the most important thing to report on the missile incident was this reassuring first-paragraph news: "An attack that never occurred created a brief alarm Wednesday after a news agency erroneously reported that Russian forces had shot down an incoming combat missile that had violated Russian air space." Not until the last paragraph of a lengthy article did the *Los Angeles Times* cite the opinion of defense expert Bruce Blair that the missile incident had disturbing implications for Russian nuclear-threat perceptions:

Moscow is especially jittery about the possibility of an attack from the North Atlantic, the Norwegian Sea or even the closer Barents Sea, said Blair, author of a recent book called *The Logic of Accidental Nuclear War*.

Historically, the North Atlantic and Norwegian Sea have been patrolled by submarines, including the Trident, equipped with powerful, accurate ballistic missiles, he said. These missiles now pose the most serious strategic nuclear threat to Russia.

"From forward locations in Greenland or Norway, they could launch a deadly missile that could land on Moscow in under fifteen minutes," Blair said. Theoretically, such a strike could decapitate Russia's nuclear command headquarters in Moscow, "so they are very nervous about this particular weapon system."

The *Washington Times* was one of the few newspapers in the West that appreciated—somewhat—the dangerous implications of the Norwegian missile incident:

> The test launch of a Norwegian research rocket on Wednesday . . . caused a major alert in Moscow. . . . President Yeltsin had his finger on the button for the first time as head of state last week. Pretty scary idea, that, given the persistent rumors that Mr. Yeltsin's finger might be just a little shaky from too much vodka these days. Not only did Mr. Yeltsin haul out the suitcase with the nuclear codes, he also accused NATO of surreptitiously trying to test Russia's military readiness. Sounds most ominous.

A short report by Jeff Berliner captured many of the essentials of the January 25 missile crisis, including the most important point—its implications for the Russian threat:

> Russian President Boris Yeltsin said Thursday he used his special internal nuclear "hotline" for the first time Wednesday to talk to his generals after a meteorological research rocket launch in Norway that some in Russia initially—and incorrectly—interpreted to be a missile launch. Yeltsin's comments . . . revealed just how far alarmist Russian reaction went to what was essentially a non-event. . . . Yeltsin's comments show the misinterpretation of the incident, perhaps even false reports, reached the highest levels of the Kremlin—raising questions about whether the Russian president himself is getting accurate information, and renewing concerns that a so-called Party of War advisors has taken up residence in the Kremlin.

"Yeltsin's comments seem to show a measure of suspicion over just how innocent the rocket launch was, betraying the kind of paranoia that marked Cold War thinking," Berliner concluded. "Yeltsin's remarks also gave credence to the growing suspicion that he has come under the influence of hawkish advisers who have inherent distrust of the West, who counseled him on invading Chechnya, and who have been reportedly insulating the Kremlin from Yeltsin's former democratic supporters."

Unfortunately, Berliner's news-service article was not published by any major paper.

The Western press, and Russian liberal journalists even more so, tended to dismiss the Norway missile incident as a crude attempt by President Yeltsin to shore up Russia's superpower reputation after the humiliating debacle in Chechnya.

Yet even this most benign explanation for Russia's nuclear alert of January 25—an explanation that assumes Russia went through the motions of a nuclear alert solely to intimidate the West—has deeply disturbing implications. Nuclear saber rattling by Russia over failures in Chechnya indicates a dangerous hypersensitivity similar to the war scare attitudes of the early 1980s. The humiliation of the Russian Army in Chechnya was a matter of merely peripheral interest in the West, yet Moscow was so sure the West was watching Russia's every move in Chechnya, looking for signs of military weakness, that the setback there moved Yeltsin to flash his nuclear sword westward as a reminder against NATO aggression.

The theory that Russia's nuclear alert was a propaganda ploy is highly unlikely. The notion that Moscow knowingly and deliberately overreacted to Norway's missile launch by going through the motions of a nuclear alert, hoping to cancel the embarrassment of Chechnya through a show of nuclear prowess, fails on the fact that such a scheme would surely backfire and would only compound Russia's military errors and make Russian nuclear forces look as inept as the Russian Army—and as dangerously unpredictable. Besides, a nuclear alert is no small thing. It runs the risk of enemy nuclear escalation, and that is why nuclear alerts rarely occur. President Yeltsin and Chief of the General Staff Kolesnikov would run the risks inherent in a nuclear alert, and expose their reputations to self-inflicted rhetorical damage, only if they believed that enemy aggression was imminent.

The most likely explanation for the events of January 25, 1995, and the explanation most consistent with the facts, is that Moscow was surprised by Norway's missile launch because of a bureaucratic snafu on the Russian side that failed to forward a foreign-missile-launch notification to the military. Recent Western moves toward an expanded NATO, East-West tensions in former Yugoslavia, Russia's military embarrassment at the hands of Chechen rebels during the Battle of Grozny, and the subsequent leadership crisis in Moscow raised Russian sensitivities about their vulnerability and fear of foreign aggression. The missile launch was momentarily misconstrued as the leading edge of a possible nuclear surprise attack. Russia went on nuclear alert, preparing to launch a retaliatory or preemptive strike.

On February 5, Nikolay Devyanin, chief designer of the "nuclear briefcase," published a blow-by-blow account of Russia's detection of the unexpected Norwegian missile and of the nuclear alert. Entitled "All That Has Happened, Alas, Had to Happen," Devyanin's article blames Moscow for bringing the world to the nuclear brink because of its unreconstructed threat perceptions. This is hardly the self-flattering stuff one expects in propaganda. He spells out the unprecedented severity of the nuclear danger on 25 January in capital letters:

> The President's admission of using his "football" [nuclear briefcase] shows unequivocally and incontestably: FOR THE FIRST TIME IN THE TEN YEARS OF ITS COMBAT OPERATION, THE "KAZBEK" AUTOMATED STRATEGIC NUCLEAR FORCE COMMAND SYSTEM AND ITS USER TERMINALS—THE "FOOTBALLS" OF THE PRESIDENT, THE DEFENSE MINISTER, AND THE CHIEF OF THE GENERAL STAFF—WERE SWITCHED INTO AN ALERT MODE, WHICH GAVE THE PRESIDENT THE TECHNICAL POSSIBILITY, FOR SEVERAL MINUTES, BY MERELY PRESSING THE BUTTON, TO AUTHORIZE THE ARMED FORCES TO USE RUSSIAN NUCLEAR WEAPONS.
>
> For the first time! What is important is that this happened not at the time when U.S. Pershings were deployed in Europe, but now, when Russia has signed the START Treaty and agreements with the United States, Great Britain, and China on the "mutual non-targeting of missiles." . . . The security of mankind cannot depend on anybody's sloppiness in notifying about launches or negligence in transferring information.

Sergey Yushenkov, as chairman of the Duma's Military Committee, was well connected to senior military officers and had access to inside information about events on January 25. Two days later, on January 27, Yushenkov expressed his "concern over the Norwegian launch. Such actions could lead to nuclear war being triggered in the event of an accident." On the same day Yushenkov told the Norwegian press that "for a while the world was on the brink of nuclear war."

The Norwegian government ordered a crash investigation to determine what happened on the Russian side, immediately after Yeltsin's Lipetsk speech disclosed that Russia had gone on nuclear alert. After two intense conferences between Norway's ambassador Per Tresselt and the Russian foreign ministry on the missile affair, the Norwegian government refused to publicly disclose its findings, except to say: "Although we supplied all the necessary information [on Norway's plans to launch a missile] and repeated the information through flight control channels on 16 January, this launch led to some alarm among the Russian missile forces, and this is cause for some concern." Ambassador Per Tresselt later said that the Russians thought Black Brant "could be a military missile, even a nuclear one. . . . I have already told the Foreign Ministry of Russia that a combination of doubtful information and misunderstanding could give some concern about the quality of the information reaching the commander-in-chief of the country that possesses Europe's most powerful nuclear forces." Norway's Conservative Party spokeswoman for foreign policy, Kaci Kullman Five, who had access to the investigation findings, was less diplomatic. She said that Russia's nuclear alert was "frightening."

Although the propaganda theory can be dismissed, one other alternative scenario cannot be entirely ruled out. It is possible that senior Russian military leaders knew in advance of Norway's impending missile launch and *still* suspected a nuclear surprise attack.

On 26 January, the day after the missile incident, General Staff chief Mikhail Kolesnikov told the press, "The Norwegian side warned the Russian authorities well in advance that this launch was expected over roughly the coming two weeks. However, no precise time for the rocket launch was given." Yet Kolesnikov was among those who feared Norway's rocket might have a military purpose, and who after the incident, despite Norwegian protests, persisted in describing Black Brant as an "operational-tactical" military missile. Taken at face value, this suggests that the Chief of the General Staff knew, by notification from Oslo, about Norway's impending missile launch some two weeks in advance—but suspected a surprise attack anyway.

General Kolesnikov and the GRU, the General Staff's military intelligence arm, both deeply distrustful of the West, would have found many circumstances surrounding Norway's missile project highly suspicious. Both the missile and the payload were financed and developed jointly with the United States, through NASA. It was the first missile launched from Norway that would have sufficient range to reach strategic targets in Russia. The launch site, Andoya Island, would mean little warning time if used for a strike on the command and control hub in Moscow, or on Murmansk, where most Russian missile submarines are based. A super-EMP warhead could conceivably fit on the missile. Chechnya and the leadership crisis in Moscow—in the view of the Russian military—created an opportunity for the U.S. to attack. It *is* possible that the General Staff was, for some two weeks or more, monitoring activities at Andoya, suspecting possible NATO preparations for a nuclear surprise attack.

Yet this hypothesis hinges on General Kolesnikov's claim that the military knew ahead of time of Norway's planned missile launch. Kolesnikov made no such claims until the Norwegian government proved that it had provided a missile launch notification to the Russian foreign ministry. General Kolesnikov may have lied about having foreknowledge of the missile launch to protect himself from blame for an embarrassing bureaucratic error.

The crisis of January 25, 1995, was the single most dangerous moment of the nuclear missile age. Never before had a leader of any nuclear power opened his equivalent of the Russian "nuclear briefcase" in earnest, in a situation where a real threat was perceived, and where an immediate decision to launch Armageddon was possible. Never before had a nuclear crisis been played out under the pressure of an actually launched ballistic missile, which reduced warning and decision time to minutes. No previous nuclear crisis—not the Cuban missile crisis or ABLE ARCHER–83—ever got to the point of a nuclear-threat conference, requiring a prompt decision on whether or not to launch a nuclear strike.

On January 25, 1995, as President Boris Yeltsin and Chief of the General Staff Mikhail Kolesnikov peered into their "nuclear briefcases" at an unidentified missile rising in the north, their hands were inches from the button.

About a year later, on a rainy Washington evening in April 1996, a small group of prominent scholars and former senior executives of the U.S. state and defense departments gathered to hear John B. Stewart speak on his monograph *Rethinking the Unthinkable: Russia's Evolving Nuclear Weapons Threat*. Stewart had recently retired as director of the Office of Foreign Intelligence at the U.S. Department of Energy; as such he had been a senior manager in the U.S. intelligence community. He had received the rarely awarded National Intelligence Distinguished Service Medal in 1994. Stewart warned, "To provide for the nation's security, we need to free ourselves from illusions dominated by escapist, wishful thinking. The end of the Cold War did not end the Soviet—now the Russian—nuclear threat. It merely changed the nature of the threat—in a real sense, making it more dangerous and confusing. . . . In January 1995 . . . Yeltsin apparently activated his football—part of a system called KAZBEK—and issued a strategic alert for Russian nuclear forces. This alert was in response to a false warning. . . . One U.S. expert described this threat miscalculation as coming closer to a Russian nuclear launch than at any previous time during the Cold War."

Not surprisingly, given the limited Western press coverage of Russia's January 1995 nuclear alert, none of Stewart's expert audience, among the best-informed defense experts in the West, had been aware of the Norwegian missile crisis.

Release of prepublication review copies of this book in 1997 created a brief international furor over the 1995 nuclear alert, prompting major press and television stories by *Time, U.S. News and World Report, 60 Minutes*, and widespread foreign media coverage. Unfortunately, the media universally neglected the larger history of the Russian nuclear war scare that makes sense of the 1995 missile crisis and that explains why such dangerous episodes are likely to happen again.

Indeed, history appeared to be about to repeat, literally, the events of January 25, 1995 just four years later. In January 1999, NASA and Norway prepared to launch another Black Brant on exactly the same mission, on precisely the same trajectory, and following much the same pre-launch notification procedures—that had failed, nearly catastrophically, in 1995. Sources in Norway informed me of the impending missile launch. I suggested to NASA that perhaps, this time, it would be prudent to inform the Russian General Staff, and not just the Russian Foreign Ministry. My suggestion was dismissed because: "It would violate diplomatic protocol. This is Norway's show." Inquiries to the U.S. Department of Defense and the Department of State about the impending missile launch drew blanks—they were unaware that another Black Brant was about to be fired. NASA, apparently, had not told them. To their credit, some in State and Defense appreciated immediately the gravity of the situation. They quickly apprised the General Staff, and several other operational levels of the Russian military—including through the U.S.-Russian Nuclear Risk Reduction Center—that a missile was about to be launched. This time, the Black Brant flew without incident. Nonetheless, our lapse in initially failing to take extra steps to warn the Russian military about another missile launch from Norway—given what happened the last time—is an astounding oversight.

The Russian General Staff's dark brooding about possible threats and recent history of nuclear overreaction—still largely unknown in the West—is "out of paradigm" for the U.S. public and policy makers, who are fixated on Russia's small band of democratic reformers and lulled into complacency by the end of the Cold War. The nuclear close call of January 1995 startled the West briefly awake in 1997, but it seems to have been almost forgotten now, vaguely remembered as an interesting exception to the trend of a strengthening peace.

And so the West continues to sleepwalk on the nuclear brink, unaware of further dangerous missteps during NATO military exercises in 1996 and 1997. We were shocked awake again in 1998 by President Yeltsin's warning that U.S. air strikes on Iraq may provoke a world war, and in 1999 by reports of a Russian nuclear alert during U.S. operation DESERT FOX. But this temporary suspicion that something is profoundly and dangerously wrong in our relations with Russia will soon pass. Our puzzlement and alarm, in the absence of understanding the perilous pattern of Russian war scares, born of Moscow's abiding pessimism, will soon find false comfort in dismissive, superficial explanations born of Western optimism. Sooner, rather than later, both sides may become victims of their fundamental failure to understand each other.

PART VI

The Future?

"Son, never promise to wage thermonuclear war for a country you cannot find on a map." . . . It is said that there are very few American congressmen and senators who know where Slovakia is and how it differs from Slovenia.

—*Segodnya*,
August 25, 1995

If NATO comes closer to Russian borders, both strategic and operational-tactical missiles could be used.

—General Lev Rohklin,
February 5, 1996

Everyone must know that in case of a direct challenge our response would be fully fledged, and we are to choose the use of means . . . including nuclear weapons.

—Ivan Rybkin,
Russian Security Council,
February 11, 1997

The most important thing is that we have firmly taken the stand of saying "no" to [the United States] using force [against Iraq]. That is impossible. That will mean a world war.

—President Boris Yeltsin,
February 5, 1998

In the past few days, the world came close to a third world war. In accordance with a secret directive, the Russian Armed Forces were placed on heightened combat alert.

—Moscow Television News,
January 17, 1999

CHAPTER 30

The West

Since the fall of the USSR and the emergence of a democratic Russia, there have been several incidents discussed in these pages in which high-ranking Russian officials have warned of an impending third world war and in which the Russian military has taken concrete actions consistent with this view in response to a number of specific crises. The Western press has briefly noted some of these, but it has never taken them seriously. The assumption that Russia no longer sees the West as an enemy and that the threat of war has therefore receded into insignificance is so universal, so strongly held among Western journalists, that they are blind to any evidence to the contrary. The blindness is not willful but the result of wide ignorance about Russian military threat perceptions and about the hazardous history of that nation's long war scare.

The United States and the rest of the West tend to regard any change in Russia, even dangerous change, as progress. No matter that Duma elections have replaced pro-Western reformers with communists and nationalists hostile to democracy and the West: at least there were elections. No matter that the Russian people hunger for bread more than ever: free enterprise will eventually provide. No matter that wars and civil wars have flared between and within the now-independent nations that were formerly the Soviet empire: at least they are free. No matter that the new Russian military doctrine relies more heavily than Soviet military doctrine did on a nuclear first strike: at least the Russian Army's 50,000 tanks are rusting near the Urals, no longer poised to overrun Western Europe.

U.S. defense and foreign policy toward Russia is no longer based on an appraisal of reality, but on hope.

Under President Bill Clinton, defense and foreign policy toward Russia is based on the best hopes of what Russia may *yet become*, and not on the reality of what Russia presently *is*, and is in fact *becoming*. For example, Vice President Al Gore, in an upbeat speech on October 19, 1995, claimed that the Clinton administration's Russia policy "was a bet on Russia's ability to turn things around. And this bet is beginning to pay off." Gore repeated President Clinton's May 1995 criticism of those who see Russia as "shackled" to its totalitarian past, and who would "deny Russia . . . the possibility of progress." Clinton's deputy secretary of state, Strobe Talbott, in a September 25, 1997, article, implied that Russia was well on its way toward becoming a nonthreatening democracy: "Russian citizens today can be more confident than a year ago that their country will make it . . . as a law-based, democratic society, increasingly integrated with the growing community of states that are similarly constituted." FBI director Louis Freeh on November 19, 1997, played down Russia's rampant organized crime as a threat to Russian democracy or the United States: "Crimes by Russians or Russian groups do not threaten the domestic or national security of the United States."

Yet a global organized crime task force headed by former FBI and CIA director William Webster issued a report that concluded Russia had become "virtually a full-fledged kleptocracy" and that failure "in reversing Russia's slide into a criminally directed society . . . would foster further instability in a major nuclear power, boding ill for the rest of the world." According to the Webster task force report *Russian Organized Crime*, by the Center for Strategic and International Studies, the United States will face "the prospect of strategic, nuclear-armed missile systems in the hands of a disintegrating military subject to criminal control. The implications of such a development are chillingly obvious." But President Clinton's public commentary on Russia implies that the future of Russian democracy is secure, rarely makes reference to Russian organized crime, and reassures the American people, as did his speech on February 5, 1998, that the United States has forged "practical partnerships with new democracies, including Russia" that are "all important steps to a more peaceful 21st century." In January 1999, Secretary of State Madeleine Albright continued to promote a hopeful view of Russia: "America wants to see Russia succeed, and to work with Russia's government and people to build a strong partnership."

Despite overwhelming evidence to the contrary, the Clinton administration, and almost everyone else, denies that Russia presently poses a threat to the United States. Russian animosity has been tamed by arms control and replaced by friendship—or at least by the hope for friendship. President Clinton's then secretary of defense, William Perry, asserted in a November 20, 1995, interview that the most profound factor in the politics of defense since the fall of the Berlin Wall has been "the reduction of the nuclear threat. . . . The United States and Russia have stopped targeting each other. . . . This dark cloud of mutual destruction has given way to new hope for friendship and cooperation." Colt Blacker, Daniel Fried, and Alexander Vershbow, special assistants to President Clinton and directors for Russian and East European affairs on the National Security Council, in an October 4, 1995, article, noted that one of their key foreign policy premises is that "Russia is no threat." William Evers, former deputy director of the Ballistic Missile Defense Organization, stated in April 1995 that "Russia, the former Soviet states, and China will not use [ICBMs] intentionally, will not launch them accidentally, and will not sell them."

In September 1997, a Russian nuclear submarine stalked the U.S. aircraft carriers *Constellation, Carl Vinson*, and *Nimitz* in the Pacific, apparently practicing to attack the carriers with advanced SS-N-19 "Shipwreck" supersonic cruise missiles, and approached within a hundred miles of Washington state, the closest to the United States since the Cold War. Secretary of Defense William Cohen was blase. Asked by reporters whether he would query Moscow about the incident, Cohen replied, "I don't intend to. They were in international waters, and to the extent they did not pose any kind of threat to our forces, I don't need to." On April 29, 1998, Secretary of State Madeline Albright, in a *New York Times* article entitled "Stop Worrying about Russia," chastised those who questioned NATO expansion as possibly dangerous in the face of a hostile and nuclear-armed Russia: "Critics who focus on Russia's opposition to enlargement are cynically assuming that Russia will always define its national interests in ways inimical to our own. They believe that Russia will always be threatened and humiliated by the desire of its former satellites to go their own way, that it will never get over the end of its empire. . . . as Secretary of State . . . I have not seen one scintilla of evidence to support the critics' fears." In January 1999, Albright offered a very positive view of a future "Russia that is confident and that will fulfill its potential as a global force for peace and justice and against crime and terror."

President Clinton himself has declared over 100 times since the missile "detargeting agreement" of 1994 that his administration has substantially reduced, or eliminated, the Russian nuclear threat. Again, on February 3, 1998, in a speech at Los Alamos National Laboratory promoting the comprehensive Test Ban Treaty, President Clinton reassured his audience that "today, there is not a single Russian missile pointed at America's children." President Clinton persists in his claim that detargeting has removed the Russian nuclear threat, despite repeated Russian strategic exercises simulating nuclear attacks on the United States.

Yet in the words of Russia scholar J. Michael Waller, the Clinton administration's claim for the missile detargeting agreement "has more to do with feel-good rhetoric than reality. . . . Detargeting makes for nice headlines, but it is impossible to verify. Retargeting can be as simple as changing a cassette tape."

The Russians themselves have contradicted President Clinton. General Igor Sergeyev, commander in chief of the Strategic Rocket Forces, interviewed in his underground bunker in June 1995 by *60 Minutes*, said that his missiles could be "retargeted and launched from this war room . . . most in a matter of minutes." Floyd Spence, chairman of the National Security Committee of the House of Representatives, in a letter dated June 12, 1996, to Secretary of Defense William Perry, challenged the Clinton administration's claim for missile detargeting. Perry's reply, in a letter of July 1, 1996, admitted that "there are no procedures to verify detargeting" and that "missile crews could quickly reconfigure equipment to prepare to launch missiles if directed."

On February 12, 1998, President Clinton's former CIA director, James Woolsey, in testimony before Congress, strongly condemned as "misleading" the president's repeated claims that missile detargeting had reduced the Russian nuclear threat: "I wish he [President Clinton] would not continue to make that statement [about Russian missile detargeting] because although it may be technically correct . . . I believe it is misleading. . . . These missiles, [based upon] everything I have known about them over the years, could be retargeted, so any of the interesting and troubling scenarios, such as a Russian response to a Norwegian sounding rocket and so forth, as I was talking about earlier, would be a circumstance in which the missiles would be quickly and readily retargeted. It is almost like saying . . . if I had a revolver here in my pocket and I took it out and pointed it at the ceiling, saying I am not targeting [anyone]. It is true, I would not be . . . I am pointing it at the ceiling. But if I lowered it, I would be. It just takes a few seconds."

Not everyone in the West agrees that the Russian threat is no more. At a forum sponsored by the National Defense University, former CIA director Woolsey, speaking on May 17, 1995, characterized Russia as "still the country most dangerous to the United States." Noting that Russian nuclear forces could annihilate the United States in the span of thirty minutes, Woolsey warned that within the next decade the odds that Russia will revert to confrontational policies are "at least two in three" against its neighbors, and "at least one in three" against the United States. Former secretary of defense James Schlesinger has said, "The standard belief in the United States that the possibility of large-scale nuclear exchanges has now disappeared is a misperception. It is time we recognize that problem." In his monograph *Rethinking the Unthinkable: Russia's Evolving Nuclear Weapons Threat*, John Stewart, holder of the coveted Intelligence Medal for Distinguished Service, concludes, "Today we are left with the choice of either taking preventative and protective measures to defend our citizens from nuclear attack—however initiated, for whatever reason—or of preparing to recover and rebuild on 'the morning after.' I believe the choice is obvious."

Bruce Blair of the Brookings Institute, one of the foremost Western authorities on Russian nuclear strategy and command and control systems, has tirelessly warned that Russian reliance on nuclear weapons and strategic and tactical early warning has grown at a time when its early-warning assets are falling into disrepair. Consequently, Blair told a Capitol Hill audience on December 12, 1997, the strategic nuclear balance is "more potentially unstable than it has been for many decades," and there is a "growing danger that Russian leaders would simply lose control over their strategic arsenals resulting in an unauthorized or mistaken launch. . . . A strong case can be made that this risk is greater today than it ever was during the Cold War. This progressive deterioration of the Russian command and early warning network represents the current most serious threat to the United States."

On February 12, 1998, another of President Clinton's former CIA directors, John Deutch, testified to Congress that "Russia continues to be our top security concern, even without the adversarial relationship of the Cold War, because Russia still possesses 20,000-plus nuclear weapons. Widespread corruption and the absence of honest and accountable internal governmental administrative functions threatens Russia's slow and erratic evolution towards democracy." On January 28, 1998, President Clinton's Director of Central Intelligence, George Tenet, offered the Senate Select Committee on Intelligence this brave testimony—albeit buried in the middle of a lengthy presentation—which appears to contradict flatly much of the administration's unworried rhetoric about Russia: "Whether Russia succeeds as a stable democracy, reverts to the autocratic and expansionist impulses of its past, or degenerates into instability remains an open question. . . . Russia retains a major nuclear arsenal—some 6,000 deployed strategic warheads. As long as there is the slightest doubt about future political stability in Russia, these weapons must be a major preoccupation for U.S. intelligence. We must also remain mindful that Russia continues a wide range of development programs for conventional and strategic forces. Finally, while Russia continues to seek close cooperation with the United States on matters of mutual concern, it is increasingly strident in opposing what it sees as U.S. efforts to create a 'unipolar' world."

Congressman Curt Weldon, a voracious reader of Russian military literature who has made numerous trips to Moscow to meet Russian officials, charges the Clinton administration with pressuring the intelligence community to understate the nuclear danger from Russia. On April 7, 1998, in a speech at the National Defense University, Weldon cautioned against the widespread misperception that the Strategic Arms Reduction Treaties would inevitably lessen or eliminate the Russian nuclear threat: "The Administration's endless mantra that Moscow is our strategic partner and that the Strategic Arms Reduction Treaties are a panacea eliminating the threat of large-scale nuclear war has, whether we like it or not, penetrated the consciousness of our political culture to such an extent that it has become politically incorrect to question the future stability of the central strategic nuclear balance. . . . Where are the numerous articles and televised debates dissecting and challenging the START treaties? Although I am a supporter of the START treaties and START process begun and executed by the Bush Administration, I think it is wrong that the Clinton Administration's direction in START has gone unremarked and unchallenged. . . . The Administration's mismanagement of the START II and START III negotiations, concessions at Helsinki, conceding asymmetries favoring Russia in tactical nuclear weapons and strategic defenses, and neglect of U.S. nuclear targeting requirements, may erode central strategic deterrence. START could be strategically destabilizing."

A 1998 article in *Strategic Review* by Richard Starr of the Hoover Institution and Boston University observes that Russia recently officially adopted "a new national security concept which openly proclaims Moscow's goal of again becoming a great power. Basic prerequisites for achieving this status include establishment of control over the so-called Commonwealth of Independent States, i.e., most of the former republics in the USSR, and a reformed Russian Army equipped with 21st century weapons." Starr notes that Russia's new national security concept allows "a first strike with nuclear weapons, even against a conventional attack."

A January 12, 1998, editorial "Russia's Nuclear Temptation" appearing in the *New York Times*—an exceedingly rare forum for this subject—warned: "The end of the Cold War has produced an alarming nuclear irony. Russia is now more dependent on its nuclear weapons than ever and at the same time those weapons are more vulnerable. That increases the chances that in a severe crisis Moscow might consider using them. . . . NATO's ill-advised expansion . . . will bring Western forces closer to the Russian border. While a NATO strike against Russian nuclear weapons now seems unimaginable, the psychology of vulnerability on the Russian side is real."

A February 10, 1999 article by David Hoffman in the *Washington Post* reports that, "Russia's early warning defense against missile attack, a key aspect of the hair-trigger doctrine of nuclear deterrence, is deteriorating. . . . Russian decision-makers are blindfolded . . . growing gaps in the area covered by Russia's early-warning satellites have increased the risk of a serious miscalculation, because Russian commanders will have less time to decide if a launch report is real. There have been several close calls . . ."

These are voices in the wilderness. Across the spectrum of opinion, political leaders are generally silent or reassuring on the subject of nuclear war with Russia. Republican majorities in the Senate and House, representing the party historically most on guard against Moscow, are viscerally ill at ease with Russia's direction and skeptical of the Clinton administration's claim that Russia is no threat. Most Republicans, however, have been reluctant to speak about the Russian nuclear threat, in part because they are afraid of being blasted as crazy Cold Warriors by the liberal press, but mainly because, with few exceptions, they lack current, specific information about the threat.

The threat of nuclear war with Russia no longer draws much scholarly attention. After the collapse of the USSR, most defense analysts refocused their attention away from Russia to the serious new dangers posed by the proliferation of weapons of mass destruction to the Third World—a danger greatly exacerbated by advanced technology spilling out of Russia. The cadre of analysts dedicated to examining the risks of a nuclear conflict with Russia has dwindled to near extinction. Journals of strategic studies, which used to be replete with articles about Soviet nuclear forces and strategy, now scarcely mention Russia as a nuclear threat—except as a proliferator of nuclear, chemical, or biological technology. Indeed, today, the phrase "Russian nuclear threat" is routinely assumed to refer to threats arising from the proliferation of Russian nuclear technology, not to the still very real possibility of a Russian nuclear attack.

Another reason for the disappearance of "Russian nuclear aggression" as a respectable topic for political and military discourse has been the desire in the West to support Russia's democratic reformers against resurging anti-Western communists and nationalists. Russian extremists would use to advantage any Western talk about the residual threat of nuclear war. A more cynical reason for silence may be that, ever since the Bush administration, Republicans and Democrats have hoped to cannibalize the defense budget for tax cuts or spending programs that would grow the economy and carry them to political glory. Draconian defense reductions have been justified by the assumption that Russia is no threat.

Unfortunately, reality is not consistent with the predominant view that Russia is now, if not a friend and ally of the United States, at least no longer an enemy. Today, right now, the United States still faces a grave threat to its existence from Russia. Indeed, just beneath the usually placid political surface of the present United States–Russia relationship lurk many of the same elements and attitudes that produced the protracted war scare that has, on several occasions, nearly brought on a nuclear Armageddon.

Hard-liners with dangerous threat perceptions still dominate the Russian military. Russian military officers and civilian hard-liners continue to espouse views reflecting deep suspicion of the West and an inordinate fear of possible Western aggression. The enfeeblement of the Russian Army, with its attendant hardships and unemployment imposed on hundreds of thousands of military officers and their families, has inflamed them against Russian democratic reformers and the United States—whom they blame for Russia's fall from greatness and for their personal misfortunes. In 1996 a poll of Russian military officers concluded that "70 percent assess the collapse of the U.S.S.R. as the greatest tragedy." A top secret CIA report titled *Prospects for Unsanctioned Use of Russian Nuclear Weapons*, leaked to the press in October 1996, states, "Russian military writings still portray Western policies as hostile. . . . Moscow's exercises have simulated short-warning nuclear attacks against Russian strategic forces and their supporting command structure." Moreover, "Moscow's potentially short fuse" was demonstrated in January 1995 when Norway's launch of a meteorology rocket "triggered a tactical warning report that automatically activated President Yeltsin's *cheget* (nuclear briefcase)."

Command and control of Russian nuclear forces remains in the hands of the General Staff. Knowledgeable Russian sources have publicly stated that the Russian military continues to hold exclusive operational control over Russia's nuclear forces, enabling it to launch a nuclear strike independently, or against the will, of Russian political leaders. The top secret CIA report cited above concludes, "Political authorities probably could neither execute a nuclear strike—even from a command post—without the cooperation of the General Staff, nor prevent the General Staff (or perhaps some other national-level command post) from launching on its own."

In the Russian view, the strategic nuclear balance remains unstable. Despite the Strategic Arms Reduction Treaties, which will greatly reduce the size of the U.S. and Russian nuclear arsenals, Russian strategists calculate that the future strategic balance will leave both sides more capable than before of destroying each other's nuclear forces in a surprise attack and therefore may well increase first-strike incentives in a future conflict or crisis.

Striking first is still the central tenet of Russian military doctrine. The new Russian military doctrine endorses heavier Russian reliance on nuclear weapons, under a broader range of circumstances than envisioned in Soviet doctrine.

Russia is still arming for World War III, bankrupting itself to build a new generation of nuclear missiles and deep underground shelters, as if a nuclear war might erupt at any moment. Russian general-purpose forces—once the mightiest on earth—are today a drain on the ruined Russian economy. They have withered away to a pathetic shadow of their former selves, increasing Russian dependence on nuclear weapons.

CHAPTER 31

Black Prophecies: Civilian Threat Perceptions

A Russian poll conducted by academic Boris Grushin for *Vox Populi* found that "the image of impending catastrophe," a sense of coming "doom" or "the end of the world," is widespread among the Russian people. The source is four popular "black prophecies" about Russia's future: civil war, anarchy, fascism, and world war. Of the last, Russians typically told Grushin, "The West intends to destroy us."

Hostile attitudes toward the West, and toward the United States in particular, are not limited to the Russian military; they are also expressed by many Russian civilian leaders, including prominent civilians in the government. The notorious Vladimir Zhirinovsky is not the only Russian politician talking about risking a nuclear war. Alexander Yanov, a retired professor at the University of New York and a leading expert on Russian ultranationalists, spent six months in Moscow interviewing communist and nationalist leaders. They described to Yanov the following "widely discussed" scenario for Russian-Iraqi conquest of Middle East oil:

> One of the first foreign policy steps of the [communists or nationalists] would be . . . to supply Iraq with enough tanks, missiles, and aircraft for another brutal invasion of Kuwait. Simultaneously, the new Russian president would warn the West that any attack against "our ally" Iraq would be considered an attack on Russia and put his strategic nuclear forces on red alert.
>
> Is it likely that anybody in Washington would think of another Operation Desert Storm in such circumstances?

Religious fanaticism among large numbers of Russians is one contributing source to intense anti-Western attitudes. In an article entitled "Against Jews and Heresies, We Will Halt the Apostates," some clergymen of the Russian Orthodox Church equated the Roman Catholic church with the Western threat: "The active expansion of Roman Catholicism and, specifically, Uniates, on the territories of Ukraine, Belarus, and especially Siberia, expressed both in the seizure of Orthodox temples and in bloody war, genocide of the Orthodox population and thousands of refugees, testifies to the immutability of the Vatican's long-standing aspirations for broadening its influence in the East."

Moscow has attempted to curry favor with the Russian Orthodox Church, whose upper hierarchy enjoyed a long relationship with the Soviet

Communist Party and the KGB, by passing laws restricting the religious liberties of other faiths and even sanctioning their persecution. For example, according to Western press and eyewitness accounts, in October 1997 in the city of Noginsk, shortly after President Yeltsin signed the new law regulating religion, "scores of leather-jacketed officers armed with semi-automatic weapons and rubber batons, burst into the [Ukrainian Orthodox] cathedral and its outlying buildings and drove the occupants into the streets. Freezing in the autumn night air, evicted elderly nuns and young priests watched in dismay as the archbishop was led away in handcuffs." Valeri Bondarenko, a student priest at the Noginsk cathedral, told London's *Independent*, "Some of us had wives with babies, but they were all thrown into the streets. Some were still in night clothes and slippers. When people saw the priest was arrested, they tried to help, but the police began to beat them." In December 1998, at the urging of the Moscow Patriarchate, the Russian government confiscated a Catholic church. Religious intolerance has always walked hand in hand with xenophobia in Russia.

The Russian Orthodox Church, for its part, appears to have resumed its historical role as a supporter of Russian imperialism. In September 1998, Aleksiy II, patriarch of the church, backed the union of Belarus and Russia, perceived by many as a first step toward recreating the Soviet Union. Russian expansion, Aleksiy implied, is a divine cause: "All the forces of Hell are rising up against every attempt to advance toward the Union."

The Russian military has attempted to win the loyalties of the religious through sometimes bizarre symbolic gestures. For instance, in January 1996 General Igor Sergeyev, then chief of the Strategic Rocket Forces, invited Patriarch Aleksiy II to visit his underground command post and bless the SRF. Saint Barbara is now the patron saint of the Strategic Rocket Forces.

Suspicion and fear of the West, so prevalent in the Russian military for so long, has finally begun to infect even Russian democratic reformers, who, since NATO's decision to expand eastward in 1995, have begun to sound like their dark cousins in the military and among the political reactionaries. For example, both Yeltsin and the maniacal Zhirinovsky warned that NATO expansion into Eastern Europe will precipitate a world war. In an interview on September 8, 1995, President Yeltsin said he "radically opposes" NATO expansion: "It will be a major political mistake of those who insist on the NATO expansion. It will definitely send the whole of Europe into the flames of war." Zhirinovsky's war warning against NATO expansion added racist overtones, describing a "third world war in Europe in which French Negroes and Chechens from Russia would fight East Europeans and the alliance." President Yeltsin repeated another theme familiar to Zhirinovsky, blaming "Western-style capitalism for corruption in Russia." On May 8, 1997, President Yeltsin declared that NATO expansion presents the most serious American challenge to Russia since the

Cuban missile crisis: "Since Khrushchev's Cuban crisis, there hasn't been such a sharp issue between Russia and the United States."

Russian academic Sergey Grigoryev proposes in an article that Russia might deal with NATO expansion by using nuclear missiles "to deliver a surprise crushing blow now." He then coyly disavows this option, but apparently only because "Russia would inevitably receive a similar response."

An article by Russian academic Sergey Kortunov concludes that Russia and the United States are natural enemies: "Russia will never have a stable and permanent strategic alliance with any of the existing or forming basic centers of power such as the United States, China, Germany, and Japan. Objectively these countries are geopolitical, economic, and military opponents with respect to Russia and with respect to each other." Even former Soviet president Mikhail Gorbachev, himself a victim of the General Staff's war scare mentality, showed vestiges of such an attitude in a February 1996 article: "The fear, realistic or not, is that the West or some politicians in the West want to deliver a coup de grace to the Russian Federation and eliminate forever a Russian challenge to United States dominance." Gorbachev cautioned, "There is a real danger that we'll restart the arms race" if NATO expands; he claimed that "some in the West have attempted to ruthlessly exploit the strains and weaknesses in Russian policy." Finally, sounding like former KGB chief Vladimir Kryuchkov, Gorbachev asked darkly, "Incidentally, why did America react so feebly to the French [nuclear] tests? Could the Americans have used the French tests to perfect their own nuclear weapons?"

A January 14, 1998, editorial by Sergey Gulyy is representative of mainstream thinking in Russian newspapers on the issue of NATO expansion and the Western threat: "One of the reasons for Russia's increased emphasis on nuclear weapons as a deterrent has clearly been NATO's not entirely successful choice of form for expansion. The Cold War is over, but the threat of a new world war is only just taking on new form."

Despite signing in 1997 the "NATO Founding Act," which made some significant concessions to Moscow intended to reduce the sting of NATO expansion, Boris Yeltsin continued his offensive against an enlarged NATO and against a "unipolar world" dominated by the United States. In February 1998, President Yeltsin warned of a possible "world war" somehow arising if the United States followed through on threats to launch missile strikes on Iraq for failing to cooperate with UN inspectors searching for hidden weapons of mass destruction.

On March 10, 1998, Yuli Vorontsov, Russia's ambassador to the United States, took the highly unusual step of publishing in the *Washington Post* a frank warning from Moscow to the American people: "Russia's attitude toward NATO enlargement has been and remains unequivocally negative. The signing of the Russia-NATO Founding Act does not alter that attitude in any manner. . . . Few people take into account the psychological factor—

the historic memory of Russians. It was from the West that real threats continuously came to Russia, bringing to our people immeasurable losses and destruction. This memory cannot be deleted or subdued by any parliamentary hearings. . . . Enlargement is a serious attempt to achieve political dominance of the Alliance in Europe, to create a NATO-centrism . . . backed-up by a military force unparalleled in the world. . . . If enlargement goes forward, there are no guarantees that everything positive we have developed in the relationship between Russia and leading Western countries will not be put in severe jeopardy."

In April 1999, former foreign Minister Kozyrev, one of Russia's most pro-Western figures, condemned Moscow for embracing an anti-democratic, anti-Western "Soviet-world outlook." According to Kozyrev, "Anti-U.S. outbursts in Russia are falling on extremely fertile soil. . . . It is easier for Russians to blame the outside world for what is going wrong instead of sorting out the real reasons for the country's problems." In May 1999, Moscow Mayor Yuri Luzhkov, a prominent reformer and presidential aspirant, saw in NATO operations in Kosovo "a second Vietnam. I do not want to forecast what is going to start there. I cannot rule out a third world war." In May 1999, envoys from Russia, China, India, Yugoslavia, Iraq, Cuba, and Libya met in Delhi "to denounce U.S.-led NATO aggression on Yugoslavia" in the words of the Indian press. Russian Ambassador Albert Tchernshyev said at the conference, "We want India and China to join us in stopping U.S. attempts to dominate the world."

The leaders of Russian democracy have probably adopted some of the rhetoric of their enemies in the General Staff, and of the communists and nationalists, in order to survive politically. It is also probable that Russian reformers have been to some extent converted to a more desolate view of the world and that they actually believe much of what they are saying. If not, if Russian democrats are lying through their teeth about the "U.S. threat" in order to get reelected, that, too, speaks disturbingly about the depth and breadth of Russia's fear.

The Russian people, although not as hard-line as the military, also have basically reactionary attitudes. The U.S. government has sponsored statistically representative polls of the Russian population. The poll results are unclassified, but the sponsoring government agency and the poll executors in Russia prefer anonymity, since they fear that the Russian government will interfere with future research if it learns who they are.

These polls of Russian civilians find that Russia's experiment with democracy is failing: "Three-quarters [of Russian civilians polled] . . . say that things are going in the *wrong* direction. . . . Most feel that the government has been doing a *poor* job of maintaining order (91 percent). . . . Three-quarters believe that Russia needs a leader who would impose strict order." Most Russians still identify the Soviet Union, not Russia, as their homeland,

and half "would support a leader who promises to create a large state like the former U.S.S.R." Most Russians "view Americans as individuals positively," but "three in five (including those with higher education) feel that the U.S. is trying to dominate the world and to reduce Russia to a second-rate power."

Even among young Russians (aged eighteen to twenty-nine), over two-thirds of those polled believe that U.S. aid to Russia is intended to foster Russian dependence and harm their country, while less than 20 percent saw U.S. aid as unambiguously benign. Over half of Russian youth mourn the demise of the USSR. Democrat Boris Yeltsin receives lower grades as a leader among Russia's young than do the communist dictators Brezhnev, Khrushchev, Stalin, or Lenin.

In the U.S. government polls, nearly two-thirds (64 percent) of the Russian people polled did not think Moscow was "meeting Russia's defense needs." Eighty-five percent of Russians "feel that Russia should do its utmost to ensure that its military might is on a par with America's." Most disturbingly, the polls indicate that two-thirds (67 percent) of the Russian people "are more worried about the possibility of war than they have been in recent years." Fear of foreign attack has grown by 60 percent since 1991: "A . . . majority (54 percent, up from 32 percent at the end of 1991) are concerned that Russia might be attacked in the next five years."

The persistence of war-scare attitudes among Russian military officers and politicians is not entirely madness. In fact, such attitudes are more understandable now than during the early 1980s. Try to see things from Moscow's perspective. Imagine that, today, the positions of the United States and Russia were reversed. Imagine that in the historic competition between capitalism and socialism, socialism had won—that socialism had proved more efficient at producing wealth and technological innovation—while the capitalist economies of the West sank farther and farther into poverty. Suppose the Soviet Union still existed and was growing stronger economically and militarily. Suppose the economic collapse of the United States fueled ethnic and regional antagonism, leading to geopolitical fragmentation, the old Confederacy and states west of the Mississippi breaking away to form independent nations. Suppose the Soviet Union recognized the Confederacy and other states as independent nations and sent Soviet businesses to exploit oil, gas, and other natural resources located in the (now independent) states of the American south and west.

Imagine that what *did* remain of the United States was so impoverished that the United States could no longer afford its armed forces: the Army and Marines becoming hollow and demoralized, without adequate arms and ammunition; the Air Force unable to fly because of lack of fuel; Navy ships rusting from disuse. Suppose Soviet general-purpose forces grew so powerful that in 1991 the USSR was able to project a Warsaw Pact coalition of 500,000 soldiers across the Atlantic for a war against Mexico—just as the United States and NATO did during the 1991 war against Iraq. Suppose that in the course of defeating Mexico, the Soviet Union approached to within a few hundred kilometers of the Texas border and demonstrated the use of futuristic conventional weapons technologically superior to anything the United States could build for years. Suppose that in 1995, and continuing today, the Soviet Union returned on a peacekeeping mission to Central America, landing thousands of troops in Nicaragua, moving powerful naval forces to the Caribbean, and bombing El Salvador, all against vehement U.S. protests—just as Moscow has protested U.S. bombing and peacekeeping activities in the Balkans.

Imagine that the NATO alliance fell apart while the Warsaw Pact remained strong, and that Britain, Germany, and other former NATO member states were now clamoring to join the Warsaw Pact. Suppose Western Europe and Canada joined the Warsaw Pact, so that the vast Soviet military alliance extended right up to the borders of the United States—just as the United States will press NATO's borders against Russia when Poland and other East Europeans are admitted to the pact.

Suppose U.S. nuclear forces were the only military means available to the United States that could still defeat the Soviet Union—providing the United States strikes first.

Under these circumstances, would the United States fear for its existence? Would the United States be on constant lookout for a Soviet surprise attack? Would Washington constantly be prepared to defend itself by the only means left: a preemptive nuclear strike? Would the possibility increase of U.S. overreaction or miscalculation leading to a preemptive nuclear strike?

If you can imagine all of these things, suppose further that U.S. political and military leaders were schooled in a ferocious totalitarian system, suspicious to the point of paranoia, and at least some senior officers on the U.S. Joint Chiefs of Staff subscribed to the view that the United States can recoup its fortunes through nuclear arms—that a nuclear war can be won. Would the possibility increase of a cold-blooded decision to reverse the verdict of history by initiating a nuclear war?

CHAPTER 32

START: A More Dangerous Balance

Two American presidents, George Bush and Bill Clinton, have declared that the Strategic Arms Reduction Treaties (START I, II, and III), which will reduce U.S. and Russian nuclear weapons to less than one-third their Cold War numbers, will virtually eliminate the threat of nuclear war. The primary basis for this claim is that START will eliminate multiple-warhead ICBMs—especially the Russian SS-18 heavy ICBMs, Russia's premier first-strike missile—which could wipe out the U.S. ICBM force in a surprise attack. The press and popular opinion makers have translated the original presidential claims about the START treaties—as eliminating the threat of nuclear war—into an already accomplished fact. But no one in the Russian military makes such grandiose claims for the START agreements.

Indeed, you do not have to be a nuclear strategist to conclude that the START treaties will not eliminate the threat of nuclear war. As of this writing, despite all the talk about future nuclear disarmament, Russia's strategic nuclear forces can still deliver to intercontinental range some 6,000 nuclear weapons. Moreover, in the next century, even after implementation of the START II "deep reductions" agreement signed in June 1992 by George Bush and Boris Yeltsin (but still unratified by the Russian Duma), Russia will still possess up to 3,500 strategic nuclear weapons—more than enough to destroy the world.

Even though the START treaties are supposed to eliminate the formidable Russian SS-18 ICBM, the treaty provisions banning multiple-warhead ICBMs will also compel the United States to gut its own ICBM force. In order to comply with START II, the United States will scrap about 80 percent of its ICBM warheads, leaving at most five hundred single-warhead ICBMs. Other proposals under consideration would eliminate U.S. ICBMs and bombers entirely, relying on U.S. missile submarines alone to deter a Russian nuclear attack under START II.

Since the purpose of Russia's SS-18 was to destroy U.S. ICBMs, Russia gives up nothing by eliminating the SS-18, because under START II the United States gives up or largely eliminates its ICBM force. Even if the United States retains five hundred single-warhead ICBMs in the year 2003, the number of U.S. ICBM weapons will be less than the number that would survive a Russian first strike today.

However, Russia may no longer be obliged to dismantle the SS-18, because of concessions made to Moscow by the Clinton administration at Helsinki in 1997. At Helsinki, President Clinton agreed to extend START

II implementation by five years, from 2003 to 2007. This could enable Moscow to retain until the end of its useful service life the SS-18, the elimination of which by 2003 was the chief accomplishment of START II. Although after 2003 the SS-18 is supposed to be "deactivated," this term is undefined in the Helsinki agreement, except that SS-18s might somehow be considered "deactivated" even if they remain in launch silos and are armed with warheads. Let us hope that the Clinton administration has not unofficially agreed with the Russians to equate "deactivation" of SS-18s with "detargeting." Statements by senior Russian officials, like commander of the Strategic Rocket Forces Vladimir Yakovlev, claim the SS-18 will remain operational until 2007. Almost immediately after the Clinton administration's Helsinki concession on the SS-18, Russia conducted SS-18 flight tests to extend the missile's service life.

START could confer on Russia a significant advantage over the United States in nuclear weapons. The United States has agreed under START II and START III to accept parity in strategic weapons at lower levels, without requiring Russia to accept parity in tactical nuclear weapons. Russia retains some ten to twenty times as many tactical nuclear weapons as the United States. U.S.-Russian parity in strategic weapons, while Russia retains a substantial advantage in tactical nuclear weapons, constitutes net Russian superiority in offensive nuclear forces.

START could confer on Russia a significant advantage over the United States in active and passive defenses. The Clinton administration at Helsinki agreed to the START III framework and to crippling technical limits on U.S. theater and national missile-defense programs without seeking concessions in Russian strategic defense programs. According to press reports, Russia is modernizing the Moscow ABM system, which protects much of the population of European Russia, where 75 percent of Russians live, and constitutes the world's only operational national missile defense. Russia continues to construct and improve numerous underground facilities designed to survive a nuclear war. As offensive nuclear forces are drawn down by START, the relative value of strategic defenses will increase. The United States has no defensive systems comparable to the Moscow ABM system or Russia's vast network of nuclear-survivable leadership and civil defense shelters.

Far from eliminating first-strike incentives, the START treaties unintentionally ratify the effects of a Russian nuclear first strike by reducing U.S. nuclear retaliatory capabilities to a minimal level. Indeed, the START treaties—especially START II and III, which entail the most radical reductions in nuclear forces—could significantly increase first-strike incentives for both sides. Calculations in *Nuclear Wars: Exchanges and Outcomes* and subsequent analysis by the author and others on strategic stability under START II and III point to increased incentives for striking first.

For both sides, START II and III will sharply decrease the weapons available to cover a still-large number of potential targets, resulting in a much less favorable ratio of weapons to targets than exists today. Therefore, the Russian military probably calculates that START offers greater opportunities for limiting damage to Russia through striking first, even if fewer enemy forces can be destroyed in a first strike. Because START force levels will not permit much, or any, redundant targeting—aiming two or more warheads at a single target, as was done previously—every U.S. warhead destroyed will guarantee the survival of a Russian target.

Under START II and III, a Russian first strike against *mobilized* U.S. forces would destroy the same fraction of U.S. forces as would have an attack made during the Cold War, prior to 1991 and the START treaties. Under START II and III, a Russian surprise attack against U.S. forces *before they can mobilize* would destroy a much larger fraction of U.S. forces than an identical attack made during the Cold War. A U.S. first strike against Russian forces would produce similar results. Therefore, incentives increase on both sides to strike early in a conflict or crisis, before the other side can mobilize.

Under START II and START III, Russia will have significant advantages over the United States in a counterforce or counterpopulation exchange, especially if Russia strikes first. Because Russian military targets are far more numerous and better protected than U.S. military targets, the U.S. needs substantially more strategic nuclear weapons to attack the same category of targets. After absorbing a Russian first strike against its military targets, the United States may be incapable of implementing its traditional counterforce strategy by retaliating against Russian military targets, since a substantial number of its weapons should be held in reserve to deter Russian attacks on U.S. population centers. In a United States–Russian counterpopulation exchange, Russia has inherent demographic advantages, because a smaller proportion of Russia's population lives in highly vulnerable urban areas. At START II and III levels, the strategic significance of these demographic differences will be magnified. Moreover, Russian military targets and population, unlike U.S. military targets and population, are protected.

Russian military analysts understand that START II and START III will impose serious targeting shortfalls on the United States. For example, Sergey Modestov, in a March 25, 1998, article, correctly observes that START II and III have required the Clinton administration to issue a new National Security Directive scaling back traditional U.S. nuclear weapon employment plans: "The revision of the content of President Reagan's previous similar directive (No. 13 October 1981) was initiated in February of this year by John Shalikashvili, who at that time held the position of Chairman of the Joint Chiefs of Staff, and by CINC Strategic Command Eugene Habiger. At that time both generals directed the President's attention to the fact that with the 3,000–3,500 nuclear weapons remaining operational under the START II Treaty it was impossible to ensure performance of missions assigned by the previous directive. And new [START III] reductions lie ahead to 2,000–2,500 warheads."

Small strategic nuclear forces, such as those that will result from START III, are inherently less stable than big nuclear forces, such as those at START I levels. Fewer warheads are available to compensate for technical or operational failure. Redundancy is also eroded because of increased dependence on a single triad leg: submarines for the United States, ICBMs for Russia. Small forces are more vulnerable to technological or operational surprise, which may result from the introduction of new weapons—such as improved antisubmarine warfare technology, ballistic missile defenses, or enhanced electromagnetic-pulse warheads—or from innovative tactics.

First-strike incentives may also increase in the future for reasons unrelated to the START treaties, because of decreased readiness of U.S. nuclear forces, erosion of Russia's early warning system and general-purpose forces, and new Russian threat perceptions. The lower readiness of U.S. strategic forces—bombers are no longer on strip alert, for example—makes them more vulnerable. Thousands of U.S. tactical nuclear weapons, constituting the majority of U.S. nuclear forces, are now located in a few vulnerable storage casernes. Previously, these weapons—including many that the Russians count as strategic, that is, SLCMs and weapons for theater aircraft—were based on mobile ships and submarines or were otherwise difficult to attack. Decreased U.S. readiness and increased vulnerability may increase Russian first-strike incentives in a crisis.

U.S. nuclear missile submarines now require an emergency action message from the president in order to launch their missiles. They cannot launch independently. An unclassified memo of September 14, 1995, from the Deputy Director of Strategy, Forces and Operations in the Office of the Assistant Secretary of Defense, states, "Under no circumstances is the commanding officer of an SSBN submarine able to launch a nuclear weapon without specific authorization from the president. Following a complete loss of communications, rigorous procedures exist to reestablish communications, but they *do not* [original emphasis] include the launch of an SLBM. This would violate the principal tenet that nuclear weapons release authority rests with the president."

U.S. nuclear missile submarines at sea have long been considered the backbone of the U.S. nuclear deterrent, guaranteeing a retaliatory strike no matter what—even if a surprise attack wipes out U.S. ICBMs and bombers and kills the president and his successors. Now, a Russian nuclear attack that kills the top U.S. leaders or severs U.S. submarine communications by destroying a handful of key nodes—one ELF (extremely low-frequency) station in Wisconsin, a few coastal VLF (very low-frequency) stations; the TACAMO (Take Charge and Move Out) aircraft base near Oklahoma City, some satellites, and electromagnetic-pulse attacks to generally suppress communications—could prevent U.S. submarines at sea from launching a nuclear retaliatory strike.

Russian forces also will be more vulnerable on a day-to-day basis. Continued deterioration of Russia's missile attack warning system through obsolescence and the loss of key radars stationed outside Russia is likely to lower sharply Russian confidence in the retaliatory use of nuclear weapons through launch-on-tactical-warning. This could press Russia to place a higher premium on nuclear first use.

Many Russian military officers, even many of those who support the START treaties, have declared that the strategic nuclear balance will be less stable in the future than today. For example, General A. V. Bolyatko, a START proponent, acknowledged in a 1993 *Military Thought* article that "as nuclear armaments are reduced, there is a discernible trend for a lessening of strategic stability." Military scientist Vladimir Zakharov, a START opponent, writes in an October 1995 article, "It should be understood . . . that deep reductions in nuclear arms substantially reduce stability of nuclear deterrence against various factors which destabilize the military-strategic balance." Igor Sergeyev, now defense minister and a supporter of START, nonetheless has written in *Military Thought* that "the military threat for Russia will hardly disappear in the near future," because the treaties do not constrain the modernization of the U.S. nuclear threat or affect U.S. war plans. "The treaties . . . on strategic offensive weapons will not make substantial changes in the development of offensive arms . . . and the conceptual views on combat employment. . . . Preserving the level of weapons combat capabilities through modernization is the main direction . . . of the U.S. strategic offensive forces under START II. . . . We must also point out that the dynamic development of the strategic nuclear forces of Great Britain and France is a substantial destabilizing factor under the conditions of the reduction of nuclear weapons."

Colonel I. A. Karpachev calculates in *Military Thought* that the sharply reduced number of warheads remaining to the sides under START will make the strategic nuclear balance much more delicate and "can lead to disturbance of parity and certain advantages for one side." General Yuri Yashin, a prominent Russian military scientist and vice president of the Russian Engineering Academy, warns that the START agreements do not remove the threat of a U.S. nuclear first strike. Yashin's logic is a classic case of "mirror imaging," attributing to the enemy one's own strategic plans and doctrine: "First and foremost we must point out that despite the significant reductions in strategic offensive weapons under the Russian-U.S. START I and II treaties, the United States has not halted its programs for the development of advanced offensive and defensive weapons systems." General Yashin claims that for the implementation period of the START agreements, the United States has a long-range strategy "which spans the period 1995–2003" and that calls for "development of U.S. ground- and sea-based missile forces, heavy bombers, and high-precision weapons, whose effectiveness was graphically demonstrated during the Persian Gulf War, and for continuing efforts to develop a U.S. ABM system—one of the main factors destabilizing parity." Yashin also notes the growing British, French, and Chinese nuclear arsenals and the trend toward nuclear proliferation and asks, "What are these things if not sources of military danger to Russia?"

General Makhmut Gareyev, one of Russia's most highly respected military theorists, argues in a November 13, 1997, article that START III will make nuclear warfighting more feasible, as it was in the "good old days" of the 1950s, and increase incentives to strike first: "At the time when the opposing sides had a comparatively limited number of nuclear weapons and the first nuclear war plans were being drawn up it was possible to assume that limited military operations, albeit involving great losses, were possible even under conditions of the use of nuclear weapons. This was mainly confirmed by experimental exercises conducted in the United States and USSR in the fifties and sixties. Running ahead, let us say that on the approach to the START III level, and given further reductions, we will return to a similar situation. . . . If we consider only the military-strategic aspect of the matter, the determination and readiness to be the first to use nuclear weapons in response to any aggression makes nuclear deterrence most effective both from the viewpoint of warning a potential aggressor and in terms of the reliable use of nuclear weapons. For it is known to be pointless from the military viewpoint to count only on counterstrikes." But the retired general is nonetheless critical of Russia's first strike doctrine and of the trend toward first use that will be exacerbated by START III: "From the viewpoint of . . . global strategic security . . . the principle of the first use of nuclear weapons also has its negative aspects. Above all, the complication and exacerbation of the international situation, the very desire not to be late and to be the first to use nuclear weapons will give rise to dangerous competition to see who will use them sooner, exacerbating the situation and provoking a preemptive nuclear strike."

In a February 12, 1998, article, "Nuclear Missile Adventurism," military analyst Petr Belov argues that the increasing vulnerability of Russian strategic forces under START will leave Russia with no alternative but to launch a preemptive strike:

> The Topol-M [SS-27 ICBM] . . . can indeed increase the probability of overcoming ABM systems. . . . This innovation is all right for the silo-based Topol-M in the event of its use for a surprise counterstrike and preemptive strike . . . but dubious for the mobile version, the combat employment of which is hardly likely to get as far as launching the missiles: They will all be destroyed beforehand because of the known location and absolute defenselessness against the enemy. . . . The probable enemy intends to eliminate any uncertainty that may arise as to the Topol-M's

> whereabouts by a range of methods—using radio and optical reconnaissance satellites of the Lacrosse and Keyhole types with 15-cm resolution, in conjunction with special technical and agent systems located along the routes of probable dispersal of the Topol-Ms. In these conditions the survivability of the mobile Topol-Ms can be "annulled" either before the use of weapons of mass destruction [by conventional weapons] . . . or else in the initial period of a nuclear attack: one high-altitude burst from a radio-frequency nuclear warhead is enough to put out of action even shielded electronic devices at distances of up to 100 km. Or a Trident missile, whose warhead would catch up with the Topol-M before it could get a safe distance away during their approach time.

The hard-line Russian Duma has, so far, opposed the START treaties, mainly because it opposes most anything that Yeltsin supports, and because it hopes that by holding START II and III hostage it can wring more concessions from the United States. Yet most senior Russian military officers support the START treaties, because in their absence Russia's continued economic deterioration will force the nation to downsize its nuclear forces unilaterally, leaving the United States in a position of superiority. Moscow needs the START treaties to maintain strategic parity, because Russia is economically incapable of sustaining modern forces above START II or III levels. Economic reality, not arms control, will compel Russia to reduce forces to START III levels. Moscow's goal is to set START III limits at low enough levels so that its ongoing strategic modernization can sustain parity with, or achieve advantages over, the United States.

The START agreements do not prohibit Russia's development of new ICBMs, like the SS-27, which will eventually replace the SS-18 and pose no less threat to the survival of U.S. strategic forces. In essence, the START treaties impose nuclear reductions only on the United States. Those Russian missiles dismantled under START must go anyway, owing to their obsolescence. Unlike Russia, the United States has no new ICBMs or SLBMs under development.

From the Russian military perspective, the START treaties, despite their flaws, are, on balance, highly favorable to Russia. The strategic balance resulting from them will, in the event of a nuclear conflict, offer Russia extraordinary and unprecedented military opportunities to destroy U.S. nuclear forces and to limit retaliatory damage to Russia—providing Moscow strikes first.

CHAPTER 33

Winning a Nuclear War

The strategic nuclear balance is fragile, because first-strike incentives will increase and retaliatory options will become riskier and less effective as the START reductions are implemented. This is well understood by the Russian military. Even more disturbing is the advocacy by some Russian officers and officials of the idea that a nuclear war can be won. For example, in an article entitled "Is There a Law of Victory?" published in *Military Thought* (1994), the flagship journal of the Russian Ministry of Defense, Colonel V. V. Kruglov argued that *striking first* and *surprise attack* are keys to victory in war. Moreover, according to Colonel Kruglov, a nuclear war can be won: "The law of victory allows us to take a new look also at such a question as victory in a nuclear war. . . . With the nuclear states reducing these amounts [of nuclear warheads] to a certain agreed level, then other warfare laws begin to operate on a par with the basic law, victory can be achieved just as in a conventional war."

Colonels V. Savchenko and S. Vasilyev, in a 1993 *Military Thought* article, proposed that the START treaties could be exploited to achieve an advantageous position for winning a nuclear war: "Nuclear weapons can become means of achieving political interests if their employment is not accompanied by negative . . . consequences for the side planning to deliver a nuclear first strike. . . . A situation is possible where, while remaining enemies, sides can begin reducing strategic offensive arms. Here a potential aggressor will strive to reduce nuclear arsenals to levels ensuring employment of nuclear weapons."

An October 1995 article by military scientist Vladimir Zakharov, subtitled "Myths about the Most Barbarous Weapon," derides as "porridge eaters" those who would use nuclear weapons "for political bluffing" and "not as a system of arms" for actually fighting and winning wars. Zakharov insists that nuclear weapons are no different from conventional weapons, just more powerful. He refutes several "myths" about the immorality and catastrophic environmental consequences of nuclear war, and he concludes, "Russia really has no other military-technical means for deterring large-scale aggression except for means of nuclear deterrence." He advocates using strategic nuclear weapons against either nuclear or nonnuclear adversaries, as allowed in Russia's new military doctrine. Another Russian military analyst, in a 1995 article, calls for unlimited use of nuclear weapons in all situations, going so far as to advocate seeding the border of Tajikistan with nuclear land mines to vaporize Afghan raiders.

In a December 1997 article, Yuriy Kozhuk describes Russia's new nuclear doctrine as a "concept of partial nuclear confrontation" that "assumes the possibility of limited use of nuclear weapons, which on the whole creates the prerequisites for escalation of the nuclear phase of the conflict." Kozhuk envisions Russia's nuclear first-strike doctrine as preventing or winning not only big wars but using the nuclear club to resolve even relatively trivial issues in Russia's favor: "The possibility of using nuclear weapons first extends . . . to prevention of a large-scale war and even, with certain assumptions, conflicts of lesser intensity, for example, for establishing conditions for the production and shipment of Caspian Sea oil that are advantageous not to third party countries, but to Russia."

Only a minority of Russian military writers overtly argue that victory can be achieved in a nuclear war. Russian civilian academics and political reformers overwhelmingly reject this view, as do Russian military leaders in *public* statements. Nonetheless, the mainstream Russian military view, which advocates nuclear first use, implicitly assumes that something *like* victory in a nuclear war is possible. After all, an advantageous outcome is supposed to derive from striking first.

The Russian president and his representatives have repeatedly reaffirmed Russia's new doctrine permitting first use of nuclear weapons under a broad range of circumstances. "Everyone must know that in case of a direct challenge our response will be fully-fledged, and we are to choose the use of means . . . including nuclear weapons," Ivan Rybkin, Secretary of the Russian Security Council, announced on February 11, 1997. Security Council Deputy Secretary Boris Berezovsky, in an interview on May 9, 1997, reiterated the doctrinal commitment to nuclear first use and claimed, "[First use of nuclear weapons] is an absolutely moral position which corresponds to current realities." The *Russian Federation National Security Blueprint*, approved by President Yeltsin in edict No. 1300 on December 17, 1997, declares, in boldface type, "**the right to use all the forces and systems at its disposal, including nuclear weapons**" and to do so "**in a decisive . . . manner until conditions beneficial to the Russian Federation for the conclusion of peace are created,**" thereby implying the possibility of victory in a nuclear war.

In an April 17, 1998, article, General Anatoliy Klimenko and Colonel Aleksandr Koltyukov, both of the General Staff's Center for Military-Strategic Research, which drafts military doctrine, applaud themselves and the new doctrine as having "candidly and honestly admitted that . . . the role of the nuclear deterrence factor increases." Alarmingly, the two nuclear hawks also credit themselves with moderation in nuclear policy, compared to some of their General Staff colleagues: "In developing the draft military doctrine, attempts were made . . . which incidentally have not stopped up to this time, to introduce into the document wording to toughen the nuclear policy."

Viktor Mikhailov, then Russia's minister of atomic energy and a still influential figure in the government, in a September 20, 1996, article appeared to share the views of nuclear enthusiast Vladimir Zakharov that Russia can use nuclear weapons for fighting wars without fear of environmental consequences. Mikhailov wrote, "In the military-technical field, Russia could strengthen its nuclear arms system: its strategic intercontinental missiles and those capable of reaching Europe . . . develop new-generation battlefield nuclear arms with relatively low capacity and reduced side effects on the environment and population located outside the hostile area. . . . Using such arms would not entail serious radiation consequences. . . . There should be no doubt that, in the event of any large-scale military attack on Russia involving conventional, let alone mass destruction arms, those arms will be resorted to."

An article of April 10, 1998, by Aleksandr Shirokorad, entitled "A Small Bomb for a Small War: The Role of Tactical Nuclear Weapons Is Objectively Increasing as Strategic Arms Are Being Reduced," agrees with Mikhailov's thinking that nuclear weapons are little different from other weapons. Shirokorad, a military historian who seems to admire the aggressive U.S. nuclear warfighting concepts of the 1950s, would cross the nuclear threshold merely to cope with U.S. reconnaissance aircraft: "And if, for example, a reconnaissance aircraft flies somewhere over Siberia at an altitude of 30 kilometers and is shot down by an air defense missile with a warhead of approximately 0.1 kilotons then, first of all, the radiation background on the ground at the epicenter of the explosion will hardly exceed the background in certain areas of Moscow and, secondly, there is not a single international agreement that would provide the basis for protest to any foreign state."

An October 1998 article by Russian journalist Sergey Sokut describes a major military exercise, conducted by General Kornukov's Long Range Aviation, that practiced a limited nuclear first strike against NATO, apparently during a "hypothetical" Balkan conflict, while NATO was actually planning for air strikes in the Balkans. "It is obvious," Sokut writes, "that the scenario of maneuvers . . . are quite realistic in light of NATO operations in the Balkans." In the exercise scenario, NATO is preparing an "aerospace offensive," but Russia launches preemptive strikes "that are designed to disrupt the enemy's concept of operations" and employs "powerful types of weapons on a limited scale." Victory is achieved as NATO "is compelled to terminate military operations and begin negotiations." Perhaps concerned about alarming NATO while it was actually in the process of real military preparations in the Balkans, the Russian commanders emphasized that their training merely simulated nuclear employment: "The

Air Force command authorities especially pointed out the fact that nuclear warheads were not extracted from their storage facilities and were not suspended from aircraft during the course of the exercise."

A May 1999 article by Pavel Felgengauer entitled "Limited Nuclear War? Why Not!" approvingly describes "Russia's new defense concept" detailed in a secret decree signed by President Yeltsin in April that calls for "radical modernization of Russia's existing nuclear arsenal, both tactical and strategic . . . to make a limited nuclear war possible. . . . the new nuclear weapons' main 'appeal' will be their ability to explode with exceptionally low yield. . . . It is being proposed to create up to 10,000 new low- and super-low-yield tactical nuclear weapons 'to counter NATO expansion in Europe.' What is more, existing strategic nuclear warheads are to be upgraded so they can be rapidly and simply reprogrammed to deliver [low-yield] strikes. . . . Nuclear pressure will once again become an effective instrument of policy. . . . To that end we must be able to carry out low-yield 'precision' nuclear strikes against military targets anywhere in the world."

Some in the West have tried to explain away Russia's new nuclear doctrine as little different from the nuclear strategy of the United States, since the United States also reserves the right to use nuclear weapons first. However, the present U.S. strategy of "Flexible Response" was not invented during the 1990s but during the 1960s and 1970s—Cold War decades—and has continued, more or less, by default. Few in the West worry about nuclear war any more, and U.S. nuclear strategy is in a state of atrophy. In contrast, Russia's aggressive new nuclear doctrine is a product of the 1990s, when the United States and Russia—the Clinton administration assures us—are no longer adversaries but strategic partners.

Besides, the comparison of U.S. Flexible Response with the new Russian nuclear doctrine is fundamentally inaccurate. In Flexible Response, the United States would have used nuclear weapons only as a last resort to stem a massive Soviet invasion of Western Europe, not as a first resort to preempt a suspected enemy nuclear or conventional attack before it happened, or to vaporize nonnuclear opponents, or to irradiate guerrillas and bandits. Russia's new nuclear doctrine more closely resembles the U.S. "New Look" nuclear strategy inaugurated by President Eisenhower, which was quickly rejected by President Kennedy as too risky. Flexible Response actually sought to reduce U.S. dependence on nuclear weapons by rebuilding U.S. conventional military capabilities.

Despite Russia's deep economic crisis, which has inflicted food, housing, and other shortages worse than those experienced by the United States during the Great Depression of the 1930s, Russia continues to invest in costly military programs designed for waging a nuclear world war. Ruinous national economic decline has made deep cuts in Russia's defense budget inevitable, forcing the General Staff to reduce greatly the size and readiness of Russian general-purpose forces and to cancel numerous military programs.

But the General Staff has protected the strategic nuclear forces and other key programs associated with waging a nuclear war, giving these projects highest priority. Today, Russia has the capability to deliver 6,000 START-accountable strategic nuclear warheads against targets in the United States and Eurasia. Moscow has kept its strategic nuclear forces at Cold War levels of proficiency, maintaining, modernizing, and training the forces continuously, at great expense to the domestic economy and the general-purpose forces. Russian strategic forces training frequently includes actual coordinated launches of ICBMs, SLBMs, and cruise missiles, including massed "ripple firing" of all missiles on an individual submarine—up to twenty intercontinental missiles have been fired in a few minutes by a Typhoon SSBN. Russia rarely did "ripple firing" during the Cold War. Although Moscow has represented these now-frequent massed SLBM firings as merely complying with START by "launching missiles to destruction," the practice provides invaluable crew training and direct operational verification of system reliability, an opportunity that has no counterpart in Western practice. Most of Russia's strategic warheads are on ICBMs and alert submarines, constantly ready, twenty-four hours a day, to launch a nuclear strike within a few minutes of being ordered to do so. Nearly all the rest can be generated for delivery to target within one day.

Under START II, Russian and U.S. strategic nuclear weapons will decline to about 3,500 apiece on each side by the year 2003, and under START III to 1,500–2,500 weapons by the year 2007. However, on the Russian side, quality will substitute for quantity, as Russia deploys more advanced and accurate missiles to deliver a smaller number of more modern and more powerful warheads. Russia will retain enough strategic warheads under START II and III to achieve its traditional damage goals against all nuclear and key military targets worldwide in a preemptive strike.

U.S. Defense Department officials have reported that Russia continues to manufacture new strategic missiles and nuclear warheads. General Eugene Habiger, commander of U.S. strategic nuclear forces, told the press in an April 1998 interview that Russia is developing a new SLBM and two new strategic cruise missiles. Habiger noted that Russia is now deploying mobile SS-25 ICBMs and the new SS-27 ICBM in silos and on mobile launchers.

Armed with a single 750-kiloton warhead—all ICBMs must be single-warhead under the terms of START II—the SS-25 is a highly reliable, solid-fuel missile with sufficient range and accuracy to destroy any nonhardened target worldwide. Presently being deployed is the SS-27; the SS-27, armed with a single high-yield warhead and having an accuracy of one to two hundred meters, will be able to destroy any hard target in the West. Warhead for warhead, the SS-27 will be twice as lethal as the SS-18 Mod 4 it replaces. Where the SS-18 Mod 4 required two warheads to destroy a U.S.

missile silo, the SS-27 can do the same job with one. A 1998 report by the U.S. Air Force's National Air Intelligence Center concludes that despite Russia's aging nuclear systems, arms reductions, and economic problems, "Russia probably will retain the largest force of land-based strategic missiles in the world."

Moscow also is developing an improved SLBM. Two advanced cruise missiles are under development for the strategic bomber force. Russia is slowly building additional Blackjack supersonic bombers. Russia is building a new class of ballistic missile submarine, the *Borey*, that has been under construction since 1996 and scheduled to be launched early in the next decade. The *Borey* project, though plagued with financial problems, is expected to produce an SSBN comparable to the most advanced in the West. Russia's GLONASS navigation satellite system is nearly complete, and it is already largely operational. By enabling ICBMs and SLBMs to make mid-course corrections, GLONASS will transform even inaccurate Russian missiles into hard-target killers, and it will impart a pinpoint precision to accurate missiles.

As Mary Fitzgerald has observed in the Hudson Institute study *The Russian Shift toward Nuclear War-Waging*, Russia assigns high priority to research and development of new "third generation" nuclear weapons that exploit "new physical principles." Enhanced electromagnetic-pulse warheads, which can paralyze an adversary's forces and command and control, are one such weapon. Russian scientists and military theorists claim that new battlefield nuclear weapons that are "cleaner" because they produce less radiation, and offer variable or very low yields to permit surgical nuclear strikes by tactical missiles, aviation, ground troops, air defense, and naval forces could multiply Russian combat effectiveness and firepower many times.

Moscow appears to be actively developing a new generation of advanced nuclear weapons through illegal underground tests. In violation of its moratorium on nuclear tests and the Comprehensive Test Ban Treaty (CTBT), Russia appears to have performed clandestine underground nuclear explosions, as evidenced by signs of recent testing on Novaya Zemlya discovered by the U.S. intelligence community in 1996. The U.S. intelligence community also reported a clandestine Russian nuclear test in August 1997, shortly after atomic energy minister, Viktor Mikhailov, visited the nuclear test site in July. But U.S. intelligence agencies, under pressure from the Clinton administration and scientists who support the CTBT, later publicly recanted and deemed the mysterious "seismic event" as probably, but not certainly, an earthquake. At minimum, the incident raises questions about the verifiability of the CTBT. The *Washington Post* reported in November 1997 that U.S. intelligence officials were concerned by the unusually high level of activity at Russia's arctic nuclear test site: "Some U.S. intelligence officials have marveled that the Russians are even now continuing their work in blowing snow and sub-zero temperatures and have speculated that the Russians have been trying to test the safety of their warheads or to investigate designs for an extremely low-yield nuclear weapon." On February 13, 1998, according to press reports, Norwegian scientists detected another seismic event at Novaya Zemlya that they suspect was a secret nuclear test. On February 23, Russian defense minister Sergeyev told the press that as a consequence of Moscow's investment in military research, "There has been an unprecedented abundance of breakthrough technologies in Russia lately, an abundance unheard of in the world. . . . The use of these technologies will increase the effectiveness of weapons and military equipment by 5–10 times."

Minister of Atomic Energy Mikhailov proposed in a September 1996 article that in the event of NATO expansion, Russia should deploy thousands of new-generation tactical nuclear weapons. Russia "could manufacture 10,000 high-safety nuclear warheads with a yield (TNT equivalent) ranging from dozens to hundreds of tons, designed for theater missiles, front-line aviation, and anti-aircraft complexes." Mikhailov claims that these new nuclear weapons could be used just like ordinary weapons, without serious risk to the environment, and "would equip the armed forces much better than they are now" by multiplying their firepower.

Mikhailov, in a 1997 interview, said that Russia was continuing to improve its nuclear weapons and is technologically ahead of the United States: "Needless to say, the United States would very much like to know what kind of [nuclear] experiments we are carrying out, given that our experience is way ahead of theirs. In order to find out they have asked us on many occasions for nuclear test site transparency, that is, openness. And our response is that there is a Comprehensive Nuclear Test Ban Treaty, which says nothing about any test site transparency. . . . The United States is still trying to 'open' us up. . . . It is extremely important to them to find out what we are doing. But it is not important to us to find out what they are doing. Russia is ahead of the United States."

Pentagon officials note that Russia continues to expand and build new underground nuclear blast shelters around Moscow and in the Ural Mountains. For example, the new deep underground facility being constructed in the Urals, at Yamantau Mountain, is designed to survive through a protracted nuclear war. The vast underground Yamantau complex, as large as a city, has a price tag equivalent to billions of dollars. Aside from surviving a nuclear war, Yamantau's purpose has been carefully concealed from the West. Despite direct requests from the Clinton administration and Congress to Russian leaders for an explanation of the Yamantau project, the very existence of which appears to contradict the premise that the Cold War is over in Moscow, the mission of Yamantau remains unknown. Yamantau is only one of numerous underground nuclear-survivable complexes being constructed or improved by Russia.

Russian nuclear-armed submarines periodically break their long hiatus on forward-area combat patrols with surprisingly aggressive forays. In December 1995, the Russian press reported that Russian nuclear attack AKULA and cruise-missile-carrying OSCAR submarines "have in recent months been displaying a level of activity unknown since the mid-80s on both coasts of the United States." Asked by Russian reporters "to explain the heightened activeness of our submarine fleet," Russian Navy chief of staff Valentin Selivanov replied, "We do not comment on our submarines' operations. As you know, secrecy is their main merit. The Americans can think what they like."

Russian interest in preparedness for World War III is not limited to nuclear arms. It also includes other weapons of mass destruction. Moscow continues to invest in the research and development of new poison gases. Val Mirzayanov, a defecting Russian scientist involved in chemical weapons development, revealed in June 1994 that the Russian military is vigorously working on "a new array of super-lethal binary chemical weapons known as Substance A-230, Substance A-232, and Substance 33, five to eight times more lethal than any previously known poison gas." Mirzayanov said that 15,000 tons of Substance 33 had already been manufactured at Novocheboksarak, a city in the Volga region.

Martin Sieff of the *Washington Times* reports of the secret Russian chemical weapons program: "U.S. intelligence sources said it was not possible to determine if the substances were being produced with Russian government approval." The military may be acting independently. In February 1999, according to press accounts, a CIA report concluded that "entities" dealing with nuclear, biological, and chemical weapons "have emerged in Russia . . . which may be operating outside the direct control of their government."

Russia ratified the Chemical Weapons Convention on November 5, 1997. Under it Moscow is obligated to destroy its chemical stocks within ten years. Nonetheless, according to a November 1997 report from the Office of the Secretary of Defense, *Proliferation: Threat and Response*, "Russian officials do not deny research has continued but assert that it is for . . . developing defenses against weapons. . . . Many of the components for new binary agents developed by the former Soviet Union are not [banned by] the CWC. . . . No permanent Russian destruction facilities [for chemical weapons] have been built. . . . Russia apparently is not spending its own funds to establish a destruction program."

In February 1998, former Russian chemical weapon scientists "produced disturbing evidence," according to Western press, "that Russian laboratories are continuing their research into new, deadlier poisons. . . . Money allocated by the United States for the chemical weapons elimination program under an accord signed by President Boris Yeltsin . . . is finding its way into the pockets of high-ranking generals in the Russian chemical weapon forces. . . . Senior figures in the program have been engaged in the sale of chemical weapons to rogue states in the Middle East. . . . [Funds were] illegally spent on building projects at 'military base 42734' at Shikany—the heart of Russia's chemical weapons testing network." Russia's declared stocks of chemical weapons amount to 40,000 tons, the largest stockpile in the world. "U.S. estimates of the Russian stockpile," according to the U.S. defense secretary's report, "generally are larger."

Russia also continues to invest in biological warfare (BW) weapons. In 1993, another defecting Russian scientist, Vladimir Pasechnik, revealed that the Soviet Union and Russia had violated the 1972 Biological Weapons Convention, which outlaws the development or production of bacteriological weapons. Pasechnik had served in a laboratory known as "Biopreparat," located in St. Petersburg, with about four hundred other scientists working on genetic engineering of germ weapons. Russia has developed a "superplague" that could kill half the population of a city in one week. Former CIA director Robert Gates testified in 1993 that the agency believes the Russian military is continuing to work clandestinely on illegal biological weapons without the knowledge of Russian civilian leaders.

On November 22, 1995, Stanislav Petrov, one of the senior managers of the Defense Ministry Institute of Microbiology, claimed in a Russian television interview that Russia was actively working on vaccines for a number of viruses and diseases that have military applications and had recently "developed a preparation to treat the ebola virus." In a ghoulish display, Petrov showed photographs of corpses, "victims of chemical attacks," which "have never been published," to impress upon his audience the importance of the Institute's work.

The April 1996 issue of the U.S. Defense Department's occasional report *Proliferation: Threat and Response*, states, "The United States continues to have concerns about Russian compliance with the Biological Weapons Convention, despite President Yeltsin's decree in April 1992 banning all activities contravening the Convention. Russia may be retaining capability for the production of biological warfare agents." A July 24, 1996, statement by the Congressional Research Service is less diplomatic about Russia's pursuit of biological weapons: "It is generally accepted that the former Soviet Union, and subsequently Russia, maintained and significantly expanded an illegal biological weapons program after its ratification of the 1975 Biological Weapons Convention. Furthermore, a series of Russian defectors have provided U.S. and British intelligence agencies with evidence that the Russian program has continued despite President Yeltsin's decree and public assurances of its demise."

In March 1998, Russian defector Kanatjian Alibekov, a scientist who had been second in command of the biological weapons program at Biopreparat, alleged that Russia, in violation of its treaty commitment, continues to work on BW, creating "genetically altered antibiotic-resistant strains of plague, anthrax, tularemia and glanders. They are working to create a strain of anthrax that will overcome the immune system . . . developing methods for genetically altering small pox virus while preserving its virulence . . . developing techniques for cultivating Marburg and Machupo viruses." In 1998, UN inspectors in Iraq uncovered at least circumstantial evidence that Russia supported Iraq's biological weapons program and may have provided Iraq with a genetically altered strain of anthrax against which U.S. vaccines might be useless.

Despite the catastrophic condition of Russia's general-purpose forces, the General Staff continues to plan for their modernization. Russia's new military doctrine calls for building a "leaner and meaner" army, which will rely on air mobility to rapidly deploy, to any point of the compass, and defeat an enemy using advanced conventional weapons and precision guided munitions. Military writings and commentaries call for abandoning the massed tank armies of the past, which proved highly vulnerable to air attack during the Persian Gulf War, and replacing the principle of mass with that of mobility and firepower. The new conventional forces are supposed to be flexible enough to wage local conflicts as well as large-scale wars. The Russian military is developing and fielding small numbers of highly sophisticated fighter aircraft, helicopters, tanks, tactical missiles and small arms.

However, reconstruction of Russia's general-purpose forces along high-tech lines is being outpaced by the accelerating deterioration of those forces. Erosion of Russia's conventional capabilities increases Russian dependence on nuclear weapons. The Russian Army could eventually collapse into anarchy or spawn another coup attempt and, again, create a nuclear crisis. A Congressional Research Service report, *Russian Conventional Armed Forces: On the Verge of Collapse?* (4 September 1997) concludes, "There is a big gap between the widely accepted (and ambitious) objectives of Russian national security policy and its diminished military capabilities, raising the danger of Russia becoming embroiled in a conflict on its periphery with which it cannot cope, with potentially dire consequences for Russia, its neighbors, and the West."

In contrast to Russia, the United States is doing nothing to prepare for, and little to deter, a World War III. America's political leaders do not believe such a war is possible—at least not in the immediate future. U.S. general-purpose forces are still the best in the world, but they have declined since their peak during Desert Storm, and little is being done to prevent the further erosion of their readiness and modernization. Russia's general-purpose forces are a wreck, far behind U.S. forces, but Moscow is doing much more than the U.S. to prepare for a nuclear conflict.

While Russia is manufacturing strategic missiles and has three improved missile types under development, the United States is no longer building any new strategic missiles and has canceled all development programs for ICBMs and SLBMs. While Russia is improving and building new deep underground command posts for surviving and prosecuting nuclear war, the United States has but three obsolete, and highly vulnerable, underground command posts—-at Cheyenne Mountain, Mount Weather, and Fort Ritchie—built in the 1940s and 1950s. Some of these U.S. command posts have actually been shut down. Unlike Russia, the United States is not researching new nuclear weapons or other weapons of mass destruction of advanced design. Indeed, a 1996 study by the U.S. Congress, *The Clinton Administration and Nuclear Stockpile Stewardship: Erosion by Design*, argues that the Clinton administration has deliberately neglected, or even sabotaged, America's nuclear industrial base. According to the study, because the United States may not be able to sustain a START II or III arsenal, future administrations may be compelled to seek further nuclear arms reductions with Russia. While Russia continues vigorously to train its nuclear forces for war by conducting major exercises, including live missile olaunches, the United States has not conducted any training of comparable scale and complexity since 1989.

Last but not least worrisome is that morale has never been lower in the strategic nuclear forces of the United States. Many officers have lost their sense of purpose. Many have grown cynical from Washington's failure to acknowledge that the officers and men manning U.S. missiles, bombers, and submarines still, every day, defend the United States from the most terrible threat in history.

CHAPTER 34

Flashpoints

Tomorrow the General Staff may well be more suspicious of potential adversaries, and more fearful of war, than it has been at any time since the war scare began in the early 1980s. In addition to traditional threats from the United States, NATO, and China, General Staff officers have expressed concern about what they see as new potential threats from a reunited Germany, a bolder Japan, new nuclear states emerging in the Middle East and Asia, from Russia's newly independent neighbors, and from within Russia itself.

The desperation and paranoia of the General Staff will only deepen as Russia continues to weaken militarily and internally, perhaps crumbling toward anarchy and civil war. The tempo of crisis in Russia and the former Soviet Union—and the threat to global security—seems to be increasing, as reflected by the occurrence in the 1990s of nuclear "close calls" during the August 1991 coup, the May 1992 Armenian crisis, the October 1993 coup, the January 1995 Norwegian missile crisis, and several more ambiguous incidents examined here. In contrast, during the Cold War decades, from 1945 through the 1970s, nuclear crises between the superpowers occurred on average about once every decade: the Berlin crisis (1948), the Suez crisis (1956), the Cuban missile crisis (1962), and the 1973 Middle East war. The frequency of nuclear crises increased in the 1980s, the last full decade of the USSR's existence, to about one war scare every five years (the 1981 Polish crisis and ABLE ARCHER–83), or one every three years, if you count as part of the previous decade the Warsaw Pact crisis of 1989–1990. Since 1991, nuclear war scares have occurred about once every two years to eighteen months.

The trend is troubling.

Can we learn anything from the history of Russia's war scares to identify circumstances that may again raise Russia's nuclear sensitivities? Future nuclear war scares are likely to arise from the same general conditions as in the past: Russian internal crises; troubles in the Baltics, Ukraine, the Caucasus, or other former Soviet republics; Western civilian or scientific aerospace activities near Russia; and Western military exercises, war and peacekeeping in the Balkans, the Middle East, or elsewhere on the periphery of Russia. The expansion of the North Atlantic Treaty Organization into Eastern Europe is a new source of tension between the United States and Russia, one that may well overshadow previous points of nuclear risk.

Russian internal troubles—such as a leadership crisis, coup, or civil war—could aggravate Russia's fears of foreign aggression and lead to a miscalculation of U.S. intentions and to nuclear overreaction. While this may sound like a complicated and improbable chain of events, Russia's story in the 1990s is one long series of domestic crises that have all too often been the source of nuclear close calls. The war scares of August 1991 and October 1993 arose out of coup attempts. The civil war in Chechnya caused a leadership crisis in Moscow, which contributed to the nuclear false alarm during Norway's launch of a meteorological rocket in January 1995. Nuclear war arising from Russian domestic crises is a threat the West did not face, or at least faced to a much lesser extent, during the Cold War.

The Russian military's continued fixation on surprise-attack scenarios into the 1990s, combined with Russia's deepening internal problems, has created a situation in which the United States might find itself the victim of a preemptive strike for no other reason than a war scare born of Russian domestic troubles. At least in nuclear confrontations of the 1950s–1970s—during the Berlin crisis, Cuban missile crisis, and 1973 Middle East war—both sides knew they were on the nuclear brink. There was opportunity to avoid conflict through negotiation or deescalation. The nuclear war scares of the 1980s and 1990s have been one-sided Russian affairs, with the West ignorant that it was in grave peril.

Russian and Western threat perceptions are likely to remain poles apart, if only because their internal realities are as different as night and day. The West takes peace and prosperity for granted; Russia knows neither of these, and is highly unstable. Russia's propensity toward aging leaders in poor health means Moscow is perpetually but a heartbeat away from another leadership crisis, with all its implications for Russian nuclear instability. For example, President Yeltsin's heart operation in 1996 became an occasion for another Kremlin wrestling match over the nuclear arsenal. Prime Minister Viktor Chernomyrdin thought he, instead of the military, should get temporary custody of Yeltsin's "nuclear briefcase," as emergency successor to the president. He did, for twenty-three hours. In 1997 and 1998, Yeltsin was again hospitalized with serious health problems that impeded his ability to govern. On March 19, 1998, Aleksandr Lebed, former secretary of the Russian Security Council, testified to the U.S. Congress that Yeltsin was mentally incompetent and that the world is endangered by a senile and delusional Yeltsin in possession of the "nuclear button." The keys to the kingdom of nuclear Armageddon seem never to be far from the minds of Russia's leaders.

Future Kremlin coup attempts may yet rock Moscow and the West. An anonymous spokesman for the defense ministry had the temerity to tell the press officially in February 1996 that if another coup happened, "Let Yeltsin not expect that the armed forces will, in a critical situation, once again step on the Constitution, as was the case in 1993." In April and May 1998, General Viktor Kulikov, who had headed the Ministry of Internal Affairs and its legions of troops, and General Lev Rohklin were accused in separate instances of plotting a military coup against the government. Some Russian journalists speculate that the reason the entire cabinet was suddenly dismissed in March 1998 was to thwart a coup by Kulikov.

President Yeltsin himself conceded another coup could be in the cards. In an August 1996 interview, when asked if another coup as in August 1991 could happen, he replied, "I do not rule out that under certain circumstances such attempts are possible." But Yeltsin also cautioned of a greater peril: "Danger rather lies elsewhere. There is still a visible trend toward the search for an enemy and an uncompromising all-out struggle in Russia. . . . These are the consequences of many years of life under the conditions of a totalitarian state. And they will not disappear overnight."

Western policy in the Baltics, the Caucasus, Ukraine, and other former Soviet republics can spark a nuclear war scare. Moscow sees the former Soviet republics as something less than sovereign nations. At best, the Kremlin views them as falling within a special Russian sphere of influence. Moscow's formation of the Commonwealth of Independent States, a military alliance comprising most of the former Soviet republics, is an attempt to institutionalize such a sphere. At worst, Russia plans eventually to reabsorb the former republics into a new Russian empire. As a 1995 study by the hard-line INOBIS think tank, a study that was "tentatively approved" by the defense ministry, according to the Russian press, concluded: "On the whole, it appears that if a judicious policy is followed, there are all grounds to count on restoration of a renewed Union state in 5–10 years made up of Russia, Belorussia, Kazakhstan, the greater part of Ukraine, as well as the Dneister region, Abkhazia, and South Ossetia. And Russia's relations with the Transcaucasus and Central Asia could develop according to the model of relations which existed earlier . . . with Moldavia, the Baltic, and Western Ukraine according to the model of Soviet-Finnish relations of 1944–1991 times." In 1997 and again in 1998, a senior official of the Russian embassy in Washington, speaking to me unofficially, endorsed the INOBIS study and predicted the restoration of Russia's lost empire within a decade. On March 17, 1998, the Russian press published a Foreign Ministry outline of the essential goals of Russian foreign policy, that included "resistance to international efforts aimed at thwarting CIS integration." One Western press report accurately observes that the plan envisions "the territory of the former Soviet Union as a Russian sphere of influence. In that context, Moscow has protested plans to integrate former Soviet states into NATO. It has also bemoaned the growing influence of the West—and especially the United States—around Russia's periphery."

Western challenges, or perceived challenges, to Russian dominance in the former Soviet republics could inadvertently provoke a Russian nuclear response. For example, Turkey's threat to intervene in the Armenia-Azerbaijan conflict resulted in the nuclear war scare of May 1992.

Russian sensitivities have not mellowed. In September 1995, maneuvers of Russia's Black Sea Fleet were justified by Admiral N. Mikhalchenko, the fleet deputy commander in chief, on the grounds of "the increased activity of NATO ships in the Black Sea region and with attempts to draw a number of coastal states into its zone of influence." In July 1996, President Yeltsin warned the West against encroaching on Ukraine and the Caucasus: "Russia will sternly react to all attempts to change the status of the Black Sea straits and to transform the Black Sea into one more springboard for navies of NATO and non-Black Sea countries." Moreover, "Russia opposes even a hypothetical possibility to extend the sphere of NATO influence to the Baltic countries." In April 1998, Russian press reports noted with alarm that the president of Azerbaijan and Turkey's chief of the general staff met to discuss the still unresolved territorial dispute with Armenia over Nagorno-Karabakh, and that Turkey's military chief voiced support for restoring "the territorial integrity of Azerbaijan." In January 1999, Russia moved additional military forces into Armenia. Azerbaijan's foreign ministry protested that "the buildup of the Russian military presence in Armenia can lead to unpredictable consequences in the region and beyond" and asked Turkey, NATO, and the United States for protection.

Relations between Russia and Ukraine remain strained, although Ukraine has surrendered all of its nuclear weapons. An unintended consequence of complex machinations of the United States to achieve a nonnuclear Ukraine could be U.S. involvement in a future Russo-Ukrainian war.

By 1994, pressure from Russia, U.S. diplomacy, and fresh financial inducements had brought a desperate and nearly bankrupt Ukraine to its knees. In January 1994, Ukraine, Russia, and the United States signed an accord giving Ukraine security guarantees and financial aid in exchange for Ukrainian agreement to return all nuclear weapons to Russia. In 1996, after delays and backpedaling by Ukraine, Kiev gave up the last of its missile warheads. However, Ukraine retains the capability to manufacture missiles and nuclear weapons, and Moscow fears Kiev might join NATO. In 1998, the Russian press accused Ukraine of conspiring with NATO against Russia: "The Ukrainian side went behind Russia's back and conspired with NATO to take at any moment the problem of the Black Sea Fleet out of the realm of Ukrainian-Russian bilateral relations and to blackmail Russia with the possibility of the . . . Fleet's presence on Ukrainian territory being examined in the UN Security Council. It is well known that the United States and the Western countries have unquestionably seized the initiative here." In 1998 Ukraine, for its part, accused Moscow of planning to sneak tactical nuclear weapons back aboard the Black Sea Fleet. "Ukraine may become the object of a tactical nuclear strike by NATO if plans for locating Russian nuclear arms on our territory are implemented. . . . This was announced yesterday by People's Deputy Sergey Terekhyn. Having analyzed [a] still classified text . . . from Moscow . . . there is a real possibility of the positioning of tactical nuclear missiles on ships in the Black Sea Fleet."

Russo-Ukrainian tensions are dangerous for the United States, because they contribute to an overall sense of growing international crisis among an already suspicious and fearful Russian military. Perhaps more importantly, U.S. efforts to help resolve the Russo-Ukrainian crisis have created the impression that Ukraine gave up nuclear weapons in exchange for substantial security guarantees from the United States. In fact, under the Trilateral Statement of January 14, 1994, the U.S. security guarantees to Ukraine were largely symbolic and probably would not legally bind the United States to side with Ukraine militarily in a war against Russia. But it is not clear that Moscow or Kiev understands the ethereal nature of the U.S. commitment to Ukrainian defense.

The potentially deadly illusion that the United States is committed by treaty to defend Ukraine could convince the Russian military that a future Russo-Ukrainian conflict, or Russian war of imperial reconquest, will inevitably involve war with the United States. This misapprehension might well lead the Russian General Staff to plan, out of mistaken military necessity, for a knockout nuclear blow against the United States at the very beginning of a war in which the United States, in reality, has no vital interest or real intention of participating.

There are other "wars of the imagination" between Russia and the United States for control of Russian or neighboring territory that Russian defense analysts are seriously preparing to fight. Anton Surikov, director of the INOBIS think tank, and General Valeriy Dementyev contend that the West is planning for war and that "three possible areas of aggression pose the greatest danger":

> First, in connection with the recent decision of Norway to extend NATO military activity to the north of the country, the Northern Axis, i.e., a NATO operation against bases of the [Russian] North Fleet on the Kolsk [Kola] Peninsula. Second, in connection with the discussed plans to create a 60,000-man Baltic Corps consisting of subunits from the FRG, Denmark, and Poland, a Northwest Axis, i.e., NATO military potential in the event of a war between Russia and the Baltic states. Third, in light of these calls to give countries of the Caspian basin NATO security guarantees similar to those which were given at one time to the countries of the Persian Gulf, a Southern Axis. Here the key role is assigned to NATO member Turkey. . . . Turkey has . . . repeatedly addressed military threats to a Russian ally, Armenia, in connection with the conflict in Nagorno-Karabakh. There is an evident

political line aimed at drawing Turkish-language and Muslim regions of the former U.S.S.R. into the sphere of Turkish influence.

In Surikov's and General Dementyev's view "the United States and the NATO countries remain the main probable adversaries of Russia" and pose an increasing nuclear threat:

> The U.S. possesses great nuclear missile potential which if used could destroy Russia as a state. It was created for the purpose of nuclear blackmail of the U.S.S.R. and was oriented chiefly toward delivery of a first nuclear strike. At present, despite ongoing reductions within the framework of [START I], not only does the first-strike orientation continue, but it is increasing.

Russian nuclear commanders may overreact to Western intelligence gathering or to Western civilian or scientific air or space activities near Russia's borders. For example, as noted, Norway's launch of a scientific research rocket in January 1995 sent Moscow into a panic over a possible U.S. nuclear surprise attack, resulting in the closest brush with Armageddon so far. When Korean Air Lines Flight 007 strayed into Soviet airspace in 1983, Moscow suspected it was a U.S. spy plane conducting reconnaissance, possibly prior to an impending surprise attack, and shot the tourists down. The KAL 007 affair contributed to the Russian war scare during the NATO nuclear exercise ABLE ARCHER–83.

The attitudes that resulted in the January 1995 war scare and the KAL 007 tragedy persist in the Russian military. Officers of the border troops told journalist Zhanna Shanurova that the "enemy," NATO, is preparing for aggression, and "with each passing year the enemy is getting bolder." They claimed that a Norwegian scientific research vessel, the *Sverdrug-2*, was recently found to be engaged in spying "although for the last ten years [Norway] had always said that it was scientific work."

Shanurova relates that in another instance Russian troops seized a Swedish research balloon that drifted over Russian territory: "The Swedes persistently requested that the container with equipment for scientific studies be returned to them. But here too, the border troops do not have a shadow of a doubt: This was a spy. It was trying to find our weak spots." The military's "hair-trigger" mentality was well-illustrated again in September 1995 when CIS air defenses shot down and killed two U.S. sports balloonists who unwittingly drifted toward an SS-25 ICBM base.

A March 23, 1998, item titled "Cold War in Cold Waters" (*U.S. News and World Report*) relates that after Russian submarines in the Barents Sea "launched a fusillade of missiles . . . Russian officials . . . complained to the U.S. Embassy in Moscow that an American submarine was nearby gathering intelligence about the performance of the Russian subs. In response, the Russian Navy gave chase, an operation said to have lasted for hours." Russian helicopters actually dropped depth charges, driving the sub away. Russian suspicions were excited again in April 1998 when Washington and Oslo announced that the United States would soon deploy in Norway, near Russian military bases on the Kola Peninsula, an allegedly harmless scientific radar intended merely "to track and catalog space junk." But even U.S. officials and scientists concede, in the words of one U.S. analyst, the radar "would be in perfect position to observe missile tests within Russia" and would "be able to warn of missiles that might be aimed outside the country" to support a future U.S. national missile defense. In January 1999, Defense Minister Sergeyev in a TV interview angrily pointed to the radar as evidence that the Cold War is still on.

Western military exercises, war and peacekeeping in the Balkans, the Middle East, and elsewhere on the periphery of Russia could be misconstrued by Moscow as preparations for aggression. For example, the NATO theater nuclear exercise ABLE ARCHER–83 sparked the Russian nuclear alert of November 1983. Routine U.S. Air Force training in Turkey contributed to Russian apprehensions about NATO intentions in the Armenia-Azerbaijan conflict amid the war scare of May 1992. U.S. air strikes in Bosnia probably contributed to Russian nervousness prior to the January 1995 missile crisis. In March 1999, General Vladimir Dworkin of the Stragegic Rocket Forces said Russia would be "much less likely to retaliate for false alarms caused by the so-called 'millennium bug' if the United States and NATO heed Moscow's demands and called off the bombings of Iraq and the threat of air strikes against Yugoslavia."

Zhanna Shanurova's conversations with officers of the border guards produced quite frank accounts of how NATO's military exercises posed a constant threat:

> The enemy is not sleeping, and is always preparing in every conceivable way to seize the northern Russian territories. He is constantly performing maneuvers to adapt himself to our climatic conditions and terrain. The unified armed forces of NATO this year have already conducted eleven training exercises in the Sea of Norway. At the present moment, there are submarines from the United States, Great Britain, the Netherlands and Sweden "training" there. . . . The foreigners have no other goal but espionage. . . . It is true, already three times U.S. atomic submarines have managed to collide with Russian ones.

Another war scare may have occurred in February–March 1996, when Moscow overreacted to a NATO land-sea exercise in Norway called BATTLE GRIFFIN–96. General Vladimir Semenov, commander in chief of the Ground Forces, stated on February 26 that NATO's training event might conceal a real threat: "NATO war exercises, which started in Norway on

Monday, jeopardize Russia's security," he said. "Up to 7,000 soldiers and officers are taking part in the land force games, including 1,900 German servicemen. The troops are part of NATO's rapid reaction force.... NATO is simultaneously staging naval exercises with more than forty warships, as well as landing units, in Norway's Arctic Circle." General Semenov was "puzzled by both the type and location of the games. Western military circles keep on thinking the way they did during the 'Cold War,' which is damaging to European security."

BATTLE GRIFFIN–96 moved Semenov to put Russia's northern forces on alert: "Because of the war games on the territory of an adjacent state, part of Russian troops will be put on alert and instructed to have a close watch on the situation." Russia must be prepared "in case of further tensions in the Russian zone of the Arctic Circle." General Semenov told Russian reporters, "The maneuvers in Norway may pose a threat to Russian national security and force it to seek suitable responses."

General Valeriy Dementyev of the Institute of Defense Studies agreed with General Semenov that BATTLE GRIFFIN–96 was a possible threat, coming as it did from one of "three possible directions of an aggression" that "are especially dangerous." In response to NATO's maneuvers, General Dementyev proposed readying missiles and aircraft: "In the interests of national security and for the sake of keeping a possible enemy away from such actions, Russia has to form an operational-tactical deterrence force.... The deterrence force may include missile and strike air force units, fitted with highly accurate weapons. In case of danger, it may be moved to the area of a possible conflict and targeted at the most important facilities."

President Boris Yeltsin was "Perturbed by NATO Maneuvers in Norway," according to a *Segodnya* headline. On March 1, 1996, Sergey Medvedev, Yeltsin's press secretary, announced that the Russian president "is following with anxiety developments near Russia on the territory of Norway." *Segodnya* reminded the reader, "It is not the first time that President Yeltsin has been worried over 'developments' near the Norwegian border. . . . When in Lipetsk last January, he became worried to such a degree that, for the first time ever, he unpacked his 'nuclear suitcase.' "

On March 14, the Northern Fleet mobilized for "large-scale maneuvers . . . timed to coincide with major NATO exercises in Norway," according to the Russian press, as "a suitable response to NATO's increased military presence near our northern borders and polar shores." On the day the Northern Fleet set sail toward the BATTLE GRIFFIN–96 task force, the Plesetsk cosmodrome in northern Russian launched a reconnaissance satellite.

At sea, the Red Banner Northern Fleet, opposite NATO's BATTLE GRIFFIN–96 forces, claimed to have chased NATO submarines intruding on the Russian zone of operations: "The ships detected foreign submarines in the course of the exercises and were able to shadow them for a lengthy period, but not remove them from the exercise zone." Russian press accurately described the situation "as close to real combat conditions as possible."

Tensions on the Russian side that may have contributed to their jitters over NATO's exercise included concerns that the United States might attack Cuba for shooting down a private U.S. aircraft. On February 28, President Yeltsin told journalists, "I am concerned over the situation around the recent incident between the United States and Cuba." Yeltsin "quite politely made it clear to the United States that war was not an answer to incidents of this type." On March 14, as the Northern Fleet set sail, the Duma condemned U.S. sanctions against Cuba as "dangerous for the world community." The foreign ministry announced Russia would "expand mutually advantageous cooperation with Cuba."

The Clinton administration seemed unaware of—or indifferent to—a potential crisis with Russia over BATTLE GRIFFIN–96. Amazingly, the focus of presidential concerns in February–March 1996 appeared to be with the Russian agriculture ministry's plans to suspend imports of U.S. poultry, which would hurt Arkansas's Tyson Foods chicken industry, an important Clinton constituent. Vice President Al Gore unsuccessfully demarched Prime Minister Viktor Chernomyrdin, in a letter on the chicken issue, which a Chernomyrdin spokesman described as having an "extremely sharp tone." Chernomyrdin refused Gore's request to hold a hotline conversation on the poultry controversy.

The United States and NATO have continued to conduct literally dozens of military exercises on the periphery of Russia, seemingly indifferent to or ignorant of the possibility of a dangerous Russian reaction.

CENTRASBAT-97 (CENTral ASian BATtalion 1997), another NATO military exercise—largely a U.S. show, with token allied participation—troubled Moscow in September 1997. In CENTRASBAT, the United States conducted the longest airborne operation in history, flying elements of the 82d Airborne Division from Fort Bragg, North Carolina, directly to the other side of the world, all the way to Kazakhstan.

Half of Russia's SS-18 ICBMs used to be deployed in Kazakhstan. The remaining half of the SS-18s are still deployed in Russia, just across the Kazakh border, where they still constitute the heart of Russia's strategic deterrent, carrying the lion's share of warheads. These missiles, in fixed silos, are zealously guarded from commando raids that the General Staff believes might come across the Kazakh border in the opening round of World War III.

After a nineteen-hour nonstop flight, U.S. paratroopers jumped and "seized" a Kazakh airport as part of a "peacekeeping" exercise. Marine Corps general John Sheehan, commander in chief of the U.S. Atlantic Command, personally led the paratroop raid and was the first to jump. Afterward, General Sheehan stated that CENTRASBAT-97 highlighted "the U.S, interest that Central Asian states live in stability" and that "there is no nation on the face of the Earth where we cannot go." Among the official goals of the exercise was to demonstrate to "neighboring countries" (a clear reference to Russia) U.S. support for the independence of the Central Asian states. Following the U.S. paratroop operation that opened the exercise, CENTRASBAT-97 involved maneuvers in Kazakhstan and Uzbekistan that lasted six days (September 15–20, 1997).

None of this was lost on Moscow.

Although there was grudging Russian participation in CENTRASBAT-97 (Russia contributed forty of the 1,400 troops that took part), the Kremlin and Duma both frowned on the event. Defense ministry official Leonid Ivashov, chief of the directorate for military international cooperation, in a televised statement on September 21 condemned CENTRASBAT-97 and all similar exercises: "Russia views very negatively even exercises held within the framework of the Partnership for Peace. . . . They facilitate the [NATO] alliance's expansion in our direction [and] to put it bluntly, the military might of NATO groups." Russian GRU (military intelligence) officials warned the press that "the scenarios of the CENTRASBAT-97 exercises, just like the SEABREEZE-97 naval exercise that was conducted in Ukraine within the NATO framework, has a nuclear . . . hidden agenda. In Ukraine, the main stage in the Ukrainian-U.S. exercises was held . . . close to the sites where launch silos of the RS-22 heavy intercontinental ballistic missiles are situated." Sergei Baburin, deputy speaker of the Duma, on September 19 complained to the press, "Under cover of statements of 'peacekeeping' nature of such maneuvers, U.S. troops are intensely studying new potential military theaters in the immediate vicinity of the borders of the Russian Federation." Baburin pointed to "SEABREEZE-97 exercises on the Black Sea, NATO games in the Baltic region, and the CENTRAL ASIAN BATTALION-97 games in Kazakhstan and Uzbekistan" as recent training events that were particularly worrisome.

Shortly after the U.S. paratroop drop, the Duma, on a virtually unanimous vote, approved a statement condemning CENTRASBAT-97 as training for war against Russia, and threatened to treat future such activities as warranting a possible Russian military response: "The State Duma was especially worried by the recent maneuvers in Kazakhstan and Uzbekistan, which involved the units of the Army of the United States of America . . . who made a non-stop flight from Fort Bragg, USA [and] landed on the territory of Kazakhstan. It is obvious that statements on the peacemaking nature of such maneuvers are camouflaging an intensive development of new potential war theaters in direct proximity to the borders of the Russian Federation by the Army of the United States of America. We cannot exclude the possibility that such super-long air-lifting operations are used to train in delivering the Army of the United States of America to the territory of the Russian Federation. . . . Intensive military activity in the form of such joint maneuvers will be inevitably regarded by the Russian Federation as a sign of hostility and engender a corresponding reaction." While CENTRASBAT-97 unfolded, on September 17–18, Duma members of the "Anti-NATO Group" advertised their departure from Moscow to reconvene in session at Kostroma, an ICBM base of the Strategic Rocket Forces.

None of this, largely unreported in the Western press, made any impression on Washington or the NATO allies, who have continued to conduct major military exercises near Russia, oblivious to Moscow's reaction and to the possibility of nuclear overreaction.

On March 9, 1998, according to a blurb on the back pages of the *Washington Times*, "NATO kicked off its largest field exercise since the Cold War . . . with 90 ships and 50,000 servicemen dealing with fictitious crises in Spain, Portugal, and Norway." STRONG RESOLVE 98, followed with great interest on the front pages of the Russian press, also involved military forces of ten Central and Eastern European countries that were former members of the Warsaw Pact and now wish to join NATO. The Russian press noted that STRONG RESOLVE 98's scenario included a conflict between Norway and the fictitious "Limonia," clearly Russia: "NATO allies are coming to [Norway's] assistance. They are transferring armed forces to the expected conflict zone and landing on disputed territories." Russian Admiral Vladimir Kuroyedov, commander in chief of the Navy, tersely commented to the press, "Such measures, involving so many men and resources, make one ponder what is going on."

In January 1999, Defense Minister Sergeyev lodged an official protest with the Norwegian defense minister over the conduct of NATO military exercises in Norway: "You probably would not like this region to become famous for intensive military actions. We think that there are no reasons for carrying out military exercises there."

Western military operations in Bosnia, the Middle East, or elsewhere on the periphery of Russia could spark another war scare. The General Staff's first reaction to foreign military operations near its borders is to question whether these might really be aimed at Russia, even if overtly aimed at another party. From Moscow's perspective, Western mobilization for operations in Bosnia or against Iraq could conceal a surprise attack against Russia.

The Clinton administration in September 1995 displayed indifference to possible Russian overreaction by authorizing cruise missile strikes in Bosnia without warning Moscow in advance. U.S. cruise missiles were launched despite Moscow's nuclear saber rattling and threats of a new world war just a few months earlier. At the time, Russian journalist S. Kurginyan portrayed the sides as "A Micron Away from Apocalypse," the title of his article, which described the United States and Russia as on the verge of war over Bosnia and NATO expansion. On September 8, President Yeltsin claimed U.S. air strikes in Bosnia proved that NATO is indifferent to life. "NATO is already showing what it is capable of. . . . It can bomb and then count how many civilians it has killed." The Russian president pointed to Bosnia as evidence of what could happen "when NATO comes right up to the Russian Federation border."

Bosnia has been relatively quiescent since the introduction of a multinational, including Russian, peacekeeping force in December 1995. But Bosnia and the Balkans remain a hotbed of unrest, ready to explode. Albania disintegrated into criminal anarchy in 1997. In 1998 and 1999, fighting in Kosovo between Serbs and ethnic Albanians threatened a wider Balkan war that could draw in Russia and the United States on opposite sides. On October 13, 1998, General Leonid Ivashov, a Russian defense ministry spokesman, reiterated Moscow's longstanding fear that NATO's presence in the Balkans is ultimately aimed at Russia. General Ivashov, speaking in "near-to-apocalyptic terms" according to press, said NATO air strikes in Kosovo would "create an absolutely new military-geostrategic situation in Europe. . . . [The] operation against Yugoslavia is also projecting the use of the Alliance's military force toward Russia. . . . Other European countries, the CIS, including Russia, can become targets of NATO intervention."

U.S. and NATO air strikes on Kosovo proceeded amid threats from Russian military officers, including Chief of the General Staff Anatoliy Kvashnin, that Russia might intervene on the side of the Serbs. Sabre rattling from the Russian military over Kosovo became so worrisome to President Yeltsin that he ordered his senior officers to desist, only to be ignored. Questions were raised about Yeltsin's control over the military—and Russian-NATO friction over NATO were further highlighted—when in June 1999 Russian troops based in Bosnia broke an understanding with NATO about how peacekeeping was to proceed in Kosovo by entering Kosovo first and racing ahead of NATO forces to occupy the airport at Pristina, the regional capitol. The Russian military planned to airlift several thousand troops into Kosovo via the Pristina airport, but could not get permission to cross Hungarian or Romanian airspace. President Yeltsin and other high Russian officials denied knowledge of this operation and claimed it was all a mistake. As of this writing, it is still unclear if Yeltsin authorized the operation and lied to the U.S. and NATO, or if the Russian military acted on its own.

Yeltsin himself, not just the Russian military, was alarmed by NATO air strikes on Kosovo and Yugoslavia despite the loud protests of Russia, a nuclear superpower. Matters were not helped when in March 1999 the United States—oblivious to the Russian reaction—after giving Moscow the standard 24-hours notice, flight-tested four SLBMs, fired off the patrolling nuclear submarine *Henry M. Jackson.* The event was widely interpreted in the Russian press as "nuclear diplomacy" over Kosovo. In April 1999,

Yeltsin cautioned "NATO, the Americans and the Germans" not to push Russia into military action in Yugoslavia as "there will be a European war for sure and possibly a world war." At a meeting of the Russian Security Council, a frustrated Yeltsin reportedly cried to his generals, "Why are they not afraid of us? We have not stopped anything!" The Kosovo crisis moved Yeltsin on April 29, 1999, to sign secret orders authorizing, according to Russian press, "the development of the nuclear weapons complex and a concept for developing and using non-strategic nuclear weapons." NATO air strikes in the Balkans moved the Russian Security Council, Russian press reported, to consider "enshrining . . . a provision" in military doctrine and operational planning "regarding a preventive nuclear strike." In May 1999, Duma Defense Committee Chairman, Roman Popkovich, declared, "We must definitely include a provision in our doctrine to the effect that Russia reserves the right to deliver a first or preemptive strike." Since Russian military doctrine already explicitly allows preemptive first use, the references to "preventive" and "first" strikes appear to endorse an additional mode of nuclear first use that may be more aggressive than preemption. In Vienna on April 30, 1999, a Duma delegation headed by Vladimir Lukin met with a U.S. Congressional delegation led by Congressman Curt Weldon to discuss the Kosovo crisis. The Duma delegation leveled a thinly veiled nuclear threat, warning that a "future" Russian government might well react to Kosovo by making a nuclear EMP attack against the United States:

> There has never been such anti-Americanism in Russia since the days of the Korean War. The situation in Russia is unstable. . . . Imagine what an anti-American dictatorship in Russia would be like. Imagine if an SSBN fired off a missile from somewhere in the Atlantic. You would not have communications. . . . You would have no internet, nothing.

On May 28, 1999, former Prime Minister Chernomyrdin, an envoy to negotiations with NATO over the Kosovo crisis, told the *Washington Post*, "The world has never in this decade been so close as now to the brink of nuclear war."

Moscow is still unreconciled to the NATO presence in the Balkans. If fighting resumes in Bosnia or Kosovo, as seems likely, or if violence elsewhere in the Balkans spreads, once again requiring the West to intervene with air strikes or large-scale occupation, the potential for Russian miscalculation will again escalate. Given the war-scare mentality of Russian political and military leaders, it may be legitimate to ask whether enough was done to forewarn President Yeltsin and the General Staff that U.S. strategic platforms would shortly attack targets a few hundred kilometers south of Commonwealth borders. If the circumstances of the nuclear superpowers were reversed, how would the Pentagon react if Russia, on twenty-four hours' notice, launched cruise missile and strategic bomber attacks on Mexico?

Ongoing Western military activities around the world provide plenty of opportunity for Russian nuclear hypertension. A particularly striking example of Moscow's tendency to misunderstand and overreact to U.S. military operations occurred in February and December 1998 and during operation DESERT FOX in 1999. In February, the United States and Iraq were in an escalating political crisis over Baghdad's obstruction and expulsion of UN inspectors seeking Iraqi weapons of mass destruction. President Clinton surged U.S. air and naval forces into the Persian Gulf to prepare for a massive cruise missile campaign to destroy suspected nuclear, chemical, and biological storage sites and to smash the Republican Guard, the loyalist military forces that maintain Saddam Hussein's dictatorship. U.S. B-1B strategic bombers, originally designed for nuclear conflict with Russia, flew into the region, ready to receive their baptism of fire.

Moscow assumed the United States was on the verge of launching a nuclear first strike on Iraq. On February 4, 1998, President Yeltsin warned in televised remarks from the Kremlin that "Clinton's actions could lead to a world war. He is acting too loudly, too loudly." Kremlin officials explained later that day that Yeltsin's warning about World War III "was referring to unnamed reports that the U.S. might use nuclear weapons to incinerate [Iraq's] chemical and biological weapons sites." On February 5, Yeltsin declared, "We must not in any event permit an American strike. I told Bill Clinton this: 'No, we won't allow it.' . . . The main thing is that we stand strong on this position, that there is no option of force. It is impossible—it would mean a world war." On February 6, President Yeltsin repeated his warning about "a new world war" a third time in as many days.

Although some initially dismissed Yeltsin's remarks as another symptom of his mental deterioration, his concern that the United States might be on the verge of starting a nuclear war in Iraq—one that could somehow escalate out of control and involve Russia—was widely shared by Russian political and military elites. At the same time Yeltsin issued his first war warning, on February 4, Foreign Minister Primakov confronted U.S. ambassador James Collins, while the Russian Foreign Ministry in Washington simultaneously demarched the White House, demanding to know if the United States was about to initiate a nuclear war against Iraq. The Russians further demanded a guarantee that the United States would not employ nuclear weapons. The Duma, according to Russian press reports, was "concerned by the possibility of the U.S. use of nuclear weapons." By a near-unanimous vote of 329 to 19, the Duma issued on February 4 a statement on the Iraq crisis condemning U.S. military preparations as "dangerous and totally unjustified actions" and announcing that "the State Duma resolutely denounces any attempts at blackmailing Iraq with the threat of the use of nuclear weapons."

Despite U.S. assurances that there were no intentions or plans to wage nuclear war on Iraq, Russia remained unconvinced.

Russian press reports speculated that the impending U.S. strike against Iraq was part of a master plan to subvert Russian interests and dominate the world. One article, typical of mainstream thinking in the Russian press, claimed that a U.S. attack on Iraq would in reality be a "Dash to the Caspian," as its title declared, part of a conspiracy with NATO to capture the oil wealth of the Caspian Sea: "Turkey and Britain are supporting the anti-Iraq, and, essentially, anti-Russian policy in the Persian Gulf. . . . The U.S. Administration is discussing different ways of 'including' the Caspian region in the European or Central Command of the U.S. Armed Forces. . . . U.S. companies are taking the lead in development of Caspian oil, and oil resources here are . . . almost 13 billion tons in the Caspian regions of Azerbaijan and Kazakhstan. . . . And for geographical reasons alone the Persian Gulf must be a secure bridgehead for Washington's possible intervention in inter-Caspian contradictions. . . . Iraq and Iran are hindering the planned U.S. 'dash to the Caspian.' " Some Duma members proposed putting Russian military forces in the Caucasus, near the Caspian Sea, on alert. On February 6, the commander of Russian border troops in Armenia had to issue a public statement to quash rumors that the Turkish army was advancing on Armenia, presumably to take over Azerbaijan and the spout for Caspian oil at Baku.

On February 10, Russian General Leonid Gulev, described as "one of Russia's leading military specialists on the U.S.," told the newspaper *Rossiskaya gazeta* that one probable reason for the U.S. attack on Iraq was to test nuclear weapons on real targets "inhabited by people." During a summit in Moscow between the U.S. and Russian military chiefs on February 12, according to the *Washington Post*, "Russian Defense Minister Igor Sergeyev forcefully lectured Defense Secretary William Cohen . . . about America's 'tough and uncompromising' stand on Iraq, warning against hasty judgments and short-lived military victories and expressing 'deep concern' about future U.S.-Russian relations if the United States takes military action against Iraq. . . . the Russian's action marked a sharp departure from usual diplomatic courtesies." Press reports described Cohen as "shocked" and "stunned" when Sergeyev asked threateningly, "Is America ready for all the possible consequences?"

The next day, Russian press carried unconfirmed reports of a Russian nuclear test at Novaya Zemlya—a mysterious seismic event was detected by Norwegian scientists. Two days after his confrontation with Secretary Cohen, on February 14, Valentine's Day, Defense Minister Sergeyev in a televised statement pledged that if the United States attacked Iraq, "we will be taking some appropriate action." That same afternoon Sergeyev told the world, in remarks immediately disseminated internationally in English, "The Russian Strategic Rocket Forces are capable of retaliating within 8 minutes after a hypothetical aggressor makes a nuclear strike . . . even if the missiles are completely untargeted." Moreover, the recent merger of the

"Strategic Rocket Forces, Space Military Force, and the missile defense forces is from seven to ten times more effective than before," Sergeyev said.

On February 17, Russia launched a military satellite, KOSMOS-2349, of unknown type, possibly a reconnaissance satellite for monitoring U.S. forces in the Persian Gulf. On February 19, a Russian nuclear submarine launched two strategic missiles from the Barents Sea and struck targets in the Kamchatka Peninsula, a "training event" that, given U.S.-Russian tensions over Iraq, seemed timed as a show of Russian nuclear strength. U.S. intelligence agencies discovered, according to Western press reports, that Russia had—in a breakthrough in biological warfare—apparently genetically engineered a new form of anthrax virus against which U.S. vaccines were useless. UN inspectors looking for weapons of mass destruction in Iraq uncovered evidence indicating that Russia may have given the new super-anthrax weapon to Saddam Hussein. Or was this "discovery" a deliberate leak by Moscow and Baghdad to deter a U.S. attack?

This time, the symptoms of a Russian nuclear war scare did not entirely escape notice of the Western press. A *New York Times* editorial on February 13 noted, "That Mr. Yeltsin . . . would prove less cooperative about opposing Iraq than [former Soviet Premier] Mikhail Gorbachev is a troubling sign. . . . The differences over Iraq reflect a broader deterioration in relations. NATO's eastward expansion into Poland, Hungary, and the Czech Republic angers many Russians, and talk of planting the NATO flag still closer to Russia in the future is even more alarming. . . . Russia's increasing reliance on nuclear weapons to defend itself, fueled in part by NATO expansion, is a dangerous development. . . . All of this is complicated by a sense that Mr. Yeltsin, after his heart problems and surgery, acts erratically at times."

As quickly as the rising tensions between the United States and Russia over Iraq arose, the crisis ended. At the end of February, the United States blinked. Unable to rally international support for air and missile strikes on Iraq, opposed by a majority of the UN Security Council, led by Russia, the United States reluctantly canceled operation DESERT THUNDER. President Clinton decided to give a new inspections agreement, brokered by UN Secretary General Kofi Annan and briefed to the United Nations on February 24, a chance to preserve peace and achieve dismantlement of clandestine Iraqi programs for weapons of mass destruction.

Almost a year later, the crisis over Iraq was back on again. In December 1998, the Clinton Administration, frustrated with Iraq's continuing obstruction of UN inspections, launched operation DESERT FOX, making large-scale air and missile strikes on Iraqi military facilities. One day after the U.S. strikes began, on December 18, Russian press reported that, according to defense ministry officials, Moscow placed its strategic nuclear forces on alert: "In view of the Iraqi crisis, the Russian Defense Ministry is taking additional steps to heighten the combat readiness of troops, including Russia's strategic nuclear forces." On the same day, presidential spokesman Dmitriy Yakushkin "confirmed that the Russian Army was put on increased military alert." Russian press justified the alert by citing former Prime Minister Primakov's denunciation of the U.S. bombing of Iraq because it "violates the entire world order established after the Second World War. . . . This action was conducted unilaterally. It cannot be tolerated."

Publicly acknowledging a nuclear alert would be highly unusual—the military prefers to keep such matters secret. Later on December 18, Defense Minister Sergeyev denied that Russian conventional military or nuclear forces were on alert. On December 25, Russia launched KOSMOS-2361, a satellite designed to provide Russian strategic forces with improved early warning of an incoming nuclear attack. On January 17, 1999, while U.S. air strikes were still going on, a Russian television news show, equivalent to *60 Minutes*, claimed Moscow had, in fact, placed nuclear forces on alert. General Anatoliy Kornukov, commander-in-chief of the Air Force and Air Defense Forces, appeared to confirm this claim:

> MOSCOW TV: In the past few days the world came close to a third world war. In accordance with a secret directive, the Russian Armed Forces were placed on heightened combat alert . . . connected with the exacerbation of the situation around Iraq.
>
> KORNUKOV: Combat alert crews at command posts were reinforced to some degree, and training sessions in arming aircraft were carried out, just in case.

According to the broadcast, "The General Staff worked with an intensity characteristic of wartime."

Russia almost certainly would not have gone to war to protect Iraq, as it in fact did not in December 1998. Behind President Yeltsin's warnings about U.S. nuclear strikes on Iraq escalating into a world war may have been unspoken concerns in the Kremlin that the United States might use Iraq as a pretext for wider aggression, or that the General Staff or lower-level nuclear commanders might overreact and launch an unauthorized nuclear attack. Yeltsin could hardly publicly admit the latter possibility. He had repeatedly assured the international community that Russia's nuclear forces are "under control" and can make no mistakes. Nonetheless, Moscow's assumption that the United States was prepared to act so precipitously with nuclear weapons betrays a suspiciousness or ignorance of the character of the United States that is profoundly dangerous in a nuclear superpower.

The United States should not assume that large-scale military operations against Iraq, or anywhere on Russia's periphery, will in every case be accurately evaluated in Moscow and perceived as nonthreatening. Moscow has made abundantly clear that mere preparations for aggression against Russia could invite a nuclear first strike.

NATO expansion to include former members of the Warsaw Pact, or of the Soviet Union, could spark another war scare. In the West, NATO expansion is not now widely seen as a dangerous proposition. During the Cold War, less than a decade ago, violation of Austrian neutrality, a minor transgression compared to the eastward expansion of NATO, was considered by most analysts to be a potential casus belli for the Soviet Union. Accordingly, NATO fastidiously respected the neutrality of Austria, to avoid provoking World War III. Virtually all Western analysts agreed that Moscow would go to war rather than lose Eastern Europe and the Warsaw Pact, and certainly to prevent the disintegration of the USSR itself. Yet these things happened, and no war came.

Today, the West thinks Moscow will suffer anything. The West's sanguine attitude toward NATO expansion, supported in the United States by both major political parties, is uninformed that the collapse of the Warsaw Pact and Soviet Union were, in fact, extremely perilous events involving grave nuclear risk for the West. That these crises ended happily for the United States and NATO was largely a matter of luck.

Somewhere to the east, an expanding NATO may well finally cross Russia's nuclear tripwire, perhaps in Bulgaria, perhaps in the Baltic states. Vladimir Lukin, chairman of the Duma's International Affairs committee, cautioned that NATO expansion eastward "is liable not to strengthen peace . . . but, on the contrary, to blow it apart." He threatened that Russia might meet NATO expansion with nuclear weapons: "Will it be better for the West to have a traumatized but still nuclear Russia again forced to withdraw into the steppes? . . . If the blind egoism of the shortsighted politicians to the west of our borders prevails, we will resort to the means we still have in our hands. These are means of some kind of desperation, but effective nonetheless."

INOBIS, Russia's Institute of Defense Studies, a think tank affiliated with the Defense Ministry, has proposed in a study a number of nuclear countermeasures to meet NATO expansion. INOBIS would target Poland and the Czech Republic with ICBMs and deploy nuclear weapons in Iran, opposite the Strait of Hormuz, to exert countervailing pressure against a Western vulnerability. The INOBIS study also proposed responding to NATO expansion by invading the Baltic states while, according to Western and Russian accounts of the proposed Russian plan, regarding "any attempt to obstruct the Russian action by NATO . . . as a prelude to nuclear war." Russian press reports claim the INOBIS plan was tentatively approved by the defense ministry.

NATO expansion could conceivably replay the Cuban missile crisis. During a high-profile visit to Cuba in October 1995, Oleg Soskovets, Russia's first deputy premier, stated that a Russian nuclear countermeasure to NATO expansion could include the deployment of "Russian missile-carrying and strike-force nuclear powered submarines in Cienfuegos." INOBIS analyst Anton Surikov, in an April 1997 article, claims the expansion of NATO to the Baltic states would constitute a provocation as dangerous as the 1962 Cuban missile confrontation.

Even pro-Western Russian leaders vehemently oppose NATO expansion. In April 1996, President Yeltsin characterized NATO's move eastward as "an attempt to keep the foreign policy and the mentality of Cold War times." In January 1997, Yeltsin again loudly protested NATO expansion and ordered his ministers to find a way to stop or counter it. In a television interview just before Christmas 1996, then Defense Minister Rodionov said that NATO plans for expansion proved that "the Cold War is not yet over." Moreover: "Russia and the United States [have] powerful nuclear potentials capable of destroying the globe and turning each other into dust. Is there a 100 percent guarantee that a possible conflict can be avoided?" More pointedly, General Lev Rohklin, chairman of the Duma Defense Committee, warned simply, "If NATO comes closer to Russian borders, both strategic and operational-tactical missiles could be used."

The very pointed nuclear threats cited here from Lukin, Soskovets, and Rohklin never appeared in the Western press, even though Moscow Interfax made them available in English.

The Clinton administration has attempted to allay Moscow's fear of NATO expansion, making concessions at the 1997 Helsinki summit in strategic arms control and allowing Russia an observer status in NATO under the "NATO Founding Act." Moscow accepted the concessions, but it still dreads NATO. On January 14, 1998, the Duma issued a formal declaration that "an analysis of the military and political situation in the world allows the State Duma to state that potential threats and challenges to Russian security have not decreased. Despite Russia's sincere desire to ease tension . . . between the West and East, NATO countries have forgotten their promise, made at the time when the Warsaw Treaty Organization was dissolved, not to . . . expand the [NATO] Alliance to the East." On January 25, 1998, Defense Minister Sergeyev announced that to counter NATO expansion, Moscow might deploy troops in western Belarus on the Polish border, a circumstance that he acknowledged "may lead to confrontation between two military alliances." In April 1998, Foreign Minister Primakov and Security Council Secretary Kokoshin met with the foreign minister of Belarus to, as the two Russian officials put it, "draw a red line against NATO's eastward enlargement, meaning that the new states which emerged on the territory of the former Soviet Union are not to join NATO." Responding after a week of silence to the U.S. Senate's April 30, 1998, vote favoring NATO membership for Poland, the Czech Republic, and Hungary, the Russian defense ministry declared simply that the Senate had committed "a fatal mistake."

Moscow is already using economic pressure on the Baltics and political support of violence in the Balkans to oppose NATO expansion. A May 1998 article, "Russia Raises Stakes against NATO" (*Washington Times*) concludes, "From the Baltic states to the Balkans, Russia and its allies are confronting new and prospective NATO members in a series of small but ugly crises. Helmut Sonnenfeldt of the Brookings Institution, formerly the State Department's chief analyst on Eastern Europe, told the *Washington Times*, "The Russian government is following a general approach of seeking to find areas where it can define itself in opposition to perceived interests of the United States and where it can find other countries that share its concern." In February 1999, Russian Deputy Foreign Minister Yevgeniy Gusarov gave an international gathering at Munich a "Cold War Flashback," in the words of the press, turning "a sleepy two-day conference on NATO's future into a controversial exchange reminiscent of the East-West conflict during the Cold War" when he said that an expanding NATO would threaten Russia and warned NATO not to cross Russia's "red line." In April, Duma Speaker Gennadiy Seleznev told the press that, "Russian nuclear arsenals prevent World War III" because "Europe's comfortable life may have made it forget World War II. . . . Nevertheless, Europe knows full well what it would be like to make war on Russia." In June 1999, in the aftermath of NATO air strikes on Yugoslavia, Strategic Rocket Forces chief Yakovlev reassurred the Russian public, in a statement also published in English, that, "There is no doubt about the reliable functioning of the troops and their ability to warn about a missile attack. . . . the Strategic Nuclear Forces [shall] destroy missiles of the enemy, the attacking objects and troops."

I have personally been on the receiving end of Russian nuclear threats over NATO expansion. In 1997 and again in 1998, a high-ranking Russian official, who has requested anonymity, warned me that NATO enlargement could trigger a nuclear war. The Russian official, claiming knowledge of military contingency plans to deal with certain scenarios of NATO expansion, said it was his personal view that these plans would be implemented if the scenarios become reality. If NATO's military forces expand into the Baltic states, he said, Russia would go to war to prevent this, and would even resort to nuclear weapons. He said Russia would go to war to preserve the Kaliningrad enclave. He said Ukraine is "part of Russia" and will be reincorporated "in 10 or 20 years" and that therefore "there is no question Russia would wage war to prevent Ukraine from joining NATO." He said Russia would wage war to prevent the former Soviet republics in the south—Georgia, Armenia, Azerbaijan—and the former Central Asia republics from joining NATO. The high-ranking official said that the "weakness of Russian conventional forces would, in the event of a war with NATO, under any of these scenarios, leave Moscow with no alternative but to launch a nuclear first strike."

The high-ranking Russian official indicated that NATO enlargement to include Poland, the Czech Republic, Hungary, Romania, Slovenia, and Slovakia would be reluctantly accepted by Russia and would not trigger a military response, providing tactical nuclear weapons or advanced conventional weapons and strike platforms are not forward-deployed to these states. If NATO moves tactical nuclear weapons or advanced conventional air power into these states, according to the Russian official, Russia would respond with military countermeasures—deploying Russian tactical nuclear weapons, returning Russian missile submarines to Cuba, moving Russian nuclear weapons into North Korea to threaten U.S. troops and allies, or basing Russian nuclear weapons in Iran to threaten the Strait of Hormuz and the global oil supply, for example. Or, the official said, Russia might "initiate a preventive nuclear war."

Poland, Hungary, and the Czech Republic, approved for NATO membership by the U.S. Senate in 1998, were admitted formally into NATO in 1999. Still more nations are in line to join NATO after 1999, pressing the alliance ever closer to Russia's borders. From the Russian General Staff's perspective, the clock is ticking, and time is running out to do something about "the NATO threat."

Shortly after an interview with then Chief of the General Staff Mikhail Kolesnikov, Russian journalist Pavel Felgengauer, who has rare regular access to senior Russian military circles, wrote in August 1995 an article entitled "The Russian Army and the East-West Military Balance: Self-Deception and Mutual Misunderstanding Did Not End with the Cold War." He concluded that during the Cold War, the West, ignorant of the Russian war scare, underestimated the threat of nuclear conflict. "Now in the mid-90s, we can conclude that the military threat in the Cold War years was fundamentally wrong. The actual conventional military threat to the NATO countries was considerably less than supposed, whereas the nuclear threat was considerably greater. . . . There was in reality a panic fear in Moscow of NATO and a possible war. . . . What is more, it was fear and the panic caused by it at the top that could have been the main cause of a nuclear war."

More importantly, Felgengauer believes, the failure to understand the erroneous nuclear threat perceptions of the past endangers the future: "The strategic errors of both parties, which could have provoked a nuclear war in Europe, have yet to be a subject of serious public analysis. And this is a bad sign. The end of the Cold War does not preclude new strategic errors—a mistaken assessment of states' intentions both in East and in West Europe." Indeed, Pavel Felgengauer offers the chilling judgment that the Russian nuclear war scare is more dangerous than ever. "Russia is still a nuclear superpower," he writes, "and the weaker its conventional possibilities, the more Moscow will be forced to rely on nuclear deterrence. . . . The West's strategic assessment of Russia's possibilities and intentions is not distinguished today, just as in the times of the Cold War, by particular accuracy. Today Russia is weaker than ever, and for this reason the likelihood of panic in Moscow is greater than in the 1970s or 1980s."

We ignore these facts at our peril.

Selected Sources

INTRODUCTION

Richard N. Cooper, "Emerging Missile Threats to North America in the Next 15 Years," *Hearings: House Committee on National Security*, HNSC 104-37 (1996). Key judgments of NIE 95-19 in "Do We Need a Missile Defense System?," *Washington Times* (14 May 96). U.S. General Accounting Office, *Foreign Missile Threats: Analytic Soundness of Certain National Intelligence Estimates*, GAO/NSIAD-96-225. Christopher Andrew and Oleg Gordievsky, *KGB: The Inside Story of Its Foreign Operations from Lenin to Gorbachev* (Hodder and Staughton, 1990), hereinafter *KGB*. Stanislav Lunev and Ira Winkler, *Through the Eyes of the Enemy: Russia's Highest Ranking Military Defector Reveals Why Russia Is More Dangerous Than Ever* (Regenry, 1998). "Yeltsin's Volatility Has Some Worried," *Washington Times* (14 June 92).

CHAPTER 1: DECEMBER 12, 1979

Joseph M.A.H. Luns, Brussels communique (12 December 79); *New York Times* (13 December 79), pp. 1, 6. Arnold Beichman and Mikhail S. Bernstam, *Andropov: New Challenge to the West* (Stein and Day, 1983). Zhores Medvedev, *Andropov* (Penguin, 1984). John Dornberg, *Brezhnev: The Mask of Power* (Deutsch, 1974). D. F. Ustinov, *Serving the Country and the Communist Cause* (Pergamon, 1983). John Kohan, "The Civilian Soldier Fades Away," *Time* (31 December 84). Celestine Bohlen, "Ustinov Guided Rise of Soviet Power," *Washington Post* (22 December 84). Oleg Gordievsky, "Pershing Paranoia in the Kremlin," *The Times* (London: 27 February 90), pp. 12–13. On Soviet nuclear superiority see Peter Vincent Pry, *The Strategic Nuclear Balance: And Why It Matters* (Crane Russak, 1990).

CHAPTER 2: OPERATION VRYAN

Andrew and Gordievsky, *KGB*. Gordievsky uses the acronym RYAN, Shvets the full acronym VRYAN: Yuri B. Shvets, *Washington Station: My Life As a KGB Spy in America* (Simon and Schuster, 1994). Death by molten metal see Murray Smith, "Courage of the Spy Who Stayed On in the Heat,"*Evening Standard* (30 March 95), p. 22. On the endorsement of nuclear first strike in Soviet military doctrine: U.S. Department of Defense, *Soviet Military Power* (March 1987); John M. Caravelli, "The Role of Surprise and Preemption in Soviet Military Strategy," *International Security Review* (Summer 1981); Mark E. Miller, *Soviet Strategic Power and Doctrine* (Advanced International Studies Institute, 1982). Colonel A. A. Sidorenko, *The Offensive* (Moscow, 1970), U.S. Air Force translation. Moskalenko,

Biryuzov, and Byely in Albert Weeks, William Brodie, and Frank Barnett, *War and Peace: Soviet Russia Speaks* (National Strategy Information Center, 1983). German Ministry of Defense, *Military Plans of the Warsaw Pact in Central Europe: A Study* (Bonn: January 1992) in German. A. Ivanko, "End of 'Surprise Nuclear Missile Attack.' Intelligence Chief Ye. Primakov Abolishes One of the KGB's Most Secret Programs," *Izvestiya* (29 November 91), pp. 1, 6. Bill Gertz, "KGB Halts Lookout for U.S. Nuclear Attack," *Washington Times* (28 November 91), p. 9. "Primakov Holds 27 November News Conference," Foreign Broadcast Information Service (hereinafter FBIS) FBIS-SOV-91-231 (2 December 1991), p. 20. Shvets in Michael Dobbs and R. Jeffrey Smith, "From Inside the KGB: A Tale of Incompetence," *Washington Post* (21 February 93), pp. 1, 26. Anatoliy Dobrynin, *In Confidence* (Times Books, 1995). VRYAN directives in Christopher Andrew and Oleg Gordievsky (editors), *Comrade Kryuchkov's Instructions: Top Secret Files on KGB Foreign Operations, 1975–1985* (Stanford University Press, 1993) and *More "Instructions from the Centre": Top Secret Files on KGB Global Operations 1975–1985* (Frank Cass, 1992). On the VRYAN computer program: William T. Lee, "The Nuclear Brink That Was—And the One That Wasn't," *Washington Times* (7 February 95), p. A19 and notes and interview.

CHAPTER 3: THE PERSHING II CRISIS

On the SS-20 threat see Jed Snyder, "European Security, East-West Policy and the INF Debate," Robert Kennedy, "Soviet Theatre Nuclear Forces," and Alan Ned Sabrosky, "America in NATO: The Conventional Delusion," all in *Orbis* (Summer 81); Paul Nitze, "The Relationship of Strategic and Theatre Nuclear Forces," *International Security* (Fall 1977). Ustinov, *Pravda*, and Andropov quotes in U.S. Arms Control and Disarmament Agency, *Soviet Propaganda Campaign Against NATO* (October 1983). On restricting SSBN patrol areas see "Excerpts from Remarks by Brezhnev on Missiles,"*New York Times* (17 March 82), p. 6. Bernard D. Nossiter, "Soviet Forswears Using A-Arms First," *New York Times* (16 June 82). "U.S. and Soviet Seek to Prevent a Surprise Attack," *New York Times* (8 December 83), p. 6. National Intelligence Council, *Dimensions of Civil Unrest in the Soviet Union*, NIC M 83-10006 (Central Intelligence Agency, April 1983). Director of Central Intelligence, *Soviet Capabilities for Strategic Nuclear Conflict, 1982–92*, National Intelligence Estimate (hereinafter NIE) NIE 11-3/8-82 (Central Intelligence Agency, 15 February 1983). Director of Central Intelligence, *The Soviet Challenge to US Security Interests*, NIE 11/4-82 (Central Intelligence Agency, 10 August 1982). Miller, *Soviet Strategic Power and Doctrine*. Peter Vincent Pry, *Nuclear Wars: Exchanges and Outcomes* (Crane Russak, 1990).

CHAPTER 4: THE POLISH CRISIS

On Jaruzelski's helicopter ride with Ustinov see John Darnton, "Jaruzelski Is Now Sorry He Ordered Martial Law,"*New York Times* (4 March 93). Drew Middleton, "Poland's Four-Star Premier," *New York Times* (11 February 81). Eric Bourne, "Wojciech Jaruzelski—A General Shaped by World War II," *Christian Science Monitor* (11 April 84). Bernard D. Nossiter, "Gromyko, At U.N., Says U.S. Fosters a New Arms Race," *New York Times* (23 September 81), p. 14. "Gromyko Speech Excerpts,"*New York Times* (16 June 82). Rudolph Boretsky, "General Dubynin," *Novoye vremya* (23 June 92), pp. 28, 29. "Soviets Were Ready to Invade Poland," *Washington Times* (14 March 92), p. 6. U.S. Arms Control and Disarmament Agency, *Soviet Noncompliance*, Pub. 120 (March 1986). Kuklinski in Benjamin Weiser, "Polish Officer Was U.S.'s Window on Soviet War Plans," *Washington Post* (27 September 92). Director of Central Intelligence, *Poland's Prospects Over the Next 12 to 18 Months*, Special NIE 12.6–82 (1 September 1982).

CHAPTER 5: THE KAL 007 CRISIS

For the best treatment of KAL 007 see Seymour M. Hersh, *The Target Is Destroyed: What Really Happened to Flight 007 and What America Knew About It* (Random House, 1986) has *TASS*, Ogarkov, and Andropov quotes. Michael R. Gordon, "Ex-Soviet Pilot Still Insists KAL 007 Was Spying," *New York Times* (9 December 96). KAL 902, Gromyko, and higher VRYAN priority in Andrew and Gordievsky, *KGB*. 1993 investigation and Kornukov in Alastair Macdonald, "Russian Air Chief Ordered KAL Downing," *Washington Times* (23 January 98), p. A17. Robert B. Cullen, "The Cautious Bully," *Newsweek* (22 November 82). Vladimir Solovyov and Elena Klepikova, *Yuri Andropov: A Secret Passage Into the Kremlin* (Macmillan, 1983).

CHAPTER 6: ABLE ARCHER

Kuznetsov in Andrew and Gordievsky, *KGB*. Director of Central Intelligence, *Possible Soviet Responses to the US Strategic Defense Initiative*, NIC M 83-10017 (Central Intelligence Agency, 12 September 1983). Director of Central Intelligence, *Soviet Capabilities for Strategic Nuclear Conflict, 1982–92*, NIE 11-3/8-82 (Central Intelligence Agency, 15 February 1983). KGB directives in Andrew and Gordievsky, *Comrade Kryuchkov's Instructions: Top Secret Files on KGB Foreign Operations*. U.S. strategic upgrades in International Institute for Strategic Studies, *The Military Balance 1992–1993* (1992). USSR Ministry of Defense, *Whence the Threat to Peace* (Moscow: Military Publishing House, 1984). "Increase Vigilance and Be Alert," *Aviatsiya i kosmonautica* (July 83) translated in JPRS 84463 (3 October 83), pp. 1–2. Ustinov in "The US in the Grip of a Military Psychosis," *Zarubzhenoye voyennoye obozreniya* (May 83) translated in JPRS 84314 (14 September 83), p. 12. Andropov in Don Oberdorfer, *The Turn: From the Cold War to a New Era, The United States and the Soviet Union 1983–1990* (Poseidon, 1991). "Lt. Colonel Petrov Saved the World from Nuclear War," *Kommersant Daily* (22 September 98) FBIS translation 19980923000048. Ian Thomas, "How I Stopped Nuclear War and Wrecked My Life," *Daily Mail* (7 October 98). Martin Walker, *The Cold War: And the Making of the Modern World* (Fourth Estate, 1993). Fred Hiatt, "Experts Report Soviet Sub May Have Hit U.S. Gear," *Washington Post* (5 November 83). David M. Alpern and Kim Willenson, "The Case of the Crippled Sub," Newsweek (14 November 83). Director of Central Intelligence, *Soviet Capabilities for Strategic Nuclear Conflict, 1983–93*, NIE 11-3/8-83 (Central Intelligence Agency, 6 March

1984). Director of Central Intelligence, *Implications of Recent Soviet Military-Political Activities*, Special NIE 11-10-84/JX (Central Intelligence Agency, 18 May 1984). William T. Lee interview and notes on still classified report by President's Foreign Intelligence Advisory Board (PFIAB) of February 1990. Ben Fischer, *The 1983 War Scare in US-Soviet Relations: Threat Perception, Scare Tactic, or False Alarm?*, paper for the 63rd annual meeting of the Society of Military History (20 April 1996). Ben Fischer, *A Cold War Conundrum: The 1983 Soviet War Scare*, CSI 97-10002 (Central Intelligence Agency, September 1997).

CHAPTER 7: THE DEATH OF ANDROPOV

Don Oberdorfer, *The Turn*. Andrew and Gordievsky, *KGB*. KGB directive of 6 January 1984 in Andrew and Gordievsky, *More "Instructions from the Centre": Top Secret Files on KGB Global Operations 1975–1985*. "Ustinov: USSR Adds Missile Subs Off US; And Will Increase Number of SS-20s If US Deploys More Euromissiles," *Current Digest of the Soviet Press*, Vol. XXXVI, No. 20; from *Pravda* and *Izvestiya* (21 May 84). Lee, "The Nuclear Brink . . . ," *Washington Times* (7 February 95), p. A19. William T. Lee, *How the Cold War Was Lost and Won*, forthcoming. Fisher, *A Cold War Conundrum*. Lev Yelin, "The Death Sentence Is a Reward for Me," *New Times* (Moscow: January 92). KOSTYAR-1 and space shuttle in Andrew and Gordievsky, *Comrade Kryuchkov's Instructions: Top Secret Files on KGB Foreign Operations*. Shvets, *Washington Station*. Ivanko, "End of 'Surprise Nuclear Missile Attack,' " *Izvestiya* (29 November 91). Gertz, "KGB Halts Lookout for U.S. Nuclear Attack," *Washington Times* (28 November 91). Gordievsky on VRYAN status in 1992 in Aleksandr Shalnev, *Izvestiya* (18 November 94).

CHAPTER 8: GORBACHEV AT 20,000 FEET

Archie Brown, *The Gorbachev Factor* (Oxford University Press, 1996). Andrew and Gordievsky, *KGB*. On the nationalities crisis and events preceding the coup see Joseph G. Whelan, *Gorbachev's Decline and Fall: From Failed Coup to Collapse of Empire August–December 1991*, Congressional Research Service 920-630 S (4 May 1992). Vladimir Pozner, *Eyewitness: A Personal Account of the Unraveling of the Soviet Union* (Random House, 1992).

CHAPTER 9: KRYUCHKOV'S COUP

For background and personalities of coup plotters see Whelan, *Gorbachev's Decline and Fall* and Pozner, *Eyewitness*. On coup plotting and military rehearsals see Andrey Ambrosimov and Andrey Zhdankin, "A Topical Interview: The Answer Is Unequivocal—There Was a Plot," *Rossiyskaya gazeta* (23 January 92) translated in FBIS-SOV-92-021 (31 January 92), pp. 37–41; and the excellent David Remnick, *Lenin's Tomb: The Last Days of the Soviet Empire* (Random House, 1993). Mikhail Gorbachev, *The August Coup: The Truth and the Lessons* (HarperCollins, 1991). Stuart Loory and Anne Imse, *CNN Reports: Seven Days that Shook the World* (Turner, 1991). For more on Kryuchkov see "Oleynikov on KGB's Role in

Coup Attempt," FBIS-SOV-91-218 (12 November 91), p. 19; David Wize, "House of Cards," *Times Saturday Review* (London: 30 November 91); Gordievsky, "Pershing Paranoia in the Kremlin," *The Times* (27 February 90). Lt. General G. Konev and Maj. General V. Pokrovskiy, "Protracted Nuclear War: According to the Views of U.S. Military Experts," *Zarubezhnoye voyennoye obozreniya* (October 87) translated in JPRS-UFM-88-003 (9 May 88), p. 5. Gertz, "KGB Halts Lookout For U.S. Nuclear Attack," *Washington Times* (28 November 91). Ivanko, "End of 'Surprise Nuclear Missile Attack,' " *Izvestiya* (29 November 91).

CHAPTER 10: THE WARSAW PACT CRISIS

De Maiziere in COMTEX, "Wire News Highlights: Soviet Hardliners Failed," *Current News Early Bird* (American Forces Information Center, Office of Secretary of Defense, 2 May 1991), p. 16. Shevardnadze interviewed Fedor Burlatskiy, *Literaturnaya gazeta* (10 April 91) translated in FBIS-SOV-91-071 (12 April 91), pp. 30–36. Helmut Kohl, *Ich wollte Deutschlands Einheit* (Berlin: Propylaen, 1996). Kevin Liffey, "German Leader Reveals KGB Plot in Book," *Chicago Sun-Times* (30 September 96). A. Krasnov and Y. Nikolayev, "On the Pendulum of the 'New Thinking': Concerning the Stance of Ex-Minister Shevardnadze," *Sovetskaya rossiya* (15 June 91) quoted in James Blitz, "Gorbachev to Purge Hardliners," *Sunday Times* (London: 16 June 1991), p. 1. "General Comments on U.S. Aims in Gulf," FBIS-SOV-91-086-S (3 May 91). Rodionov and Chernavin interviewed by Aleksandr Prokhanov, "A Visit to General Rodionov's Office," *Den* (May 91), p. 1. "Gorbachev Warns Against 'New Cold War,' " FBIS-SOV-91-092 (13 May 91), pp. 27–28. Marshal O. Losik, "Where the Limits of Reasonable Sufficiency Are," *Krasnaya zvezda* (5 March 91) translated in FBIS-SOV-91-045 (7 March 91), pp. 57–58. Natalie Gross, "Soviet Press Review: Reasonable Sufficiency Reappraised," *Jane's Soviet Intelligence Review* (May 91), pp. 238–239. Kapronov in Jim Danneskiold, "Top Soviet Advisor: Military Officials Rethink Promise Not to Use Nuclear Weapons First," *Los Alamos News Bulletin* (12 April 91), p. 5.

CHAPTER 11: TWILIGHT

For further examples of Soviet hardliner threat perceptions see G. V. Titov interviewed by Viktor Andriyanov, "From the Viewpoint of Counterintelligence: And Its Leader's View of the Processes Occurring in Society, the World and the Country," *Rabochaya tribuna* (30 March 91) translated in JPRS-UTA-91-006 (9 April 91), pp. 5, 6 and speech by Strategic Rocket Forces chief in "Maksimov Speech on Missile Troops Day," FBIS-SOV-89-224 (22 November 89), pp. 122–124. Secret Yazov order reprinted in *Komolskaya pravda* (27 August 91) translated in FBIS-SOV-91-166 (27 August 91), p. 59. Graham Hall Turbiville, Jr. (editor), *The Voroshilov Lectures: Materials from the Soviet General Staff Academy* (National Defense University, 1989), chapter 4. "General Says Half of Army Backed Coup Attempt," FBIS-SOV-91-173 (6 September 91), pp. 59–60. Increased Combat Readiness implemented among bunker and chemical troops: Maj. General Vladimir Podelyakin interviewed in *Rossiskaya gazeta* (30 August 91), p. 3; V. Ivanov, "USSR KGB 'Bunker' Directorate, 1015 Hours, 18 August," *Komsomolskaya pra-*

vda (27 August 91) translated in FBIS-SOV-91-169 (30 August 91), p. 47; Chemical weapons mobilized in N. Burbyga, "They Wanted to 'Mark' the Defenders of the White House," *Izvestiya* (28 August 91) translated in JPRS-UMA-91-028 (14 November 91), pp. 7–8. Barton Gellman, "General Withdrew Missiles to Shelters During Coup," *Washington Post* (28 August 91), p. 18. Bill Gertz, "U.S. Missed Soviet Nuclear Alert in Coup," *Washington Times* (12 May 92), p. 1. Kobets quoted in Ivan Yelistratov, "Army in August Putsch: It Was There But Did Not Participate," *Izvestiya* (19 February 92) translated in FBIS-SOV-92-035 (21 February 92), pp. 63–65. V. Litovkin, "Army General Yu. Maksimov: 'One Republic Cannot Maintain a Nuclear Shield,' " *Izvestiya* (30 August 91) translated in FBIS-SOV-91-169 (30 August 91), pp. 79–81. Kaysin in " 'Serving the Fatherland' Examines Military Life," FBIS-SOV-91-175 (10 September 91), pp. 48–55. Maltsev in "General Reviews 19 Aug Events at Crimean Airport," FBIS-SOV-91-165 (26 August 91), pp. 34–35. Colonel M. Ponomarev, "World Remains a Dangerous Place," *Krasnaya zvezda* (19 September 91) translated in FBIS-SOV-91-185 (24 September 91), pp. 5–6. Lisov in Abrosimov and Zhdakin, FBIS-SOV-92-021, pp. 37–41. USSR Defense Minister D. Yazov, "Greatness of the People's Feat: Victory, Memory and Truth," *Pravda* (9 May 91) translated in FBIS-SOV-91-090 (9 May 91), pp. 42–44. Yazov on Gorbachev in Remnick, *Lenin's Tomb*. Sergui Verona, *Soviet Union: A Chronology of Events Surrounding the Coup Attempt August 1–September 15, 1991*, Congressional Research Service 91-705 F (27 September 1991), p. 5. Whelan, *Gorbachev's Decline and Fall*. "After the Coup: Three Harrowing Days That Shook the World, Hour by Hour," *New York Times* (22 August 91).

CHAPTER 12: OPERATION THUNDER AND THE FALL OF THE OLD GUARD

Ponomarev, FBIS-SOV-91-185, pp. 5–6. On GRU giving false warning of a U.S. nuclear alert during the coup see Bill Gertz, "Russian Renegades Pose Nuke Danger; CIA Says Arsenal Lacks Tight Controls," *Washington Times* (22 October 96). Yakovlev, Shakrai, and Sakharov quoted in Remnick, *Lenin's Tomb*. Loory and Imse, *CNN Reports*, pp. 16, 41. Andrey Krayniy, "This Is No Business for Generals . . . But All the Same It Is a Good Thing That the People and the Army Are United," *Komolskaya pravda* (27 August 91). "Shaposhnikov: Yazov 'A Madman,' " FBIS-SOV-92-033 (19 February 92), p. 56. "Yazov's Involvement in Coup Attempt Explored," FBIS-SOV-91-166 (27 August 91), p. 58. Pugo and Akhromeyev suicides in Abrosimov and Zhdakin, FBIS-SOV-92-021, pp. 37–41; "After the Coup; Phone Call, Then a Suicide," *New York Times* (24 August 91). Clifford Krauss, "Sergei F. Akhromeyev: Complete Soviet Soldier, Well-Liked in West," *New York Times* (26 August 91). Crowe remarks at briefing (7 August 1989). Kryuchkov disinformation in Gerald Nadler, " 'Victim' Stands Accused: Gorbachev Aided Coup, Plotters Say," *Washington Times* (3 February 93); "Kryuchkov-Yeltsin: The Thunder Sounds Louder in the Silence of Matrosskaya Tishina," *Pravda* (11 July 92), p. 1.

CHAPTER 13: THE COVER-UP

Gellman, "General Withdrew Missiles," *Washington Post* (28 August 91). Mobile ICBMs can launch from garrison: U.S. Department of Defense, *Soviet Military*

Power: An Assessment of the Threat (1988), p. 47. Secret Yazov order reprinted in *Komolskaya pravda* (27 August 91) FBIS-SOV-91-166, p. 59. Moiseyev in Paolo Valentino, *II Corriere della Sera* (31 August 91) translated in FBIS-SOV-91-165 (26 August 91), p. 32. Tom Mathews, Carol Bogert, Andrew Nagorski, Douglas Waller, and Tony Clifton, "The Coup Maker's Secrets," *Newsweek* (9 September 91). Burbyga, JPRS-UMA-91-028, pp. 7–8. Gennadiy A. Pavlov, Testimony before the European Affairs Subcommittee of the Senate Foreign Relations Committee (24 September 1991). R. Jeffrey Smith, " 'Nuclear Suitcase' Disabled During Coup, Hill Told," *Washington Post* (25 September 91). On Soviet nuclear command and control see Kurt Campbell, Ashton Carter, Steven Miller, Charles Zraket, *Soviet Nuclear Fission: Control of the Nuclear Arsenal in a Disintegrating Soviet Union* (Harvard University, November 1991). "Coup Leaders Controlled Nuclear Warhead Codes," FBIS-SOV-91-165 (26 August 91), p. 33. O. Volkov and V. Umnov in "Nuclear Briefcase Designer Interviewed," FBIS-SOV-92-019 (29 January 92), p. 7. Batenin in Allen Levine, "Soviet General Says Unrest May Spark Nuclear Terror," *Atlanta Constitution* (16 October 91), p. 2 and unpublished transcript of interview.

CHAPTER 14: THE NEW RUSSIA

Chronologies detailing the disintegration of the Soviet Union are: Julie Kim, *Soviet Disintegration: Chronology of Events September 16–December 31, 1991*, Congressional Research Service 92-39 F (13 January 1992); Beth Gerard, *Post-Soviet Transformation: Chronology of Events: January 1–February 15, 1992*, Congressional Research Service 92-230 F (24 February 1992); Julie Kim, *Post-Soviet Nation-Building: Chronology of Events February 16–May 31, 1992*, Congressional Research Service (17 June 1992). Nick Cook, ". . . and Marshal Shaposhnikov," *Jane's Defense Weekly* (28 September 91). On Shaposhnikov's nuclear role see Michael Dobbs, "Gorbachev Waits in a Gilded Cage," *Washington Post* (17 December 91); John-Thor Dahlburg, "Gorbachev Steps Down; Nuclear Button to Yeltsin; Red Flag Lowered; Transition," *Los Angeles Times* (26 December 91), p. 1. Gerald Nadler, "First C.I.S. Summit Could Be Last," *Washington Times* (22 January 93). "Address to the Nation on United States Nuclear Weapons Reductions," *Public Papers of the Presidents of the United States: George Bush*, Book II (1992). Ann Devroy and R. Jeffrey Smith, "President Orders Sweeping Reductions in Strategic and Tactical Nuclear Arms," *Washington Post* (28 September 91), p. 1. Ter Petrossian in "Armenia, Casting Wary Eye on Azerbaijan, Seeks Closer Ties with Turkey," *Washington Post* (14 November 91), p. A42. Russian strategic forces remained on alert and programs continued, see Major A. Dolinin, "Society in Alarm. Economy in Crisis. Army Maintaining Combat Capability," *Krasnaya zvezda* (24 January 92) translated in FBIS-SOV-92-017 (27 January 92), pp. 18–19. Lawrence K. Gershwin, "Threats to U.S. Interests from Weapons of Mass Destruction" (Central Intelligence Agency, 23 September 1992). Gertz, "KGB Halts Lookout for U.S. Nuclear Attack," *Washington Times* (28 November 91). Andrew and Gordievsky, *KGB*. GRU pursues VRYAN "to an even greater extent" than KGB in Gordievsky, "Pershing Paranoia in the Kremlin." French intelligence on GRU in Andrew Borowiec, "NATO Leaders Face Spectre of Revived Russian Military," *Washington Times* (10 January 94). "Germany Says Russia Increasing Espionage," *Washington Times* (9 April 97). H. Andrew Boestling and Richard A. Best, Jr., *Russian Foreign Intelligence Capabilities*, Congressional Research Service 96-982 F (19 December 1996). "GRU Analysis: Directions of Development of Deck-Based Naval Aviation" and "GRU Analysis: NATO Aviation in the Balkan Conflict," both in FBIS-UMA-96-138-S (17 July 96); "GRU Analysis: French Nuclear Weapons Complex" and "GRU Analysis: Status, Future, Development of NATO Navies," both in FBIS-UMA-96-090-S (8 May 96). "General Staff Discusses Resolving Military Conflicts," FBIS-SOV-96-032 (15 February 96), p. 40. Maj. General V. A. Ryaboshapko, "Geopolitics and Security," *Military Thought* (July–August 1996) translated in FBIS-UMA-97-075-S. Stanislav Lunev testimony in *U.S./Russia National Security Issues*, Hearing before the R&D Subcommittee of the House National Security Committee, HNSC No. 105-38 (1998). "Russian Strategic Bombers Train to Attack United States," *Russia Reform Monitor* (Washington, D.C.: American Foreign Policy Council, 19 June 98) hereinafter *Russia Reform Monitor*. Belous in "Strategic Missile Launch Postures Examined," JPRS-UMA-94-010 (16 March 94), pp. 16–17. "Cosmos Launch Linked to Warning System Revamp," FBIS-UMA-98-125 (5 May 98). "Despite Economic Collapse, Russia Has Found Cash for These Projects," *Foreign Aid Advisory* (Washington, D.C.: American Foreign Policy Council, 1 June 98). See also testimony of former Director of Central Intelligence John Deutch and James Woolsey in *Threats to United States National Security*, Hearing before the House National Security Committee, HNSC No. 105-4 (1998) and of Richard Pipes and James Wooley, *Challenges Posed by Russia to United States National Security Interests*, hearing before the House Committee on National Security, HNSC No. 104-40 (1996). Michael R. Gordon, "Despite Cold War's End, Russia Keeps Building a Secret Complex," *New York Times* (16 April 96); "Sense of Congress on the Need for Russian Openness on the Yamantau Mountain Project," *National Defense Authorization Act for Fiscal Year 1998*, 105–340 (27 October 1997).

CHAPTER 15: THE U.S. THREAT

"Navy Launches Its Last Trident," *Washington Times* (2 December 97). Sergeyev in "Don't Count Them Out, Russia Continues to Prepare for War by Upgrading Missile Systems, as Does the United States," *60 Minutes* (18 June 1995). Lt. Colonel A. Dokuchayev, "Why Does the United States Need First Strike Weapons?," *Krasnaya zvezda* (26 June 92); "U.S. Nuclear Strategy Still Remains the Same," *Krasnaya zvezda* (28 October 93); Colonel V. V. Kruglov and Colonel M. Ye. Sosnovskiy, "On the Role of Nonstrategic Weapons in Nuclear Deterrence," *Voyennaya Mysl* (September 97); Shaknazarov and coauthors in "Academics Take Apocalyptic View of Future," FBIS-SOV-98-007. On cruise missile threat see "Aerospace Defense," FBIS-UMA-95-139-S (20 July 95); "Current Problems of Creating Precision Weapons," FBIS-UMA-96-018-S (26 January 96). Vladimer Vasilyev, "Moscow's ABM Defense: Yesterday, Today, Tomorrow," *Segodnya* (14 October 95) translated in FBIS-UMA-95-226-S (24 November 95), pp. 21–23. Sergey Grigoryev, "Russia's New Strategic Course on the Western Axis," *Nezavisimoye voyennoye obozreniye* (January 96) translated in FBIS-UMA-96-026-S (7 February 96), pp. 1–6. "Latvia Radar Loss Leaves Russian Gap," *Washington Times* (30 August 98).

CHAPTER 16: THE GREAT DEBATE

Amberin Zaman, "Battle for Enclave Escalates," *Daily Telegraph* (24 February 92). Amberin Zaman, "Pressure on Turkey to Back Azerbaijan," *Daily Telegraph* (2 March 92). Michael Dobbs, "Key Town in Karabakh Seized by Armenians; Azerbaijanis Pledge Swift Counterattack," *Washington Post* (10 May 92). Ponomaryov and Sheinis in "Investigation Commission Holds News Conference," FBIS-SOV-91-248 (26 December 91), p. 42. Kobets in "Lopatin Says Army Beyond Civilian Control," FBIS-SOV-92-033 (19 February 92), pp. 56–57. "Velikhov Discusses Nuclear Safety, Arms Control," FBIS-SOV-91-180 (17 September 91), p. 1–2. Unpublished remarks by Maj. General Yuriy Kirshin at the Hudson Institute (Washington, D.C.: 27 September 91). Rear Admiral V. Prozorov and Captain S. Kozyrev in A. Orlov, "Where Have Our Missiles Been Retargeted?" *Sovetskaya rossiya* (7 February 92) translated in FBIS-SOV-92-028 (11 February 92), pp. 3–4. Mary Fitzgerald, "A Russian View of Russian Interests," *Air Force Magazine* (October 92). For more on Rodionov see "Rodionov Urges Legal Framework for Military Reform," FBIS-UMA-95-234-S (6 December 95), pp. 6–7; "Rodionov's Remarks to Senior Officers," FBIS-SOV-96-146 (25 July 96), p. 25; "Defense Minister Rodionov Interviewed 27 July," FBIS-SOV-96-146 (29 July 96), p. 21. "Makhmut Gareyev: Nuclear Weapons in Today's World," *Krasnaya zvezda* (29 July 94); General Makhmut Gareyev, "The Problem Cannot Be Resolved with Nuclear Weapons," *Krasnaya zvezda* (5 August 94) translated in JPRS-UMA-94-033 (17 August 94), pp. 53–55; General Makhmut Gareyev, "Why Russia Needs a Military Doctrine," *Rossisyskiye vesti* (4 March 93); Marshal Viktor Kulikov and General Makhmut Gareyev, "Some Issues of Military-Technical Policy," JPRS-UMA-94-009-L (17 June 94), pp. 36–40; "Gareyev Interviewed on Nuclear Arms' Role, Purpose in Future War," JPRS-UMA-94-029 (8 July 94), pp. 10–13. Colonel A. Klimenko, "CIS: Does It Need a Common Military Doctrine?," *Krasnaya zvezda* (26 December 91), see also John T. Banks, "The Russian General Staff Reconsiders New Military Doctrine: Questions about 'No First Use'," *FSRC Analytical Note*, A92-006/UL (Science Applications International, 20 February 92). Korotchenko and Grachev in Colonel G. Miranovich, "Russia's Armed Forces Today and Tomorrow," *Krasnaya zvezda* (2 June 92), pp. 1, 3. "Foundations of Russia's Defense Doctrine," *Voennaya mysl* (Special Edition, May 1992).

CHAPTER 17: THE RUSSO-UKRAINIAN NUCLEAR CRISIS

Luke Sallow is a pseudonym for a U.S. intelligence officer. Interview with Ukrainian Vice Premier Konstantin Masik, *Nezavisimaya gazeta* (24 October 91). "Report of Russian-Ukrainian Arms Threats Rejected," FBIS-SOV-91-206 (24 October 91), p. 37. Kobets in "Possibility of Nuclear Strikes Said Unfounded," FBIS-SOV-91-202 (18 October 91), p. 1. " 'Nuclear Strike' Rumors Blamed on Media, Yeltsin," FBIS-SOV-91-207 (25 October 91), p. 12. M. Porovskiy, "Ukraine and Its Defense Policy," *Narodnaya armiya* (3 January 92), p. 1. "Further Reportage on Black Sea

Situation," FBIS-SOV-92-008 (13 January 92). "Strategic Air Division Goes Over to Ukraine," "Ukraine Official Comments," and "Military to Investigate," all in FBIS-SOV-92-033 (19 February 92), pp. 23–24. "Ukraine Said in Control of Strategic Air Unit," *Washington Times* (18 February 92). Jonathan Lyons, "C.I.S. Nukes Said to Be Firmly Under Control," *Washington Times* (19 February 92). "Ukraine Controls Nuclear Bombers, Rebel General Says," *Washington Times* (19 March 92). Bomber pilots appeal to Shaposhnikov in A. Polyakov, "Will We Really Divide Up the Strategic Forces, Too?," *Krasnaya zvezda* (20 February 92). Strategic forces troops take oath in Major A. Dolinin, "Agreements Say One Thing, But Another Is Actually Done," *Krasnaya zvezda* (26 February 92). Natalia Feduschak, "Ukraine Seeks to Get Control of Nuclear Arms," *Wall Street Journal* (26 March 92). Maksimov in Viktor Litovkin, "Commander of Strategic Forces Accuses Ukrainian Leadership of Attempts to Wreck International Accords," *Izvestiya* (11 June 92) translated in FBIS-SOV-92-113 (11 June 92), p. 2. Asanbayev in Servet Kabakli interview, *Istanbul turkiye* (10 April 92) translated in FBIS-SOV-92-077 (21 April 92), p. 42. Nazarbayev in Edith M. Lederer and Sergei Shargorodskiy, "Nukes Still Hot Issue in Ukraine," *Washington Times* (14 June 92). Gerald Nadler, "Ukraine Won't Ship Any More Nukes to Russia," *Washington Times* (13 March 92). Andrey Ostalskiy, "Nuclear Ukraine Not End of the World," *Izvestiya* (28 Match 92). Pavel Felgengauer, "Ukrainian Missiles Will Not Be Moved to Russia. They Can Fly There Themselves," *Segodnya* (6 August 93). Pavel Felgengauer, "Ukraine Seeks Nuclear Independence," *Nezavisimaya gazeta* (14 March 92). Bill Gertz, "Cheney: Future Looks Murky for Soviet Nukes," *Washington Times* (16 December 91).

CHAPTER 18: WAR IN THE CAUCASUS

"Pentagon Preparing Scenario of War Against Russia," *Izvestiya* (21 February 92) translated in FBIS-SOV-92-037 (25 February 92), p. 22. Barton Gellman, "Pentagon War Scenario Spotlights Russia," *Washington Post* (20 February 92). Aleksin in Viktor Litovkin, "Foreign Submarines Feel Increasingly Free in Russian Territorial Waters," *Izvestiya* (27 March 92), p. 2. On depth-charging see Andrey Naryshkin, ITAR-TASS (26 March 92). Rowan Scarborough, "Cold War-Style Spying Cited in Sub Collision," *Washington Times* (19 February 92). "C.I.S. Navy Claims It Chased Away U.S. Sub," *Washington Times* (27 March 92). "Fleet Finishes Submarine Investigation," "Protest Note Sent," and "U.S. Official Confirms Accident," FBIS-SOV-92-033 (19 February 92), p. 5. Manki Ponomarev, "United States Steps Up Patrols by Nuclear Submarines," *Krasnaya zvezda* (20 October 93). Gates and Clapper in George Lardner, Jr., "Republics' Procurement Said to Plunge," *Washington Post* (23 January 92). Steve Ginsberg, "CIA Director Robert Gates Address to a Conference Sponsored by the Nixon Library," *Reuters Transcript Report* (12 March 92). Vanora Bennett, "Karabakh Violence Masks Power Struggle," *Reuters* (25 May 92). John Lloyd, "Cauldron in the Caucasus: The Wider Ramifications of the Armenia-Azerbaijan Conflict," *Financial Times* (26 May 92). "Shaposhnikov Against Interference in Karabakh Conflict," *Moscow Radio World Service*, in English (20 May 92). Gerald Nadler, "C.I.S. Warns Turkey to Stay Out of Fighting," *Washington Times* (21 May 92), p. 7. "Commonwealth Threatens Turks; Says

Hands Off Armenian Conflict," *The Record* (21 May 92), p. A40. "Stay Out of Enclave, Russia Tells World, Warning Seems Aimed at Turkish Threat," *St. Louis Post-Dispatch* (21 May 92), p. 12A. Dahlburg, "Gorbachev Steps Down," *Los Angeles Times* (26 December 91). Shaposhnikov's character in David Evans, "New Defense Chief First of New Breed," *Chicago Tribune* (29 August 1991). David Ljunggren, "C.I.S., Turks Put Security Forces on Alert," *Washington Times* (22 May 92), p. A7. Alert, Sadarak, and Gareyev in Aydyn Mekhtiyev, "Internationalization of the Conflict," *Nezavisimaya gazeta* (23 May 92), pp. 1, 3. Turkish alert from interview with U.S. defense attache stationed in Ankara at time of crisis. Alert, Nakichevan, chemical attack, Gasonov in "Moscow TV Reviews Nagorno-Karabakh Situation," Teleradio Kompaniya Ostankino Television First Program Network, "Novosti" newscast (21 May 92) FBIS UNCLAS 3R/PMU-STV/SU-811-291-297, Serial LD2105103192. "Armenia Accused of Bacteriological Warfare," FBIS-SOV-92-053 (18 March 92), p. 75. "Incirlik Said Used to Supply Armenia with Arms," FBIS-WEU-92-104 (29 May 92). "Majority of MPs Are for Military Solution," *Hurriyet* (Ankara: 21 May 92). Giray and Sener in "Aliyev Criticizes Shaposhnikov's Warning to Turkey," FBIS-SOV-92-100 (22 May 92), p. 57. "Spokesman, Chief of Staff React to Shaposhnikov Statement," Ankara TRT Television Network (21 May 92) FBIS UNCLAS 7Q/LD PMU, Serial TA2105165792; "Shaposhnikov Statement Criticized," FBIS-WEU-92-100 (22 May 92), p. 41. "Kozyrev Warns Turkey Against Attacking Armenia" and "Kozyrev Expresses Gratitude," FBIS-SOV-92-101 (26 May 92), p. 5. "Turkish Intervention Could Lead to Disaster," *Izvestiya* (23 May 92) translated in FBIS-SOV-92-103 (28 May 92), p. 5. Grachev in Roman Zadunaiskiy, *ITAR-TASS* (1 June 92). James M. Dorsey, "Turkey Beaten Back by Resurgent Bear," *Washington Times* (25 September 93). On Turkish threat in Georgia see "Turkey Broadens Presence in Transcaucasus," FBIS-SOV-96-014-S (22 January 96). Krivokizha and Felinskiy in "Russian Naval Strategy," FBIS-UMA-96-002-S (3 January 96). "Armenia Signs Military Alliance with Russia," *Monitor: A Daily Briefing on the Post-Soviet States* (Washington, D.C.: Jamestown Foundation, 2 September 97) hereinafter *Monitor*. "Official Refutes Azerbaijani Claims of Armenian Nuclear Arsenal," *INTERFAX* (6 October 97). "Yeltsin Asserts Rights in Caucasus: He Challenges Rising U.S. Role," *Washington Times* (21 August 97). "Azerbaijani Turkey Concerned Over Unsettled Nagorno-Karabakh Problem," FBIS-SOV-98-105 (15 April 98). "Azerbaijani to Stay Out of CIS Security Pact," *Monitor* (8 February 99). "Baku Looking West for Security," *Monitor* (3 February 99). Stephen Kinzer, "Azerbaijan Asks U.S. to Establish Military Base," *New York Times* (31 January 99). "Irrendentism Enters Armenia's Foreign Policy," *Monitor* (22 April 98). Mikhail Gerasimov, "Ankara Proposing Close Cooperation with Tbilisi—Turkish Military Presence in Georgia Possible in Near Future," *Nezavisimaya gazeta* (27 December 95) in FBIS-SOV-96-014-S. Pavel Felgengauer, "Caucasian War at Center of World Policy in the Year 2000," *Segodnya* (4 January 94) translated in JPRS-UMA-94-004 (26 January 94), pp. 3–5.

CHAPTER 19: DEMOCRACY OF THE GENERALS

Ralph Boulton, "Grave of Akhromeyev Rallying Point for Hardliners," *Reuters* (19 August 92). Maj. General Vladimir Dudnik, "700 Extra Generals; Everything Else

Is in Short Supply," *Novoye vremya* (March 93) translated in JPRS-UMA-93-016 (19 May 93), p. 1. "Journalist Repeats Accusations Against Grachev," FBIS-SOV-95-206 (25 October 95). Paul Bedard and Bill Gertz, "Status of Nukes a Concern to U.S.," *Washington Times* (10 December 91). "Missile Carrying Convoy Stopped at Border," FBIS-SOV-92-007 (10 January 92), p. 58. "Soldier Kills Commander, Comrades at Nuclear Site," FBIS-SOV-94-058 (25 March 94), p. 8. Margaret Shapiro, "Russian Missile Center Has Electricity Cut Off," *Washington Post* (22 September 94). Oleg Falichev and Aleksandr Dolinin, "Emergency on All-Russian Scale," *Krasnaya zvezda* (23 September 94), p. 1. Lebed, homeless officer, and Rogov in Serge Schmemann, "Parliament Attack Exposes Divisions," *New York Times* (28 November 93). Kokoshin in "Deputy Defense Minister on Reform, Conversion, Politics," JPRS-UMA-94-031 (3 August 94). Martin Sieff, "U.S. Says Russia Isn't Coming Clean with Poison Gas Data," *Washington Times* (24 June 94). Bill Gertz, "Russia Has Biological Weapons, Defector Says," *Washington Times* (22 January 93). Rowland Evans and Robert Novak, "Yeltsin in the Dark," *Washington Post* (24 June 92). "Russia Denies Report of New Germ-War Agent," *Washington Times* (29 March 94). "Alksnis and Bogomolov on Future of USSR," FBIS-SOV-91-237 (10 December 91), pp. 29–31. Teresa Cherfas, "Iron Man," *New Statesman and Society* (5 April 91), pp. 12–13.

CHAPTER 20: RUTSKOY

"Rutskoy to Run for Presidency; Blames CIA for Economic Collapse," *Pravda* (14 May 93) translated in British Broadcasting Corporation Transcript (18 May 93). Rutskoy 1991 coup hero see Vasily Izgarshev, "At the Service of the Fatherland—Three Nights from the Life of Aleksandr Rutskoy," *Pravda* (7 September 91), pp. 1–2. "Rutskoy Accuses Yeltsin Allies of 'Booziness,' " *Herald* (Glasgow: 1 September 93). Alan Cooperman. "Rutskoy Would Be 'Demagogic, Imperialist' President: Brzezinski," *Associated Press* (25 March 93). "Admits Threatening Shevardnadze with Tbilisi Bombing," Ostankino Channel 1 TV (Moscow: 15 July 1993) translated in British Broadcasting Corporation Transcript (17 July 93). Nikolay Burbyga and Viktor Litovkin, "Pavel Grachev: Things Are Hard for the Army Today," *Izvestiya* (23 February 93), pp. 1, 5; see also *Argumenty I Facty* (February 93), pp. 1–2. Ivanov in Roman Zadunayskiy, "Russia Will Keep Its Powder Dry," *Rossisyskiye vesti* (31 March 93), p. 7. Minister of Defense Pavel Grachev, "Urgent Problems of Organizational Development and Training of the Russian Armed Forces at the Current Stage," *Voennaya mysl* (June 1993). Col. General Igor Sergeyev, "The Strategic Missile Troops: Organizational Development and Reform Problems," *Voennaya mysl* (June 1993). Captain Gorbachev interviewed in Andrew Vasilyev, "From the Nuclear Abyss to Catastrophe for Russia—That Is Where the START II Treaty Is Leading," *Pravda* (4 March 93). Colonel Yevgeniy Morosov, "Officers Against Yeltsin," lecture (20 March 1993) translated in JPRS-UMA-03-016 (19 May 93), pp. 5–6. "Stanislav Terekhov: Third World War Is Underway," *Sovetskaya rossiya* (29 June 93), p. 3. Manki Ponomarev, "SDI: Life After Death?," *Krasnaya zvezda* (27 July 93). V. Nikolayev, "General V. Achalov: 'I Put My Trust In Facts,' " *Pravda* (11 February 93), p. 7. Anatoliy Verbin, "Foreign Spies Accused of Influencing Russian Policy," *Reuters* (27 January 93). Sergey Sherykin, Commentary on

Radio Rossi Network (Moscow: 5 February 93). Zhirinovskiy on U.S. as evil empire in Henry Urbanowski, "Saddam, We're Proud of You," *Sztander mlodych* (Warsaw: 1 February 93), p. 5. "Russian Volunteers Are in Baghdad, Ready to Fight," *Washington Times* (28 January 93). R. Jeffrey Smith, "Missteps by U.S. Military Posed Threat During Cuban Missile Crisis, Book Says," *Washington Post* (20 September 93). Scott D. Sagan, *The Limits of Safety: Organizations, Accidents and Nuclear Weapons* (Princeton University Press, 1993).

CHAPTER 21: THE WARNING

Notes from seminar given by General Vladimir Dworkin and Alexei Arbatov, "Emerging Russian Nuclear Strategy and Doctrine," Center for Naval Analyses (11 June 93). Grachev, "Urgent Problems of Organizational Development," *Voennaya mysl* (June 1993). Bill Gertz, "Russian Nuclear Exercises Include Mock Hit on U.S.," *Washington Times* (14 September 93), pp. A1, A24.

CHAPTER 22: WHO'S GOT THE BUTTON?

Kraemer in Gertz, "Russian Nuclear Exercise," *Washington Times* (14 September 93). Unpublished transcript of interview with Maj. General Geliy Batenin, quoted partially in Allen Levine, "Soviet General Says Unrest May Spark Nuclear Terror," *Atlanta Constitution* (16 October 91), p. 2. Pavlov, Senate Testimony (24 September 91) see notes chapter 13. For an example of how Pavlov's disinformation on Russian command and control has been popularized, see "Controlling Nuclear Arms," *USA Today* (29 August 91). Nikolay Devyanin interviewed by Volkov and Umnov, *Komsomolskaya pravda* (28 January 92), p. 2. See chapter "USSR President Was Not the Only One Who Had Access to the Nuclear Button" in Valentin Stepankov and Yevgeniy Lisov, *Kremlin Conspiracy* (Ogonek, 1992) the chief investigators of the August 1991 coup who had unfettered access to military secrets. Campbell, Carter, Miller, and Zraket, *Soviet Nuclear Fission: Control of the Nuclear Arsenal in a Disintegrating Soviet Union.* Bruce Blair, *The Logic of Accidental Nuclear War* (Brookings, 1993). Michael Boldrick, "Dr. Strangelaunch," *Reason* (June 1994). Ryzhkov in Kensuke Ebata, "CIS Spells Out Defensive Plan," *Jane's Defense Weekly* (20 June 92). "Flash: CIA Reassesses Danger of Russian Missile Strike, Concludes 'Unsanctioned' Attack on U.S. Is Possible," *Coalition to Defend America* (22 October 96). Bill Gertz, "Russia's Nuclear Arsenal, Storage Deemed Unsafe By U.S. Experts," *Washington Times* (27 July 95), p. 12. Bill Gertz, "Russia's Nuclear 'Football' Easy to Block: General Staff Could Override Yeltsin's Order, CIA Says," *Washington Times* (22 October 96), p. A18. Bill Gertz, "Russian Renegades Pose Nuclear Danger: CIA Says Arsenal Lacks Tight Controls," *Washington Times* (22 October 96), p. A1. "Dead Hand's" existence questioned in "Strategic Nuclear Forces Battle Management System, " *Voprosy bezapasnosti* (15 November 98) translated in FBIS-UMA-99-031. Notes from seminar given by General Vladimir Dworkin and Alexei Arbatov, "Emerging Russian Nuclear strategy and Doctrine," Center for Naval Analysis (11 June 93). "Lobov Removed Due to 'State of Health,' 'Conspiracy' Reported," FBIS-SOV-91-236 (9 December 91), p. 25. "Arbatov Views Disarmament, Nuclear Weapons," FBIS-SOV-91-232 (3 December 91). Boldyrev in Vladimir Umnov, "The Man with the Suitcase," *Moskovskiye novosti* (5–12 June 94) translated in JPRS-UMA-94-029 (8 July 94), pp. 13–16. Alexei Arbatov, "The Mysteries of the Nuclear Button," *New Times* (January 92). "Decree Sets Up 'Strategic Deterrence Force,' " FBIS-SOV-91-223 (19 November 91). "Further on Plan for New Strategic Troops" and "Manilov Comments on Forces," FBIS-SOV-91-224 (20 November 91). Makismov on OGK SSS in *Krasnaya zvezda* (17 February 99). "Sergeyev on Uniting Command of Nuclear Forces," *INTERFAX* (10 February 99).

CHAPTER 23: UKRAINE AND THE HOT SEPTEMBER

"Provisions of Russian Military Doctrine 'Cause Concern,' " *INTERFAX* (30 November 93). G. Sapozhnikova, "Every Estonian Must Know Where Missile Will Come From," *Komsomolskaya pravda* (13 March 93), p. 5. "Alksnis and Bogomolov on Future of USSR," FBIS-SOV-91-237. "Government Statement Slams Ukrainian Nuclear Policy," *ITAR-TASS* (4 August 93). Felgengauer, "Ukrainian Missiles Will Not Be Moved to Russia," *Segodnya* (6 August 93). Marta Kolomayets, "Ukraine Agrees to Deal on Fleet: Would Give Russia Ships, Nukes," *Washington Times* (4 September 93). Celestine Bohlen, "Ukraine Agrees to Allow Russians to Buy Fleet and Destroy Arsenal," *New York Times* (4 September 93). Robert Seely, "Ukrainian Retreats on A-Pledge," *Washington Post* (20 October 93), p. 31. "Kravchuk, Plyushch Comment on Russia's Military Doctrine" and "Further Kravchuk, Plyushch Comments," FBIS-SOV-93-214 (8 November 93), pp. 58–59. Ralph Boulton, "Russia Strikes New Harsh Tone in Relations with CIS," *Reuters* (26 November 93). "Kozyrev Says Russia Can Defend Ukraine" and "Kozyrev on Russian Foreign Policy Toward CIS," FBIS-SOV-93-231-A (3 December 93). Poll in *INTERFAX* (10 February 92); see also "Poll Views Possibility of Nuclear Weapons Use," FBIS-SOV-92-038 (26 February 92); pp. 4–5. Serhiy Pavlenko, "Bombers Over Chernihiv?," *Holos ukrayiny* (November 1993), p. 4. Background to coup, nuclear control declared intact: Stuart D. Goldman and Jim Nichols, *Yeltsin Disbands the Russian Parliament*, Congressional Research Service 93 851 F (27 September 1993); Jim Nichol, *Yeltsin and the Russian Congress of Peoples Deputies: Outcome and Implications for U.S. Interests*, Congressional Research Service 92-988 F (30 December 1992). Steven Erlanger, "Yeltsin's Weakness: Failure to Convert Early Popularity into Political Base," *New York Times* (23 March 93). Serge Schmemann, "Yeltsin and Rivals Are in a Standoff in Power Struggle," *New York Times* (24 March 93). Operation Hard Sign in "GRU Restructuring: Army Concentrating *Spetsnaz* Units in Moscow Area," *Kommersant Daily* (15 December 92) translated in JPRS-UMA-93–005 (9 February 93), p. 15. U.S. Department of Defense, *Soviet Military Power 1987* (March 1987), p. 89. "Struggle for Control over 'Alfa' Spetsnaz Unit," JPRS-UMA-94-003 (19 January 94). Ralph Boulton, "Yeltsin Suspends His Vice President from Office," *Washington Times* (2 September 93). Serge Schmemann, "Yeltsin and Legislature Act to Oust Each Other; Clinton Backs President," *New York Times* (22 September 93). Fred Hiatt and Margaret Shapiro, "Yeltsin Defies Legal Trap Set by His Hardline Opponents," *Washington Post* (26 September 93). Margaret Shapiro and Fred Hiatt, "Yeltsin Forces Set Monday Deadline," *Washington Post* (30 September 93). Jim Nichol, *Russia's Violent Show-*

down of October 3–4: Analysis and Implications, Congressional Research Service 93-884 F (6 October 1993). "Yeltsin Controls Nuclear Button—Defense Ministry," *Reuters* (22 September 93). Craig Covault, "Russia Launches Three Spy Satellites," *Aviation Week and Space Technology* (27 September 93), p. 24. TSENTER in Vadim Byrkini, *ITAR-TASS* (22 September 93). TSENTER, forgetting Yeltsin, and protecting nuclear depots in "Grachev: Defense Ministry Guarantor of Stability," *Moscow Mayak Radio* (22 September 93) FBIS UNCLAS 3XX/PMU/SUP RUSS 866 864 710 MK. "Volga, Ural, Siberian Troops Conclude Military Exercises," *Radio Rossi Network* (16 October 93). TSENTER repels aerospace attack in I. Krondo and G. Makarychev, "Grachev, Army Command View Recent Exercises, Possible Cuts," *Russia Television Network* (22 October 93) UNCLAS 3B/RUSSTV MILT LEADER 865 866, Serial PM2710134393. "Moldova Puts 14th Army on Alert," FBIS-SOV-93-183-S (23 September 93), p. 51. Submarine alerted in "Provincial Chronicle," *Segodnya* (28 September 93), p. 2.

CHAPTER 24: LIVE, ON *LARRY KING*

"Kozyrev," *Reuters Transcript Report* (28 September 93). General John Shalikashvili, testimony during confirmation hearings before the Senate Armed Services Committee (22 September 93). "Shalikashvili," *Reuters* (22 September 93). Grachev, "Defense Ministry Guarantor of Stability," *Moscow Mayak Radio* (22 September 93). Grachev on Achalov, "Grachev: Defense Ministry Will Not Obey Supreme Soviet," *ITAR-TASS* (22 September 93). Shapiro and Hiatt, "Yeltsin Forces Set Monday Deadline," *Washington Post* (30 September 93). Day by day accounts of coup events are in *New York Times* and Nichol, *Russia's Violent Showdown*. Serge Schmemann, "Riot in Moscow amid New Calls for Compromise," *New York Times* (3 October 93). Dudnik, fighting, Makashov, Generals reluctant to back Yeltsin, hourly chronology and much detail in *Washington Post* (5 October 93); Stephen Foye, "Confrontation in Moscow: The Army Backs Yeltsin, For Now," *Radio Free Europe Research Report* (22 October 93). Street fighting, Makashov, shelling of White House, Zlobin, singing, Rutskoy panics in "Red October," *Time* (18 October 1993). General Staff uncommitted until 10:00 P.M. in Pavel Felgengauer interview, *Los Angeles Times* (8 October 93). Irina Savvateyeva, "Army Reportedly 'Bided' Its Time," Yeltsin orders Grachev in Vasiliy Kononenko, "The Prospect of Presidential Rule?" "Grachev's Reluctance Highlighted," Igor Chernyak, "Seen Waiting for People's Support," "Commentary Calls for Calm, Cohesion of Army," "Grachev Reviews Actions, Status of Troops at Press Conference," all in FBIS-SOV-93-192-S (6 October 93), pp. 21–22, 24–26. "Colonel General Kolesnikov Interviewed," JPRS-UMA-94-031 (3 August 94), pp. 17–18. 1,500 dead reported in David Satter, "Yeltsin: Shadow of a Doubt," *National Interest* (Winter 1993/94), p. 52. Makoklyuyev in Aleksandr Ivanov, "How Many Spy Satellites Are There in Space Today," *Krasnaya zvezda* (20 October 93), p. 2. TSENTER in "Radio Salvyanka," *Moscow Radio Rossi* (16 October 93); "Vesti," *Moscow Ostankino Television* (22 October 93); "Regimental Tactical Exercise Begins in Moscow District," FBIS-SOV-93-182-S (22 September 93), p. 16. Bruce Blair, "Russia's Doomsday Machine," *New York Times* (8 October 93), p. 35. "Military Cadets Said Disaffected with Yeltsin," JPRS-UMA-94-032 (10 August

94), p. 4. "Grachev on Verge of Despair," FBIS-SOV-94-134 (13 July 94), p. 22. "Reportage on Coup, 'Health' Rumors," FBIS-SOV-94-056 (23 March 94), pp. 8–11. "Events of 19–20 June Seen as 'Coup Attempt,' " FBIS-SOV-96-123 (25 June 96). "Chernomyrdin Investigates Coup Allegations Against Lebed," *Monitor* (17 October 96). Stuart D. Goldman, *Russian Conventional Armed Forces: On the Verge of Collapse?*, Congressional Research Service 97-820 F (4 September 97), pp. 46, 50–54; quote from Goldman letter to author, "New CRS Report on Russian Conventional Armed Forces," (18 September 97). Starovoitova and Primakov in *Russia Reform Monitor* (9 February 99), (8 December 98), and (27 January 99).

CHAPTER 25: DANGEROUS MEN

Pavel Felgengauer, "General Kolesnikov: Armed Forces Are Only a Tool in the Hands of the Government," *Nezavisimaya gazeta* (3 July 92). Pavel Felgengauer, "Military Expect Intervention by the West. Grim Prospects for Russian Foreign and Defense Policy," *Nezavisimaya gazeta* (1 August 92), p. 1. Col. General M. P. Kolesnikov, "The Development of Military Strategy in the Years of Great Patriotic War," *Voennaya mysl* (May–June 95), p. 10. "The Bolshevik Who Came in from the Cold," *Los Angeles Times Magazine* (6 October 91). Ruth Marcus, "Senior U.S. Official Voices Doubts About Yeltsin," *Washington Post* (14 July 92). Alessandra Stanley, "Strange, Alarming Behavior of Leaders Shows Strain of Russia's Troubled Times," *Washington Times* (31 January 95). Col. General Viktor Barynkin, "Is Russia at Risk of War?," *Krasnaya zvezda* (1 November 95) translated in FBIS-SOV-95-213 (3 November 95). "Col-Gen Barynkin on Military Operations to Settle Military Conflicts," FBIS-UMA-95-244-S (20 December 95), p. 6. "Final Part of Barynkin Article on Defense Published," FBIS-SOV-95-217 (9 November 95), p. 35. On Russian nuclear command and control, see Chapter 22 and notes. Prudnikov in "Aerospace Defense," FBIS-UMA-95-139-S (20 July 95), pp. 2, 4. Malcolm Browne, "2 American Balloonists Die When Shot Down in Belarus," *New York Times* (14 September 95). Rodionov in "Cold War Continues, Russia's Defense Minister Says," *Baltimore Sun* (22 December 96). Sergeyev, "The Strategic Missile Troops," *Voennaya mysl* (June 1993). On utility of nuclear weapons see General Igor Sergeyev, "History of Strategic Missile Forces Assessed," *Voennaya mysl* (January 1993). Rattles nuclear sabre in "Strategic Missile Forces Commander on 35th Anniversary," JPRS-UMA-95-001 (11 January 95). Nikolai Sokov, "Rocket Union?" *Jane's Defense Weekly* (10 February 99). Kvashnin anecdotes as related by reliable witnesses. Mark Galeotti, "Russia's Military Under a New Master" and "Chief of the General Staff Anatoliy Kvashnin," *Jane's Intelligence Review* (1 September 97). Kornukov in Alastair Macdonald, "Russian Air Chief Ordered KAL Downing," *Washington Times* (23 January 98). Kornukov on Nuclear Alert during DESERT FOX in FBIS-SOV-99-027 (27 January 99). Cuban missile crisis and stealthiness in General Vladimir Yakovlev, "The SMF's Special Mission," *Armeyskiy sbornik* (May 1997) translated in FBIS-SOV-97-137-S (1 May 97).

CHAPTER 26: AURORA BOREALIS

Purpose of Black Brant XII and main scientists from NASA, see also "Massive Blunders by INTERFAX," FBIS-WEU-95-018-A (27 January 95). "Shaposhnikov

Has Nuclear Button Taken Away from Him," *Moskovskiye novosti* (25 July 93), p. A10. Maksim Chikin, "Whose Hand Is Reaching for the Nuclear Button?" *Komsomolskaya pravda* (5 November 95) translated in FBIS-SOV-95-214 (6 November 95), pp. 38–39. "Mutual Detargeting of Strategic Nuclear Systems," *U.S. Department of State Dispatch Supplement* (January 1994), p. 25. Yesin in "Missiles Are Not Now Targeted at Each Other, but Missileman's Alert Duty Is Not Being Abolished," *Krasnaya zvezda* (20 January 94), p. 1. Surikov in "Official Comments on Problem Concerning Missile Retargeting," *ITAR-TASS* (10 March 95). "Russian Missile Detargeting," *National Defense Authorization Act for Fiscal Year 1997*, Report of the House National Security Committee 104–563 (1996), pp. 355–356. Office of the Secretary of Defense, *Report to Congress on Detargeting* (16 May 1997). J. Michael Waller, "The Russian Nuclear Threat Is Not Gone," *Wall Street Journal* (17 July 1996). J. Michael Waller, "The Missiles Pointed at America," *Washington Times* (24 September 96). *Basic Provisions of the Military Doctrine of the Russian Federation* translated in FBIS-SOV-93-222-S (19 November 1993), pp. 2, 6, 8. "Rogov: Russia's New Military Doctrine, Part II," JPRS-UMA-94-033 (17 August 94), pp. 56, 61, 65. "Makhmut Gareyev: Nuclear Weapons in Today's World," *Krasnaya zvezda* (29 June 94) translated in JPRS-UMA-94-029 (8 July 94), pp. 10–13.

CHAPTER 27: DARK HISTORY

General P. A. Zhilin, *The History of Military Art* (Istoriya Voyennogo Iskusstva, 1986) translated in JPRS-UMA-87-004-L (27 March 1987). "Yeltsin Issues Warning to Estonia Over Ethnic Russians," FBIS-SOV-93-121-A (25 June 93), p. 2. "Kozyrev Warns U.S. on Interfering in Estonia Relations," FBIS-SOV-94-143 (26 July 94), p. 6. "Grachev Rattles Sabre at Latvia," *Washington Times* (11 January 94), p. 11. P. Lloyd, "Russian Military in Troubled Mood," *Financial Times* (8 September 94). Colonel V. Cheban, "Armed Conflict and Russian Security," *Voyennyy vestnik* (April 94) translated in JPRS-UMA-94-034 (19 August 94), pp. 8–11. U.S. attacks on Bosnia aimed at Russia in "Academicians Criticize U.S., NATO Bosnia Policy" and "Deputies on NATO's 'Lesson for Russia,' " FBIS-SOV-95-127 (3 July 95). "Kozyrev: Chauvanistic Wind Blowing in the U.S.," FBIS-SOV-94-056 (23 March 94), pp. 5–6. "Grachev Criticizes Bosnia Air Strikes," *Washington Times* (26 April 94). "Russia Opposes Lifting Bosnia Muslim Sanctions," *Reuters* (14 June 94). Margaret Shapiro, "Bosnia Arms Vote Risks World War, Russian Warns," *Washington Post* (15 June 94), p. 31. "Yeltsin Probably to Attend Missile Staff Exercise," *INTERFAX* (21 June 94). "Yeltsin, Grachev Observe Missile Launch," FBIS-SOV-94-120 (22 June 94), p. 28. Pavel Felgengauer, "Russian Nuclear Triad Ready for Action. President Yeltsin Pushes 'Red Button' for First Time," *Segodnya* (23 June 94) translated in FBIS-SOV-94-122 (24 June 94), pp. 31–32. Kolesnikov, Grachev, and official purpose in "Yeltsin Observes Nuclear Forces 'Combat Vigil' Procedures," *ITAR-TASS* (22 June 94) in FBIS-SOV-94-120 (22 June 94), p. 29. Launch depicted and date "not accidental" in Aleksandr Gerasimov, "Today," *Moscow Ostankino Television* (22 June 94). "Northern Fleet Conducts Missile Exercise," "Yeltsin Observes Strategic Missile Exercise," and Corfu "Notes Agreement's Historical Importance" in FBIS-SOV-94-122 (24 June 94).

"Churkin Warns of Large-Scale War in Former Yugoslavia," FBIS-SOV-94-121 (23 June 1994), p. 8. Viktor Litovkin, "On Land, in the Air, and at Sea the Supreme Commander in Chief Tests the Nuclear Forces," *Izvestiya* (23 June 94) translated in FBIS-SOV-94-120 (22 June 94), pp. 25–26. *Russia's Nuclear Doctrine*, presentation by Russian Assistant Minister of Defense for Military Policy, General G. D. Ivanov to Mr. Ash Carter of the U.S. Office of the Secretary of Defense (October 1994).

CHAPTER 28: BLACK BRANT XII

Fred Hiatt, "Russia's Spy Chief Warns West: Don't Oppose Soviet Reintegration," *Washington Post* (22 September 94). "Primakov Unveils Intelligence Report on CIS, Russia," *ITAR-TASS* (21 September 94) translated in FBIS-SOV-94-184 (22 September 94), pp. 5–6. Paul Bedard, "Walesa to Clinton: Russians Coming," *Washington Times* (7 July 94). Veto in Martin Sieff, "Yeltsin Fears 'Cold Peace' in Europe" and Nicholas Doughty, "Russia Warns of Freezing Relations," *Washington Times* (5 December 94). Coup possible over Chechnya in James Rupert, "Brute Images of Chechnya's War," *Washington Post* (4 January 95). Yegor Gaidar, "Destination Disaster on the Road to Chechnya," *Washington Times* (9 January 95). Valery Vyzhutovich, "Boris Yeltsin Joins the Party of Force," *Moscow News* (30 December 94–5 January 95) in JPRS-UMA-95-001. Clapper in Bill Gertz, "Russian Heads Likely to Roll," *Washington Times* (18 January 95), p. 11. Sergeyev in "Strategic Missiles Forces Commander on 35th Anniversary," JPRS-UMA-95-001 (11 January 95), pp. 9–10. Chechnya in "Chronology of Russian-Chechen Crisis," *Reuters* (16 February 95); John Keegan, "How Kremlin Got It Wrong in Chechnya," *Daily Telegraph* (7 January 95); "Battle Engulfs Grozny as Russian Helicopters Crash," *Reuters* (25 January 95). Russia-Norway border dispute in Stanislav Bartnikas, "Back to Pre-Petrine Rus?," *Moscow News* (5 August 94). Zhilin in Sergei Strokan, "Disarmament/Environment: 'Lively' Russian-Norwegian Military Talks," *Inter Press Service* (11 December 95). Per-Aslak and Sergei Strokan, "Norway: Where NATO Rubs Shoulders with Suspicious Russia," *Inter Press Service* (25 March 96). Russian military uninformed in "Norway Asks Russia for Assurances Over Missile Scare," *Agence France Presse* (27 January 95); "Norwegian Rocket: A Real Threat or a Played-Out Spectacle?," *Izvestiya* (28 January 95) translated in JPRS-TAC-95-006-L. "Official on 'Misunderstanding' Over Norwegian Missile," FBIS-SOV-95-020 (30 January 95). Havnen and Adolfsen in "Norway Regrets Yeltsin Remark on Research Missile," *Reuters* (27 January 95). Demurin and anonymous Russian General in *Izvestiya* (28 January 95) translated in JPRS-TAC-95-006-L (28 January 95). For an authoritative technical description of the missile incident, by the chief designer of the "nuclear briefcase," see Nikolay Devyanin, "All That Has Happened, Alas, Had to Happen," *Moskovskiye novosti* (29 January–5 February 95), pp. 1, 12. For an authoritative eyewitness account of the missile incident by the commander of Russia's early warning radars, General Anatoliy Sokolov, see Oleg Falichev, " 'Iron Cucumbers' in Dangerous Orbits. Necessary Postscript to Norwegian Missile Incident," *Krasnaya zvezda* (7 February 95) translated in FBIS-SOV-95-027 (7 February 95). Black Brant used discarded NATO boosters in "Norwegian Rocket Had Military Look, Russians Say," *Reuters* (28 January 95). On launching from Norwegian Sea and decapitation see "Journalist Visits Moscow ABM Defense HQ," FBIS-UMA-96-090-S (8 May 96), p. 21. On Rust affair see Devyanin and Richard Balmforth, "Moscow Says Missile Scare Was Just a Misunderstanding," *Herald* (Glasgow: 26 January 95). Browne, "2 American Balloonists Die When Shot Down in Belarus," *New York Times* (14 September 95). Maj. General V. S. Belous, "Third Generation Nuclear Weapons" and Col. General I. N. Rodionov, "On Certain Problems of Development of Military Science" in *Voennaya mysl* (December 91) translated in JPRS-UMT-92-005-L. Sergei Ivanko is a pseudonym for a serving officer in the Russian Strategic Rocket forces.

CHAPTER 29: DANGEROUS MINUTES

Authoritative technical account of missile incident by chief designer of "nuclear briefcase" in Devyanin, "All That Has Happened, Alas, Had to Happen," *Moskovskiye novosti* (29 January–5 February 1995). Authoritative eyewitness account by General Sokolov in Falichev, " 'Iron Cucumbers' in Dangerous Orbits," *Krasnaya zvezda* (7 February 95). Kolesnikov, anonymous General, Chernikov, ballistic curve, and Kolesnikov notified in "Norwegian Rocket," *Izvestiya* (28 January 95). Vasily Kononenko, "Yeltsin Leaves Chechnya Behind in Lipetsk, but Takes 'Black Attache Case' with Him," *Izvestiya* (27 January 95), p. 1. Boris Grishchenko, "Colonel General Mikhail Kolesnikov: 'Reaction to Norwegian Rocket Launch Was Appropriate and Effective," *Krasnaya zvezda* (28 January 95), p. 2. "Massive Blunder by INTERFAX," FBIS-WEU-95-018-A (27 January 95). INTERFAX blames military source in Anatol Lieven and Andrew Glasse, "Norway Rocket Gives Russian Defences Cold War Reminder," *The Times* (26 January 95). Sonni Efron, " 'Missile Attack' on Russia Was Just a Science Probe; Defense News Agency Is Falsely Informed That a Weapon Was Shot Down. Norwegian Rocket Is Untouched," *Los Angeles Times* (26 January 95), p. 1. "Report That Russia Shot Down Missile Proves to Be False," *Atlanta Journal and Constitution* (26 January 95). "Dr. Strangelove in Spitzbergen, etc.," *Washington Times* (28 January 95), p. C2. "A major security alert in Russia" was reported in connection with the Norwegian rocket incident, seven months later, buried in "Yeltsin 'Recovering Quickly,' Will Leave Hospital Monday," *Washington Post* (13 July 95), p. 18. Jeff Berliner, "Yeltsin: Russia Tracked 'Missile,' " *United Press International* (26 January 95). Incident dismissed as propaganda in Andrew Higgins, "How Boris Saved the Kremlin," *The Independent* (3 February 95); "Yeltsin's Use of Attache Case a 'Farce,' " FBIS-SOV-95-018 (27 January 95); Aleksandr Gamov, "Yeltsin Uses the Nuclear Briefcase with the Button for the First Time," *Komsomolskaya pravda* (28 January 95). Yushenkov in Halvor Tjonn, "Moscow Silent on Missile," *Aftenposten* (Oslo: 27 January 95), p. 6. Per Tresselt in "Norway Embassy: Russia 'Timely Informed' On Missile Launch," *ITAR-TASS* (27 January 95) and "Norwegian Rocket Incident Settled," FBIS-SOV-95-019 (27 January 95). "Norwegian Official on 'Concern' at Reaction to Missile Launching," *Moscow 2x2 Television* (26 January 95) FBIS Serial LD2601221795. Per Tresselt on Russian reaction in Irina Laguina, "Norway Plays Down Rocket Incident," *Moscow News* (3 February 95). Yushenkov and Kullman Five in "On the Brink of Nuclear War," *Arbeiderbladet*

(Oslo: 27 January 95), p. 17. Stewart remarks of 11 April 1996 in John B. Stewart, Jr., *Rethinking the Unthinkable: Russia's Evolving Nuclear Weapons Threat* (George C. Marshall Institute, 1996). Examples of stories prompted by 1997 prepublication release of *War Scare*: Tim Zimmermann, "Just When You Thought You Were Safe . . . ," *U.S. News and World Report* (10 February 1997); Bruce W. Nelan, "Nuclear Disarray," *Time* (19 May 1997); television documentaries *Doomsday* on Discovery Channel and on *60 Minutes.*

CHAPTER 30: THE WEST

Strobe Talbott, "The Struggle for Russia's Future," *Wall Street Journal* (25 September 97). "FBI Director Downplays Russian Crime," *Monitor* (21 November 97). "FBI Director, in Moscow, Downplays Russian Organized Crime Threat," *Russian Reform Monitor* (28 November 97). Douglas Farah, "Freeh Says Russian Mafia Growing Threat to U.S.," *Washington Post* (2 October 97). Albright in Thomas Lippman, "U.S.-Russian Talks Expose Growing Differences," *Washington Post* (28 January 99). Webster in *Russian Organized Crime* (Center for Strategic and International Studies, 1997) and Webster testimony in *Nuclear Terrorism and Countermeasures*, Hearing before the Military R&D Subcommittee of the House National Security Committee, HNSC No. 105-221 (1998). Martin Sieff, "Russian 'Kleptocracy' Risks Spread of Nuclear Weapons," *Washington Times* (30 September 97). "Remarks by the President and Prime Minister Blair upon the Prime Minister's Arrival," The White House, Office of the Press Secretary (5 February 1998). Perry and Holum in *Defense News* (20–26 November 95). Bill Gertz, "Perry: Missile Defense Unnecessary," *Washington Times* (26 April 96), p. A6. Coit Blacker, Daniel Fried, and Alexander Vershbow, "U.S. Offers Moscow an Alliance with an Expanding NATO," *Christian Science Monitor* (4 October 95). Evers in "House Panel to Examine Russian Command and Control Issue," *External Affairs Digest* (Ballistic Missile Defense Organization, 26 June 95). "Russian Sub Stalks Three Carriers, Practices Attack on USS Carl Vinson," *Monitor* (1 December 97). Bill Gertz, "Cohen Downplays Sub's Stalking of U.S. Ships," *Washington Times* (26 November 97). Bill Gertz, "Russian Sub Stalks Three U.S. Carriers," *Washington Times* (23 November 97). Madeleine K. Albright, "Stop Worrying About Russia," *New York Times* (29 April 98). "Clinton Still Says No Russian Missiles Threaten 'America's Children,' " *Russia Reform Monitor* (19 February 98). J. Michael Waller, "The Russian Nuclear Threat Is Not Gone," *Wall Street Journal* (17 July 96). Testimony of Bruce Blair, J. Michael Waller, and Mary Fitzgerald, "Russian Missile Detargeting and Nuclear Doctrine," Hearing before the R&D Subcommittee of the House National Security Committee (12 March 1997). *Report to the Congress on Detargeting*, Assistant Secretary of Defense, International Security Policy (16 May 1997). Sergeyev in "Don't Count Them Out," *60 Minutes* (18 June 95). Letter from Chairman Floyd D. Spence, House National Security Committee, to Defense Secretary Perry on missile detargeting (12 June 1996). Letter from Secretary of Defense William Perry to Chairman Spence, House National Security Committee, on missile detargeting (1 July 1996). Woolsey in *Threats to United States National Security*, hearing before the House National Security Committee, HNSC No. 105-40 (12 February 1998). "Statement on Nuclear Weapons by International Generals and

Admirals," *State of the World Forum* (5 December 96). Speech by former DCI Woolsey to forum sponsored by National Defense University (16 May 95). Jamie Dettner, "Thatcher Calls for Trans-Atlantic Anti-Missile System," *Washington Times* (10 March 96). Zbigniew Brzezinski, "Running Out of Illusions," *Washington Times* (4 February 96). Schlesinger in Stewart, *Rethinking the Unthinkable* (Marshall Institute, 1996), p. 6. "Strategic Nuclear Balance Increasingly Unstable—Blair," *Armed Forces Newswire Service* (12 December 97). "CIA's Tenet Warns Against U.S. 'Complacency' About Russia," *Monitor* (9 May 97). Curt Weldon, "Command and Control for the 21st Century," Speech, Conference on Assured Strategic Command and Control (National Defense University, 7–8 April 98). Richard F. Starr, "Russia's New Blueprint for National Security," *Strategic Review* (Spring 1998). Moynihan in Barbara Slavin, "Unlikely Cast Gathers to Oppose NATO Growth," *USA Today* (24 April 98). "Russia's Nuclear Temptation," *New York Times* (12 January 98). For CIA report, see Gertz references in Chapter 22.

CHAPTER 31: BLACK PROPHECIES

Boris Grushin, "The Manipulating of Public Awareness Continues: The Image of Impending Catastrophe in Russia as a Weapon in the Political Struggle," *Nezavisimaya gazeta* (12 January 96) translated in FBIS-SOV-96-028-S (9 February 96), pp. 37–41. "Against Jews and Apostates . . ." article in "Patriarch Asked to Halt 'Catholic Threat,' " FBIS-SOV-96-057-S (22 March 96). "Ukrainian Orthodox Archbishop Warns of 'Many More' Victims," *Russia Reform Monitor* (24 October 97). "Persecution of Christians Begins Anew Across Russia," *Russia Reform Monitor* (21 October 97). " 'Forces of Hell' Oppose Russia-Belarus Union," *Monitor* (28 September 98). Saint Barbara in "SRF Commander: START II to Russia's Advantage," FBIS-UMA-96-031-S (14 February 96), p. 4. "Zhirinovskiy Threatens Europe with 'New World War,' " FBIS-SOV-96-029 (12 February 96). "Yeltsin Warns on NATO Expansion," *Associated Press* (8 May 97). Sergey Grigoryev in "NATO Expansion Seen as Serious Threat to Russian Security," FBIS-UMA-96-06-S (7 February 96), p. 2. Kortunov in "Balanced Relations with Other Powers Urged," FBIS-SOV-96-044-S (5 March 96), p. 7. On Adamov see *Associated Press* and *Dow Jones Newswires* (4 March 98). "Anti-American Undertone in Yeltsin's Remarks," *Monitor* (27 March 98). Yuli M. Vorontsov, "One Thing All Russians Agree On," *Washington Post* (10 March 98). Sergey Gulyy, "America Promises Baltic Something," *Novyye izvestiya* (14 January 98). "Academics Take Apocalyptic View of Future," FBIS-SOV-98-007.

CHAPTER 32: START: A MORE DANGEROUS BALANCE

R. Jeffrey Smith, "Nuclear Arms Doctrine to Be Reviewed," *Washington Post* (19 October 93). "Nuclear Dyad?," *Wall Street Journal* (8 July 94). Helsinki Agreement in *Joint Statement on Parameters on Future Reductions in Nuclear Forces*, The White House, Office of the Press Secretary (21 March 97). "U.S. and Russia Sign Arms Control Documents," *Monitor* (29 September 97). "The Helsinki Summit: Arms Control Triumph or Tragedy?," *National Security Report*, Office of the Chairman, House National Security Committee (April 1997). "Amended START-

2 Allows Russia to Keep SS-18s Until 2008," *Russia Reform Monitor* (15 April 98). "New Strategic Missile Chief Interviewed," FBIS-TAC-97-183. "ICBM Test Success Enables Possible Service Life Extension," *ITAR-TASS* (11 June 97). Vladislav Kuznetsov and Mikhail Shevtsov, "Russian Missile Troops: START II Not to Compromise Them," *ITAR-TASS* (25 September 97) translated in FBIS-UMA-97-268. Russian tactical nuclear advantage in Vince Crawley, "Russian Nuclear Weapons Called 'Headache' for NATO," *European Stars and Stripes* (18 December 96). "Tactical Nuclear Weapons in Russia," FBIS-SOV-98-064 (5 March 98). Peter Vincent Pry, *Nuclear Wars: Exchanges and Outcomes* (Crane Russak, 1990). Deteriorating Russian radars in "Vointsev: Development of Missile Attack Warning System," JPRS-UMA-94-008 (23 February 94). Sergey Modestov, "Additional Arguments for START II Proponents," *Nezavisimaya Gazeta* (30 January–5 February 98), p. 1. Unclassified memo on SSBN launch procedures, Office of the Assistant Secretary of Defense; Deputy Director of Strategy, Forces, and Operations (14 September 95). General A. V. Bolyatko, "On the Question of Strategic Stability," *Voennaya mysl* (10 October 93). "Zakharov in Favor of Strong Nuclear Force, Reconsideration of START II," FBIS-UMA-95-216-S (8 November 95). Sergeyev, "The Strategic Missile Troops," *Voennaya mysl* (June 1993). Colonel I. A. Karpachev in "For the Question of Military Parity and Arms Sufficiency," JPRS-UMT-93-005-L (18 May 93), p. 19. Gareyev, "Nuclear Weapons and Russia's Security," FBIS-TAC-97-322 (18 November 97). Petr Belov, "Nuclear Missile Adventurism," *Nezavisimaya gazeta* (24 February 98) translated in FBIS-TAC-98-055. For an example of START as a U.S. conspiracy to win a nuclear war see "Scientists Oppose START II Ratification," FBIS-SOV-95-091 (11 May 95). "Communist Backs START-1 If New Missiles Are Funded," *Russia Reform Monitor* (26 June 98). "Need to Ratify START II Examined," FBIS-SOV-95-214 (6 November 95), p. 23.

CHAPTER 33: WINNING A NUCLEAR WAR

Lt. Colonel V. V. Kruglov, "Is There a Law of Victory?," *Voennaya mysl* (January 94), p. 37. Colonel V. V. Kruglov and Colonel M. Ye. Sosnovskiy, "Nonstrategic Weapons in Nuclear Deterrence," *Voennaya mysl* (September 97), pp. 11–14. Colonel V. Ya. Savchenko and Lt. Colonel V. Vasilyev, "Consideration of External Threats to State Security in Substantiating the Permissible Level of Reduction of Strategic Offensive Arms," *Voennaya mysl* (July 93) translated in JPRS-UMT-93-010-L (17 September 93). Vladimir M. Zakharov, "A Problem: Should Russia Remain a Nuclear Power? Myths About the Most Dangerous Weapon," *Nezavisimaya gazeta* (12 October 95) translated in FBIS-UMA-95-216-S (8 November 95), pp. 11–15. Nuclear landmines in "Tactical Nuclear Weapons as Deterrent to Peripheral Conflicts." FBIS-UMA-95-239-S (13 December 95), pp. 10–11. Yuriy Kozhuk, "By Hook or by Crook," *Flag Rodiny* (10 December 97) translated in FBIS-SOV-98-009. Dworkin in Aleksandr Golts, "The Last Attribute of a Superpower," *Itogi* (16 December 97) translated in FBIS-SOV-98-020. David R. Markov, "The Russians and Their Nukes," *Air Force Magazine* (February 97). Rybkin in "Russia May Use Nuclear Arms in Conventional War," *Reuters* (11 February 97). Berezovsky in Adam Tanner, "New Russian Doctrine Includes Nuclear First Strike," *Reuters* (9 May 97). David Hoffman, "Yeltsin Approves Doctrine of Nuclear First Use If Attacked," *Washington Post* (10 May 97). Andrey Vaganov, "Test Run for National Security Blueprint. In His Document Russian Federation Security Council President Consciously or Unconsciously Returns to Cold War Times," *Nezavisimaya gazeta* (7 May 97). *Russian Federation National Security Blueprint* in *Rossiyskaya gazeta* (26 December 97), pp. 4–5. Klimenko and Koltyukov in "General Staff Draft on Organizational Development," FBIS-SOV-98-107 (17 April 98). Yakovlev in Gennadiy Miranovich and Aleksandr Dolinin, "We Are All Responsible for the Security of the Fatherland," *Krasnaya zvezda* (13 March 98) translated in FBIS-UMA-98-075. Nikolayev in "Gareyev, War, Modern International Conflict," FBIS-SOV-98-040 (9 February 98). Viktor Mikhailov, Igor Andryushin, and Alexander Chernysov, *NATO's Expansion and Russia's Security* (20 September 96). Aleksandr Shirokorad, "A Small Bomb for a Small War: The Role of Tactical Nuclear Weapons Is Objectively Increasing as Strategic Arms Are Being Reduced," *Nezavisimaya voyennoye obozreniye* (10 April 98) translated in FBIS-SOV-98-100. Sergey Sokot translated in "LRA Global Exercise to Disrupt Aerospace Offensive," FBIS-UMA-98-300 (27 October 98). "Yeltsin Decides on Financing New Strategic Missile Force," *Russia Reform Monitor* (13 July 98). "Russia Stages Massive Mock Nuclear Attack," *Russia Reform Monitor* (23 October 98). "Russian Exercises Involve Missile Strikes by Land, Sea, Air," *INTERFAX* (2 October 97). Bill Gertz, "Russian Bombers Train to Strike U.S.," *Washington Times* (9 June 98). "Russian Navy Test Fires Ballistic Missiles," *Monitor* (2 July 96). "Pacific Fleet Submarines Test Fire Cruise Missiles," *INTERFAX* (23 July 97) translated in FBIS-UMA-97-204. "Russia to Destroy 20 Ballistic Missiles in December," *ITAR-TASS* (1 December 97). "Naval Exercise to Feature 'Massed' Missile Firing," FBIS-UMA-98-105 (15 April 98). Habiger in "U.S. Military Surveys Russian Strategic Nuclear Modernization," *Russian Reform Monitor* (3 April 98). "Russians Deploy First of Missiles: New ICBMs Said to Be World's Best," *Washington Times* (25 December 97). "Russian Air Force to Get New Blackjack Strategic Bombers," *Monitor* (29 October 97). "Strategic Air Force to Skip a Generation,"*Monitor* (19 June 97). "Russia Designs New Long-Range Bomber," *Xinhua* (19 June 97). Jacques Isnard, "Russia Develops Three New Nuclear Missiles," *Le Monde* (13 March 98) translated in FBIS-TAC-98-072. "First Borey-Class Sub to Be Launched Early Next Century," *Nezavisimaya voyennoye obozreniye* (10–16 April 98) translated in FBIS-UMA-98-105. Mary Fitzgerald, *The Russian Shift Toward Nuclear War Waging* (Hudson Institute, 1993). Bill Gertz, "U.S. Officials Suspect Russia Staged Nuclear Test This Year," *Washington Times* (7 March 96), p. 3. Bill Gertz, "Perry Cites Evidence of Russian Nuke Test," *Washington Times* (8 March 96). Bill Gertz, "Suspicion Grows of Russian Nuke Test," *Washington Times* (29 August 97). Bill Gertz, " 'Seismic Event' Raises Questions of Verifying Nuclear Test Ban," *Washington Times* (30 August 97). William J. Broad, "Hints of a Nuclear Test in Russia Are Disputed," *Wall Street Journal* (21 October 97). R. Jeffrey Smith, "U.S. Formally Drops Claim of Possible Nuclear Blast," *Washington Post* (4 November 97). "Norwegian Experts—Arctic Tremor May Be Russia Weapons Test," *Moscow NTV* (13 February 98) in FBIS-SOV-98-044. "Norwegians Suspect Another Secret Nuclear Test in Arctic," *Monitor* (20 February 98). "Russia Nears Completion of Doctrine," *BMD Monitor* (23 February 98). Mikhailov in Aleksandr Khokhlov, "U.S. Nuclear Secrets Are Old Hat for Russia," *Novyye izvestiya* (18 November 97) translated in FBIS-SOV-97-322 (18 November

97). Bill Gertz, "Moscow Builds Bunkers Against Nuclear Attack," *Washington Times* (1 April 97). Carey Scott, "Kremlin Refurbishes Nuclear Bunkers as Fear of NATO Grows," *Sunday Times* (London: 13 April 97). Mark Walsh, "U.S. Suspects Russia Is Building Super-Bunker," *Defense News* (28 July–3 August 97). "Sense of Congress on Need for Russian Openness on the Yamantau Mountain Project," *National Defense Authorization Act for Fiscal Year 1998*, House National Security Committee, HNSC No. 105-340, Sec. 1227 (27 October 1997). James Hackett, "Underground Readiness for War," *Washington Times* (16 July 97). Selivanov in "Navy Aide: No Comment on U.S. Russian Submarine Reports," FBIS-SOV-95-239 (13 December 95), p. 25. Bill Gertz, "Russian Submarine Is Spotted Off Coast: Boat Was Closest to U.S. Since 1987," *Washington Times* (23 June 95). "NATO Concern Over Russian Submarine Patrolling Noted," JPRS-UMA-94-038 (14 September 94). Martin Sieff, "U.S. Says Russia Isn't Coming Clean with Poison Gas Data," *Washington Times* (24 June 94). CIA Report on "Spotlight Turned on Illegal Russian Arms Dealings," *Monitor* (10 February 99). Office of the Secretary of Defense, *Proliferation: Threat and Response* (November 1997). Clifford Kraus, "U.S. Urges Russia to End Production of Nerve Gas," *New York Times* (6 February 97). Owen Matthews, "Russia Using U.S. Funds for Chemical Weapons Research, Say Scientists," *The Scotsman* (27 February 98). Bill Gertz, "Russia Has Biological Weapons, Defector Says," *Washington Times* (22 January 93). Rowland Evans and Robert Novak, "Yeltsin in the Dark," *Washington Post* (24 June 92). Steve Bowman, *Russian Biological Weapons Program*, Congressional Research Service (24 July 1996). Ken Alibek, "Russia's Deadly Expertise," *New York Times* (27 March 98). David Hoffman, "Russia Challenged to Disclose Status of Biological Weapons," *Washington Post* (26 February 98). "Moscow Invests $12 Billion in New Weapons," *Russia Reform Monitor* (2 September 97). "Russia to Show Its Su-37 Fighter in LeBourget This Week," *ITAR-TASS* (18 June 97). "Russia's New Supersonic Anti-Ship Missile Revealed," *Agence France Presse* (6 August 97). *The Clinton Administration and Nuclear Stockpile Stewardship: Erosion by Design*, Office of the Chairman, House National Security Committee (30 October 1996). Yuriy Karnakov, "Russian Nuclear Triad to Demonstrate its Combat Readiness Tomorrow," *Russkiy Telegraf* (2 October 97) translated in FBIS-UMA-97-276.

CHAPTER 34: FLASHPOINTS

Lebed in "Russia Nuclear Security Issues," hearing before the R&D Subcommittee of the House National Security Committee (19 March 1998). Laura Myers, "Opponent Says Yeltsin Too Unpredictable," *Associated Press* (19 March 98). David Hoffman, "Yeltsin Antics Growing Harder to Follow," *Washington Post* (2 April 98). Military will not again rescue Yeltsin in "Generals Said Angered by Rumored Chechnya Withdrawal," FBIS-SOV-96-029 (12 February 96), p. 5. "Yeltsin Sums Up Five Years since August Coup Attempt," FBIS-SOV-96-163 (21 August 96), p. 13. Mikhalchenko in "NATO Black Sea Activity Cited as Reason for Fleet Training," FBIS-UMA-95-192-S (4 October 95). "Azerbaijani Turkey Concerned Over Unsettled Nagorno-Karabakh Problem," FBIS-SOV-98-105 (15 April 98). Paul Bedard, "Ukraine Agrees to Give Up Nukes: U.S., Russia Ensure Security in Pact," *Washington Times* (11 January 94). Ukraine-NATO conspiracy in Sergey Andreyev,

"Kiev Ignores Previous Agreements," *Nezavisimaya gazeta* (3 February 98) translated in FBIS-SOV-98-036. "Yeltsin Reassures Baltic Fleet, Kaliningrad of Support," FBIS-SOV-96-159 (15 August 96), pp. 14–15. "Moscow Regrets Turkey's Support of Chechen Separatists," FBIS-SOV-96-163 (21 August 96). Terekhyn in Anatoly Sychko, "That Is Just What We Need—Russian Nuclear Warheads," *Vseukrainskiye vedomosti* (Kiev: 26 March 98) translated in FBIS-SOV-98-100. *Trilateral Statement by the Presidents of the United States, Russia and Ukraine* (Moscow: 14 January 1994). Paul Bedard, "Ukraine Agrees to Give Up Nukes: U.S., Russia Ensure Security in Pact," *Washington Times* (11 January 94). "Dementyev, Surikov 'Army of Future,' " FBIS-UMA-96-090-S (8 May 96). Zhanurova in "Border Troop Officers Claim U.S. Espionage," FBIS-SOV-96-155-S (9 August 96), pp. 4–5. "Cold Wars in Cold Waters," *U.S. News and World Report* (26 March 98). "Russian Navy Fired Depth Charges at U.S. Submarine," *Russia Reform Monitor* (8 May 98). Daniel Dupont, "Air Force 'Have Stare' Radar May Be Deployed Along Russian Border," *Inside Missile Defense* (15 April 98). "Sergeyev Urges Norway to 'Be Rid of Military Facilities,' " *INTERFAX* (28 January 99) translated in FBIS-UMA-99-028 (28 January 99). "Russian Counterintelligence Claims Successes," *Monitor* (1 August 97). "Moscow Complains of Increased Spying," *Monitor* (9 May 97). "Yeltsin Approves Program to Protect State Secrets," FBIS-SOV-96-046 (12 March 96), p. 27. Semenov in Anatoliy Yukin, *ITAR-TASS* (26 February 96) translated in "Army Commander Says NATO Exercises Threaten Russia," FBIS-SOV-96-039 (27 February 96), p. 10. "NATO Exercise 'May Pose Threat' to Russian Security," FBIS-SOV-96-044 (5 March 96), p. 13. Dementyev in "NATO Activity in N. Europe Concerns Military," FBIS-SOV-96-043 (4 March 96), pp. 32–33. Vladimir Abarinov, "Boris Yeltsin Perturbed by NATO Maneuvers in Norway," *Segodnya* (1 March 96) translated in FBIS-SOV-96-043 (4 March 96), p. 10. "Northern Fleet Starts Exercises in Barents Sea," FBIS-SOV-96-052 (15 March 96), p. 34. "Northern Fleet Exercises in Barents Sea End," FBIS-SOV-96-058 (25 March 98), p. 35. "Yeltsin Remarks on Cuban Downing of U.S. Planes," FBIS-SOV-96-041 (29 February 96), p. 13. "Moscow to Develop 'Mutually Advantageous' Ties to Cuba," FBIS-SOV-96-052 (15 March 96), p. 11. "Lukin: NATO Maneuvers in Norway 'Clearly Aimed at Russia,' " FBIS-SOV-96-058 (25 March 96), p. 17. "Karasin Says Russia 'Concerned' Over Norway-U.S. Exercises," FBIS-SOV-96-016 (24 January 96), p. 13. "Gore's 'Sharp Tone' Noted in Letter to Chernomyrdin," FBIS-SOV-96-044 (5 March 1996). CENTRASBAT-97 and Sheehan in "Historic U.S.-Led Military Exercise Begins," *Monitor* (17 September 97). "U.S.-Led Military Exercise Ends Successfully in Uzbekistan," *Monitor* (22 September 97). R. Jeffrey Smith, "U.S. Leads Peacekeeping Drill in Kazakhstan," *Washington Post* (15 September 97). Ivashov in "Senior Defense Official Repeats Russia's Opposition to NATO Exercises," *TV6 Moscow* (21 September 97) in British Broadcasting Corporation Summary of World Broadcasts (23 September 97). GRU in Andrey Korbut, "U.S. Landing Force in Central Asia," *Nezavisimaya gazeta* (13 September 97) translated in FBIS-UMA-97-259. Baburin and "Anti-NATO Group" in Vladimir Kuznetsova and Sergei Ostanin, "Lawmakers Concerned About NATO Maneuvers Near Russia," *ITAR-TASS* (19 September 97) translated in FBIS-UMA-97-262. "NATO-Sponsored Exercise Underway in Ukraine," *Monitor* (26 August 97). Carey Scott, "NATO Wargame Kicks Russia in Soft Underbelly," *The Times* (London: 17 March 97). Duma statement in "Is It Truly a Partnership for Peace?,"

Rossisskaya gazeta (8 October 97). "NATO Field Exercise Largest Since Cold War," *Washington Times* (10 March 98). "Limonia" and Kurodyedov in Viktor Lukin, "Military Said 'Jealous' of NATO Maneuvers," *Izvestiya* (12 March 98) translated in FBIS-UMA-98-072. "Russia's Sergeyev Reacts to U.S. 'Military Actions' in Norway," FBIS-UMA-99-028 (28 January 99). S. Kurginyan, "A Micron Away from Apocalypse," *Zavtra* (September 95) translated in FBIS-SOV-95-198-S (13 October 95). "Moscow Continues to Bristle with Cold War Rhetoric Over Kosovo," *Monitor* (14 October 98). Akchurin in Anatoliy Yurkin, *ITAR-TASS* (5 February 99). "Official: Russian Army to Attack NATO Ships if FRY Struck," *BETA* (19 February 99). "Russian Foreign Minister Issues Fresh Warning to NATO," *Monitor* (26 June 98). Steven Lee Meyers, "Jinxed Bomber at Last on Duty in Persian Gulf," *New York Times* (3 January 98). Yeltsin on world war over Iraq in *INTERFAX* (4 February 98); Igor Shchegolev, "Yeltsin—Russia Must Not Permit U.S. Strike on Iraq," *ITAR-TASS* (5 February 98) translated in FBIS-SOV-98-036. "Yeltsin: A U.S. Attack on Iraq Might Start World War III," *Russia Reform Monitor* (11 February 98). "Yeltsin Criticizes Clinton Over Iraq Policy," *Monitor* (6 February 98). "International Issues Also on Agenda," *Monitor* (11 February 98). Sergei Shargorodsky, "Yeltsin Says Clinton May Provoke World War Over Iraq," *Associated Press* (4 February 98). Primakov and U.S. denial in Michael Specter, "Yeltsin Says Clinton Could Blunder into a World War," *New York Times* (5 February 98). Nuclear assurances in Konstantin Eggert, "Russia Will Not Approve Strike Against Iraq for Anything. Yevgeniy Primakov Makes This Promise to State Duma," *Izvestiya* (5 February 98) translated in FBIS-SOV-98-035. Chrystia Freeland, "Russia Deputies Speak Up for Iraq," *London Financial Times* (4 February 98). "Duma Urges Withdrawing from Sanctions If Iraq Attacked," *INTERFAX* (4 February 98) translated in FBIS-SOV-98-035. "Statement of the State Duma," Embassy of the Russian Federation, Press Release #4 (6 February 98). "U.S. Says It Has No Plans to Use Nukes on Iraq," *Reuters* (5 February 98). Aleksey Chichkin, "The Iraq Crisis: The Economic Aspect. From Desert Storm to 'Dash to the Caspian?,' " *Rossiyskaya gazeta* (5 February 98) translated in FBIS-SOV-98-036. Natalya Panshina, "Zhirinovskiy Proposes Air Defense System for Iraq," *ITAR-TASS* (4 February 98) in FBIS-SOV-98-035. "Russia Refutes Report of Turkish Moves on Armenian Border," *INTERFAX* (6 February 98) in FBIS-SOV-98-037. Gulev in "Russian Military Specialist on Iraqi Crisis," *Rossiyskaya gazeta* (10 February 98). Bradley Graham and David Hoffman, "Russian Rebukes U.S. Over Iraq," *Washington Post* (13 February 98). "Russian Defense Chief Assails U.S. for Iraq Policy," *Monitor* (13 February 98). "Norwegian Experts—Arctic Tremor May Be Russian Weapons Test," *Moscow NTV* (13 February 98) in FBIS-SOV-98-044. "Sergeyev Pledges 'Appropriate Action' If Strike on Iraq," Moscow Russian Public Television *First Channel Network* (14 February 98) in FBIS-UMA-98-045. "Sergeyev Cites 8-minute Response Time for Missile Forces," *INTERFAX* (14 February 98) in FBIS-UMA-98-045. "Russia Launches Military Satellite," *Associated Press* (17 February 98). "Nuclear Submarine Test Fires 2 Strategic Missiles," *ITAR-TASS* (19 February 98) in English, see FBIS-UMA-98-0050. "Russian Lab Develops Anthrax Strain that Might Defeat U.S. Vaccine," *AET* (13 February 98). "Russia Again Denies Biological Weapons Charges," *Monitor* (3 March 98). "Russia Reportedly Has New Poison," *Washington Post* (4 April 97). R. Jeffrey Smith, "Did Russia Sell Iraq Germ Warfare Equipment," *Washington Post* (12 February 98), p. 1. "The Faded Romance with Russia," *New York Times* (13 February 98). Mikhail Shevtsov, "Russia's Strategic Nuclear Forces on Heightened Alert," *ITAR-TASS* (18 December 98). Yakushkin in *INTERFAX* (18 December 98). "Def Min Denies Russian Forces on Heightened Alert," *Reuters* (18 December 98). Satellite Launch in *Russia Reform Monitor* (5 January 99). Kornukov in "General Staff Rehearsed World War Scenarios," *Moscow TV* (17 January 99) transcript translated in FBIS-SOV-99-027 (27 January 99). INOBIS in Institute of Defense Studies, *Conceptual Provisions of a Strategy for Countering the Main External Threats to Russian Federation National Security* (Moscow: INOBIS, October 1995). " 'Theses' May Underlay New Military Doctrine," FBIS-SOV-95-208 (27 October 95), pp. 23–24. "NATO Expansion Could Prompt Czech, Polish Targeting," FBIS-SOV-95-195 (10 October 95), p. 34. Pavel Felgengauer, "Russian Generals Are Not Concerned About the Good Intentions of the NATO Countries," *Segodnya* (23 June 95). "Military Plans Nuclear Counter to NATO," (3 October 95). Richard Beeston, "Russia Has a 'Nuclear Answer' to Wider NATO," *The Times* (London: 30 September 95), p. 14. Soskovets in "Visit May Bring Russian Subs Back to Cuba," FBIS-SOV-95-202 (19 October 95), pp. 24–25. Surikov in "Baltic Accession to NATO Would Equal Cuban Missile Crisis, Senior Russian Analyst Says," *Monitor* (22 April 97). Martin Sieff, "Yeltsin Orders Effort to Defeat U.S. Goal of NATO Expansion," *Washington Times* (7 January 97). "Yeltsin Warns on NATO Expansion," *Associated Press* (8 May 97). Rodionov in "Cold War Continues, Russia's Defense Minister Says," *Baltimore Sun* (22 December 96). Rokhlin in "Duma Committee Plans to Examine START II Treaty," FBIS-SOV-96-024 (5 February 96), p. 41. Bill Gertz, "Russia Practiced Nuclear Attack on NATO," *Washington Times* (8 July 97). "Duma Wants Army, Defense to Adapt to New Security Threats," FBIS-SOV-98-014 (14 January 98). "Sergeyev Warns of Anti-NATO Move in Belarus," *Monitor* (30 January 98). "Uneasy Russian-NATO Relations Continue," *Monitor* (11 May 98). "Russia, Belarus 'Draw Red Line' Against NATO Enlargement," *Monitor* (6 April 98). Martin Sieff, "Russia Raises Stakes Against NATO," *Washington Times* (4 May 98). Gregory Piat, "Group Gets Cold War Flashback," *European Stars and Stripes* (9 February 99). Pavel Felgengauer, "The Russian Army and the East-West Military Balance: Self-Deception and Mutual Misunderstanding Did Not End With the Cold War," *Segodnya* (18 August 95) translated in FBIS-SOV-95-164-S (24 August 95), p. 4.

Index

Abkhazia, 275
ABLE ARCHER military exercise: communications anomalies and, 39; DEFCON-1 and, 39; first-strike and, 44; National Intelligence Estimates and, 42–43; Pershing II missiles and, 3–34; Soviet alert and, 41–44; Soviet threat perception and, 33, 36, 37–44; toning down of, 38
Achalov, Vladimir, 141–42, 143, 171–72, 178
Achalov, Vladislav, 163
Adolfsen, Kolbjoern, 217, 218
Afghanistan, 4, 92, 137, 162
"Against Jews and Heresies, We Will Halt the Apostates," 249
Air Defense Forces, 190, 191, 193, 219–20
Air-launched cruise missiles (ALCMs), 35–36, 111, 211
Akhromeyev, Sergey, 47, 59, 78, 80–81, 131
Albania, 284
Albright, Madeleine, 242, 243
Alekseyevich, Viktor, 190
Aleksin, Valeriy, 117
Aleksiy II, 250
Alibekov, Kanatjian, 270–71
Aliyev, Geydar, 121, 123
Alksnis, Viktor, 131, 136, 158–59
"All That Has Happened, Alas, Had to Happen," 234–35
Alpha Group, 78, 178
Ames, Aldrich, 47
Anarchy, 134
Andoya Island, 222, 236
Andropov, Igor, 5
Andropov, Irina, 5
Andropov, Yuri: assassination attempt on, 18; background of, 3–4; Brezhnev replaced by, 30; death of, 47; health decline by, 45; Korean Air Lines flight 007 and, 31, 32; Kryuchkov and, 61–62; NATO arms expansion and, 3; Pershing II missiles and, 17; political violence by, 4; Pugo and, 58; Reagan administration and, 12–13; threat perception by, 1, 5, 37; VYRAN and, 9
Annan, Kofi, 288
Antiballistic Missile Defense, 162
Antikainen, Toivo, 4
Anti-NATO Group, 283
Arbatov, Alexei, 129, 145–47, 151, 152, 154
Argentina, 189
Armenia, 89, 104, 113, 114, 115, 124, 205
Armenian-Azerbaijan conflict, 92, 102, 276; balance of power and, 94; birth of, 115–16; Felgengauer and, 124–26; as grassroots conflict, 116; peace talks and, 123; Russian forces in, 119–20; Russian threat perception and, 117; Ter-Petrosyan and, 94; Turkish forces in, 119–20; war warning and, 121–23, 126–27
Asanbayev, Erik, 112
Aspin, Les, 141
August coup: confrontation with Gorbachev and, 59–61; conspirators of, 57–59; disinformation about, 83–85; failure of, 78–81, 90–91; first-strike policy and, 81; Maksimov and, 156; Maltsev on, 51;

Moscow Television Network on, 51; nuclear briefcases and, 84–85; obedience to launch and, 85–86; Operation THUNDER and, 77–78; press report on, 102; Rutskoy and, 138; Soviet strike capabilities and, 84–85; Soviet threat perception and, 73–74, 75, 77; suicides and, 79–80, 81; Union Treaty and, 60, 61, 69; war preparation command and, 70–76; Warsaw Pact collapse and, 69; Yeltsin and, 77–78
Aurora borealis, 195
Austro-Hungarian Empire, 208
Azerbaijan: breakup of Soviet Union and, 89; Caspian oil and, 287; nuclear weapons in, 113; Ottoman Turks and, 114; Rodionov and, 104; Russian "peacekeeping operations" in, 205. *See also* Armenian-Azerbaijan conflict

Baburin, Sergei, 282
Bacteriological warfare, 14
Baikonur Cosmodrome, 90, 133, 165
Baklanov, Oleg, 59, 60
Baku, Azerbaijan, 89, 114, 116
Baltic Fleet, 133
Baltic Sea, 89
Barents Sea, 278
Barranikov, Viktor, 163, 174, 178
Barsukov, Mikhail, 215
Barynkin, Viktor, 95–96, 187, 189–90, 191, 207
Bashkirov, Mikhail, 109, 111
Basic Provisions of the Military Doctrine of the Russian Federation, 199–200
Batenin, Geliy, 85, 149–50, 151, 154
Baton Rouge, 117
BATTLE GRIFFIN–96, 279–81
Battle of Austerlitz, 203–4
Belarus, 89, 109–10, 112, 249, 250
Belorussia, 275
Belous, Vladimir, 98, 221
Belov, Petr, 260–61
Berezovsky, Boris, 263
Berlin crisis, 273
Berliner, Jeff, 233–34
Biological warfare, 136, 270–71, 288
Biological Weapons Convention, 14, 270
Biryuzov, S. S., 11
Black Berets, 56
Black Brant XII rocket. *See* Norwegian missile crisis
Black Colonel, 131, 136, 137
Black Sea Fleet, 111, 112, 159, 276–77
Blacker, Colt, 242
Blair, Bruce, 84, 153, 232–33, 244–45
Boldin, Valery, 60
Boldyrev, Yuri, 151
Bolshevik Revolution, 115
Bolyatko, A. V., 259
Bondarenko, Valeri, 250
"Boris Yeltsin Joins the Party of Force," 215
Bosnia, 206, 208–10, 215, 283–85
Bradley, Ed, 100
Brezhnev, Leonid, 5–6, 9, 17, 30
Brezhnev Doctrine, 6
Britain, 9, 115, 189, 286
Brzezinski, Zbigniew, 138
Bulygin, Yuri, 103
Burbulis, Gannadiy, 121
Bush, George, 38, 87, 92–93, 94, 99, 112–13, 255
Butcher of Tbilisi, 192
Byely, B. A., 11

California, 143
Capitalism, 134
Carl Vinson, 242–43
Carter, Ash, 213
Caspian Sea, 89, 287
Caucasian War, 87
"Caucasian War at Center of World Policy in the Year 2000," 125
Center for Naval Analysis, 145–47
Center for Operational Strategic Studies (COSS), 107
Center for Strategic and International Studies, 242

Central Aerological Observatory, 229
Central Asia, 275
Central Council of Trade Unions, 58
Central Intelligence Agency (CIA), xvii, x–xi; August coup and, 77; chemical weapons and, 269; GRU and, 205; Korean Air Lines flight 007 and, 28–29, 31; National Intelligence Estimates and, xi; Polish crisis and, 25; Russian command and control and, 152–53; Russian military perceptions and, 247; Rutskoy and, 137; Zhirinovsky and, 142
CENTRASBAT-97, 281–82, 283
Cetin, Hekmit, 118
Charles XII, 114
Cheban, V., 207
Chechnya, 181, 187, 214, 215–16, 217
Chemenko, Andrei, 142
Chemical Troops, 72
Chemical weapons, 120, 269–70
Chemical Weapons Convention, 269
Cheney, Richard, 92, 93
Chernenko, Konstantin, 54
Chernavin, Vladimir, 67
Chernikov, A., 229
Chernomyrdin, Viktor, 197, 274, 285
"Chief Conclusions and Views Adopted at the Meeting of Heads of Service," 13
Chikin, Maksim, 197
China, 92, 200, 242, 251, 252
Christianity/Christians, 92, 114
Christopher, Warren, 149
Churkin, Vitaliy, 212
CIS Army, 168–69
Civil war, 69, 92, 172, 205
Clapper, James, 117–18, 215–16, 217
Clinton, Bill: Iraq and, 286; Poland and, 214; START and, xiii, 255–59; threat perception by, 97–98, 243; U.S.-Iraqi 1998 conflict and, 288; Ukranian crisis and, 160
Clinton administration: BATTLE-GRIFFIN-96 and, 281; Bosnia and, 283; Iraq and, 286; NATO expansion and, 216; NIE 1995 report and, xi–xii; Russian nuclear tests and, 267; threat perception by, 241–44, 245; Yamantau project and, 268
Clinton Administration and Nuclear Stockpile Stewardship: Erosion by Design, The, 272
Cohen, William, 243, 287
"Cold War in Cold Waters," 278
Cold War, The, 37
Collins, James, 286
Committee for State Security. *See* KGB
Commonwealth Armed Forces, 122
Commonwealth of Independent States (CIS), 90, 124, 246, 275. *See also names of specific states*
Communist Party, 91
Comprehensive Test Ban Treaty (CTBT), 267, 268
Conference on Security and Cooperation in Europe, 217
Congress of People's Deputies, 57, 161
Congressional Research Service, 270, 271
Constant Combat Readiness, 97, 226–27
Constellation, 242–43
Conventional Forces in Europe (CFE) Treaty, 55, 58, 74
Cooper, Richard N., xi–xii
Corfu summit, 211–12
Coups, 274–75. *See also* August coup; October coup
CPSU Central Committee, 72
Crimean War, 115
Croats, 208
Crowe, William J., 80–81
Cruz, Edith, 27
Cuba, 37, 281
Cuban missile crisis, x, 143–44, 193, 273
Czech Republic, 288, 290
Czechoslovakia, 4, 6, 9, 24, 26, 64

Danilchenko, Sergey, 211
"Dash to the Caspian," 286
David, Jacques Louis, 203–4

DEAD HAND, 153, 180
DEFCON, 39, 77
Defense Council, 84
Defense Intelligence Agency, xi
De Maiziere, Lothar, 64–65
Dementyev, Valeriy, 277–78, 280
Demirel, Suleyman, 102
Democratic revolutions, 64–66
Demurin, Mikhail, 218
Deneiken, Petr, 172
DESERT FOX, 193, 238, 286, 288
DESERT STORM, 66–68, 106
DESERT THUNDER, 288
Deutch, John, 245
Devyanin, Nikolay, 183, 218, 222, 223, 224–25, 230, 234–35
Dimensions of Civil Unrest in the Soviet Union, 17–18
Disinformation, 63, 79, 83–85, 94–95, 150–51
Dneister region, 275
Dobrynin, Anatoly, 12
Dubynin, Viktor, 25
Dudnik, Vladimir, 132, 172
Duluth, Minnesota, 144
Dunaev, Andrey, 163
Dworkin, Vladimir, 129, 145–47, 151, 152, 199, 279

East Germany, 64, 67
East Prussia, 204
Eastern Europe, 55, 64–66, 189. *See also names of specific countries*
Eisenhower, Dwight D., 265
El Salvador, 34
Elchibey, Abulfez, 123
Electromagnetic-pulse (EMP) attack, 220–22, 230
Emerging Missile Threats to North America during the Next Fifteen Years, xi
"Emerging Russian Nuclear Strategy and Doctrine," 145–47
Enterprise, 29
Estonia, 59, 89, 91, 158, 204–5
European Union, 211–12
Evers, William, 242
Falichev, Oleg, 219
Falklands War, 189
Felgengauer, Pavel, 124–26, 159, 175, 265
First-strike policy: ABLE ARCHER military exercise and, 39, 44; 1993 Alexandria conference and, 145–47; Arbatov and, 129; August coup and, 75, 81; Baryinkin and, 189–90; Fisher and, 46–47; future threat and, 274, 285; Gareyev and, 103, 105, 106, 107, 201; General Staff 1996 policy on, 95–96; Grachev and, 107, 140, 188–89; ICBMs and, 10–11; Iraq and, 285; Kozhuk and, 263; military planning documents and, 11–12; missile attack warning system and, 101; National Intelligence Estimates and, 19; new military doctrine and, 98, 198–202, 212–13, 241, 248, 262, 263; non-nuclear states and, 125; Norwegian missile crisis and, 228; nuclear balance and, 248; Pershing II missiles and, 22; Persian Gulf War and, 67; policy revision and, 67–68, 69–70, 285; Polish crisis and, 26; Rodionov and, 104,106, 192, 198; Rogov and, 201; Russian Army's weakness and, 102–3; Russian military exercises and, 265; Ryaboshapko and, 96; Soviet ideologists and, 11; SS–18 ICBM and, 255; Starr and, 246; START and, 256–61, 266; treaties prohibiting, 17; Ukraine and, 110, 158; victory and, 262; VRYAN and, 10, 14, 15, 22; Yakojlev and, 194; Yeltsin and, 198, 212
FISHBOWL, 220–21
Fisher, Ben, 43, 46–47
Fisk, Robert, 208
Fitzgerald, Mary, 105–6, 267
Five, Kaci Kullman, 235
Flexible Response, 265
Florida, 143
Foreign Intelligence Service (SVR), xiv, xv, 94

Foreign Missile Threats: Analytical Soundness of Certain National Intelligence Estimates, xii
Fort Bragg, North Carolina, 281, 282
Foye, Stephen, 174
France, 115
Freeh, Louis, 242
Fried, Daniel, 242
"From the Nuclear Abyss to Catastrophe for Russia—That Is Where the START II Treaty Is Leading," 140
Future threats: Balkan conflicts and, 284–85; coup attempts and, 274–75; first-strike policy and, 274; NATO expansion and, 239, 273, 276, 287; NATO military exercises and, 279–83; Russian internal troubles and, 274; Russian military attitudes and, 278–79; Ukraine and, 276–77; Western policy on Russian periphery and, 275–76

Gaidar, Yegor, 161, 163, 215
Garayev, Makhmut: first-strike policy and, 105, 201–2; military doctrine debate and, 102–3, 104, 105, 106, 107, 108, 198, 200–201; START and, 260; suspicion of West by, 200
Gareyev, Tamerlane, 122
Gasonov, Gasan, 120
Gates, Robert, 117–18, 136, 137, 270
General Accounting Office (GAO), xi, xii
General Staff: Armenian-Azerbaijan conflict and, 125; army modernization and, 271; August coup and, 70, 83–84; command posts of, 70; communist influence in, 103, xiv–xv; control of nuclear arsenal by, xv, 85, 147, 149–51, 152, 153, 154–55, 156, 162, 170–71, 187, 196, 212, 248; coup preparations by, 162–63; defense budget and, 265–66; electromagnetic-pulse weapons and, 221; Falklands War and, 189; Felgengauer and, 126; first-strike policy and, 56, 67–68, 69–70, 95–96, 147; Gorbachev and, 54, 55; Increased Combat Readiness and, 168; 1993 intelligence policy and, 95–96; Iraq and, 285; missile launch exercise by, 209; NATO expansion and, 216; NATO military exercises and, 283; new military doctrine and, 147; Norwegian missile crisis and, 217–18, 222; nuclear war limitations and, 43; October coup and, 165, 167, 172, 175–76, 178, 179–80, 198; 1999 science missile launch and, 237–38; renaming of, xiv; source of U.S. nuclear attack and, 220; SS-18 ICBMs and, 281; Strategic Defense Initiative and, 7, 141; threat perception by, xiii, xvi, 63, 273; Ukraine and, 158–59, 277; VRYAN and, 95; Warsaw Pact collapse and, 64–66; Yeltsin and, 154, 158; Yeltsin's staff and, 191. *See also* Kolesnikov, Mikhail
General Staff Academy, 105, 132, 204, 71–72
General Staff Command Post, 187, 224
Georgia: breakup of Soviet Union and, 89; civil war in, 92; nuclear weapons in, 113; Ottoman Turks and, 114; Rodionov and, 56, 104–5, 192; Russian "peacekeeping operations" in, 205; Rutskoy and, 138; Turkey and, 124; Union Treaty and, 59
German Ministry of Defense, 12
German reunification, 64–65
Germany, 107, 115, 160, 251, 273
Giray, Safa, 120–21
Glasnost, 54, 115
Global Navigation Satellite System (GLONASS), 98, 267
Gorbachev, Anatoliy, 140–41
Gorbachev, Mikhail: Akhromeyev and, 80; Andropov and, 45; Armenian-Azerbaijan War and, 15; background of, 53; Bush and, 93, 94;

CFE Treaty and, 55; communism and, 53; communism's collapse and, 55–56; decentralization and, 91; domestic reforms by, 55; General Staff and, 55; German reunification and, 65; hypocrisy by, 80; Iraq and, 288; Persian Gulf War and, 67; political rise by, 54; threat perception by, 62, 251; threat reduction measures by, 54–55; Warsaw Pact crisis and, 64, 65; Yanayev and, 57; Yazov and, 58, 74. *See also* August coup
Gorbachev, Raisa, 53, 60
Gordievsky, Oleg, xiii; ABLE ARCHER military exercise and, 33, 38, 39, 41, 44; Andropov's health and, 45; betrayal of, 47–48; British elections and, 36; Guk and, 47; Korean Air Lines flight 007 and, 28, 31–32; missile dispersal indicator and, 47; National Intelligence Estimates and, 19, 21; Soviet betrayal by, 9; Soviet threat perception and, 7; Strategic Defense Initiative and, 36; U.S. intelligence community and, 18–19; VRYAN and, 9, 12, 13, 48, 49, 63, 95
Gore, Al, 241, 281
Gouré, Leon, 154
Grachev, Pavel: Achalov and, 171; Armenian-Azerbaijan conflict and, 119, 121, 122, 123; arms policy of, 140; August coup and, 78, 86; background of, 132; control of nuclear arsenal by, 157, 187, 188–89; corruption by, 188; first-strike policy and, 107, 147, 148, 188–89; independent military action and, 135; Kolesnikov and, 186; loyalty to Yeltsin by, 180–81; missile attack warning system and, 100; missile launch exercise and, 210; mutiny in Russian military and, 132–34; NATO expansion and, 188; Norwegian missile crisis and, 224; October coup and, 164–65, 167–68, 176–77; removal of, 191; reputation of, bad, 132; Russian Army's communist orientation and, 131–32; Rutskoy and, 163; Shaposhnikov and, 196; threat perception by, 139–40, 143, 168; TSENTER and, 171; Vyzhotovich and, 215; Yeltsin and, 188
Great Depression, 265
Greenham Common, 47
Greenland, 233
Grenada, 37–38, 67
Grenfell, Carol, 27
Grenfell, Neil, 27
Grenfell, Noelle Ann, 27, 28
Grenfell, Stacey Marie, 27, 28
Grigoryev, Sergey, 101, 251
Gromov, Felix, 190
Gromyko, Andrei, 24, 30, 32
GRU: ABLE ARCHER military exercise and, 34; August coup and, 77; conspiracy theories by, 205; NATO military exercises and, 282; Norwegian missile crisis and, 236; pre-missile war strategy by, 97; size of, 10; threat perception by, 97, 205–6; VRYAN and, 9, 10, 14, 62, 95
Grushin, Boris, 249
Guk, Arkadi, 47
Gulev, Leonid, 287
Gulyy, Sergey, 251
Gures, Dogan, 121
Gurinov, Georgiy, 172
Gypsies, 208

Habiger, Eugene, 257, 266
HARD SIGN, 162–63
Havnen, Ingvard, 217
Helms, Jesse, 28
Helsinki Final Act, 25
Henry M. Jackson, 284
Hero of the Soviet Union, 137
Hersh, Seymour, 29, 31
Hetai, George, 4
History of Military Art, 204
Hitler, Adolf, 89, 115, 160
Hoffman, David, 246
Holtet, Jan, 195
Hungarian Revolution, 4

Hungary, 4, 24, 26, 64, 288
Hussein, Saddam, 142, 286, 288

"I Put My Trust in Facts," 141
I Spit on the West, 143
Implications of Recent Soviet Military-Political Activities, 42
"Increase Vigilance and Be Alert," 35
Increased Combat Readiness, 71–76, 77, 81, 83, 85–86, 168, 169
Independent, 250
India, 252
INOBIS, 275, 290
Institute of Microbiology, 270
Intercontinental ballistic missiles (ICBMs): ABLE ARCHER military exercise and, 43–44; August coup and, 76, 83; Bush and, 93, 99; capabilities of, 76; Cuban missile crisis and, 143; current Russian production of, 266–67; detargeting agreement and, 210; Evers and, 242; first-strike strategy and, 10–11; in Kazakhstan, 112; Norwegian missile crisis and, 228; Russian command and control and, 152; Russian military exercises and, 210–11, 266; Russian nuclear buildup and, 98; SS-18, 255, 256, 281; SS-24, 159; SS-27, 192; START and, 255–56, 258; Ukranian crisis and, 112, 159–60; upgrade of, 34; VRYAN and, 261; Zhirinovsky and, 143
Interfax news, 232
Intermediate-range ballistic missiles (IRBMs), 16
Intermediate-Range Nuclear Forces (INF) Treaty, 54, 220
Iran, 92, 107, 287, 290
Iraq: biological weapons and, 271; Persian Gulf War and, 66–67; Russian political leaders and, 249; Russian threat perception and, 141, 238, 279, 286–87, 288–89; U.S. 1998 conflict with, 286–89; Yeltsin and, 238, 239, 251, 286–89; Zhirinovsky and, 142
"Is Russia at Risk of War?" 189
"Is There a Law of Victory?" 262
ITAR-Tass news building, 175
Ivanko, Sergei, 225–26
Ivanov, G. D., 139, 143, 213
Ivanova, Valentina, 79–80
Ivashov, Leonid, 282
Izgarshev, Vasily, 138
Izvestiya, 83, 117, 122, 211
Izvestiya, Novyye, ix

Japan, 38, 186, 251, 273
Jaruzelski, Wojiech, 23–26
Jews, 208

Kadar, Janos, 4
Kaliningrad, 89
Kalugin, Igor, 111, 190
Kamchatka Peninsula, 27, 30, 169, 211, 288
Kapranov, Nikoloai, 67
Karpachev, I. A., 259
Karpukhin, Viktor, 78
Kars, Turkey, 125–27
Kars Treaty, 121
Kaysin, Yuri, 73
Kazakhstan: Baikonur Cosmodrome and, 165; breakup of Soviet Union and, 89, 91, 90; Caspian oil and, 287; NATO military exercises in, 281, 282; new Russian military doctrine and, 160; nuclear weapons in, 109, 110, 112–13; restoration of union and, 275
KAZBEK, 225, 226
Kennedy, John F., x, 143, 265
KGB: ABLE ARCHER military exercise and, 34; August coup and, 72; German reunification and, 65; Operation THUNDER and, 78; renaming of, xiv; size of, 10; VRYAN and, 9, 10, 13, 14, 95; Zhirinovsky and, 143. *See also* Andropov, Yuri; Kryuchkov, Vladimir
KGB: The Inside Story of Its Foreign Operations from Lenin to Gorbachev, xiii
Khasbulatov, Ruslan, 154, 163–64, 178

Khrushchev, Nikita, 81
Kirghizia, 113
Kirshin, Yuri, 104
Kissinger, Henry, 30
Klepikova, Elena, 30
Klimenko, Anatoliy, 106, 107, 263–64
Kobets, Konstantin, 72, 103, 110, 174
Kohl, Helmut, 45, 64–65
Kokoshin, Andrey, 135
Kola Peninsula, 28, 277, 279
Kolesnikov, Mikhail: control of nuclear arsenal by, 154–55, 156–57, 168, 185, 186, 187, 191, 228; coup and, 168, 172, 175–76, 180; missile launch exercise and, 210; Norwegian missile crisis and, 224, 228–29, 230, 231–32, 234, 236, 237; replacement of, 192; threat perception by, 186–87; Turkey and, 124
Koltyukov, Aleksandr, 263–64
Komsomol, 3
Komsomolskaya pravda, 85
Kononenko, Vasilily, 175, 231
Korean Air Lines flight 007, 27–32, 36–37, 193
Kornukov, Anatoly, 29, 193, 265
Korobushin, V., 153, 180
Korotchenko, Igor, 95, 107
Kortunov, Sergey, 251
Korzhakov, Aleksandr, 196–97, 215
KOSMOS-2262, 166
KOSMOS-2263, 166
KOSMOS-2264, 166
KOSMOS-2349, 288
KOSMOS-2361, 289
Kosovo, 252, 284–85
KOSTYAR-1, 48
Kosygin, Alexei, 6
Kozhuk, Yuriy, 263
Kozryev, Andrey, 121–22, 142, 160, 198, 205, 208–9, 212, 252
Kozyrev, S., 104
Kraemer, Sven, 149
Krasnaya zvezda, 73, 110, 133, 158
Kravchuk, Leonid, 110, 111, 112, 113, 159, 160
Kremlin building, 78
Krimsky Bridge, 173
KROKUS, 224, 226
Kruchina, Nikolai, 79
Kruglov, V. V., 262
Kryuchkov, Vladimir: ABLE ARCHER military exercise and, 38–39; arrest of, 79; August coup and, 59, 61, 75, 78–79; disinformation by, 79; first-strike policy and, 75; influence of, 57; Operation THUNDER and, 78; Persian Gulf War and, 66; political rise by, 61; threat perception by, 1, 33, 45–46, 61, 62, 69; Warsaw Pact collapse and, 64; VRYAN and, 36, 48
Kuklinski, Ryszard, 25–26
Kulikov, Viktor, 12, 24–25, 275
Kurginyan, S., 283–84
Kurile Islands, 29
Kuroyedov, Vladimir, 283
Kuwait, 66–67, 249
Kuznetsov, Valeriy, 37
Kvashnin, Anatoly, 193, 284
Kyrgyzstan, 89

Large Phased-Array Radars (LPARs), 100, 101
Larr, Mart, 158
Larry King Live, 170
Latvia, 59, 89, 91
Launch-detection satellites, 37
Lebed, Aleksandr: army of, 168–69; attitude toward West by, ix; August coup and, 78; defense ministry and, 180–81, 191; dictatorship and, 129; Moldovo and, 133–34; rhetoric by, 133; Yeltsin denounced by, 274
Lee, William T., 43, 46, 47
Leninsk, Kazakhstan, 165
Liberal Democratic Party of Russia, 142
Libya, 49
"Limited Nuclear War? Why Not!," 265
Limits of Safety, The, 143
Lipetsk, Russia, 230–31, 280
Lisov, Yevgeniy, 73–74, 79–80, 81
Lithuania, 59, 89, 91
Lobov, Viktor, 104
Lobov, Vladimir, 154, 215

Logic of Accidental Nuclear War, The, 233
London Sunday Times, 197
Long-Range Aviation, 72, 75, 111, 156, 190, 265
Los Angeles Times, 119, 232
Losik, Oleg, 67–68
Lukin, Vladimir, 285, 290
Lunev, Stanislav, xiii, 96–97
Luns, Joseph, 3
Lusitania, 32
Luzhkov, Yuri, 252

Maine, 32
Makashov, Albert, 174
Makoklyuyev, Yevgeniy, 179
Maksimov, Yuri, 73, 112, 156
Maltsev, Igor, 73
Marxism-Leninism on War and Army, 11
McFarlane, Robert, 38
Medvedev, Sergey, 197, 280
Mein Kampf, 141
"A Micron Away from Apocalypse," 283–84
Middle East, 273, 283. *See also names of specific countries*
Middle East War, 273
Midway, 29
Mikhailov, Viktor, 264, 267, 268
Mikhalchenko, N., 276
Military Plans of the Warsaw Pact in Central Europe, 12
Military Thought: electromagnetic-pulse weapons and, 221; first-strike policy and, 262; Grachev and, 139; Kolesnikov and, 187; local conflicts and, 207; new military doctrine and, 107–8, 147; START and, 259, 262
Miller, Mark, 20–21
Minuteman ICBM, 34, 37, 99
Mirzayanov, Val, 135–36, 269
Missile Attack Warning System (MAWS), 100–101, 162, 192, 219, 218, 219–20, 222–24
Missile Defense Forces, 287
Mladič, Ratko, 208
Modestov, Sergey, 257–58
Moiseyev, Mikhail, 83, 84
Moldavia, 275
Mongols, 203
Morosov, Yevgeniy, 141
Moscow ABM system, 256
Moscow Declaration, 198
"Moscow-Kiev Clash. This Seems to Be Washington's Persistently Pursued Aim," 158
Moscow Patriarchate, 250
Moscow Television News, 239
Moscow Treaty, 121
Moskalenko, K. S., 11
Moskovskiye novosti, 110
Mount Ararat, 114
Muscovy, 203
Muslims, 92, 208
MVD troops, 163, 168–172, 173–74
M. V. Frunze—Military Theorist, 105

Nagorno-Karabakh, 102. *See also* Armenian-Azerbaijan conflict
Nagy, Imre, 4
Nakhichevan Autonomous Republic, 118, 120
Napoleon, 203–4
National Air Intelligence Center, 267
National Defense University, 105
National Intelligence Council, xi
National Intelligence Estimates (NIEs): ABLE ARCHER military exercise and, 42–43; assassinations and, 18; Cooper's report and, xi–xii; escalation theory by, 22; first-strike strategy and, 19; Gordievsky and, 19, 21; Pershing II missiles and, 19, 33–34; Poland and, 26; 1995 report by, xi–xii; Russian spy satellite launch and, 165; SDI and, 33; sources for, xi; Soviet social unrest and, 17–18; threat perception by, 19–21; VRYAN and, 19
National Security Agency, xi
National Security Directive, 257
Nazarbayev, Nursultan, 112–13, 160
Nazis. *See* World War II
New York Times, 28, 180, 243, 246, 287

Nicaragua, 34, 37
Nikolayev, Andrey, 213
Nimitz, 242–43
Noah's Ark, 114
Noginsk, Russia, 250
Non-Proliferation Treaty, 160, 199, 213
North Atlantic Treaty Organization (NATO): Achalov and, 141; airspace violations and, 29; Armenian-Azerbaijan conflict and, 120, 123, 124; Black Sea region and, 124, 276; Bosnia and, 209, 284, 285; 1979 communique by, 3; Dementyev and, 277–78; first-strike policy and, 146; Korean Air Lines flight 007 and, 32; Kosovo and, 252, 284–85; Kvashnin and, 193; Large Phased-Array Radars and, 101; military exercises of, 279–83 (*see also* ABLE ARCHER military exercise); Morosov and, 141; Norway and, 216; Norwegian missile crisis and, 232, 233, 236; Pershing II missiles and, 16; Polish crisis and, 25, 26; Russian military exercises and, 265; Turkey and, 115, 119, 200; Ukraine and, 160, 276; Yugoslavia and, 208–9, 252; Yzov and, 58. *See also* ABLE ARCHER military exercise
NATO expansion: Baryinkin and, 189; Duma on, ix; General Staff and, 216; Gorbachev and, 251; Grigoryev and, 251; Mikhailov and, 268; NATO military exercises and, 282; Norwegian missile crisis and, 214, 216–17; Poland and, 214–15; reversal of fortune and, 254; Rohklin and, 239; Russian dependence on nuclear might and, 288; Sergeyev and, 216, 217; Vorontsov and, 252; Western threat perception and, 243, 246; Yeltsin and, 188, 215, 250–51; Zhirinovsky and, 250
NATO Founding Act, 251, 252
North Pole, 236
Northern Fleet, 216, 277, 280, 281
Northern lights, 195, 218
Norway, 115, 216, 280, 283
Norwegian missile crisis: Devyanin on, 234–35; electromagnetic-pulse weapons and, 220–22, 230; first-strike policy and, 213; 1999 launch and, 237–38; NATO expansion and, 216–17; notification before launch and, 217–18, 234, 235–36; nuclear alert and, 183, 226–27, 228–29, 232, 234, 235; press coverage on, 232–34, 237; Russian detection of launch and, 222; Russian propaganda on, 231–32; Russian threat perception and, 222–25, 228–30, 231–33, 234–36; selection of launch site and, 195; Western threat perception and, 237–38
Norwegian Sea, 222, 233
Novaya Zemlya, 267, 268, 287
Novocheboksarak, Russia, 269
Novolipetsk Metallurgical Combine, 231
Novozhilov, V. I., 72
Nuclear arms race, 268
Nuclear briefcase ("football"): August coup and, 69, 84–85; Chernomyrdin and, 274; Grachev and, 156–57, 187, 188–89, 196; Kolesnikov and, 155–57, 185, 186, 187, 228; Kvashnin and, 193; launch capability and, 151–52, 189; Norwegian missile crisis and, 224–25, 229–30, 231, 233, 235, 236–37; Rodionov and, 192; Shaposhnikov and, 154; Yeltsin and, 229, 231, 233, 235, 237, 274
"Nuclear Missile Adventurism," 260–61
Nuclear threat. *See* Russian threat perception; Soviet threat perception; Western threat perception; *specific subject matter*
"Nuclear Ukraine Nor End of the World," 113
Nuclear Wars: Exchanges and Outcomes, 256

Oberdorfer, Don, 38, 41
October coup: Achalov and, 171–72; communications and, 171–72, 173;

control of nuclear arsenal and, 163–64; Defense Ministry and, 175–76; General Staff and, 172, 175–76, 178, 179–80, 198; Grachev and, 176–77; military indecisiveness and, 172–73; Ostankino Television station and, 174; Petsnaz commandos and, 176; press reports on, 164–65, 174–75, 177; Russian threat perception and, 165–69, 178, 179; Rutskoy's rioting legion and, 173–74; spy satellite launch and, 165–67; Ukrainian crisis and, 159; Western threat perception and, 178–79, 180, 181; White House barricade and, 164
Offensive, The, 11
Ogarkov, Nikolai, 29, 31
Old Testament, 114
Operation Barbossa, 204
Operation Morning Dew, 168
Organized crime, 242
Osipovich, Gennadi, 28
Ostalskiy, Andrey, 113
Ostankino Television, 120, 173, 174
Ottoman Turks, 114, 208
Ozal, Semra, 118
Ozal, Turgut, 118

Pacific Fleet, 133, 169, 172
Partnership for Peace, 124, 282
Pasechnik, Vladimir, 135–36, 270
Pasha, Enver, 115
Pavlov, Valentin, 59, 79, 83–84, 150
Peacekeeper ICBMs, 36, 93, 99
Pearl Harbor, 204
Penkovsky, Oleg, 9
Perestroika, 54, 65
Permanent Operational Assignment to Detect Signs of NATO Preparations for a Nuclear Attack on the U.S.S.R. as Reflected in the Activity of Special Services of the NATO Bloc, 13–14
Perry, William, 242, 243
Pershing II missiles: ABLE ARCHER military exercise and, 33–34; Andropov and, 5; capabilities of, 34; deployment of, 16; first-strike and, 22; launch-detection satellites and, 37; National Intelligence Estimates and, 19, 33–34; Norwegian missile crisis and, 229; removal of, 54; Soviet military adjustments and, 46; U.S. intelligence community and, 18–19; Ustinov and, 6, 16–17; VRYAN and, 16
Persian Gulf War, 66–68, 271
Peter the Great, 90, 114
Petrov, Stanislav, 270
Plan for Basic Measures to Step Up Still Further the Effort to Combat the Subversive Intelligence Activities of the United States Services, 46
Plekhanov, Yuri, 60
Pokrovskiy, V., 62
Poland, 23–26, 214–15, 288, 290
Poland's Prospects over the Next 12 to 18 Months, 26
Pollack, Craig, 195
Ponomarev, Manki, 73, 77, 158
Ponomaryov, Lev, 103
Popkovich, Roman, 285
Porovskiy, Mykola, 110
Possible Soviet Responses to the U.S. Strategic Defense Initiative, 33
Pravda, 17, 137
Preemption. *See* First-strike policy
President's Foreign Intelligence Advisory Board, 43
Primakov, Yevgeniy, xiv; Iraq and, 286, 289; replacement of, 181; restoration of union and, 214; VRYAN and, 12, 49, 62–63, 94–95
Pristina, 284
Proliferation: Threat and Response, 269, 270
Prospects for Unsanctioned Use of Russian Nuclear Weapons, 247
Prozorov, V., 104
Prudnikov, Viktor, 190–91, 220
Pry, Ruthie, 115–16
Pugo, Boris, 57, 58–59, 78, 79–80

Rada, 110
RC-135 intelligence aircraft, 28, 29
Reagan, Ronald, 7, 31, 36, 38, 257–58

Reagan administration, 12–13
Red Army, 4, 6, 23, 64–65, 117
Red Banner Northern Fleet, 280
Republican Party, 246
Rethinking the Unthinkable: Russia's Evolving Nuclear Weapon Threat, 237, 244
Rodionov, Igor: DESERT STORM and, 67; dismissal of, 192; electromagnetic-pulse weapons and, 221; first-strike policy and, 102, 103, 106, 198; Georgia and, 56, 104–5; Grachev's dismissal and, 191; military doctrine debate and, 104, 105–6, 107–8
Rogov, Sergey, 129, 135, 200, 201, 202, 206
Rohklin, Lev, 239, 275
Roman Catholic Church, 249
Rossiskaya gazeta, 287
Russia: Armenia and, 114; arms production by, 266–67; capitalism's failure in, 134–35; intelligence investment by, 97; missile attack warning system of, 100–101; nuclear arsenal of, 245; nuclear force investment by, 97–98; organized crime in, 242; religious freedom in, 249–50; social problems in, 134–35; Soviet breakup and, 89–91; Turkey and, 114–15; underground complexes in, 268–69; vulnerability of, 91–92; war history of, 203–4. *See also* Yeltsin, Boris
Russia-CIS: Does the Western Position Need Correction?" 214
Russian Army: Chechnya and, 215–16, 234; communist orientation of, 132; decline of, 131, 271; future of, 246; military doctrine debate and, 107; mutiny in, 132–34; poverty in, 135; World War I and, 204
Russian Constitution, 275
Russian Conventional Armed Forces: On the Verge of Collapse, 181, 271
Russian Defense Ministry, 175–76. *See also* Grachev, Pavel
Russian Duma, xiv, 261, 282–83, 286–87
Russian Duma Resolution, ix
Russian Federation National Security Blueprint, 263
Russian Foreign Ministry, 238
Russian military: budget for, 265–66; chemical weapons and, 269–70; command and control system in, 149–57; conspiracy theories and, 205; conventional modernization plans by, 271; democratic reformers and, 247; doctrine debate by, 102–8; first-strike exercises by, 265; hard-line influence in, 247; independent action by, 135–36; modernization of, 272; new doctrine of, 145–47, 160, 198–202, 212–13, 241, 248, 262–64; nuclear testing by, 267–68; nuclear victory and, 263; October coup and, 172–73; Orthodox Church and, 250; START and, 255, 259–61, 262; submarine exercises by, 269; threat perception by, 141, 277–78 (*see also specific names under* Russian threat perception); Ukraine and, 277; Yeltsin and cadets in, 180. *See also* General Staff; *specific military branches, leaders*
Russian Ministry of Foreign Affairs, 159
Russian Ministry of Interior, 172
Russian Navy, 117, 155, 164, 190, 220, 269, 279
Russian Organized Crime, 242
Russian Orthodox Church, 249–50
Russian parliament: antipathy for U.S. by, 142; Iraq and, 286; NATO military exercises and, 282–83; October coup and, 171; power struggle by, xiv, 153–54; START and, 261; Yeltsin opposed by, 134, 161–62, 163–64
Russian Shift toward Nuclear War-Waging, The, 267
Russian Special Operation Forces, 97
Russian threat perception: by Achalov, 141–42; Armenian-Azerbaijan conflict and, 117; by Barynkin, 189–90; Bush's disarmament gesture and,

99; Chechnya and, 234; by civilians, 249–53; by democratic leaders, 251–52; by Gorbachev, 251; by Grachev, 139–40, 143, 168; GRU and, 205–6; individualism *v.* collectivism and, 160–61; Kirshin and, 104; by Kolesnikov, 186–87; local conflicts and, 206–7; logic of, 253–54; Lunev and, 96–97; by Morosov, 141; NATO expansion and, 250–51, 252; Norwegian missile crisis and, 197, 222–25, 228–30, 231–33, 234–36; nuclear shelters and, 98; October coup and, 165–69, 178, 179; poll on, 161; by populace, 252–53; by Prudnikov, 191; by Sergeyev, 279; source of nuclear attack and, 220; START and, 259–60; by Terekhov, 141; U.S. advanced conventional weapons and, 100; U.S.-Iraqi 1998 conflict and, 285–87; Ukraine and, 158–59; Velikhov and, 103–4; weakened Russia and, 139; Western threat perception and, 241; World War III preparation and, 271–72; by Yakolev, 193; by Yeltsin, 251–52. *See also* Future threats
Russia's Nuclear Doctrine, 213
"Russia's Nuclear Temptation," 246
Russification, 91, 114
Russo-Turkish war, 114
Rust, Matthias, 219
Rutskoy, Aleksandr, 137–38, 159, 161, 163, 168, 171–72
RYAN. *See* VYRAN
Rybkin, Ivan, 239, 263
Ryzhkov, Viktor, 152

Sagan, Scott, 143
Sakhalin Island, 27
Sakharov, Dmitri, 79
Sallow, Luke, 109
Samsonov, Viktor, 154–55, 192
Sarajevo, 206
SATAN SS-18 ICBM, 76
Saudi Arabia, 66
Savchenko, V., 262
Savvateyeva, Irina, 174–75
Schlesinger, James, 244
Scruton, Rebecca, 27
SEABREEZE-97, 282
Second Air Force, 119, 120
Sedognya, 87, 123, 280
Selivanov, Valentin, 269
Semenov, Vladimir, 190, 279–80
Senate Armed Services Committee, 117
Sener, Abdullatif, 121
Serbs, 206, 207, 208, 284
Sergeyev, Igor: defense ministry and, 192; launch exercise by, 210–11; military technological advances and, 268; NATO expansion and, 192, 216–17; NATO military exercises and, 283; Orthodox Church and, 250; reorganization by, 156, 192–93; retargeting missiles and, 243; Spetsnaz commandos and, 162; START and, 259; threat perception by, 279; Trident missile and, 100; U.S.-Iraqi 1998 conflict and, 287–89
Sergeyevich, Mikhail, 81
Shakrai, Sergei, 79
Shalikashvili, John, 170–71, 178, 257
Shanurova, Zhanna, 278, 279
Shaposhnikov, Yevgeniy: Armenian-Azerbaijan conflict and, 118–19, 121–23, 125; August coup and, 72, 78, 86, 90–91, 119; breakup of Soviet Union and, 89; defense responsibility by, 90–91; Grachev and, 196; nuclear briefcases and, 154; Ukraine and, 111
Sheehan, John, 281–82
Sheinis, Victor, 103
Shenin, Oleg, 60
Shevardnadze, Eduard, ix, 64, 65, 138, 142
Shevykin, Sergey, 142
Shirokorad, Aleksandr, 264
Shultz, George, 28, 32
Shumeiko, Vladimir, 163
Shvets, Yuri, 12, 49
Siberia, 173, 249
Sidorenko, A. A., 11
Sieff, Martin, 269
Simonenko, V., 123–24

60 Minutes, 100, 237, 243
Slaton, Jessie, 27
Slavin, Boris, 137
"A Small Bomb for a Small War: The Role of Tactical Nuclear Weapons Is Objectively Increasing as Strategic Arms Are Being Reduced," 264
Slovakia, 239
Slovenia, 239
Sokolov, Anatoliy, 222–23, 224, 228, 229
Sokov, Nikolai, 193
Sokut, Sergey, 265
Solidarity, 24–25
Solovyov, Vladimir, 30
"Some Approaches to Developing Russia's Military Doctrine," 105
Sonnenfeldt, Helmut, 30
South Ossetia, 138, 275
Sovetskaya Rossiya, 65
Soviet Capabilities for Strategic Nuclear Conflict, 1982–1992, 19, 33–34
Soviet Capabilities for Strategic Nuclear Conflict, 1983–1993, 19, 42
The Soviet Challenge to U.S. Security Interests, 20
Soviet economy, 66
Soviet-Finnish relations, 275
Soviet Navy, 72, 75
Soviet Pacific Fleet, 27
Soviet Propaganda Campaign Against NATO, 19
Soviet Strategic Power and Doctrine, 20–21
Soviet threat perception: ABLE ARCHER military exercise and, 33, 36, 37–44; by Andropov, 1; August coup and, 61, 73–74, 75, 77, 85; Brezhnev's 1981 speech and, 9; British elections and, 36; first-strike policy change and, 68, 69–70; by General Staff, xvi, 63; by Gorbachev and, 54, 62; Greenham Common missiles and, 47; Grenada and, 37–38; Korean Air Lines flight 007 and, 28, 29–30, 31–32, 36–37; by Kryuchkov, 45–46, 61, 62, 69; National Intelligence Estimates and, 19–21; Pershing II missiles and, 4–5; Persian Gulf War and, 66–67; by Pokrovskiy, 62; Reagan administration and, 7, 12–13; SDI and, 7; Soviet social unrest and, 17–18; space shuttle and, 48; threat indicators and, 46; U.S. military buildup and, 34, 35–36; U.S. nuclear weapon modernization and, 7–8; Victor III submarine and, 40–41; by Yazov, 74. *See also* Pershing II missiles; VRYAN
Soviet Union, breakup of, 89–91
Space Military Force, 287
Spence, Floyd, 243
Spetsnaz commandos, 162, 176
Spitsbergen archipelago, 230
Stalin, Joseph, 6, 23, 115
Starovoitova, Galina, 181
Starr, Richard, 246
State Committee for the State of Emergency, 60, 61, 74–75, 77
Statement for the Record to the U.S. Congress, xi
Stealth technology, 100
Stepashin, Sergei, 181, 215
Stewart, John B., 237, 244
"Stop Worrying about Russia," 243
Strategic Arms Limitation Treaty (SALT I), xv
Strategic Arms Reduction Treaties (START): Bush and, 93; Clinton's concessions and, 255–56; first-strike policy and, xiii, 256–61; retaliatory strikes and, 258–59; Russian advantage and, 256, 261, 266, 257; Russian inventory and, 111; Russian military and, 262; Russian threat perception and, 140–41, 259–60; START I reductions and, 54–55; START II reductions and, 255–56, 266; START III reductions and, 258, 266; strategic balance and, 259–60, 261; submarine-launched ballistic missiles and, 99–100; threat

reduction and, xv; U.S. capabilities and, 272; U.S. threat perception and, 255; Weldon and, 245–46
Strategic Defense Initiative (SDI), 7, 18–19, 33, 36, 48, 55, 141
Strategic Deterrence Forces, 155–56, 192
Strategic Missile Forces Command Center, 133
Strategic Missile Forces Staff, 162
Strategic Missile Troops, 216
Strategic Review, 246
Strategic Rocket Forces: August coup and, 72, 73, 75, 76; command posts of, 70; control of nuclear arsenal by, 190; leaders of, 156; Maksimov and, 155–56; retaliatory capabilities of, 287–88; Russian command and control and, 152–55; training of, 85; Yakolev and, 193–94. *See also* Sergeyev, Igor
Strategic Rocket Forces Academy, 111
STRONG RESOLVE 98, 283
Submarine-launched ballistic missiles (SLBMs): electromagnetic-pulse weapons and, 221; first-strike policy and, 10, 11; Norwegian missile crisis and, 223; Russian command and control and, 152–53; Russian development of, 267; Russian launch exercise and, 211; Russian military exercises and, 266; source of U.S. attack and, 220; START and, 99–100; U.S. and Russian, compared, 169
Submarine-launched cruise missiles (SLCMs), 35–36
Suez crisis, 273
"Suitcase" bombs, 97
Supreme Soviet, 161, 163
Supreme Soviet's Council of the Union, 91
Surikov, Anton, 198, 278, 290–91
Surikov, Viktor, ix
Sverdrug-2, 278
Sweden, 278
Syria, 66
Tadzhikistan, 113
Tajikistan, 81, 91, 92, 205, 263
Talbott, Strobe, 241–42
Target is Destroyed, The, 29
Tashkent treaty, 122
Tass, 29
Tbilisi, Georgia, 138
Tchernshyev, Albert, 252
Teekhov, Stanislav, 141
Tenet, George, 245
Terekhov, Stanislav, 131
Terekhyn, Sergey, 277
Ter-Petrosyan, Levon, 94, 121
Test Ban Treaty, 243
Thatcher, Margaret, 36, 37
Third World, 68, 246
Through the Eyes of the Enemy, xiii
THUNDER, Operation, 77–78, 85
Time, 237
Tito, Josep, 208
Tizyakov, Aleksandr, 79
Tolubko, V., 111–12
Transcaucasus, 275
Tresselt, Per, 235
Tribe, William, 208
Trident C-4, 34–35
Trident II SLBMs, 99–100
TSENTER, 169, 171, 178–80
Turkey: Cold War and, 115; future threats and, 277–78; Iraq and, 286; NATO and, 200; Russia and, 114–15; Russian military doctrine debate and, 102, 107; World Wars and, 115. *See also* Armenian-Azerbaijan conflict
Turkish Army, 119–20, 122
"Turkish Military Presence in Georgia Possible in Near Future," 124
Turkmenistan, 89
Turn, The, 38, 43
Typhoon SSBN, 266
Tyson Foods, 281

Ukraine: breakup of Soviet Union and, 89, 91–92; Catholicism and, 249; future threats and, 276–77; NATO military exercises in, 282; restoration

of union and, 275; Turkey and, 123; Union Treaty and, 59
Ukrainian crisis: Bashkirov and, 109; Black Sea Fleet and, 111, 112; ICBMs and, 159–60; Kazakhstan and, 112–13; loyalty pledge and, 111–12; new Russian military doctrine and, 160; October coup and, 159; Porovskiy and, 110; press report on, 110, 113; Russian threat perception and, 158–59, 160–61; weapons claim and, 111, 158–60
Ukrainian 43rd Army, 159
Ukrainian Ministry of Defense, 159
Ukrainian parliament, 159, 160
Uniates, 249
Union Treaty, 56, 59, 61
United Nations: Armenian-Azerbaijan conflict and, 120, 121; Bosnia and, 207; first-strike policy and, 17; Iraq and, 251, 288; Persian Gulf War and, 66; Soviet states and, 91; Yugoslavia and, 208
UN Security Council, 215, 276, 288
United States. *See* North Atlantic Treaty Organization; Western threat perception; *names of U.S. leaders*
U.S. ABM system, 260
U.S. Air Force, 143
U.S. Arms Control and Disarmament Agency, 19, 25
U.S. Congress: August coup and, 83–84; Bosnia and, 209; Lebed and, 274; Lunev and, 97; military modernization and, 272; NIE 1995 report and, xi–xii; Yamantau project and, 268
U.S. Congressional Research Service, 74, 181
U.S. Defense Department, 117, 162, 238, 266, 270
U.S. military, 271–72
U.S. National Aeronautics and Space Administration (NASA), 213, 218, 236, 237–38
U.S. National Defense University, 71
U.S. Navy, 117
U.S. News and World Report, 237, 278
U.S.-Russian Nuclear Risk Reduction Center, 238
U.S. State Department, 91, 238
U.S. Strategic Air Command, 143
Ural Mountains, 6, 268
Ustinov, Dmitri, 5, 6, 13, 16–17, 23, 24, 30, 35
Uzbekistan, 89, 282

Vandenberg Air Force Base, 143
Vasilyev, Vladimir, 100–101
Velikhov, Yevgeniy, 103–4
Vershblow, Alexander, 242
Victor III submarine, 40–41
Volk Air Field, 144
Volkov, Lev, 206;
Voronstov, Yuli, 251–52
Vox Populi, 249
VRYAN: ABLE ARCHER military exercise and, 38, 40; Bush's disarmament gesture and, 94; continuation of, 45–46, 62–63, 94–95; disinformation about, 94–95; establishment of, 9, 13; first–strike and, 22; Gordievsky and, 12; Greenham Common missiles and, 47; GRU and, 95; Korean Air Lines flight 007 and, 32; Kryuchkov and, 48, 62; National Intelligence Estimates and, 19; new Soviet leaders and, 48; 1984 conference and, 45; Pershing II missiles and, 16; Primakov and, 49 priority of, 36; purpose of, 10, 15; Ryaboshapko and, 96; Soviet acknowledgment of, 12; threat indicators and, 10, 14, 15; U.S. intelligence community and, 18; Warsaw Pact crisis and, 65
Vulliamy, Ed, 208
Vyzhotovich, Valery, 215

Walesa, Lech, 214–15
Walker, Martin, 37, 41–42
Waller, Michael J., 243
War scare. *See* Russian threat

perception; Soviet threat perception; Western threat perception; *specific subject matter*
Warsaw Pact: CFE Treaty and, 55; dissolution of, 64–66; first-strike policy and, 11–12, 67; Solidarity and, 24, 26; Yazov and, 58. *See also names of Warsaw Pact countries*
Warsaw Poles, 23
Washington Post, 87, 214, 246, 251, 267–68, 285, 287
Washington Station, 49
Washington Times, 153, 233, 269, 283
Webster, William, 242
Webster's, 195
Weinberger, Caspar, 38
Weldon, Curt, 245–46, 285
Western threat perception: BATTLE GRIFFIN-96 and, 281; biological warfare and, 270–71; by Blair, 244–45; blindness of, 241; by Clinton, 160, 197–98; by Clinton administration, 241–44, 245; control of nuclear arsenal and, 197; Cuban missile crisis and, 143–44; defense budget and, 247; detargeting agreement and, 197–98, 243–44; by Deutch, 245; escalation theory and, 93–94; first-strike policy and, 265; future and, 274; by Gates, 117–18; by Hoffman, 246; intelligence officers' preparation and, xii–xiii; local conflicts and, 94; NATO expansion and, 246; NATO military exercises and, 281, 283; Norwegian missile crisis and, 213, 232–34, 237–38; October coup and, 165, 178–79, 180, 181; Republican Party and, 246; Russian Army's decline and, 215–16; Russian threat perception and, 241; by Schlesinger, 244; scholarly attention and, 246–47; by Shalikashvili, 170–71; by Starr, 246; START and, 255; by Stewart, 244 by Tenet, 245; Ukrainian crisis and, 160; by Weldon, 245–46; by Woolsey, 244. *See also* National Intelligence Estimates (NIEs)
"White House," 77–78, 168, 171–72, 174. *See also* October coup
"Whose Hand Is Reaching for the Nuclear Button?" 197
Wilson, Woodrow, 32
Woolsey, R. James, xi, 244
World War I, 32, 115, 204, 208
World War II: Akhromeyev and, 80; Andropov and, 4; Brezhnev and, 6; intelligence information and, 21; Jaruzelski and, 23; Russia and, 204; southern Soviet states and, 89; Turkey and, 115; Ustinov and, 6; Yugoslavia and, 208

Yakovlev, Aleksandr, 78
Yakovlev, Vladimir, 156, 193–94, 256
Yamantau Mountain, 98, 268
Yanayev, Gennadiy, 57–58, 59, 60, 79
Yanov, Aleksandr, 249
Yashin, Viktor, 225–26
Yashin, Yuri, 259–60
Yazov, Dimitry: arrest of, 79; August coup and, 57, 58, 59, 78–79, 84; first-strike policy and, 75; Gorbachev and, 74; Operation THUNDER and, 78; threat perception by, 74; war preparation command by, 70–76, 85–86; Warsaw Pact collapse and, 64
Yeltsin, Boris: Akhromeyev and, 131; assassination attempt on, 153; August coup and, 77–78, 83; biological warfare and, 270; Bosnia and, 284; Bush and, 93; Chechnya and, 215, 234; Clinton and, 160; commitment to democracy by, xiv; control of nuclear arsenal by, 170, 187, 274; Corfu summit and, 211–12; Cuba and, 281; decentralization by, 91; democracy and, 187–88 economic failure and, 134; Estonia and, 204–5; European alliance and, 251–52; first-strike policy and, 147,

198, 212; future coup attempts and, 275; General Staff members and, 103; Grachev and, 132, 180–81, 188; heart operation of, 274; impeachment vote against, 163; Iraq and, 239, 251, 286; Korzhakov and, 196; Kosovo crisis and, 284–85; Lebed and, 133–34; military's loyalty to, 132; missile launch exercise and, 209–10; NATO expansion and, ix, 188, 215, 250–51, 265, 276; NATO military exercises and, 280; Norwegian missile crisis and, 183, 224, 225, 227, 228, 230–32, 233, 234, 237; nuclear parity and, 251–52; nuclear victory and, 263; parliamentary opposition to, 134, 161–62, 163–64; power struggle by, xiv, 153–54 (*see also* October coup); Rodionov and, 105, 192; Samsonov and, 192; Shaposhnikov and, 90; START and, 141, 255; threat perception by, 251–52; Ukraine and, 110; U.S.-Iraqi 1998 conflict and, 286–87, 288, 289; Yugoslavia and, 212; Zhirinovsky and, 142–43. *See also* October coup; Ukrainian crisis

Yerevan, Armenia, 116

Yerin, Viktor, 164, 215

Yesin, Viktor, 198

Young Communist League, 3

Yugoslavia, 141, 207–9, 212, 252, 279, 284–85

Yushenkov, Sergey, 183, 235

Zakharov, Vladimir, 262–63, 264

ZAPAD-81, 25

Zheltyakov, Aleksandr, 211

Zhilin, Alexander, 216–17

Zhilin, P. A., 204

Zhirinovsky, Vladimir, 142–43, 249, 250

Zlobin, Konstantin, 177

Zorkin, Valeri, 177

ABOUT THE AUTHOR

PETER VINCENT PRY, formerly with the CIA, is currently a professional military advisor to the U.S. House of Representatives on national security issues. In an award honoring his years of service, the CIA stated: "A noted expert in his field, Dr. Pry conducted groundbreaking research that illuminated one of the most important issues of our time, the U.S.-Soviet nuclear competition. On the vanguard of strategic intelligence analysis during the Cold War, he developed much of what the U.S. government knows about Soviet planning for nuclear war, including Soviet views of the character of war, perceptions of U.S. intentions, assessment of the nuclear balance, and operational plans. In the post-Cold War period, his work has been central to the U.S. government's understanding of evolving Russian threat perceptions and military doctrine, and the construction of new paradigms for strategic warning and stability assessments." He lives in Annandale, Virginia.